D1566168

Signs of Diaspora
Diaspora of *Signs*

The Commonwealth Center Studies in American Culture
series is published in cooperation with the
Commonwealth Center for the Study of American Culture
at the College of William and Mary,
Williamsburg, Virginia,
by Oxford University Press,
New York

Pillars of Salt, Monuments of Grace:
New England Crime Literature
and the Origins of American Popular Culture, 1674–1860
Daniel A. Cohen

"Littery Man":
Mark Twain and Modern Authorship
Richard S. Lowry

Signs of Diaspora / Diaspora of Signs:
Literacies, Creolization, and Vernacular Practice
in African America
Grey Gundaker

Signs of Diaspora

Diaspora of *Signs*

Literacies, Creolization,

and Vernacular Practice

in African America

GREY GUNDAKER

New York   Oxford

Oxford University Press

1998

Oxford University Press

Oxford   New York
Athens   Auckland   Bangkok   Bogota   Bombay
Buenos Aires   Calcutta   Cape Town   Dar es Salaam
Delhi   Florence   Hong Kong   Istanbul   Karachi
Kuala Lumpur   Madras   Madrid   Melbourne
Mexico City   Nairobi   Paris   Singapore
Taipei   Tokyo   Toronto   Warsaw

and associated companies in
Berlin   Ibadan

Copyright © 1998 by Grey Gundaker

Published by Oxford University Press, Inc.,
198 Madison Avenue, New York, New York 10016

Oxford is a registered trademark of Oxford University Press

Library of Congress Cataloging-in-Publication Data
Gundaker, Grey.
    Signs of diaspora/diaspora of signs : literacies, creolization, and
vernacular practice in African America / by Grey Gundaker.
        p.   cm.—(Commonwealth Center studies in American culture)
    Includes bibliographical references and index.
    ISBN 0-19-510769-1
    1. Afro-Americans—Language.   2. English language—United States—Foreign elements.
3. African languages—Influence on English.   4. Afro-Americans—Communication.
5. Afro-Americans—Civilization.   6. Literacy—United States.   7. Black English.
I. Title.   II. Series.
PE3102.N4G86   1997
408'.996073—dc21   96-51560

Printed in the United States of America
on acid-free paper

[There was a] policeman in the gate and he opened a book, I saw my name . . . written in the book. He turn over the leaf, I saw it mark "Welcome." He turned a leaf and I saw it mark "Fear." He told me this is my record. I asked the meaning of "Welcome," he said my work is Welcome. I asked the meaning of "Fear," he told me "You must not fear anything." (Norman Paul, quoted by Smith 1963:80)

Preface

*I*n Bahia, Brazil, in the early years of the nineteenth century, Hausa and Yoruba Muslim slaves precipitated a series of revolts. Schooled in Arabic literacy through memorization of the Qur'an, the rebels also wore into battle protective amulets containing sacred verses and prayers. The rebels thus paired literate technology with the doctrines of esoteric Islam. At about the same time, famed slave insurrection leader Nat Turner, awaiting execution in a Virginia jail, expressed his mission to lead African Americans to freedom by stressing knowledge of both Roman script literacy and sacred hieroglyphics in which God's instructions to revolt were written in blood on the leaves of trees. Today, in Washington's National Museum of American Art in Washington, D.C., James Hampton's spiritual masterpiece, the monumental Throne of the Third Heaven of the Nations Millennium General Assembly, surmounted by the forceful injunction "Fear Not," flashes out a message of transcendence and power through countless layers of shimmering, script-encrusted foil and paper (fig. P.1; all sketches in illustrations are drawn by me. Unless otherwise noted, they are based on my own photographs).

On Hampton's Throne, as in Turner's narrative, two scripts interact:

FIGURE P.1. Sketch of James Hampton's Mercy Seat (collection of the National Museum of American Art, Smithsonian Institution).

one the conventional Roman alphabet, the other an undeciphered revealed script (fig. P.2). Different scripts and graphic practices in the African diaspora also interact in less dramatic circumstances. Consider a message scratched on a sea wall in Roseau, Dominica: parallel lines of abstract emblems and Roman-lettered words together forming a prayer for the basic necessities of life (fig. P.3). Or, on a smaller scale, a hand-painted sign on a chain-link gate in Tennessee: the words "Beware of Dog" ringed by bold Xs and Os in red and black (fig. P.4). Or the red letter V alongside material signs, a white wheel and palmetto in the yard of Victor Melancon in Hammond, Louisiana (fig. P.5). The retired autoworker's yard also contains a miniature burial ground commemorating the passage through his life of various roles—welder, barber, sailor, seer—and personal and spiritual guides (fig. 4.34).

These cases illustrate some of the ways that different scripts and approaches to reading and writing interact in African America. Several are easy to write off as instances of simple decoration, the kind of aesthetic en-

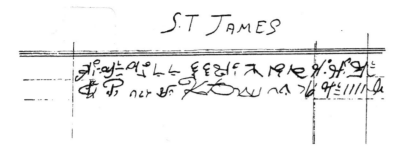

FIGURE P.2. James Hampton used both the Roman alphabet and his own

what MORE foR GOD too Do AGAIN TO GET THE FOODS CLOTHE AND SHELTER 1988 IT IS TIME NOW

FIGURE P.3. Emblems and an alphabetic prayer in a Spiritual Baptist inscription, Roseau, Dominica, June 1989.

FIGURE P.4. Warning sign, Chattanooga, Tennessee.

FIGURE P.5. Found object
initial V, Hammond,
Louisiana

hancement that lacks real substance but makes everyday existence more interesting. Several also involve claims of supernatural communication and agency. Although some form of "literacy" is manifest, the behavior of the participants diverges significantly from conventional rationalist and empiricist models of "being literate." One aim of this book is to propose more constructive ways of approaching such phenomena and taking seriously the information they yield.

The obvious link among these cases is that they combine at least two modes of inscription in a single object, ensemble, or episode. Thus, though each remains distinct in numerous other respects, all mark a confluence between at least two powerful and complex historical currents: the traditions, innovations, and practices of people of African descent in the Americas; and the ideologies of alphabetic literacy that have taken shape among the Arab, European, and European American merchants, slavers, soldiers, and schoolteachers with whom Africans and their descendants have circulated through a prolonged, often violent and oppressive cultural choreography, with profound effects on all parties. To explore the interaction of modes of inscription in the diaspora, then, is to explore the politics of culture.

The sources I draw on for this study include published accounts and my own fieldwork in the southeastern United States—and, to a lesser extent, the West Indies—over a six-year period. In a sense, however, although I worked in eleven states and five countries and pulled as much information as I could from several research libraries, I did very little research specifically for this book.

My initial intention was to work on two projects that seemed to have very little in common. One was an investigation of yards and gardens that

African Americans had dressed for beauty and protection. The other was a more or less straightforward ethnography of literacy within a limited geographic area, preferably one community.

As I traveled in search of a field site, documenting yardwork along the way, I began to notice overlaps between the two projects. Because of racial stereotypes, the potency of "illiterate" as a pejorative label, and the use until recently of literacy tests as a means of disenfranchising black voters, I found that literacy was an uncomfortable topic for me, a white outsider, to raise with African American consultants whom I had known for only a short time. I also found, though, that they enjoyed talking about their yards, collections of objects, and artwork. These topics took off from visible accomplishment rather than an unjust past, and they quickly led in other directions—including the recollections of schooling, informal instruction, and day-to-day reading and writing I had hoped to learn about for my other project. Given the co-constructed nature of conversation, this outcome was predictable, but it surprised me nonetheless. In my travels I also noticed that the two projects overlapped in material ways. Writing and print appeared in yards and home exteriors, and sometimes, especially in the deep South and the West Indies, a printed message appeared alongside other marks that I could not interpret. I began keeping track of such cases.

Meanwhile, between field trips I also read anything that might help to fill in the historical and cultural backgrounds of African American literacy and land use, including travel accounts, oral histories, autobiographies, ethnographies, folklore collections, and novels. Many of these sources contained descriptions that recalled events and objects I had encountered myself, in which alphabetic literacy or its artifacts intersected black vernacular customs, procedures, and innovations. Gradually, instances that seemed anomalous individually began to make sense together and to clamor for their own accounting. Together they challenge some venerable presuppositions about the nature and consequences of literacy; together they also weave a backdrop for vernacular African American literacy. This backdrop is not a seamless fabric, nor does it lend itself to progressive narration. A better analogy might be a loose, strong, boundless net or, perhaps, a genre of performance orchestrated from provisional coherences, memories, appropriations, maskings, jokes, and invocations of transcendence.

The "method" of this book, then, is simply to notice, recount, group, and attempt to interpret interactions between different modes of inscription in the diaspora, following where they lead without claiming definitiveness or closure. Because this book traces a particular kind of interaction across disparate objects and events, it is inherently interdisciplinary and is not preoccupied with texts in the ways that cultural studies and documentary histories usually are. Rather, my orientation is *ethnographic* even when looking at historical material, and preoccupied with *modes of participation* and with culture as *activity*. Integral to this orientation is the assumption that the material contains cues to its own interpretation. Some of these cues index African diasporic associations that have had little say in canonical conceptualizations of "oral" or "literate" activities, or the continua and gaps between these categories. I strive to foreground these cues here and hope others will pursue them further in the future. Thus I include considerable "data" for readers to work through, argue, visualize, recall. The book roves across diverse times, places, and materials in order to foreground cultural dynamics that are more difficult to see when one follows the usual procedure of looking incrementally at one era, one region, one revolt, one book, one throne, or one graphic system at a time.

I am deeply indebted to a number of people for information, encouragement, and constructive criticism. At Teachers College, Columbia University, Ray McDermott set in motion my fascination with literacies and anthropology, offering ideas and encouragement throughout the years that followed my studies there; Paul Byers introduced me to visual anthropology and changed forever my assumptions about communication; Hervé Varenne provided much-needed support. At Yale University, John Szwed contributed enormously through his generosity with information and by sponsoring this project from its inception, as a seminar paper for his course "The Creolization of Literatures," through its expansion into a dissertation and through numerous revisions. It is impossible to imagine what the history of art in Africa and the Americas would be like without the encyclopedic learning and kindness of Robert Farris Thompson pushing so many of us forward. Also at Yale, Keith Basso, Michael D. Coe, and H. W. Scheffler read drafts of parts of this work in early stages and made helpful suggestions. Paul Alfred Barton patiently explained the history and workings of his outstanding achievement, developing the Afrikuandika script, and generously allowed me to reproduce an illustration. Judith McWillie deserves deep thanks for sharing her knowledge, fieldwork, and humor for the past decade. Thanks also go to Flossie Bailey, Edna Jones, Johnson Smith, Ruby Gilmore, Victor Melancon, and my mother, Martha Gundaker.

I also appreciate financial support: for fieldwork, from Sigma Xi, The Scientific Research Society; the Williams Fund, Yale University Department of Anthropology; and the estate of Nell D. Turner; for writing, a Mellon Dissertation Fellowship in 1991–92; for additional research, a residential fellowship in 1992–93 in Studies in Landscape Architecture at Dumbarton Oaks; and for revision of the manuscript, a postdoctoral fellowship in 1993–95 at the Commonwealth Center for the Study of American Culture, College of William and Mary. Chandos Michael Brown, editor of this book series and director of the Center; Arthur Knight; Mechal Sobel, George Henderson, and Sharon Ghamari offered their insights; Brian V. Street and two anonymous readers provided suggestions for revisions. As Bakhtin says, our words are all half someone else's, but I claim errors of fact and judgment as my own.

Contents

1 Introduction: "Conventional" Literacy and "Vernacular" Practice   3

2 Creolization, Double Voicing, Double Vision   15

3 African Scripts, Graphic Practices, and Contexts of Learning and Use   33

4 Diaspora of Signs: A Transatlantic Network   63

5 Narratives of Literacy Acquisition and Use   95

6 Alternative Modes of Participation with Text and Artifacts of Literacy   123

7 Contrasting and Complementary Scripts and Graphic Signs   163

Notes   201

References   237

Index   279

Signs of Diaspora
Diaspora of *Signs*

1

Introduction

"Conventional" Literacy and "Vernacular" Practice

In the Afro-Atlantic diaspora, and perhaps all complex cultural networks and encounters, events involving literacies arise that incorporate resources with different histories and different relationships to spoken language within a single event, narrative, or object. The expressive interaction that results registers these differences but also generates new associations keyed to the immediate situation.[1] These associations feed back into the sociocultural context, help to reconstitute it, and provide metacommentary on the conditions, such as pressured culture contact, that gave rise to the interaction in the first place.

Thus, for example, Carolyn Cooper has pointed out that the printed text of an enslaved eighteenth-century Jamaican woman's song registers both the "truncation" of her voice to fit English conventions of verse and at least some residue of her embodied performance (1993:20–30). Although tensions between the worlds of the outsider recorder and the insider performer are to a degree interpretable by projection from hierarchies of gender and colonialism, the specific ways these tensions are built into the document, the song text, are not self-evident. They require engaging this artifact of literacy from a bicultural or intercultural critical stance unavailable to either the eighteenth-century English bookkeeper who transcribed the song or the enslaved Jamaican who performed it.

This book is also concerned with intercultural forms. Specifically, it looks at the recurring differentiation and cross-fertilization between "conventional" (shorthand for a maze of institutionally sanctioned practices and events) Roman script literacy, with its *canonical* approaches to text, and a host of practices that fall outside literate canons or school-backed rubrics of literate practice. I call these alternative practices "vernacular" for convenience, because of their basis in indigenous, often noninstitutional activities (Camitta 1993). "Conventional" and "vernacular" are "floating signifiers," categories with shifting content partly defined through contrast, partly through orientation toward different bases of power, and partly through the resources that participants bring to bear on their situations.

Research on literacy has often failed to take vernacular practices into account, especially those of economically and politically oppressed peoples like African Americans, because only conventional, institutionally backed forms of literacy seem to have positive educational, economic, and political value. Indeed, in the old, implicitly evolutionist rhetorics of assimilation and acculturation, conventional literacy assumed redemptive proportions as a prescription for a variety of supposed social ills. Such rhetoric implies that literacy itself, not jobs and economic opportunity, can propel the poor into prosperity.

Whatever its causes, lack of attention to indigenous and vernacular forms has serious consequences. Failure to take into account both sides of any interaction masks reciprocity and conflict between them, and ultimately masks participants' resourcefulness in dealing with the imbalances of power that shape their lives. The interaction of modes of inscription[2] in the diaspora resonates with other aspects of African American expression[3] and pulls reading, writing, print, and literate artifacts into the fabric of culture while the abstraction "literacy" floats outside, packed with ideological clout but detached from important referents.

African American vernacular practices that usually fall outside rubrics of literacy include reading and writing linked to divination, trance, and possession; writing in charms; the use of personal and nondecodable scripts; the strategic renunciation of reading and writing as communicative tools; the incorporation of reading and writing into performances of music and ritual; and nonschooled methods of literacy acquisition. Interaction between conventional and vernacular forms encompasses practices that many African Americans themselves regard as unusual,[4] as well as those that emerge from a background of struggle for literacy, education, and justice.[5]

Fundamentally, the interaction involves the intersection of "outsider" conventions with "insider" knowledge and practice, registering the ways that literacies and graphic practices actually take shape locally, culturally, and in individual lives. By tracing this interaction we can see how African Americans have used literacy and its artifacts to construct cohesions, distinctions, and differences that elude description through familiar "divides" like orality versus literacy, literate versus illiterate, or writing versus marking.[6]

I argue that interactions of literate and vernacular practices and signs that Nat Turner, James Hampton, and countless others have orchestrated in many parts of the diaspora signify efforts to change the ground rules of European and Euro-American–based literate ideology, adaptively mastering and reconfiguring its components to fit African American values and circumstances. Expressive cultural modes—narrative, material production, performance—provide resources and means of orchestration, of fine-tuning to circumstance, and are worth exploring in their own right. But working across these modes can also illuminate literacies from angles inaccessible through other approaches.

Divides like oral-versus-literate have been subjected to numerous critiques. Yet they persist. Perhaps because they are part of popular culture as well as scholarly discourses, perhaps because we "know" speech and writing are qualitatively different, this one kind of difference overshadows others and makes alternative frames seem counter to common sense. Nevertheless, the harder one looks at reading and writing in context, the harder it is to reconcile complex activities with either/or accounts.[7] Real-life complications massively overload the conventional have/have-not, can/cannot, literate/nonliterate grid. As Michel de Certeau has pointed out, these polarities have contributed to a mythic equation between certain forms of what he terms "scriptural practice" and Western (read European and American) identity.

> Scriptural practice has acquired a mythical value over the past four centuries by gradually reorganizing all the domains into which the Occidental ambition to compose its history, and thus to compose history itself, has been extended. . . . "Progress" is scriptural in type. In very diverse ways, orality is defined by (or as) that from which a "legitimate" practice—whether in science, politics, or the classroom, etc.—must differentiate itself. The "oral" is that which does not contribute to progress; reciprocally, the "scriptural" is that which separates itself from the magical world of voices and tradition. A frontier (and a front) of Western culture is established by that separation. (de Certeau 1984:134)

De Certeau has summarized a set of common-sense fallbacks in cultural process: categories that have a life of their own sustained through self-validating assumptions and distinctions between haves and have-nots that endure despite changing terminology. One of the tensions that drives the interaction of conventional and vernacular approaches in African America has long been, and continues to be, the notion that institutionally backed practices are "legitimate" while "voices and tradition" are counterprogressive.

Anthropology has certainly contributed to this trend by assigning human groups to various topologies and classification systems with thinly veiled political agendas. Although anthropologists pride themselves on their respect for native terms and indigenous distinctions, until quite recently the warrant for anthropology's existence rested on the collection of data from the other side of a purported "great divide" between "complex" and "traditional" societies. The parallel "literate" versus "oral" distinction permitted anthropologists to imagine that their job was to write about Others without the Others reading, writing, or talking back. Many anthropologists have shared with historians of writing (Diringer 1948; Gelb 1963; Havelock 1976, 1986) the assumption that the West (intrepid intellectual descendant of classical Greece) contributes the "theoretical" and "analytic" side of research while the rest—not only indigenous populations and ethnic minorities but also working-class British youth, Appalachian coal miners, and other labeled groups—contribute the "data."[8] This patronizing attitude is crumbling as massive border-crossing diversifies populations from the city to the academy and as ethnic and cultural studies recognize the astute ways that indigenous peoples and "the folk" reflect on their own situations. When people seem inarticulate it is more than likely that powerlessness, not naiveté, renders them so (McDermott 1987).

Research on literacies and writing systems in the past decade has become far more sensitive to these issues. In African American studies, the importance of the spoken word and "speakerly" text has resuscitated oral and literate categories while exploring the spillover between them. This blurring of old divides is positive; more worrisome is the tendency to equate the African American vernacular in blanket fashion with "orality," itself a misleadingly lump-sum category.

The music and verbal arts of people of African descent have contributed so extensively to the day-to-day texture of American life that American culture would be unrecognizable without them. Yet the media that preserve and transmit music and verbal art, though they seem so much more replete than the written word, continually siphon away the other channels of communication like gesture, movement, and spatial reckoning that are integral to performance. The historical durability and importance of other avenues of expression, particularly visual and material ones, have until recently been seriously underestimated. This book is concerned with many material, performative, and graphic forms that do not directly involve speech but nevertheless recontextualize conventional literate as well as oral communication.

We need richer metaphors to conceptualize complex interaction if we hope to account for—let alone reformulate—the entrenched conceptual hierarchies. I suggest we draw an analogy between the interaction of literate and vernacular practices and interference patterns at the juncture of complex systems—the ambiguating effect that results when disjunctive networks overlay, interface, and shift, with changing points of view.[9] This conceptualization of the multivalent underpinnings of African American literacy, and literacies in general, is, I think, more apt.

However, let me stress that by suggesting that vernacular practices "interfere" with conventional literacy, I do not mean that vernacular forms somehow subvert individuals' ability to read and write. Nor do I imply mere knee-jerk forms of resistance to oppression. The evidence against either interpretation is compelling. Given the opportunity, African Americans have readily mastered reading and writing, turned these skills to wide-ranging purposes, and held education in high esteem whether or not they received formal schooling and whether or not conventional literacy has promised any practical benefits. Most of the cases I discuss in subsequent chapters involve people who could and did read and write in a conventional manner, but who selected or switched to the vernacular under certain conditions—conditions we need to explore.

For all their variety and expressivity, vernacular practices can be a touchy subject because they have been mystified, exoticized, and used in adverse stereotypes. Africans and African Americans have been dehumanized to construct a "front" or "frontier" for the/a Western identity, positioned as contrastive others, and polarized from the "civilized." Much of this othering work rests on the notion that Africans came to this hemisphere from a "preliterate" continent, Africa as a homogeneously vague void from which the history of African American literacy emerges in linear progression. The story is a familiar one. Beginning with capture on a continent without writing, Africans and their descendants traversed by ingenuity and determination through the bitter plantation era, in which reading and writing were forbidden, and into the battle for literate ascendancy against racism and economic hardship in the twentieth century. While this narrative attests to the tremendous obstacles that African Americans have faced, it also omits questions about the knowledge and behaviors that African captives may have brought with them and about the specific adaptive strategies they may have employed. What legacy, if any, in addition to sheer force of will, might have interfered with a lineal progression from "preliterate" to "postliterate"? And is straightforward progression an appropriate way to conceptualize literacy or learning in the first place? By accepting the notion of progression—"progress" in de Certeau's scenario—this narrative tacitly accepts evolutionary premises that cannot do justice to the complex, interactive ways in which people learn and come to terms with reading and writing.[10] Furthermore, notions of preliterate societies fit all too well with totalizing notions of nonliterate and illiterate persons.

The statuses accorded to writing systems also broadly parallel the statuses that evolutionary accounts ascribe to people. Accounts of both privilege a- or decontextual abstractions. For example, evolutionists assume that "reason" is a higher-order faculty that emerges not from practical experience but from the syllogistic manipulation of discrete, arbitrary, and decontextualized units. A comparable position holds that alphabets are more "efficient" than syllabaries because alphabets supposedly encode smaller units of sound and use graphic representations that are abstract and context-independent. This position fails to take into account either the highly variable fit between the units of a writing system and those of spoken language or the contextual cues that must be mastered in order to interpret what has been written (Coe 1992). Evolutionary accounts therefore rule out questions about historical and cultural particulars before they are asked. Yet these particulars are precisely what make literacies multiplex, not unitary, facets of a larger graphic repertoire or economy (Basso 1974; Szwed 1981; Woods-Elliot and Hymes n.d.).

The recurring interaction between conventional and vernacular forms in African American practice shows that *the relationship between the old and the new is recursive, not a matter of simple displacement*. Material potentially relevant to this relationship in African America abounds. To begin with, of course, Africa is by no means homogeneous or a void. Most (if not all) African Americans can trace their ancestry to areas with rich scriptural and graphic traditions—which, however, include practices excluded from prevailing rubrics of literacy. Furthermore, peoples of West and Central Africa who did not use alphabets or syllabaries during the era of the slave trade routinely combined verbal and visual expression in gestural and textile codes, graphic renderings of proverbs, the graphic invocation of spiritual powers, punning with material objects, and intricate divination systems. In the face of contact through capture, invasion, and trade, all these communicative modes offered resources for embedding outsider scripts in local systems of values, and vice versa. I review some of these resources in chapter 3.

Interaction between African, African American, and European-derived practices and knowledge systems also resists unilinear notions of transatlantic continuity—*not* because there are too few connections, although the forms connections take are quite diverse and often convoluted; rather, the fruits of the relatively new enterprise of African American studies suggest that there is *too much* information on too many levels—and too much more to learn—to expect anything less than a wide-ranging network of connections and disjunctions between the old and the new.

In short, linear and progressive notions of cultural process are as out of step with African American studies as they are with research on literacy. The interference metaphor sketched earlier is a more workable conceptualization. Multileveled and relational, it dispels seeming contradictions such as old versus new and historically durable versus innovative with the reminder that they are not inherent states but contextual, contingent descriptions of relations. Flesh out the interference metaphor further with specific economic, political, and racial pressures experienced by black Americans, and it becomes easier to see why authors from Frederick Douglass to W. E. B. Du Bois to Gerald Early have viewed the tensions involved in living a "double" life as generative forces in African American literature and experience.

In any case, remaining open to interaction among African precedents, emergent African American practices, and European-derived literate conventions amounts to little more than a claim that literacies inscribe traces of their histories and contexts of use. Although the first African settlement in North America predated the *Mayflower* (Bennett 1966), illegal slavers continued to smuggle captive Africans into Southern ports as late as 1858 (see Fauset 1925; Imes 1917). This extended period of transatlantic contact alone cannot explain African American vernacular approaches to literacy and texts, but it should not be ignored.

An inclusive, transatlantic outlook also opens insights on the recurring features of functional groupings into which vernacular African American graphic practices cohere. When we attend to cues such as indigenous terms, the design of signs, material composition, and the context of use, African American practices seem to exhibit considerable redundancy and patterning. Broadly, three functional groupings emerge from a wide range of events and locations. They are, with considerable code- or style-switching among them: (a) linear messages and narrative; (b) modes of tying, wrapping, and enclosure; and (c) emblems that invoke and project identities. The groupings are usually tacit and encompass adaptations to local circumstances. To adopt Brian Street's (1984) usage functions and contexts of use frame reading, writing, artifacts, and graphic practices *ideologically* from "inside" the African American vernacular, while canonical, schooled, literate conventions frame a putative "mainstream" from the outside. (See fig. 1.1.)

I argue that together these groupings encompass the broad contours of an African American graphic repertoire that overlaps, but is not isomorphic with, that of canonical literate conventions. Cultures around the world may well make comparable distinctions and generate similar modes of inscription. The main divergence between these groupings and literate conventions arises not from signs themselves, but because conventional literate ideology devalues or brackets from relevance virtually all aspects of reading or writing that are context-dependent or not directly involved in the encoding and decoding of units of sound. In other words, this ide-

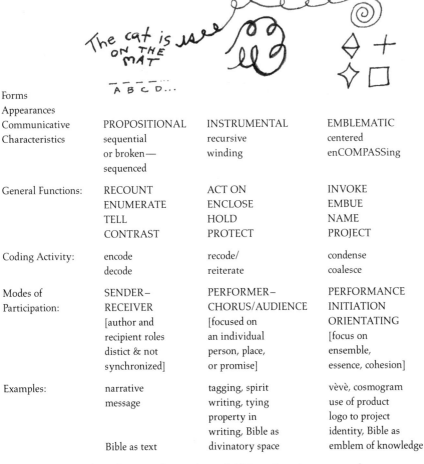

Forms Appearances			
Communicative Characteristics	PROPOSITIONAL sequential or broken— sequenced	INSTRUMENTAL recursive winding	EMBLEMATIC centered enCOMPASSing
General Functions:	RECOUNT ENUMERATE TELL CONTRAST	ACT ON ENCLOSE HOLD PROTECT	INVOKE EMBUE NAME PROJECT
Coding Activity:	encode decode	recode/ reiterate	condense coalesce
Modes of Participation:	SENDER– RECEIVER [author and recipient roles distict & not synchronized]	PERFORMER– CHORUS/AUDIENCE [focused on an individual person, place, or promise]	PERFORMANCE INITIATION ORIENTATING [focus on ensemble, essence, cohesion]
Examples:	narrative message Bible as text	tagging, spirit writing, tying property in writing, Bible as divinatory space	vèvè, cosmogram use of product logo to project identity, Bible as emblem of knowledge

FIGURE 1.1. Three functional groupings of African American vernacular inscriptions

ology functionally isolates components associated with literacy from those of other potentially relevant communicative repertoires. (See fig. 1.2.) Each interaction between entrenched literate conventions and the emergent African American vernacular thus poses a challenge (not unlike the ways that modernist expressions influenced by jazz and African art challenged earlier representational orthodoxies). Readers of a book like this one come to the text well supplied with knowledge of literate conventions that have a built-in orientation toward European values and institutions. In order to understand the interaction from both sides we must therefore strive for balance from a foothold within the black vernacular. For this purpose, I turn to three recurring concepts that have served their users well as shorthand for salient aspects of black experience: (1) *creolization*; (2) authors' accounts of *double voicing* in African American literature and experience; and (3) *double vision*, the ability to see across cultural and physical boundaries.

Creolization has theoretical and practical aspects. Theories of creolization differ, but they share a baseline concern with intersections of two or more previously unrelated languages, cultures, or traditions and the interaction of small- and large-scale phenomena with disparate histories. Given this focus on cultures and language-in-use, the concept of creolization can also help to link the study of African American literacies to other aspects of anthropological theory and ethnographic investigation in the diaspora. Because it crosscuts disciplines and traditions, creolization encompasses literacy-related practices that might otherwise seem merely anomalous. The term is also helpful because it refers to a *process*, a dynamic pattern

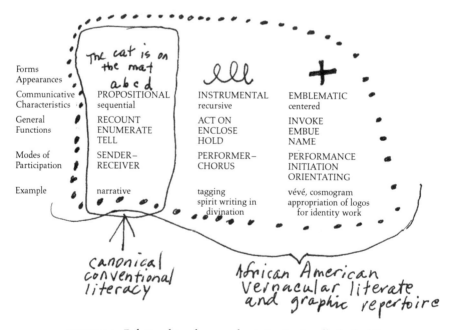

FIGURE 1.2. Relationship of vernacular to institutionally backed literate conventions.

that emerges when interference among different cultural systems becomes systematized in new languages and cultural orders.[11]

The notions of double voicing and double vision have been applied to so many situations and taken up by so many academics in recent years that they have become virtual clichés. But, though these terms have lost their freshness as literary metaphors, in nuanced use they continue to bring indigenous insight to bear on a specific kind of sociocultural positioning, called hybridity by Paul Gilroy and other theorists of the Black Atlantic, which is a critical issue in the contemporary diasporic world along with race, class, and gender.

The word "hybridity" is sometimes used interchangeably with "creolization." However, the terms differ significantly in the kinds of interaction they imply, thus in the relationship they imply among a creole/ hybrid event (or object or culture) and its contributing sources (Szwed 1996). Whereas hybridization is often said to "blend" formerly divergent sources into a new entity (new varieties of corn and livestock being classic examples), creolization draws on sources to make new forms but does not necessarily obliterate them in the process. Indeed, the new form may involve a pointed commentary on its sources, or it may transform them by association in new contexts. These potentials of creolization are central to the modes of expression this book examines.

I use the terms "double voicing" and "double vision" in fairly literal ways to refer to two or more ways to say/hear, inscribe/interpret, or see/represent. These terms help to describe processes of creolization because they take into account the dual or multiple factors that interaction involves, yet they work against either/or, is/isn't polarization. "Doubling" establishes an oscillation between contrasting perspectives but does not reify them into entities. Double voicing refers to the articulation of a dual cultural consciousness, shaped through social and personal conflict and expressed in oral and written mediums. Double vision is itself a double-voiced concept, in that speakers and writers use it to refer to both bicultural existence and to special powers of sight that cross the boundaries between the visible and the invisible, the material and the immaterial dimensions of reality. By extension, double voicing and double vision offer ways to talk about relationships between two (or more) sign systems, modes of inscription, and ways of approaching literate texts and artifacts. Sometimes they take on a more concrete character when two voices, two scripts, two systems of meaning occur side by side.

*C*hapters 1 through 4 sketch some of the signs, functions, and contexts that inform the interaction of conventional literacy and vernacular practices in African America. These chapters are not about proving specific African retentions or origins; some transatlantic connections I mention are well established, while others are more speculative. The purpose of these chapters as a group is to suggest the historical and geographic scope of an extended intercultural relationship that was, and is, too complex to describe in full, yet is all too often treated as insubstantial, trivial, or nonexistent.

Chapter 2 expands the themes of creolization, double voicing, and double vision, especially in relation to the varied ways African Americans have displayed mastery of outsider forms attributed to European sources and then displaced them through emphasis on insider knowledge.

Chapter 3 is about "resources," a term I use to designate material (whether physical, graphic, conceptual, or behavioral) that is excerpted, quoted, revitalized, reinterpreted, or recontextualized by a shift from one interpretive frame to another. For example, the Bible as a resource is used for conventional literate reading as well as divination. As an object, the Bible can be moved physically to a different setting, or its function can change while it remains in one place. Yet it also retains certain important associations whether it is read aloud or probed with a fingertip. Thus resources provide means of embedding aspects of one situation inside another, an important cultural dynamic (Herskovits 1958). Chapter 3 focuses on scripts; graphic signs; literate and graphic practices, values, and ideologies; and approaches to learning that I believe have transatlantic implications. The chapter opens with a review of the literature on African graphic systems.

Chapter 4 shows how one network of graphic signs with well-established African connections functions in the United States and the Caribbean independently of and in interaction with Roman alphabetic messages. This chapter uses material from my fieldwork and published sources to explore relationships among the crossmark, the four-eyes sign, and the cosmographic sun. My aim is to describe semantic networks that emerge when we look at specific African American graphic and material signs in detail.

Chapters 5–7 focus on the ways that the interaction of conventional literacies and vernacular practices figure in African American expressive culture. These chapters contain a series of brief interrelated case studies, many drawn from standard sources.[12]

Chapter 5 looks at narratives of literacy acquisition and use, dating from the late eighteenth century through the turn of the twentieth century. Two themes recur in these narratives. First, the relationship between literacy, personal liberty, and political and economic freedom is a subject closely scrutinized by scholars. The second theme, which has received much less attention, involves occasions when the narrator makes a point of *not* reading or *not* writing, even though he or she struggled successfully to acquire literate skills. These occasions sometimes also involve intense spiritual or religious experience. Chapter 5 shows that these two themes intersect in important ways. In the short run, provisional renunciations of reading and writing privilege insider knowledge and relegate conventional literacy to a position of secondary importance—as do the creolized expressive activities I discuss in chapter 2. In the long run, however, such renunciations may have the opposite effect, helping to fortify participants in the fight for economic, political, and educational opportunity. The interacting themes of purposeful reading and not-reading, writing and not-writing, suggest transatlantic dimensions that are also important to the inquiry of this book.

Whereas chapter 5 deals with narrative, chapter 6 examines modes of participation with texts and artifacts of literacy. These modes involve texts and artifacts used (1) as metaphors; (2) in ritual performance; (3) as talismans, charms, or instruments in healing; and (4) as components of divination and revelation. From a Eurocentric perspective, these are precisely the kind of activities that mark the "backward" end of the continuum of progress. Chapter 6 suggests other ways of conceptualizing these modes of participation, attempting to take into account the creolizing processes in which texts and artifacts are embedded and the double vision that such participation entails.

Double vision and creolizing processes also inform the texts and activities I discuss in chapter 7. Here I focus on the combining of contrasting kinds of script and graphic signs in cases that are quite diverse. They include revealed and personal scripts, writing in trance, wordplay, and reconfigured spelling and punctuation. What the cases share is that they render double vision concrete, placing conventional literacy alongside alternative forms of inscription. The interaction between two kinds of script binds together different sets of values and points of view. Writ large, the interaction reconstitutes patterns in material and graphic form that also cut across the narratives and modes of participation discussed in the previous chapters. Overall, the patterned interaction of reading and not-reading, writing and not-writing, coded and nondecodable renders more noticeable a coherent yet open-ended and inclusive African American vernacular repertoire that brings literacy into an alternative mythic zone, not "the West" but "home," wherever that may be.

> "The Book speaks in many languages," said the Devil. "A lifetime can be spent in the worthwhile pursuit of the wisdom of the Book. There are special situations with no rules, and special rules for no situations."
>
> (Dumas 1988:237)

2

Creolization, Double Voicing, Double Vision

*T*he writer Henry Dumas imagined an exegetical devil pronouncing on the "wisdom of the Book." Presumably, this Book numbers among texts that, according to anthropologist Jack Goody, place an unchanging record of the word of God and fixed rules for living at the center of religions like Christianity and Islam. Goody argues that this textual basis distinguishes "religions of conversion" from nonliterate or preliterate religions that acquire followers by birth and location (1968, 1977, 1987). Yet, as Dumas's Devil implies, one can't rely on the Book for fixity and closure. The search for the wisdom of the Book can consume a lifetime; indeed, its promise of worthwhileness amounts to a devilish temptation because the rules in the text and the situations in life do not mesh.

This disjunction must have been readily apparent to enslaved black congregations as they listened to the passages about good masters and dutiful servants that white preachers selectively intoned in the service of the plantocracy of the American South. But zigzag breaks and tied-up commitments thwart the devil, and African Americans have refined the arts of hearing the unsaid and transforming situations and rules that their oppressors overoptimistically treat as givens. This chapter reviews three fluid strategies that African Americans have used on occasion to characterize such experiences, including among others the relationships and disjunctions among conventional literate and vernacular practices in written texts and expressive activities.

Creolization

The concept of creolization offers a way to talk about complex cultural and linguistic interaction. A concept with this capacity is essential for coming to terms with reading, writing, text, graphic signs, and literacy-related artifacts in African America. Consider the problems involved in comparing literacies and studying changes in their functions over time:

> It is clear that any kind of literacy is initially dependent upon a given graphic code or set of codes. If that were all there was to it, however, then encoding and decoding techniques between the grapheme and the phoneme would exhaust literacy. The introduction of graphemes does not lay innocently upon the complex of preexisting codes. It assumes some of the representational burdens of preexisting codes but is powerless with respect to others, and a reshuffling goes on. Each channel of communication depends for its complete encipherment on what it excludes as well as what it includes of the total communicative act. When channels change . . . there is a redistribution between what is explicitly represented or notated and what is not. . . . When a culture changes historically, the channel it uses for specific kinds of messages, the relations between utterance and situation, are brought to the fore and possibly radically reconstrued. (Kittay 1990:165–166)

Here, Jeffrey Kittay gives a clear summary of the situational and cultural specificity of communicative channels and codes. But the assessment stops short of the additional complexity in situations of extended cultural interchange where each grapheme, and each act of encoding, also has the potential to inscribe conflicted histories and imbalances of power. Debates about standardizing orthography for Haitian Creole are exemplary:

> [A]rguments about orthography reflect competing concerns about representations of Haitianness at the national and international level, that is, how speakers wish to define themselves to each other, as well as to represent themselves as a nation. . . . The orthography debates about kreyòl share . . . structural and symbolic properties of dichotomizing discourses. Critical to the debates is who counts and who does not, who is "us," and who is "them." In terms of nation building, these oppositions often point to serious social divisions and ambivalences that have deep historical roots. . . . Furthermore, orthographic choice here is a statement about a nation's potential connections to other communities. (Schieffelin and Doucet 1994:176–77).

Representations of language thus go hand in hand with representations of nation and culture. But what might happen if we let go altogether of the notion of *a* culture as lump sum and treat the change of codes and boundaries among communicative channels as integral to cultural process? Deterritorializing culture as a unitary construct envisions a world in which contact and variation are not aberrations from norms or catalysts for reshuffling but, rather, givens against which human strivings for stable and

recognizable realities constantly pit themselves. Orthographic standardization is a node of contestation in these strivings, and so is the rubric
"culture." Like "literacy," the content it covers is flexible.

As I use the concept here, creolization is a form of cultural process
rooted in the politics of contact, color and class stratification, and vernacular expressive forms that emerged in the former slave societies of the West
Indies under colonial rule (Brathwaite 1971).

As a research paradigm, creolization draws on linguistic theory, but
follows creole linguistics instead of older structural theories.[1] Creolization
"suggests that internal variation and change, rather than uniformity and
synchronicity, are distinctive features of languages" and "that cultures are
neither structures nor plural amalgams, but a . . . set of intersystems"
(Drummond 1980:34).[2]

Intersystems arise in lived experience. During creolization, participants
reconfigure relationships among intersecting, interfering, and often hierarchical cultural systems to fit new circumstances. When Africans from different ethnic groups encountered each other and the representatives of
metropolitan, colonial powers on the plantations, they often made the most
of similarities and redundancies among cultural systems. At the same time
they also selectively loosed components from their moorings in these systems, treating them as resources to draw on as situations warranted.

West Indian societies differ among themselves and from that of the
United States in how they envision a society composed of diverse populations. Creolization is relevant in the United States because a creolist perspective presupposes that permeable social and disciplinary boundaries,
border-crossing, and cultural mobility are the ways of the world, not mere
aberrations.[3] Although the North American and West Indian experiences
are by no means interchangeable, important commonalities exist in the
histories of people of African descent in the two regions.

From the linguistic standpoint, creoles are new languages that emerge
in (usually pressured) contact among peoples whose languages (and cultures) previously had little or no contact (French, Fon, and KiKongo, for
example). In addition to their association with the pressures of African and
European encounters in the Americas, several other points about creole
languages are relevant to literate and graphic practices.

Although creoles are autonomous, "new" (not "deficient" versions of
"standard") languages, the metropolitan languages that contributed to the
formation of a creole under colonialism frequently remain associated with
schooling and conventional literacy in societies where creoles are spoken,
much as in the United States many people consider standard English essential to school success. The standard language (Haas 1982) retains an
aura of relative prestige because standard language and conventional literacy are, often accurately, perceived as adjuncts of social, political, and economic mobility. However, in the West Indies, Creole has its own forms of
prestige among "nationalistic peoples who believe that the extreme Creole
varieties preserve their historical and cultural experience and allow for
more genuine expression of things West Indian" (Roberts 1988:13).

The different forms of appreciation and social distinctions associated with standard and creole languages generate areas of cultural and linguistic ambiguity (Reisman 1970; B. F. Williams 1987). As Karl Reisman put it, "syncretisms increase the area of conscious or unconscious *double statement* and the possibility of symbolic play" (1970:131, my emphasis). Reisman also noted that the strength of creole languages comes from their use for communication among the enslaved and their descendants. "This is the source of the force of Creole languages which from the beginning of our records made those who wished to communicate with the slave populations feel the need to adjust to it even while it belonged to a powerless section of the society" (1965:34–35).

This contrast of insider and outsider communication, of inward-directed cultural and (inter)personal life playing with and against mythic and practical aspects of literate ideology, recurs again and again across African American expressive forms and biographies.

The poet and historian Edward Kamau Brathwaite found a double-sided approach to literacy in accounts of the 1831–32 slave revolt in Jamaica, and especially the ambiguous position of Sam Sharpe, its leader, a mission-educated mulatto who cast his lot with the more African-oriented black slaves.

> Sam Sharpe could read, and to this extent he was involved in the Liberal Metropolitan intrusion [liberal non-slave-owning missionaries who taught slaves and free blacks]. He was also a deacon in the Baptist church, which gave him an even more intimate relationship with metropolitan values. But . . . [he] was one of the "ingrates." . . . And when he used the press or print, he used it not to browse or graze but to *confirm*: "Sharpe said I know we are *free*, I read it in the English papers." Besides, the oral context of knowledge in which Sharpe was rooted meant that . . . Sharpe absorbed and converted into the communal literacy of his time, what the books call *rumour*. So that the *ship*, which was used . . . to identify [the masthead of] a particular newspaper, was also the *freedom ship* . . . bringing the Freedom Paper from [the British government] . . . and is the same ship that the present day Rastafari know will come to take them back to Ityopia. Here, in other words, was subversive material that couldn't be charged with seditious libel; which couldn't even be controlled. (1977:51–52)

The recruitment of English newspapers into local approaches to literacy had unanticipated consequences and subversive power. Brathwaite's "prismatic" view of creolization (1974, 1977) encompasses unintended consequences, nonevolutionary reversals, and shifting allegiances.

> [T]he idea of creolization as an ac/culturative, even interculturative process between "black" and "white," with the (subordinate) black absorbing "progressive" ideas and technology from the white, has to be modified into a more complex vision in which appears the notion of *negative or regressive creolization*: a self-conscious refusal to borrow or be influenced by the Other, and a coincident desire to fall back upon, unearth, recognize elements in the maroon or ancestral culture that will preserve or apparently preserve the unique identity of the group. This quality of consciousness is recognized in all modern societies as one of the roots of nationalism. (1977:55)

Violent revolt is one of the occasions that fosters group consciousness and nationalistic impulses. These impulses are grounded in what Brathwaite calls *nam*: that combination of

> (1) *lore* (direct conscious teaching), (2) *behavior* (energy patterns of expression, speech movement and sociointellectual praxis), and (3) *ideological myth* . . . which have somehow kept Afro-Caribbean cultural expression "African" and/or "black," especially at moments of crisis or in the so-called margins of the society, despite the obvious material and social advantages of Afro-Saxonism, for instance. (1977:41)

"Somehow" is the operative word here. Even at those so-called margins and crises where "blackness" is most palpable, continuities and discontinuities with the African past in creolization resist neat, global claims about origins, content, or scope. However, African American adaptations and innovations in the social climate of creolization do often seem to fall into a pattern of dualities or double statements that highlight difference and recur across various kinds of activity. Though "duality" is a convenient rough-and-ready term to sketch this pattern schematically, the "components" of dualities do not consist of paired, reified units, but of loosely coupled networks whose moments of contrast are occasioned by purposeful participation, not top-down systematicity.[4]

Students of African American expressive culture have observed that when doubling patterns unfold in particular sequential events in time, the semantic loading of an event often tends to shift away from a "European" orientation and toward an "African" one as activity progresses (Abrahams and Szwed 1983:29; Marks 1971; Pitts 1986, 1989, 1991, 1993). Thus doubling can involve something like Brathwaite's "negative creolization." To give just one example from Monserrat:

> *(C)ountry dance* orchestras . . . play for social dancing, but the same music is also used for inducing possession on other occasions, called "jombee dances." On these latter occasions quadrille dance rhythms [which spread to Monserrat from Europe] are intensified and gradually "Africanized" in order that individuals may become possessed and convey the messages of the spirits. Secular customs such as suppers for guests are transformed into ritual sacrifices for spirits, and the mundane lyrics of quadrille songs become part of the mechanism for possession. But the ritual occasion has become so "masked," reinterpreted so extensively that the traditional European elements of the dance seem predominant to the casual observer. (Szwed and Marks 1988:29)[5]

The shift to a more "African" style in the jombee dance, church services, street carnivals, and other performances is also of course a shift toward insider knowledge and communication, comparable to the social functions of Creole.

However, a literal-minded attitude toward what is "really" African in origin in performance shifts can be confusing, because what may signify or emblematize African identity in a particular situation may have nothing do with actual origins.[6] (For example, popular streetwear in the late

1980s were green, red, and black leather pendants of the map of Africa made in Asia from North or South American or Australian hides.)[7]

Double Voicing

Code and style shifts are dynamic, contrastive events that foreground two or more languages, resisters, or behavioral styles, and pivot on the contrast between them. As stylized events themselves, style shifts usually seem to unfold effortlessly, even naturally, despite their aesthetic and performative complexity. But they also embody tensions of class, language, and cultural markedness (Abrahams 1970–71). "I don't talk that talk," said an African American Yale student to protest stereotypes that impute "lower-class" speech styles to black speakers generally. This statement is a dual articulation that sums up the tension very well: the student briefly talks "that talk"—the adaptable black vernacular of toast and tale, signifying and marking—in order to say that she doesn't.[8] This episode can be read as a case in point of the double voicing that several black authors have said characterizes their literature and lives.[9] Perhaps best known is the phrase "double consciousness," which W. E. B. Du Bois introduced in *The Souls of Black Folk* to sum up what he termed the unreconciled "twoness" of being American and Negro.[10]

Although "twoness" and "double consciousness" have gained widespread currency as metaphors and models of African Americans' cultural situation, these concepts have rarely been probed ethnographically, as ways of characterizing style switching in actual utterances, events, and patterns of activity. Yet numerous African American speakers and writers have grappled with the issue, leaving a trail of double voicing in their works. For example, as Joanne Braxton has pointed out, the poet Paul Laurence Dunbar strove to capture the sounds of black dialect in some of his poems and wrote others in a European-oriented high style, creating powerful works in both styles (1993). But reviewers such as William Dean Howells praised only the poems in dialect, which could be easily reconciled with stereotypes of the "primitive," and dismissed Dunbar's standard English verse as second-rate. Other reviewers, struggling to excoriate stereotypes, tended to underestimate Dunbar, relegating his work to the category of sentimental plantation literature. What matters most about Dunbar for present purposes is that, whether one views him as an unreconcilably ambivalent writer to his detriment or a master of two voices to his favor, the marks of Dunbar's voices register in print. The dashes and apostrophes of dialect contrast visibly with the regular spacings of standard English spelling on the page.

Literature, then, is a category of conventional literacy that also registers the tensions that shape and segment a particular literacy from within. According to M. M. Bakhtin, such tensions shape dialogic forms like the novel into polyphonous arenas in which the multiple voices of the author's world clamor against each other to have their say (1981). Other forms and genres are more stable, tending toward monologic utterance: epic poetry and essays, for example. However, although Bakhtin was attentive to the social life of language, he was not writing from a world that was polyphonous in the same deeply rifted and silted way as the African diaspora.

When black authors speak of double voicing, they seem to be saying that in their world, their African America, not only the dialogic novel but even supposedly "monologic" genres—essays, toasts, sermons—have at least two voices. Furthermore, although double voicing permeates these genres, the relationship between voices in them is *not* necessarily "dialogic," in the sense of an open-ended conversation, a dialogue. Metropolitan voices do not call-and-respond or discuss or debate with African American voices. Rather, one voice systematically *displaces* another, moving from the standard voice to the inside voice and back again as situations warrant. The standard is so familiar to its speakers that it can mask the inside voice, especially from those predisposed to think that no such voice exists in the first place.

In this view, then, even black monologue and the quintessentially monologic essay form are double. The essayist Gerald Early explains:

> The black essayist is caught between acting and writing . . . as he uses language he becomes both mascot and scribe, an odd, ambivalent coupling of the purloined and the purposeful. Hazrat Inayat Khan, Sufi philosopher and musician, spoke wisely when he said, "the nature of creation is the doubling of one." . . . Those systems of doubleness in our culture are what generates the vital syncretism that makes it function. (1989:xii-xiii)

Thus literacy, as the infrastructure of literature, is deeply if tacitly implicated in reconstructing dualities, and sometimes covering as much as it reveals.[11]

Early also discusses doubleness in the novelist and anthropologist Zora Neale Hurston's autobiographical account of her teenage days as the sole black person on tour with a white theatrical company (1989:xi). For company members she was a mascot, but also a chronicler and entertainer-of-the-entertainers who left tweaking, gossipy messages on the company callboard. As Hurston recalled the experience, blackness wasn't all that set her apart.

> I was a Southerner, and had the map of Dixie on my tongue. . . . It was not that my grammar was bad, it was the idioms. [Northerners] do not know of the way an average Southern child, white or black, is raised on simile and invective. They know how to call names. It is an everyday affair to hear somebody called a mullet-headed, mule-eared, wall-eyed, hog-nosed, 'gator-faced, shad-mouthed, screw-necked, goat-bellied, puzzle-gutted, camel-backed, butt-sprung, . . . razor-legged, box-ankled, shovel-footed, unmated so-and-so! . . . When they get through with you, you and your whole family look like an acre of totempoles. (Hurston 1942:145)

Here Hurston demonstrates another potential of double voicing: new meanings made from double-sided associative packages. Her vivid images feel solid enough to be physically built.[12] Moving down the list, found objects, fish, fauna, flotsam, and body parts retain their old, separate identities while playing new roles in paired combinations—a doubling of histories within an overarching transformation.

Although Hurston attributes this form of wordplay to black and white Southerners alike, in African American parlance the type of insult she describes is known as *specifying* and is associated especially with black women. Refined to a cutting edge, this name-calling gains part of its force from its ever-pending threat to spin out of control. Another permutation (or analogue) of specifying is *reading*, a term that probably derives from the practice of "reading out of the church" or "reading out of fellowship." Reading out involves calling the names of sinners and backsliders and listing their transgressions one by one before an assembled congregation (Washington 1972:65). But the term "reading" also implies a comprehensive insult, a total perusal of all aspects of the subject, top to bottom and margin to margin.

Hurston's written specifying/reading relates better to Brathwaite's ambiguous image of a newspaper ship that becomes a freedom ship than to beliefs like those of some literacy scholars that alphabetic writing inherently promotes clarity and cements meanings in place (cf. Olson 1977).[13] On the contrary, depending on context, writing can fuel rumor and unanticipated turns of events. Hurston seems to underscore this idea by calling her autobiography *Dust Tracks on a Road*. With this title her double voice implies not only the track of a life, steps taken, but steps that can be picked up and used, as dust tracks can be used by one's enemies in hoodoo, conjuration. As in the case of hair, blood, sweat, toenails, and excreta, writing down a life creates a residue to conjure with. Writing is a double-sided, dangerous, and changeable medium.[14]

Double Vision

The term "double vision" refers to the perception of more than one plane of existence at a time. Ralph Ellison aligned double vision with double consciousness to talk about the experience of being black and American (Ellison 1964). But the semantic history of the concept in African American folk tradition is also rich in usages in which double vision refers to seeing across the boundary between material and spiritual worlds. Sometimes African Americans have used the term *four-eyed* for this capacity.[15] Newbell Niles Puckett explored a narrow sense of the concept, the gift of seeing ghosts, under the heading " 'double-sighted' folks" in his account of Southern Negro folk beliefs (1926:137–138). Persons with this gift were said to be born with a caul or veil over the face, and various states of the caul—kept after birth, torn, bought, sold, lost—determined the extent of the gift, and whether the owner could speak with the ghosts or merely see them. Thus, broadly, double sight includes clairvoyance and the ability to divine the hidden causes of illness and assaults by negative influences.[16]

Double vision also generates a watershed in perceptiveness, sorting viewers according to what they can and cannot see and leaving room for even mundane objects and events to have meanings that outsiders cannot recognize. For example, during fieldwork in Mississippi I met an elderly man, Johnson Smith, who had arranged ordinary objects in his yard—wheels, water hoses, reflectors, chairs—to make double-entendre references to his double-sighted powers and also to make his scrap resale businesses more entertaining.[17] Mr. Smith was quite purposeful in these activities and proud of his eyesight, which was perfect despite his eighty-five years. Many of his butt-sprung, puzzle-gutted conglomerations (fig. 2.1) fit Hurston's material specifications exactly, but Mr. Smith relished their invisibility to a general audience: "They can't see it; they can look all day and they still can't see it. But it's all right there *looking at them*" (interview, December 1991).

I asked Mr. Smith if he would instruct me about double sight as he saw fit. In reply he brought out an old wooden box containing a stereoscopic viewer and cards bearing pairs of identical photographs. The set had belonged to his mother. He inserted cards into the viewer and told me to describe the content of each scene in turn, including everything I saw. I did as he asked but was disappointed; it seemed that he had either not understood or purposefully misunderstood what I meant by "double sight" and was simply sharing a family heirloom. But at his insistence I continued to describe each scene aloud. There must have been thirty or more. Gradually the words changed from description to a litany of physical toil. Each of the stereoscopic cards that I described showed double photographs of turn-of-the-century black labor: people picking cotton under a glaring sun, baling and ginning cotton, sawing pine trees, distilling turpentine, darning worn clothing beside a cabin fire—romanticized scenes that lost their nos-

FIGURE 2.1. Sink-face, Lumberton, Mississippi, 1989.

talgic aura through the naming of their subjects. Mr. Smith did not comment on this episode directly. He said, "See how real those pictures look. I walked all over Mississippi back in those times" (interview, November 2, 1990). He left interpretation open-ended, like the objects in his yard, there to be noticed or not.

Double vision as Johnson Smith explained it is a form of visual signifying.[18] Insights come between the lines, and clouds of ambiguity become sharp points. Smith's lesson in double vision used visual signifying not to insult but to instruct, to orchestrate a transition in values. He saw to it that my exhaustion and eventual empathy with the black workers would displace the (almost certainly white) photographer's nostalgic view of the past.

This transition parallels other African American performances that style-shift toward a "deeper," more in-group or "African" orientation as the performance intensifies. Some shifts, like the "downward" transition in the jombee dance, also involve spirit possession. All begin with displays of expertise in forms that participants consider primarily European-derived. These forms are displaced by those that highlight important African American values; for example, individual virtuosity, spiritual insight, and ancestral reciprocity.

The concept of double vision furthers possibilities for noticing and describing parallel shifts in the ways some African Americans have attuned their literacy acquisition, texts, and scripts to similar values. Often these approaches concretize double vision by aligning two (or more) types of graphic signs. Such signs appeal to the eye, but vision coexists with hearing, the tactile quality of rhythm, and other responses of the senses in performance.

The traditional sung sermon style of African American preachers offers an example of this dynamic.[19] The sung sermon is also a mode of performance in which conventional literacy interacts with vernacular signs of spirituality. Jeff Todd Titon notes, in his afterword to a collection of sermons by the Rev. C. L. Franklin, that two streams of preaching have persisted in African American communities since the pre-Emancipation period. One descends from learned orators and seminarians; the other descends from enslaved preachers—"exhorters," whose style has variously been described as "old-time," "folk," "performed," and "spiritual" (Franklin 1989:213). In the latter stream as it appears today, and in sermons like those of C. L. Franklin, which combined both streams, performance style shifts often highlight, then displace, an approach to written text associated with European American conventions.[20]

William Ferris described the transition in style and evaluative loading built into traditional black sermon structure. The preacher begins with a text from the Bible but moves away from the text and textuality as the sermon progresses. Wordings carried over from week to week replace the text's particularity. The phrases with which the preacher builds the sermon become shorter and more rhythmic. Call-and-response with the congregation increases. In the eyes of preacher and congregation, the mark of a successful sermon is the arrival of the Holy Spirit amid the congregation. "When a person 'falls out' [s]he has received direct communication from God and [her] experience is evidence that the preacher has succeeded with his sermon" (1972:39).

The arrival of the Spirit requires changing the ground rules for participation away from those associated with conventional literacy. This kind of change is not absolutely tied to any one communicative mode or to qualities "internal" to speech or writing (Bledsoe and Robey 1986; Shuman 1986).

Obviously, sermon style is not dependent on actual reading. The preacher need only quote the text in a measured, authoritative manner in order to open the sermon. However, by calling into play those qualities conventionally associated with literacy—textual stability, institutional backing, multiply mediated relations with the author "behind" the text, the distanced roles of active reader and passive listener—the doubling pattern of the sermon aptly foregrounds the alternatives—flexibility, improvisation, individual voices, direct spiritual communication with those who reciprocally help to make such communication possible—and furthers a shared, active involvement with the Spirit, in which the preacher's role as leader intertwines with the responsive encouragement of his or her flock.[21]

In sum, the sermon's shift in emphasis contributes to the *visibility* of the Spirit. Within the framework of responsive participation, the shift helps to "open the eyes" of the congregation[22] in a microcosm of initiation.[23]

In many churches another aspect of the service also resembles initiation. Although preacher and congregation move together, the shift away from two crisply defined roles—reader and listener—also accentuates more complexly differentiated and stratified groupings among the churchgoers. These groupings include the preacher, elders, worshippers who receive the Spirit, usherboard members who assist them, and various gradations of persons upon whom the Spirit does not directly manifest, including candidates for membership, the recently baptized, guests, and children. The churchgoers' dress may also signal these gradations and groupings: large hats for mature matrons, white uniforms for the usherboard, dark skirts and white blouses for young women.[24]

The importance of knowledge and membership can also be stated very concisely by adapting literate and graphic conventions. For example, a church sign from Chattanooga, Tennessee, combines double-voiced associations (including "that talk," in the dialect spelling j-e-s for "just" and the emphatic preaching intonation Jeeeez-us) with double-visual readings to enfold an in-group within the outstretched arms of Jesus and the cross (fig. 2.2). Variations on the theme of the in-group, "just us," also play against a word of special import for African Americans, "justice." For example, the name of one black-owned publishing house specializing in Afrocentric literature is Just Us. The rap performer Just-Ice doubles the concepts of justice and cool in his name.

Double vision, therefore, not only implies a capacity to see multiple planes of existence and how they relate or conflict with one another; it also lays claim to deep knowledge, initiates' knowledge, whether of religious matters or the secular concerns of a self-aware, self-defined community.

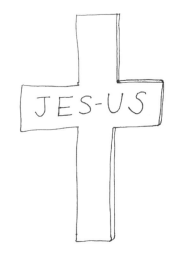

FIGURE 2.2. Jesus / Jes-us sign,
Chattanooga, Tennessee.

Style shifts between conventional and alternative approaches to literacy, text, and script not only foreground the value of insight; they also foreground a participant's claims to knowledge. These claims can be linked to other domains in a number of ways. Visual doubling sometimes indexes the existence of knowledge without betraying its content; or doubling can overtly inform and instruct, using visual and aural puns to layer insider meanings within conventional literate decoding.

Past into Present

The vernacular literate and graphic repertoire of African Americans parallels other expressive modes by drawing on resources from the past without being reducible to them. Debates continue about how best to characterize transatlantic connections, disjunctions, and the nature of African American history; I will not dwell on the various lines of argument here.[25] What matters for my argument is that *when people draw on their past, we are dealing with patterns of relationship, and configurations that remain relatively stable, but not necessarily with a specific or restricted body of content.* Relationship is qualitative, not quantifiable; it is not a "thing." The "things" related vary more than *how* they relate, and how they relate is the "somehow" that as Edward Kamau Brathwaite has shown, can transform the ship pictured on the masthead of an English Jamaican newspaper into a promise of freedom for black slaves. This approach to things (units of any kind) is inclusive; it does not categorically rule out anything from possible relevant combination. It can recruit the image of an English ship, but it can also recruit things with clear connections to specific African societies and regions—daynames, loan words, foodways—and things that index broader African-oriented skills and sensibilities—yards tied with fences and words, heavy objects carried on the head, dyed and painted colors placed for maximum differentiation ("loudness"). The sweep of possibilities is enormous, and to exclude anything categorically from the realm of possibility seems only to guarantee single vision for the scholar.

Thus I do not agree with the claim that no significant African ideas, practices, or institutions crossed the Atlantic. This claim categorically excludes African but not European historical resources from consideration in the complex relationships that render "African American" and also "American" recognizable and relatively stable qualifiers.

Furthermore, the claim that relationships and configurations remain more stable than the things configured should not be confused with the notion that meaningful continuities between Africa and the Americas exist solely or even primarily as unconscious "deep structures" analogous to the hidden, abstract grammar of a language system distinct from its "surface" lexicon-in-use (cf. Mintz and Price 1976). It seems far more plausible that the activities and choices that post facto become identified with African and African diaspora peoples (for example, facility with indirect speech or with percussion) recur for about the same reasons as many activities and choices that acquire no particular cultural associations (for example, not bumping one's head on a low lintel or becoming accustomed to certain sounds); people become habituated, actions become familiar. Acting "out of awareness" is thus simply *routine*.

The highly abstract notion of deep structure derives from an outdated and heavily critiqued split between theory and practice, system and event. Historically, it derives from the same preoccupation with "pure" and "impure" languages and cultures that predisposed colonial powers to treat those they colonized as inferiors. In anthropology explanations based on deep structure have resulted, perhaps more by default than design, from a conjunction between Chomskian structural linguistics of the late 1950s and early 1960s, a symbolic turn within anthropology that treats cultures as "wholes" roughly comparable to Saussure's *langues*, and the collapse of the dominant paradigm for research in sociocultural anthropology as a field. Dating from at least the nineteenth century, this paradigm has sent forth one anthropologist to study one "culture" in one place and to produce a written account (Clifford and Marcus 1986). Since this paradigm treats cultures as essentially discrete units, they can only be "compared" on the basis of abstracted traits and structures (see, for example, the catalog of the Human Relations Area Files). By definition, diasporic, migratory, and transnational populations fall outside the paradigm's purview; they involve mobility and mixture and thus require different research premises. Recently, anthropologists have recognized the importance of population movements. Many anthropologists now work in multiple sites or accommodate diversity in other ways.

The notion of deep structure perhaps emerged as a way to appear to accommodate to recent developments without altering old premises. Invoking "deep structure" permits the anthropologist who has studied a community as a singular unit under the traditional paradigm to "explain" why peoples in various distant locations along a migration route or across a diaspora seem to do things the "same" way or make the "same" things.

Without accounting for historical or ethnographic linkages, and without having to work across traditional anthropological boundaries, the anthropologist nevertheless can comment authoritatively on a wide area. Above all, he or she can retain the "ethnographic authority" that remains vested in the unitary paradigm and its ideal of pure, remote others.

I argue that we do not need notions like deep structure. Rather, we can observe recurring terms, practices, concepts, and configurations of objects more or less on the surface, as part of what people actually do, use, and say. Take, for example, the term "deep." In contrast to its use in academic terminology derived from structural linguistic models, no invisible abstract structure is necessary to show that the term "deep" is an important indigenous ascription of seriousness and discretion in locations across West and Central Africa and the diaspora. Indigenous connotations of "deep" usually involve layers of knowledge, portentous discernment, and access through initiation. Practices that selectively hide and reveal, and distinguish surface from depth, continually reconstitute the significance of "deep" as a cultural construct (Bellman 1984:144; Nooter 1993).

Creolization is selective in what it retains from the past but inclusive in its approach to new material. Thus creolization can involve redistribution among multiple strata, what is deep but also what is in your face.

The practice of tying and wrapping is one case in point. Tying and wrapping are observable ways of constituting a particular kind of relationship, a particular way of differentiating *in* from *out*, while making the material of enclosure an indexical sign for the act of enclosing. This practice of marking an ensemble as tied is so widely distributed in the diaspora and so widespread in its intersections with inscription that I view it as the mediating functional group of African American vernacular inscriptions, connecting narration to emblematization and to diachronic and synchronic modes of representation.

As far as I know, the Africans ravaged by the slave trade in the seventeenth, eighteenth, and early nineteenth centuries did not outline or wrap the boundaries of their property in lines of linear Roman script. But ubiquitous West and Central African symbolic, protective, and therapeutic uses of objects, and the combination of speaking with wrapping motions in the creation of power objects, provide a helpful background for interpreting the actions of some contemporary African Americans who do "tie" their property in writing in ways that persons of European descent in the same region—at least as far as I have observed—do not.[26]

The paintings of the late Mary Tillman Smith have been shown in major museums and avidly collected in conjunction with the art market's "discovery" of what has been variously labeled "grassroots," "visionary," and "outsider" art. Mrs. Smith came to notice in part because of her fences (fig. 2.3). Before art dealers removed most of the larger panels, her property was encircled with vertical and horizontal pieces of plywood and corrugated metal that zigzagged up and down gentle slopes of manicured grass. Most of the panels had bright white backgrounds inscribed with the faces and figures of family, Jesus, and Mrs. Smith herself. Most of the panels also contained block-printed messages of inspiration and occasion-

FIGURE 2.3. Part of Mary Tillman Smith's fence, 1989.

ally warning. Removed to venues of art display, the panels seem self-contained, but in situ they called and responded visually and thematically, like the colorful cloth strips in a string quilt, in ways that removal could only rupture.

Claude Davis's squatter's compound (discussed again in chapter 7), was in many ways the stark opposite of Mary T. Smith's deeded property. A homeless man, Davis staked out his domain of residence under an interstate highway, tagging trees around its periphery with a personal emblem, somewhat as an urban graffiti writer might mark off territory (fig. 2.4).

Smith and Davis have both been labeled "outsiders": Smith, to benefit an art market that privileges discontinuity among art products, producers, and their communities; Davis, to account for his homelessness and his purported eccentricity in rejecting overtures from social service workers. However, it should be clear that Smith and Davis approached their living space in a similar way. Both went beyond marking terrain to inscribe enclosures that displayed their personal commitments, buffered their homes against negativity, and revealed their standing, as a gospel song puts it, "in the safety zone."

The tying and wrapping gesture extends across the diaspora and across the Atlantic, linking acts of inscription with other forms of material culture. For example, the anthropologist Allen Roberts is currently investigating a West African mosque built from bundled blades of straw. The builders explained to Roberts that straw pens write the word of Allah in the Qu'ran and that the zigzag banded walls of the mosque represent the sacred word unfolding in time and space (Roberts 1995).

So similar are the gestures of the straw mosque and Mary T. Smith's fence that it is tempting to leap time and space and claim that somehow mosque and fence are the "same." However, what has apparently recurred,

FIGURE 2.4. Emblem boundary markers placed by Claude Davis, Chattanooga, Tennessee, 1990.

or co-emerged, is not objects themselves but a mode of relating values and materials. This relationship is not intangible "deep grammar" but, rather, a concrete articulation of what has mattered and continues to matter to people in their practical actions. To study the relationship is to learn the correlates of *mattering* embodied in configurations of ideas, actions and materials.

At best, the problems this task presents are irreducibly multivalent. At the same time that we consider the transatlantic dimensions of tying and wrapping property, we must also bear in mind that, spatially and temporally and conceptually, in between a wrapped/tied power-object in Kongo (or Yoruba or Mende) terrain and wrapped yards in Tennessee or Mississippi there exists a vast array of tied and wrapped candles, trees, fences, statuary, charm bundles, grave mounds, light fixtures, hairstyles, and even quilt-wrapped human bodies, that fans out in locally nuanced permutations across Africa, Europe, Latin America, the West Indies and North America. This spread means distance, yes, but also an enormous array of purposeful actions and their material residues. Picking one's way through this maze along a trail of *direct* retention is difficult—*not* because connections between Africa and the New World do not exist (patently they do), but because *indirect* modes of expression are characteristic of many of the phenomena we are interested in; and *not* because there is too little information linking Africa to the New World, as most critics of the theory of "retentions" have contended, but because there is *too much* information to map onto a unilinear grid without serious distortion.[27] The apparent one-to-one correspondences that we encounter on the surface are nested in diverse interactions that stabilize them as such. As *reinterpretations* that use new materials to sustain old ideas, these correspondences may well differ across time and space, their differences registering what matters in particular lives.[28]

When a contemporary American homeowner wraps her property in written messages, it is thus misleading to label this practice either old or new, or to call the psychic locus of the practice either surface or deep. Oldness and newness exist within each other and realize each other recursively according to one's point of view. Activity and its organizing principles intertwine. Recall Hurston's puzzle-gutted, double-sided, double-voiced specifying and Johnson Smith's concrete enactment of the same relationship.

Terms like double vision offer ways to comprehend these multiple planes of existence. In this regard, the expanded capacity of initiate vision has practical benefits. Since initiation is a social as well as personal rite of passage, this aspect of it is not surprising. Double vision is also one aspect of a broader vernacular vocabulary for talking about and constructing the transatlantic continuities and intercultural interference that are manifest in creolized forms. In the more technical vocabulary of creolization studies, double-voiced, double-visual forms might be classified as reinterpretations, remodelling, calques, or loan translations (see Abrahams and Szwed 1983:29; Dalby 1970/71). This is because words that seem to have transparent meanings to speakers of the metropolitan language of an enslaving or colonizing power (such as English or French) also have locally nuanced usages. One example is the word *mark*, which I discuss in chapter 6. Another is the use of objects to "write" specific signs (chapter 4).

It is probably natural for a theologian to perceive the text as just as important inspirationally as the rhythm . . . but . . . it is the rhythm that especially gives us the feeling of power. . . . Since black people have not had raw political and economic power, we have been dependent on gleaning our psychological empowerment by theological means and from cultural resources—respectively, text (ethical righteousness) and rhythm (rhythmic confidence).

(Spencer 1995:188–89)

3

African Scripts, Graphic Practices, and Contexts of Learning and Use

*T*his chapter briefly reviews some of the transatlantic resources that may inform African American vernacular practices and interact with conventional literacy. It also lays groundwork for several case studies in later chapters.

Resources, as I use the term, include African writing and graphic systems, individual signs and sign complexes (see chapter 4), remnants of Arabic literacy and Muslim magic, functions and contexts of use and learning, and ideologies of inscription. Assessing the relevance of resources involves examining both the geographic distribution of sign systems—and people who use/d them—in West and Central Africa and the diaspora, and the recurrence of certain configurations of signs, functions, and contexts of acquisition and use. The claim that a "resource" has been "used" depends on configurations, not mere resemblances. This protects against overly simplistic claims and accommodates creolization by allowing for the possibility that new information—aspects of conventional literacy, for example—is taught and learned through procedures familiar to Africans, or that durable elements fit into new settings to serve historical purposes.[1]

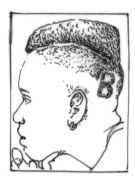

FIGURE 3.1. Inscribed hairstyle, 1990.

FIGURE 3.2. Hairstyle inspired
by Dennis Rodman, Chicago Bulls
basketball team, 1996.

Consider, for example, building facades and body surfaces. Including clothing, and especially hair and headgear, these are focal points for designs that combine decoration with emblems and scripted messages in Africa, the West Indies, and black communities in the United States. (For example, Denyer 1978; Bravmann 1983:29; Prussin 1986). It also seems true—though this is no more than an impression—that black Americans are more likely to initiate styles that place emblems, logos, print, and slogans on the head and elsewhere on the body, and on homes and other buildings, than their white counterparts (figs. 3.1, 3.2).

Such placements seem to be predicated on a similar ideology of inscription. Sometimes, as in the late 1980s style in figure 3.1, the hair, not merely the hat, has a graphic sign or word carved into it. Communicative strategies that align silhouette, image, and graphic sign have long histories in West Africa. Initially the practice of "writing" on the head may have crossed the Atlantic not only in sculpted hairstyles but in the form of message-bearing headties whose wrapping correlates with a proverb or, like the *harsa* turbans of Hausa aristocrats, the loops of the word "Allah" in Arabic script (Perani and Wolff 1992). I am not suggesting direct lines of influence so much as relatively stable criteria for what is expressively possible and appropriate. Inscriptions on body and building surfaces are a perfect example of a network of transatlantic associations that involves too much information to fit in a simple linear grid.

Before I turn to the resource potentials of specific graphic systems, let me make clear what I do and do not argue. I do not argue that indigenous African writing or graphic systems traveled in their entirety to the United States during the era of the Atlantic slave trade, surviving intact to the present. I have not found sufficient evidence for such a claim, although I would not rule out new evidence coming to light in the future. Nevertheless, there is good reason to claim that interaction with conventional literacy exists, as transatlantic and locally adapted resources inform vernacular practices. That is one of the points I make in this and later chapters. My concern is mainly with African Americans whose ancestors were brought to this country in the mid–nineteenth century or earlier. For other parts of the diaspora, and for more recent emigrants of African descent, the situation is somewhat different. For example, practitioners of Afro-Cuban religion have brought their graphic system with African roots, *anaforuana*, to Miami, New York, and other U.S. cities.

African and diaspora resources often do not fit conventional literate expectations. As Christopher L. Miller has written:

> The verbal arts of Africa are as numerous and varied as the peoples and cultures of the continent, encompassing sign systems that stretch and violate the Western categories of writing and speech. . . . [T]he verbal arts in Africa tend to blur the distinction between absolute orality and absolute literacy; therefore the evolutionary model of transition from primitive orality to civilized writing is clearly inappropriate. (Miller 1990:72–73)

This blurring of categories poses several comparative questions for any study of the interaction between African American conventional literacy and vernacular practices. What factors, besides transatlantic continuity, might account for similarities—such as, for example, similar forms of European and African magic that have been excluded from investigations of literacy? And, over and above commonalities in learning, content, function, and context of use, is there evidence that African Americans stretch and violate the Western categories of writing and speech in a fashion similar to what Miller describes Africans doing? Are there similarities in the contours of stretching and violation across the diaspora?

Indigenous Graphic Systems and Scripts

African script and graphic systems are richly varied. Even more important than the graphic signs themselves are the ideologies of inscription associated with these systems and the values in which they are rooted. In creolization, these values and ideologies are resources for new practices, and they underwrite the double voicing that emerges from the interaction of African American vernacular and conventional literate forms. The concepts of double vision and multiple realities are built into many of these ideologies. From the Dogon, to the Vai, to the Luba and Kongo peoples of

Central Africa, numerous African literate and graphic ideologies distinguish between surface signs, which are prone to duplicity and manipulation, and deep signs, which allude to hidden truths.

Graphic signs for communicative purposes exist throughout Africa, as they do throughout most of the world. A richly illustrated compendium of these systems and contemporary African writing in graphic and electronic media was compiled by David Dalby for an exhibition in Paris and a catalog published in 1986. Readers seeking detailed information will find this volume indispensable. In West and Central Africa—the areas of the continent most profoundly affected by the slave trade—most signs are emblematic, semasiographic, or mnemonic in character, in contrast to the linear, phonological syllabaries and alphabets for which the term "script" is conventionally reserved. But several phonological scripts also exist in the area.[2]

The main indigenous West African scripts of the Vai, Kpelle, Mende, Loma, and Bassa peoples cluster in Liberia and Sierra Leone, with the exception of the Bamum script of Cameroon (Dalby 1967, 1968, 1970, 1986).[3]

The indigenous scripts of West Africa are syllabaries. In their present linear, phonological form, all emerged in the early nineteenth century or more recently. Older markings reminiscent of individual graphs of the syllabaries appear in decorative motifs and inscriptions on stone dating back hundreds of years. Since Arabic and Roman script literacy already existed in the area, the desire to compete effectively with outsiders seems to have been a major impetus toward the development of linear forms of the scripts, but preexisting indigenous graphic symbols and Islamic talismans probably also influenced their design (Dalby 1968:194-195).

The dates of "invention" of the scripts rule out any wholesale transfer across the Atlantic. In the Americas, phenomena related to these scripts, if any, would therefore involve similarities in functions and contexts of use, and individual graphic symbols that predate the emergence of the linear form of the scripts.

There is a remote possibility that the Vai script might be an exception, for the coastal Vai were active brokers in the latter days of the slave trade. After 1808, when the trade became illegal and the price of slaves increased sharply, numerous captives from further inland passed through barracoons in Vai territory. A few were Vai themselves, mainly those enslaved as punishment for adultery or some other offence (Holsoe 1977). While by no means unique to the Vai or the United States, certain suggestive parallels exist in script use between Vai and African American vernacular practices, particularly regarding the learning (which I turn to later) and placement of the script. The Vai script became known to Europeans when a colonial officer noticed writing on the exterior wall of a house.[4] An intriguing photograph that Scribner and Cole reproduce, but do not discuss, shows women wearing sashes bearing Vai script tied around their heads during a Sande society parade, in effect tying their persons in the power that Sande assigns to the script (1981: n.p.).[5] This kind of use for the Vai script parallels certain uses of Arabic among nearby ethnic groups. For example, masks attributed to the male Poro society of the Toma of Guinea are inscribed with powerful magic squares on their inner surfaces (Bravmann 1983:44).[6]

David Dalby also includes the Djuka (Afaka) script of the Surinam Maroons with the West African syllabaries because it was created among people of African descent and resembles the African scripts in many particulars.[7] The origin narratives surrounding six of these seven scripts are remarkably similar. They claim that the writing systems were revealed to their inventors in dreams or visions, and that white spirit messengers brought books and graphic signs to some of the inventors. Magical and mystical practices were also associated with the scripts. African writing and graphic systems often marked an intersection between an indigenous belief system and either Islam or Christianity, depending on the locale.

> The taboos associated with the revelation of the Vai and Loma scripts are reminiscent not only of the taboos of Islam, but also of the taboos associated with initiation into the traditional secret societies of West Africa—just as the adoption of personal "book-names" by the inventor of the Vai script and his colleagues, and by the inventor of the Djuka script, may be compared to the adoption of post-initiation "society" names in West Africa, or of new Muslim or Christian names on conversion to one or other religion. There is no clear dividing-line between "God" and the traditional "spirit-world," both of which appear to lie behind the revelation of the scripts. (Dalby 1968:164)

Not surprisingly, vernacular graphic practices mark similar intersections in the diaspora. Revealed origins, potions, and special procedures weigh into the balance of power between indigenous scripts and the outsider Roman and Arabic alphabets by anchoring the new scripts in venerable lines of descent from God and the spirits. The incursion of the Roman and Arabic alphabets into West Africa—the former associated with colonial powers, the latter backed by Islam—probably spurred the development of linear, phonological scripts at least in part because they represented conquering powers whose strengths were worth emulating and appropriating to local use.

But the fact that the African inventors knew of Roman and Arabic writing does not explain why their own scripts took the form of syllabaries rather than alphabets.

There are at least two partial explanations. First, the inventors may have been seeking a closer fit with the consonant-vowel structure of their spoken languages. The components of the syllabaries have changed over time, but usually range between one and two hundred graphs, sometimes more. These graphs fit closely with spoken sound units; they also minimize or totally eliminate ambiguities like /threw/through/ that arise as Roman script spelling adapts to changes in spoken English.

However, because these scripts are syllabaries, some scholars have had the temerity to claim that they are evolutionary inferiors to alphabets because the sound units that syllabaries encode are larger than the phonemic units that alphabets—supposedly—encode. Yet because there is wide variation in how closely or loosely the characters in an alphabet fit the phonemes of a given language, a considerable amount of interpretive work remains for the reader, whatever the script. Moreover, this qualification of alphabetic "efficiency" refers only to the wide variations in fit between alphabets and so-called standard languages—that is, varieties with which a script and also technologies like printing have had a stabilizing interaction. The qualification fails to take into account dialects, creoles that draw lexically on a given metropolitan standard, or other variations in actual use. Conventional literate ideology, therefore, tacitly maintains an evolutionary perspective on language itself, implicitly aligning languages and language varieties relative to each other, on the basis of their presumed efficiency of encoding through standardized/conventionalized alphabetic transcriptions. Even through a basic premise of contemporary linguistics is linguistic relativity—roughly, that languages are different but equal—this relativity depends on treating each language as a stable and autonomous system (langue) in contrast to variable speech (*parole*). As Ferrucchio Rossi-Landi has written, "the notion of a language replaced the notion of language-in-general (*langage*)" (1973:64). Through their cultural loading, writing systems attune to the built-in ambiguities of parole and langage. But the adaptations of scripts and speech that are the results of this process tend to be obscured by literate ideology preoccupied with the closeness of the fit between *a* language (langue) and *a* writing system: that is, the relation of one putatively autonomous system to another.

All writing systems involve ambiguous relations with speech that can only be resolved contextually and, ultimately, culturally.

Thus ambiguity is distributed differently depending on which aspects of the relationship between sign and sound a given system encodes and which it leaves to context. Here cultural functions, values, and ideologies of inscription enter the picture, and here African and European orientations seem to foreground different values, though in some respects these orientations have much in common.

In particular, many West and Central African societies foreground ambiguity, indirection, and flexibility in achieving balanced social relationships. Attitudes toward writing and signs also involve these values. In contrast, Western literate ideology tends to reject ambiguity as a positive value except in certain so-called artistic genres. From at least the mid–seventeenth century, European grammarians, British essayists, and their intellectual heirs have valued clarity, explicitness, and invariance above other qualities. From their perspective, alphabetic script represents the evolutionary pinnacle of explicitness. But from the perspective of some African script designers and sign users whose ideology of inscription places a premium on subtlety and indirection, this emphasis on explicitness and the fixity associated with alphabets may seem constraining, even rather crass.

Perhaps for this reason, when alphabetic literacy became part of the African American expressive repertoire, so did a variety of adaptations—altered functions, juxtapositions of different sign systems, wordplay, and so forth—all of which ambiguate literate conventions.

The second possible explanation for the emergence of syllabaries rather

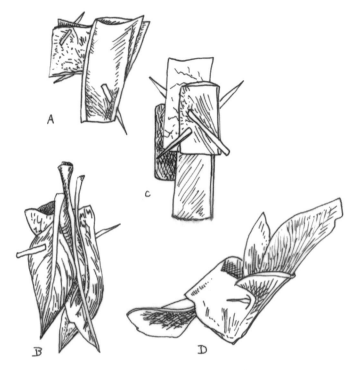

FIGURE 3.3. Folded and pierced leaf messages (after Béart 1955:729).
(a) "Il faut suivre celui qui a l'expérience."
(b) "Amis, mefiez-vous des hypocrites?"
(c) "Aimez-vous les uns les autres?"
(d) "Pouvez-vous venir?"

than alphabets in West Africa also relates to ambiguity, indirection, and flexibility as ideologies of inscription. Graphic signs often become accessible through secret society initiation, and also involve dietary and gender-linked restrictions. The emergence of syllabaries may trace indirectly back to secret society practices, for across West Africa puns, secret languages, and wordplay involve syllabic units, rebuses, and homonyms as in figure 3.3, in which pierced leaves cue specific readings.

Wordplay is relevant to writing systems in at least two ways. From the standpoint of the development of writing systems, rebuses and homonyms link and help to stabilize relationships between certain speech syllables and various visual and material forms such as folded leaves, pictograms, and communicative object ensembles. For example, the folded and pierced leaves in figure 3.3 relate to proverbs and serve as love letters. Among the Yoruba a gift of salt (iyò) is a traditional sign of joy or rejoicing (yò) because the words for salt and joy sound similar (Dalby 1968:168n). Symbolic messages were also employed by the Jebu of Nigeria. Figure 3.4, for example,

is a message from a native prince of Jebu Ode to his brother residing abroad. It consists of six cowries, all turned in the same direction; the

FIGURE 3.4. Jebu message (after Bloxam,
1887, p. 296).

quill of a feather is passed through them from front to back, and the shaft turned back towards the end of the quill, and fixed to the side of the cowries.

Six in the Jebu language is *E-fà*, which is derived from the verb *fà*, to draw; Africans are in the habit of cleansing their ears with a feather, and look upon it as the only instrument by which this can be effectively done; the whole message, therefore, is as follows.

Efà yi ni mo fi *fà* o mora, ki 'wo na sì *fa* mi girigiri.

"By these six cowries I *do draw* you to myself, and you should *draw* closely to me."

Iye yi ni mo fi *nreti*, ni kankansì ni ki nri o.

"As by this feather I can only reach to your ears, so I am expecting you to come to me, or hoping to see you immediately." (Bloxam 1887:295–296)

Part of the Jebu message is language-dependent: the syllable *fà*. Part is not: the feather *drawn* through the cowrie shells could be called either morphosemantic or semasiographic because although one must know how the sign works, one need not speak the same language as the Jebu in order to interpret that part of the message correctly. Jebu signs comprise a *system* because the rebus and morphosemantic elements became stable in use and in concert with particular contexts.

In addition to stabilizing relations through recurring rebuses, wordplay keeps possibilities open for new relationships between words, syllables, objects, and pictographic representations. Like their transatlantic counterparts, African American graphic and literate practices also provide the systemic and contextual loopholes for ambiguity that are so important to achieving balance in social relations. Revealed origins, access through initiation and fraternal organizations, double-entendre, punning, wordplay, and

FIGURE 3.5. Tree with shoe soles / souls in the yard of Edward Houston, Center Star, Alabama, 1988.

the use of objects to encode messages recur in African American graphic and literate practices from the slave era to the present. Sometimes witty, sometimes profound, they imply coexistent material, spiritual, and social realities and assert that navigating successfully among these realities is a precondition for personal well-being and privileged social standing.

Figure 3.5 shows a tree in the yard of the late Edward Houston of Center Star, Alabama (cf. Thompson and Cornet 1981:181). Houston attached red and white shoe soles to a large oak, as if walking up the trunk. In addition to creating an irregular path that negative influences cannot follow (see chapter 6 and Thompson 1983:221), Houston may very well have intended an object pun between the words *sole* and *soul* by making footprints ascending toward heaven. The fact that right and left feet are reversed also has otherworldly connotations. The idea of ascent was plainly important to Houston because under another huge oak he placed a homemade rocket pointing toward the sky with a tire encircling its nose cone—a probable reference to eternity and the four cardinal directions, themes repeated in other assemblages throughout the yard (see chapter 4).

Houston's work is only one instance of the very widespread phenomenon of object coding in African America. This type of expressive endeavor resembles initiate access to writing in that objects convey different messages to different audiences and often, with works such as Houston's, direct deep readings to prepared viewers, but not to the unprepared. In the folk art literature it is not uncommon to find sculptures like Houston's rocket described as "whimsical," a diminution of seriousness that ironically sustains differential access to works that art promoters sometimes describe as transparently "naive."[8]

The notion of stratified graphic signs and readings is highly developed

FIGURE 3.6. Sudanese graphic signs (after Béart 1955:207): (a) stillborn or deceased infant; (b) uncircumcised; (c) circumcised; (d) young man; (e) man; (f) old man; (g) impotent or flaccid old man.

among the peoples of Mali. The Bambara, who are linguistically related to the Vai, have at least three nonlinear graphic systems.[9] The most complex consists of signs "believed to be primordial, and instrumental in the actual creation" (Dalby 1968:180). Access to these signs comes only at high levels of initiation.

The graphic systems of the Sudan involve considerable abstraction, but rather than representing the sound system of a language, graphs represent sets of interrelated concepts and distinctions. Their appearance can be misleading. At first glance the series of composite graphs in figure 3.6 resembles phonological scripts that modify baseline alphabetic or syllabic graphs with diacritical markings (as in Arabic). But in this case the basic graph is a morphosemantic sign for the noun "man," and the graphic variables beneath and beside the basic graph are roughly analogous to adjectives that classify the kind of man that each graphic composite represents.

Numerous other West and Central African graphic systems communicate through nonphonological graphic signs. Perhaps the best known system of this kind is *nsibidi,* the signs of the Calabar Ejagham and neighboring peoples of the Cross River district of southeastern Nigeria and western Cameroon (fig. 3.7).

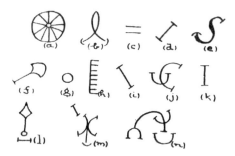

FIGURE 3.7. Nsibidi signs (after Dayrell 1910:114): (a) Young boys sitting in Nsibidi house; (b) two young women prostitutes; (c) boys the women send out to bring them men or money. (d) One of the boys took (e) a chewing stick, (f) a bottle of *tombo,* (g) a glass, (h) to the young men; (i) who sent their boy to bring (j) a bag containing rods (money). (k) The young men's boy took the rods to the women's two boys, who took it to the women. (l) The young men sent their boy to arrange a meeting with the women. (m) One of the young men met one of the women for sex. (n) But the next day the young man saw her with a different man and learned she was unfaithful.

Since the literature on nsibidi is extensive,[10] I will simply mention the three aspects of nsibidi that seem to resonate most strongly with African American practices: (1) access through secret society membership; (2) use in performance in conjunction with other expressive modes and communicative channels; and (3) important relationships between graphic signs and other channels. Through these relationships nsibidi create redundancy that reinforces message content. Nsibidi also generate ambiguities, particularly since variations in knowledge of the signs among members of the audience make nsibidi a sorting mechanism as well as a communication system.

The disposition to treat writing as one aspect of an unfolding performance, and one communicative channel working in concert with or against other channels, is again quite at odds with the literate ideology of alphabetic writing as an autonomous system. This disposition lends itself to new combinations and contrasts in creolization.

In the Ejagham language the word *nsibidi* means approximately "cruel letters," a form of "justifiable terror in the service of law and government" (Thompson 1983:227). Among the Ejagham, members of the Nsibidi or Ngbe (Leopard) Society bore responsibility for policing and punishing offenders in the community. P. Amaury Talbot, a British colonial district commissioner, who was fascinated with nsibidi and Cross River peoples, recalled:

> On another occasion a prominent member of the "Egbo" [Leopard Society], who had the reputation of knowing more "Nsibidi"—a primitive secret writing now much used in this part of the world—than any man now alive, was asked to give me a little help in the study of this script. He refused point blank, though a good remuneration had been offered for his services. He added as an "aside" to another member of the society, with no idea that his words could be understood by the "white man," "If I taught D. C. Nsibidi, he would know all the Egbo signs, and the secrets of the animals." He refused to give any further information, and soon after went away. (Talbot 1912:39)

This account suggests that the signs encoded some of the deepest knowledge to which the Ejagham could aspire. Nevertheless, nsibidi were sometimes on view to outsiders, if not understood by them.

> [At Nchofan on the Cross River] the children came to give a very charming "play." The performers numbered about fifty boys and girls, dressed in gay-coloured cloth and chains of beads, with ceintures, to which were attached little bunches of brass bells, or tiny rattles, made from the seeds of the "Agara" tree, with three big pods brightly painted in red and white, caught together by strings and tied just below each knee. In their right hands they bore thin play-swords of white wood, decorated with Nsibidi writing, with long fringes of palm fibre dyed red. (Talbot 1912:217)

Thus, although the signs had secret aspects, Talbot also observed the signs in the "plays" that foreshadowed the future roles of children in the community.

When adult men of the Ngbe Society perform, they make gestural signs that parallel graphic nsibidi. In a "responsorial" competition, the men challenge each other to display progressively deeper knowledge until one combatant or another finds himself unable to answer (Thompson 1974:180–181). In this performance, graphic signs and gestures are complementary, in that display of one attests to knowledge of the other. Nsibidi performance lays claim to double vision and navigation among multiple realities by serving as test and attestation for what cannot be revealed in public or to initiates of lower degree.[11]

Gerhard Kubik's surveys of African graphic systems, focusing on Bantu language areas, include object codes made from twists of cloth, nuts, leaves, or feathers (1984, 1986). Pictographs surround the periphery of traditional healing and religious centers for communicative and psychotherapeutic purposes. Healing designs of this type find transatlantic parallels in such diverse settings as Jamaican balmyards, Vodou hounfors, the healing and worship center of Bishop Washington Harris and his followers in Memphis, Tennessee, and the writings of Joe Light and Mary T. Smith. These graphic narratives not only convey sequential information but contribute synchronically to a visual environment that restores balance to the afflicted.

In addition to building interiors and exteriors, more ephemeral signs for healing, worship, and judgment are also inscribed on the ground (see Dalby 1986:4; MacGaffey 1990:22). In the United States, Ruby A. Moore reported a healer's cure for disease that involved "drawing a mystic symbol on the ground" (1892:230–232; also quoted in Puckett 1926:360).[12] *Tusona*, a form of groundwriting that extends to mathematical formulations, is now found in eastern portions of Central Africa, but may formerly have covered a wider area.

The west coast of the Congo-Angola region supplied one-quarter to one-third of the Africans enslaved in the southern states of the United States as well as a sizable proportion of those sent to Brazil and Haiti.[13] In Congo-Angola, graphic and object coding systems link proverbs and morphosemantic units with pictographic, material, gestural, and scarified sign repertoires (see Vaz 1970; Martins 1968; Cornet 1980; Faïk-Nzuji 1992). As a resource in the Americas, a major graphic/object sign complex from Central Africa is the Kongo cosmogram, or *dikenga*. Robert Farris Thompson and Wyatt MacGaffey have described the Kongo cosmogram in detail through material, graphic, and gestural permutations (Thompson 1983, 1994; Thompson and Cornet 1981; MacGaffey 1988). The cosmogram (figure 3.8) is a visual summary of key concepts of Kongo cosmology that resonate with aspects of cosmologies among other peoples, ranging from Angola northward to Edo Olukum worshippers in Nigeria (see Rosen 1989). The various graphic and object-embedded renderings of this sign compound the analogous paths of the sun and the human soul in one spatial-temporal equation, beginning at dawn with birth, progressing across the horizon toward the apex of human strength at noon, and descending at sunset into a spirit world under the Kalunga River water that mirrors the world of the living—whence the spiral of life begins again. In material

FIGURE 3.8. Variations of the Kongo cosmographic *dikenga* sign (after Thompson 1994: 49).

and graphic form the cosmogram is often expressed as a circle enclosing a sun or cross, clock, spiral, or diamond with disks at the four points.

African American articulations of the cosmogram's guiding principles come in many guises, for example the famed "Sun Do Move" sermons of John Jasper (Courlander 1976:351–359) or the following passage by Boston Napolean B. Boyd, who was born into slavery in 1860:

> Perpetual motion is the repeating of history, bodies repeating bodies of their kind, based upon positive and negative forces, one presupposing the other. Night presupposing day; winter, summer; salt water presupposing fresh water; a hill, a plain; two hills, a valley; crooked, straight, good, bad; bitter, sweet. . . . Fall and spring are the intermediates of winter and summer. . . . Dark nights presuppose light nights; there would be no light nights if the moon did not die and come to life again. . . . So it is with the sun and all nature, mankind included. If there is no death there is no resurrection. If there is eternal life, there is also eternal death. One cannot exist without the other. There cannot exist white people without black people, and the colored races are intermediate. A perpetual motion are these and many other principles in which this world revolves. (Boyd 1924:12)

Like Kongo cosmology, Boyd's vision of the universe is cyclical and dynamic, built upon interdependent, opposed elements. His interest in perpetual motion links him to several other African Americans of the same period who actually tried to build perpetual motion machines. These efforts, in turn, resonate with the tires, whirligigs, and solar charts that articulate the cosmographic principles in African American yards and graveyards today (chapter 4). Complementing Christian notions of eternity, the cosmogram's merger of abstract principle with material expression is also characteristic of African religions. As Herskovits says of the Dahomean *vodu*, the spirit is "localized" and "while philosophically conceived as existing everywhere in space, must also have definite places to which it can be summoned, where it can be commanded . . . and from which it can go forth to achieve those things desired of it" (1967 vol.2:171).[14]

In this sense the cosmogram marks a *point*: the meeting of spiritual and earthly powers (Thompson 1983:108–131). The point marks the place at the crossroads for offerings and oathtaking, and in the Americas serves as the fundamental gesture in making the Afro-Cuban *prenda*—a charm vessel that activates a spirit servant for its owner (Thompson 1983:122; Cabrera 1954:120–134); the *pwe*, a group of potent charms and a link between the focused power of the point and the power of naming (Brown 1975:14, 241–260); and an array of other protective signs.

Thanks to Thompson's transatlantic initiative, the four moments of the sun and other variants of the Kongo cosmogram are fast becoming the most thoroughly documented and longest-attested facets of the Afro-Atlantic visual tradition (Wahlman 1987; McWillie 1991; Fenn 1985; Nichols 1989). Closely argued papers by the archaeologist Leland Ferguson suggest that African Americans enslaved in South Carolina used bowls bearing cosmograms in rituals as far back as the eighteenth century (1989, 1992). Ferguson determined that Colono Ware bowls with crossmarks inscribed inside and on the circular bottom of the bowl were found under water—suggesting ritual submersion—in areas where African Americans outnumbered whites and Congo-Angolans made up nearly half of the total population (1989:18). Colono Ware bowls from other areas were not similarly marked, so it seems unlikely that the crossmarks were simply maker's marks. A small proportion of the bowls have counterclockwise "tails" at the end of the crossmarks or other indications of counterclockwise directional movement.

In addition to indicating the directional path of the sun, this movement parallels that of the circling ring shout, a ritual involving both sacred and secular participation (see chapters 5 and 6). Sterling Stuckey links the African American shout explicitly to solar movement and affirms that "the circle imported by Africans from the Congo region was so powerful in its elaboration of a religious vision that it contributed disproportionately to the centrality of the circle in slavery" (1987:11).

Like nsibidi, then, graphic cosmograms translate into movements that can engage parts of the body, the whole body, or entire social groups. Indigenous African graphic and script traditions are resources saturated with spatial, temporal, and performance associations.

Arabic Script and Islam

Thus far I have reviewed indigenous West and Central African systems and signs; Arabic script and esoteric Islam were also important in parts of West Africa affected by the slave trade. Some Muslims profited from the trade; others were innocent victims, taken prisoner and shipped overseas during the wars that accompanied Islam's spread. In her study of African American cultural history in the Sea Islands, Margaret Washington Creel (1988:38–44) surveys the ethnic distribution of Islam in West Africa dur-

ing the era of the slave trade and assesses the role of Muslim jihad in ethnic displacements and escalation of the trade. Although Creel is concerned
with Senegambian interconnections with the Sea Island Gullah of North
America, she seems unconvinced that Senegambian Muslims exerted
significant influence in the United States. However, in an earlier and more
speculative book, Paul Oliver proposed that enslaved Muslim musicians
from the Senegambian savannah contributed distinctive song styles and
musical instruments to the blues music of southern blacks (1970). More
recently, Michael Coolen also discussed Senegambian influences on African American music (1991). Writing in the 1930s, Lydia Parrish considered the Muslim presence sufficiently representative to warrant using
Arabic script in the illustrative endpapers of her classic collection, *Slave
Songs of the Georgia Sea Islands* (1942). Allan D. Austin makes a strong
case for the existence of an influential but chronically underresearched
Muslim minority in antebellum America (1983). He compiled source materials on fifteen enslaved West African Muslims, with shorter entries on
fifty others (1983:vii). Several of these men managed to return to Africa,
including the remarkable Prince Abd Rahman Ibrahima for whom the
quest for repatriation lasted over forty years (Alford 1977). Descendants
of two Muslims enslaved in coastal Georgia, Salih Bilali of St. Simon's Island and Bilali of Sapelo Island, were photographed and interviewed well
into the twentieth century (Georgia Writers' Project 1940; Courlander
1976:282–285).

It is hard to estimate the number of Muslims brought to the South or
the number who were literate. Records are unclear, and information about
Muslims may have been suppressed. One reason for this suppression was
that a popular nineteenth-century justification for slavery—conversion of
polytheistic "fetishists" to monotheism—did not apply to Muslims. (In
the seventeenth and eighteenth centuries, little effort was made to convert
slaves regardless of their religious background; only a few were baptized
Christians.) Another difficulty stems from the planters' unease with enslaving persons thought to have Arab (i.e., Caucasian) blood.[15] Planters
with Muslim slaves were sometimes pressured by those who opposed
slavery in general or indiscriminate enslavement of monotheists to return
them to their homes. After sifting conflicting sources, Austin suggests
that about 10 percent of the West Africans sent to America from 1711 to
the end of the legal trade in 1808 were "to some degree, Muslim." He proposes 29,695 as a plausible total, including those smuggled in after the
official close of the slave trade (1983:35–36).

Muslim literacy made planters uneasy. Often the same documents that
yield information about Arabic literacy are concerned with obtaining
slaves' release. Unless the skill proved useful to planters for recordkeeping
or entertainment for their guests, Arabic literacy was no doubt suppressed
with as much zeal as Roman script literacy on the plantations.[16]

However, we know from surviving documents that a number of enslaved Muslims across a wide geographic area could read and write Arabic
to varying degrees. In recognition of this ability the name of the ethnic
group Mandinga also meant "bookman" before the nineteenth century

(Austin 1984:30), and Bookman as a personal name, along with Booker, may reflect a legacy of Muslim literacy echoing down the years. As a group, the skills of captured Muslims spanned considerable range: reciting passages from the Qur'an, decoding written passages, copying out the Qur'an entirely from memory, keeping plantation records, and even composing detailed autobiographies. A slave called London, about whom little else is known, used Arabic script to transcribe in English the hymns and New Testament verses he heard from other slaves in Georgia and Florida, thus effecting a relationship between Arabic and Gullah that bypassed standard English and Roman script altogether (Austin 1983:40).

The best-known document in Arabic by an African in the United States was written by Bilali, or Ben Ali, of Sapelo Island, Georgia (see Courlander 1976:plate 10). Bilali was captured and sold while he was still a student. Some have contended that when he arrived on Sapelo he may have attempted to retain what he had learned from the Muslim system of rote education by writing down what he remembered in his manuscript (Greenberg 1940; Courlander 1976; Austin 1983:265–307). However, on the basis of a broad view of African and African American literate and graphic practices and ideologies, it also seems possible that Bilali composed the manuscript as a focusing device for prayer and meditation—a function also compatible with an education designed to promote deeper understandings of Islamic wisdom as students learned to read and write.

Initially, Bilali's book was thought to be a diary. In the 1930s, the linguist Joseph Greenberg took a copy to Africa. His research led him to claim that the document was instead a legal treatise, set down from memory and checkered with errors (Greenberg 1940). Recently, Ronald A. T. Judy has challenged Greenberg's interpretation through a close comparison of the manuscript with several African-Arabic orthographies. Judy makes a case for viewing those aspects of the manuscript that Greenberg calls "misspelling" as intentional heterography and indeterminacy. According to Judy, the manuscript is writing as *writing*, not the encoded speech that linguists like Greenberg tend to privilege. Although Judy does translate the manuscript word by word, he argues that as a *text* it remains "untranslatable," that its "meaning is never immediate and apparent" (1993:216–273).

If Judy is correct about the intentional indeterminacy of the document, both the rhythmic, open-ended use of language apparent in the translation Judy provides and the actual script in which Bilali wrote resonate with other works produced before and after his time. Some were produced in close geographic proximity to the Sea Islands. However, these works are not, for the most part, the slave narratives that attract scholars interested in the formation of an African American literary canon. Rather, most, if they have been noticed at all, command attention under the rubric "visual art" because they pose even more blatant challenges to textual coherence and literate decoding than the work of Bilali. Indeed, Bilali's manuscript seems to fall within a continuum of West African and African American graphic practices that extend from conventional literate activities through invented scripts like that of the late Leroy Person (Manly 1989), through writing in alphabetic or personal signs that "ties" and protects property or persons, to writing that "ties" the writer to the divine, to undecoded (possibly nondecodable) inscriptions like those of James Hampton, to the graphic glossolalia of J. B. Murray, a healer and artist from central Georgia (see chapter 7).

Whether or not indeterminacy is built into certain forms of Arabic inscription, it stands to reason that if commitment to Islam was a matter of degree, Bilali and others who read and wrote Arabic would constitute the stricter end of the scale.[17] The same process of memorization by which they learned Arabic script would ensure prolonged exposure to Muslim ritual and the teachings of the Qur'an. With subsequent generations, worship of Allah and the notion of book religion could fade into or be masked by Christian parallels.

This change may also have occurred in a single lifetime. In late 1850s up to 1863, accounts of the life of "Uncle Moreau," (or Moro)—Omar Ibn Said—appeared in the press. Moreau was a captive Fulah who had taught the Qur'an and basic arithmetic in his homeland before, enslaved, he landed at Charleston in 1807. For many years, Moreau held strictly to Muslim feasts and practices, but (according to a nineteenth-century biographer whose opinion is questionable), Moreau gradually "began to lose his interest in the Koran" as he was taught "the elements of a better faith." Nevertheless, Moreau continued to be "a fine Arabic scholar, reading the language with great facility, and translating it with ease" (in Blassingame 1977:472–473).

But changes that seem to erase the Muslim heritage may also be temporary, or include institutional adaptations and new theological teachings that remain within Muslim nomenclature, as for example in the Nation of Islam, Moorish Science, and Moorish Masonry, which have generated their own literatures and repertoires of graphic signs (see Wilson 1993).

Esoteric Islam may also have served as a resource for African American graphic practices, particularly in magical formulae that call for eating, drinking, or divining with written text and for wearing texts as charms (see Bravman 1983; El-Tom 1985; Prussin 1986; Mommersteeg 1988; Bledsoe and Robey 1986). Practices drawn from esoteric Islam are well documented among Hausa and Yoruba Muslims in Brazil (Reis 1982, 1993; Monteil 1965, 1966, 1967a, 1967b), although debate surrounds their relationship to literacy (cf. Goody 1986). Nonconventional forms of writing and charms, along with conventional literacy, also figured in slave revolts in Haiti (where Boukman was the name of one famed rebel leader), as well as elsewhere in the West Indies (Brathwaite 1977; Craton 1982:110–113) and in the United States (Starobin 1971, Cornelius 1991:17–41).

Figures 3.9 and 3.10 illustrate a West African Muslim talisman in Arabic and in translation into French. After inscription, pages such as this were ritually folded and enclosed in packets and pouches, often made of elaborately decorated leather.[18]

To a more integral extent than ideologies of inscription associated with the Roman alphabet, the ideology of written Arabic makes an explicit con-

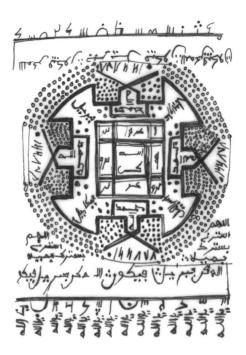

FIGURE 3.9. West African talisman (after Béart 1955:397).

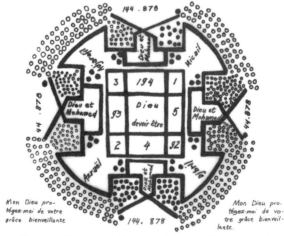

FIGURE 3.10. Translation of figure 3.9 (Béart: 1955:397).

nection between the appearance of the script and its religious, esoteric, and pragmatic functions. European script and print styles index various interpretations and functions—Gothic = church, Times Roman = newspaper, swirly copperplate = love letter—that anyone literate in the language and the script can read. But a poorly crafted version of one of these is just that: bad workmanship. In strict Islam, however, ugly writing is a more serious matter; it offends the sight of Allah, who gave the gift of writing to humans and infused the idea of power into writing for any purpose.

Arabic script has also spawned numerous magical offshoots that cannot be decoded without special instruction. Ibn Washiya composed a compendium of mystical alphabets of the tenth century (1977; see also Dornseiff 1925; Marques-Riviere 1950). Dalby suggests that West Africans may have incorporated graphs from these alphabets into local graphic systems (1968:195).

North African magic also used special scripts drawn from Jewish mysticism and Egyptian hermetic traditions. The Jewish Kabbalah knits together Africa, Europe, and later the Americas with overlapping spheres of influence. Cabalistic seals form the backbone of the *Sixth and Seventh Books of Moses,* a work of uncertain origin that purports to date from a fifteenth- or sixteenth-century manuscript compiled from antique materials. (See fig. 3.11.) This book and seals derived from it became standard parts of the repertoires of American hoodoo and West Indian obeah specialists early in the twentieth century (Elkins 1986), as in the following sinister spell:

> [W]hensomevah dis individ'al is filing dese fingahnails. . . . Git dis snakehead which is a powdah compounded. . . . An when yo' git in yore possession, yo' take *Six Books of Moses,* den yo' call de *alphabets* of de individ'al name an' whensomeveah yo' call de alphabets . . . dey shadah will come befo' yo' an yo' corked it up as yo' lookin' on it—cork dis powdah up. . . . Now dat individ'al are gonna leave dis worl'. (Hyatt 1970–78, vol.3:1951)

To the present, Spiritual Baptists in the Caribbean incorporate signs from the book with other forms of writing; it also serves as a text for the Aladura movement in western Nigeria (Probst 1987). In the United States the *Sixth and Seventh Moses,* and more recent variations, sell briskly in religious supply stores today, along with gold-dipped seals based on their diagrams, which come packaged with appropriate prayers and invocations.[19] In Haitian Vodou, where biblical figures pair with or serve as translations for spirits of African derivation, Moses was associated with the father of Damballah, the serpent god of Dahomean and Dahomean-influenced religions (Jacobs and Kaslow 1991:85). In a sermon at his Israelite Divine Spiritual Church of Christ in New Orleans's ninth ward, where a statue of Moses appears on the high altar, Archbishop Ernest J. Johnson said, "Moses was the biggest hoodooer, God taught him" (Neeley 1988:724; Jacobs and Kaslow 1991:198). He elaborated: "God taught Moses many things. So many things mean different things. And God told Moses how to put these symbols together. The spiritual man knows what the average man does not know" (Neeley 1988:724–725).

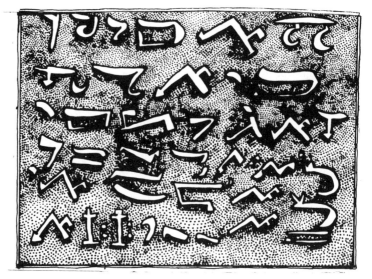

General Citation of Moses on All Spirits

FIGURE 3.11. Seal from the *Sixth and Seventh Books of Moses.*

Moses links the herbal and material knowledge of the "old people" with the Bible and also with hermetic beliefs said to derive from ancient Egypt. Shops that sell the books of Moses also sell numerology books that instruct readers in the magical properties of numerical equivalents between numbers and letters. Equivalents in Arabic and Hebrew numerology foreshadow contemporary texts.[20] Masonic symbols and rites are indebted to Egyptian, Jewish, and Islamic traditions as well, and they, too, have spread across European and African America; for example, the Masonic symbols in vèvè (invocatory drawings and emblems) for the *lwa* (spirits) of Haitian Vodou.[21]

Speech and Writing

A recurring theme in West and Central African and African American literate and graphic ideologies is that visible markings can contribute to or disrupt vital balances of psychic, social, and spiritual power. The process of maintaining balance must take subtle, even invisible factors into account as well as everyday events. All sorts of objects and expressive forms can contribute to the balancing process—dress, gesture, spatial arrangements, performances—and graphic practices are bound up with of all them, sometimes indexing a particular line of interpretations, and sometimes leaving loopholes of ambiguity that promote flexibility and help interpersonal relations flow smoothly.

Although only a few African graphic systems are scripts by conventional definition—that is, phonological representations of speech—all are *related* in some way to speech and also to what cannot or should not be spoken aloud: graphic signs permit unspoken communication even when

FIGURE 3.12. Two versions of Daniel in the lion's den:
(a) stained glass window;
(b) with thickness of lines correlated to depth of significance (after
Victor Melancon, Hammond, Louisiana)

they encode spoken sounds. Thus graphic ideologies and ideologies of
speech have much in common, although they differ as well. One of the
most important areas of common ground is the concern with indirection
and ambiguity and with the potential danger of both speech and writing.

The distinction between clarity and indirection thus parallels that between surface and deep writing. Many African script and graphic traditions are sensitive to this contrast. Lightly drawn nsibidi can be used in
sweet-talking love letters, but darker markings warn against idle talk and
danger, even death (Thompson 1983:238–247). In the United States the
familiar typographic conventions of newspaper headlines and advertising
copy use darker print to command greater attention. But two of the
African Americans I interviewed interpreted light and dark marks similar
to readings of nsibidi. Claude Davis said that he used darker colors and
heavier paint to write messages about justice and judgment on the highway overpass where he lived (interview, November 1989).

Victor Melancon demonstrated a strategy he used to read religious
messages in photographs of stained-glass windows (figure 3.12). The
darker and thicker the lines, the deeper the significance of that part of the
design. When Melancon's understanding of deep ideas in a Bible story varied from those coded in the lead lines of an actual window, he metico-
lously redrew the image in pencil with the corrected distribution of dark
and light, thin and heavy lines. For example, Melancon copied a scene of
Daniel in the lion's den so that thick, dark lines entered the den from
above; these, he explained, were the tracks of the secret words that God
used to give Daniel encouragement (interview, June 1991).

Melancon's strategy involved separating or uncoupling the structural function of lines of lead from their communicative function. Since he knew how stained-glass windows are constructed, he made the separation purposefully. He partly detached a resource from an old context both to use it in a new way *and* to underscore a significant aspect of the old context, creolizing the image and the strategy of interpretation to accommodate deep and surface readings.

Object codes and African American variants, like the punning soul/soles on Edward Houston's tree, also promote dual surface and deep readings. The Vai syllabary, the practical tool of letter-writers, also has its deep side, available only to those instructed by the Sande society. Sylvia Ardyn Boone, who researched Sande and art among the Mende, noted that for the Mende *"initiation is a condition of seeing. . . .* Everything is out in the open; nothing is purposefully hidden. . . . Initiates have had their eyes opened so they have . . . an informed intellect, a widened vision, a deepened discernment" (1986:xi). This premise, that nothing is hidden but few are privileged to know the explanation and meaning of things, helps to account for why the Mende, who have had multiple means of writing available to them for generations, seem to prefer not to write about themselves.

> Mende have written almost nothing about their life experiences or about their concepts and ideas. They have the distinction of being one of the West African groups which invented its own ideographic and syllabic writing system. Despite this noteworthy development, little of what was recorded in the Mende script has ever become known to scholars. In the present day, although many Mende families have been literate in Arabic or western alphabets for six or seven generations and hold advanced degrees from western and Islamic universities, we still have only a handful of literary materials published by Mende writers. (Boone 1986:xii)

Ambivalence about words also forms a layered or hierarchical organization for Mande speakers in Mali. As Christopher Miller has explained,

> The Mande attitude toward the word . . . is complex and ambivalent; it can be explained in shorthand by saying that speech is dangerous because it releases *nyama* [vital force, sometimes characterized as malevolent] when it transforms silence into noise. The general term for the spoken word is *kouma*, but *kouma* is only that speech that is associated with the outermost organs of speech—the mouth, the tongue, and the throat; other, deeper types of the word correspond to other bodily organs, in a hierarchy that equates interiority and depth with truth and trustworthiness. . . . Speech from the mouth can be sweet and seductive but also dangerous. . . . True knowledge is held in silence, safe from the transformation into speech that releases *nyama*. The Mande attitude toward speech reveals a sign system that is both dualistic and laden with danger. (Miller 1990:81)

Mande speech is layered from the depths of meaning and depths of the body to the surfaces of articulation, the lips and the tongue.[22] One implication of this layering, extended to literacy, is that deep writing is not merely an elite, "restricted" layer of meanings over or underneath a desirable skill, but rather that *depth* is also necessary to meet the criteria for trust that prevail throughout the writer's society (compare to Clanchy 1979, 1988), just as some Western scholars contend that *explicitness*—surface clarity—is a necessary condition for truth in conventional literate texts. Among the Vai, the Ejagham, and the black community of Center Star, Alabama, trust is not given lightly, and deep writing is not used—or written—lightly either.

*T*he surface-versus-deep distinction in talk and writing is not characteristic of any particular type of system, or any particular type of phonological orientation, but rather occurs with morphosemantic signs, semasiographic signs, syllabaries, and alphabets. In one of the most thorough explorations of deep talk and deep writing, Beryl Bellman showed how the distinction also carries over into a Roman script letter sent by a Kpelle relative to a Liberian student living in the United States. The letter, according to Bellman, "exemplifies how instructions for interpretation can be embedded in a text. . . . [The writer] uses deep message forms to communicate the most important items of news from home" (1984:63).

Bellman's analysis of indirection and ambiguity in writing, and of Kpelle secrecy and deep talk, is too complex to review here. For our purposes, the Kpelle letter is a clear indication of the way that writing interacts with preexisting values. Literacy has consequences, to be sure, but these cannot be predicted on the basis of European-oriented literate ideology. Thus, in contrast to the Western convention that literacy is a major mark of cultivation and civilization, in many African and American contexts, writing is more akin to the unpredictable wilderness and crossroads forces that command caution and threaten disruption of social order.

One way to cope with the unruly potentials of writing and reading is to refine the code. For the British essayists and for contemporary academic writing, to do so has meant reducing ambiguity by "saying what you mean" lexically and grammatically: conforming to conventions for "clarity" in given contexts. But for Paul Alfred Barton, an Afro–West Indian born in St. Lucia and now living in the United States, refining the code has meant creating a new writing system that remains attuned to culture across differing languages. This system, Afrikuandika, aims to accurately represent sounds as they move out of the body through places of articulation in the mouth (fig. 3.13). In the inventer's own words, in Afrikuandika:

> The glyphs represent parts of the mouth that we all have. It is quite easy to remember how to write a glyph if we can relate it to the position of the speaking parts that produces the sound represented by that glyph. . . . The Afrikuandika system uses drawings to show the speaking parts as they are when producing a sound or word. . . . This *alphabet* was designed specifically for the writing of African languages and for the African peoples all over the world. . . . The *sing-song* dialects of some types of Caribbean English, the *drawl* of the American southerner, the rhythms of Afro-American English, or the exact dialect of any language can be written as spoken. (Barton 1991:12)

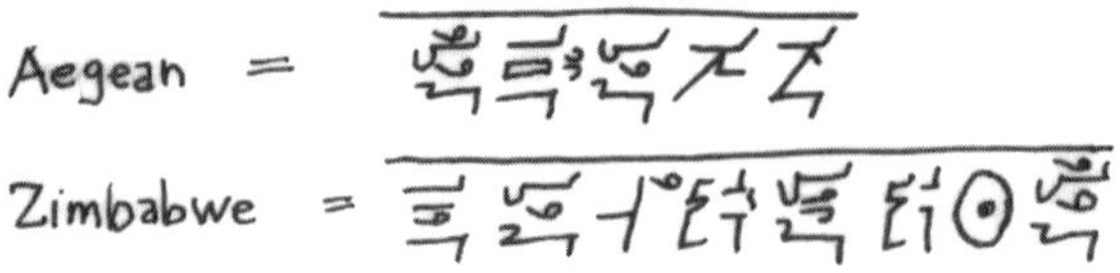

Aegean =

Zimbabwe =

FIGURE 3.13. Afrikuandika glyphs designed by Paul Alfred Barton (1991:16).

Barton's script appears to be unique among the world's writing systems because, as far as I know, it is the only nonsemasiographic notation system—excepting the phonological system used by linguists—designed purposefully to accommodate multiple languages and linguistic *variations*. Barton's description of himself and his script as "Afro–West Indian" is thus a telling reminder that the script has roots in a complex linguistic setting where speakers command multiple registers of St. Lucian Kweyol and English.

Barton's aims for his script thus differ from what we know of the motives of the Ndjuka script designer, Afaka, the only widely known creator of a script in the Caribbean region. Afaka's syllabary corresponds closely to the consonant-vowel structure of Ndjuka (Dubelaar and Pakosie 1993:239). It is "a" script designed with "a" language in mind. Although that language is a creole, the script is more a result of the emergence of Ndjuka Creole as a new language than it is an attempt to accommodate creolization as an open-ended process.

Pan-Africanist in its goal of providing an international system for Africans on the "same level as English, Chinese, Amharic, Arabic [and] Hebrew" (1991:1), Afrikuandika invites unity among peoples of African descent without simultaneously erasing their diversity. Afrikuandika thus shares with older African syllabaries and graphic systems a moral and ethical orientation. Barton designed this remarkable script not only to aid communication across borders, but to aid language instruction and to help hearing-impaired persons learn to speak.

Contexts of Learning

Divergences in the values that inform African, African American and European-oriented ideologies of inscription help to explain why we have so poor a sense of how these ideologies have interacted in practice in the United States. In addition to creating problems with definitions—of script, sign-to-speech relations, and literacy—difficulties in learning how African Americans may have used resources from the past arise because scholars too often conflate or confuse the effects of schooling, literacy, and other informal and formal modes of learning. In their seminal investigation of multiple literacies among the Vai of Liberia and Sierra Leone, Scribner and Cole found that many of the so-called consequences of literacy in fact derived from schooling, and schooled communicative conventions, not from inherent properties of literacy or alphabetic script (1981). Vai literates could read and (usually) write one or more of three scripts: Roman, taught in American English in mission schools; Vai, often acquired informally from a relative during short breaks at work; and Arabic, taught by Muslim religious instructors through copying, memorization, and recitation of the Qur'an.

Enslaved and freed African Muslims captured in Senegambia and other areas recalled learning Arabic script in much the same way as the Vai who attended Qur'anic schools. According to Salih Bilali (b. 1770) of Hopeton Plantation in Georgia, in his home of Massina, "All the children are taught to read and write Arabic, by the priests (Maalims). They repeat from the Koran, and write on a board, which when filled is washed off" (Hodgson 1844, Curtin 1967:146).[23] In this system, learners can read and recognize passages in the Qur'an long before they can write. Salih Bilali had mastered this form of reading before his enslavement at age twelve, and he read regularly until his death. However, it seems likely that he could not write Arabic, or had lost the skill, because he dictated his memoirs to a planter who reported them in a letter. What is important here is that instruction "in Arabic" in West Africa is above all instruction *in the Qur'an* and the Muslim religion. The goal is to familiarize children with a particular book; and both the language and the script of the Qur'an are unfamiliar to the children at the outset because they are native speakers of African languages, not Arabic.

When freed black children in coastal Georgia and South Carolina began attending school behind Union lines in 1862 (see also chapter 5), the perspectives of the teachers and the students were, predictably, quite divergent. For the northern Protestant missionary teachers, the challenge was to teach reading, writing, and arithmetic in a manner that approximated the one-room schooling of New England. For the children the learning situation, initially at least, had a great deal in common with African Qur'anic schooling. Interestingly, the children excelled in the skills that such schooling promotes, easily learning the alphabet and numbers. However, they were almost totally unfamiliar with the words used in northern primers (Rose 1964:230).

For the children, then, school involved rote learning, copying text, and grappling with a foreign language—for these children were native speakers of Gullah, a creole with a lexicon partly of English but also made up of a host of local usages and African words (Turner 1949). While their heritage of verbal art may help to account for their aptitude for memorization, it is worth bearing in mind that at least a few had parents or neighbors like Bilali and Salih Bilali for whom formal instruction and religious instruction were virtually the same.

The following episode in the Sea Islands illustrates one of the ways such values may have played out in practice. The historian Janet Cornelius also mentions the episode in passing as an example of "learning to read as a religious act." She points out that sometimes blue-back spellers were used interchangeably with the Bible, and some preachers even conducted marriages with the speller in hand (1991:93).[24]

Monday, June 9 [1862]. Found that Bacchus' brother Lester had been taken sick Sunday morning and died at night. . . . Just after dinner we saw the people assembling at their burying-place and H. and I went down to witness the services. Uncle Sam followed us, book in hand and spectacles on nose, reading as he walked. As we grew near to the grave we heard all the children saying their A,B,C through and through again, as they stood waiting around the grave for the rest to assemble and for Uncle Sam to begin. Each child had his school-book or picture-book Mr. G. had given him in his hand—another proof that they consider their lessons some sort of religious exercise (Ware 1969:65).

This important episode (see Raboteau 1978:240) consists of children singing the ABCs at the funeral of one of their schoolmates. Harriet Ware, the teacher who observed the scene, interpreted it as evidence that the children saw educational activity as spiritually efficacious (Ware 1969:62–68). Since the teachers in the Sea Islands were missionaries, this interpretation is hardly surprising. However, the scene also indicates what the children and perhaps their families already regarded as appropriate. Yet it would be misleading to attribute the ABC-at-the-funeral scene to pure "Muslim influence." The historical and ethnic background of the Sea Islanders and their coastal neighbors was far too complex. Right up to the outbreak of the Civil War, the area received intermittent illegal cargoes of slaves from the West Indies and West and Central Africa, who were usually sold in semiclandestine fashion directly from ships docked near Beaufort and Charleston, South Carolina. According to Daniel Littlefield's figures, between 30 and 40 percent of the black population of the coast came from Congo-Angola; about the same number from Liberia and Sierra Leone (the latter being especially favored because of their expertise in rice cultivation); and the remainder from other areas such as the Gold Coast and the Bight of Biafra, with a scattering of Muslims among all of them (Littlefield 1981:20–21, 109–114; Wood 1974:95–130, 333–341). In addition to the sizable cultural contributions of Congo-Angolans, the former residents of Sierra Leone and Liberia either lived in or passed through the very areas where Poro and Sande societies were active (Creel 1990:77–78, 90–91).

Over the last two decades articles by scholars including David F. Lancy (1975, 1980), John D. Studsill (1979), and F. Niyi Akinnaso (1992) have asserted that in various African societies, secret societies and divination systems have provided formal instruction that can resemble, but is not isomorphic with, formal education in Western schooling. Lancy has also shown that secret society–like procedures appear to carry over from the Poro Society into the Liberian public schools (1975:379). Akinnaso has stressed that societies lacking literacy may nevertheless have formal learning and schooling, which he has characterized as "relatively standardized and based on values deriving from a group's collective representations." However, he has pointed out that "early anthropologists, with the possible exception of Melville Herskovits . . . did not consider schooling a traditional institution; rather, they regarded schooling as a colonial intrusion" (1992:70); thus they overlooked indigenous forms of schooling. In addition, the "adoption of the distinction between 'oral' and 'literate' culture has . . . [led] to a focus on the differences between the two cultural traditions," which has had the consequence of obscuring similarities between traditional African methods of formal instruction and those of Europeans (Akinnaso 1992:69–71).[25]

In addition to the Poro and Sande schools, these similarities are apparent in secret society instruction among the Luba (Studsill 1979; Roberts and Roberts 1996) and in Ifa divination (see Bascom 1969, 1980; Abimbola 1977), to name only two of many other comparative possibilities. In the Luba school, pupils learn nonphonological signs and then participate in a situation that is more like Western education in the higher grades—they learn how to use a sign system that both records information and promotes multiple, contextual interpretations (also see Roberts and Roberts 1996). This process also resembles learning to read nsibidi: during instruction in deep writing, learners master signs as they receive instruction in the social responsibilities that accompany successive degrees of knowledge.

Although education researchers are attracted to formal and informal learning *procedures*, they often seem less comfortable with the *content* of instruction or some of its adjuncts. Lancy points out that Kpelle secret society instruction results in indoctrination into social patterns of ritual and secrecy: instruction is not conducted "in terms of facts" (1980:273). Akinnaso excludes from consideration noninstitutional forms of knowledge and "spiritual knowledge."

> Spiritual knowledge is a form not mediated by humans but comes directly from those supernatural powers, spiritual forces, and other agencies believed to control the ability to reveal the secrets of the universe to man. . . . The acquisition of spiritual knowledge is often linked with some form of dissociation or inspiration; a detached setting, such as the shrine, the woods, or the bedroom; unusual times, such as the dead of the night; or some kind of psychophysical transformation, such as visions, trances, and dreams. (Akinnaso 1992:82)

While the exclusion of spiritual knowledge may help Akinnaso hold fast to certain points that he wishes to make about formal methods and learning, the exclusion is hard to sustain when one looks at divination systems themselves. As Philip Peek has written, divination is a "non-normal mode of cognition" that the diviner brings into line with ordinary community life through his interpretive skill and, especially, his skill in interaction with clients (1991:193–212). Messages come to the diviner in a number of ways: "Whether the message emerges through spirit possession, a numerical configuration, or a pattern of symbolic objects, it is the diviner's role to translate these esoteric codes" (1991:200).

Note the varied factors—some labeled spiritual, some labeled practical—that can contribute to formal and informal learning. This variety makes it risky to decide in advance how these resources will inform actual practice. While it is possible to exclude various approaches to knowledge for heuristic and analytical purposes—just as it is possible to maintain an oral-versus-literate cultural divide for such purposes—these exclusions are precisely what obscures the *interaction* of formal and informal learning, and of conventional—"Western," "mythic"—literacy and vernacular practice in African America and elsewhere.

In the United States, opportunities for formal and informal learning in plantation slavery were limited by demands on time and limits on movement and communication among enslaved people. Any formal learning they managed to organize around alphabetic literacy could not go forward as recognizable "schooling" or "education" unless it was hidden from whites. Nonetheless, a few such schools did exist, like the one that Mrs. Mandy Jones of Harrison County, Mississippi, recalled during an interview in the 1930s:

> De slaves would run away sometimes, an hide out in de big woods. Dey would dig pits, an kiver the spot wid bushes an' vines, an mebbe lay out fer a whole year. An' dey had pit schools in slave days too. Way out in de woods, dey *was* woods den, an de slaves would slip out o' de Quarters at night, an go to dese pits, an some niggah dat had some learnin' would have a school. (Rawick 1977 vol. 8:1246)

Schools like this were not widespread. A few black secret societies also existed in the antebellum era, but more emerged after freedom as fast-growing fraternal organizations. The regalia, rituals, and teachings of some of these fraternities have demonstrable links to African precedents (Kuyk 1983). On the whole, however, the circumstances of plantation life compelled the acquisition of alphabetic literacy through informal channels. Friends and relatives cautiously shared knowledge among themselves in a manner not so different from the way twentieth-century Vai teach each other the Vai script in brief interludes among other activities.

Informal activity like play among free schoolchildren and enslaved children also included breaks into formal instruction. During these breaks white children and black children and occasionally adults "played school," sometimes in hiding, sometimes in the plantation yard, despite the punishments that awaited if white adults observed them. When white children playacted school on the plantation, they usually assumed the role of the teacher, passing along basic information: numbers, counting, the alphabet, and spelling. From that point on, some African American learners proceeded rapidly on their own.

> I was much pleased with the account I got of a negro blacksmith in this neighborhood [Mobile], whose passion for learning made him allure the white boys into his smithy, as they passed to and from the school. The boys wrote on the blackened wall the alphabet, and taught him the sound of the letters. Thence he proceeded to syllables and words, under the same youthful instructors. Having learned to read, he taught himself writing and arithmetic, algebra and geometry, and was studying Latin and Greek, when he was discovered by a Christian gentleman. . . . The sum of eighteen hundred dollars was raised. . . . The liberty of himself and family was purchased, and he was sent out to Liberia. . . . [H]ere there is no idea of liberation without expatriation, as if to render the sweets of liberty as bitter and undesirable as possible, and to present no

alternative to the poor negro but helpless bondage or hopeless exile. (Lewis 1845:176–177)

Such were the rewards of learning for black Americans in the antebellum South.

These varied perspectives on learning and instruction show that we cannot assume that activities with the characteristic formality of schooling were, or are, preoccupied with conventional literacy through instruction in either a phonological alphabet or syllabary. This preoccupation does prevail in European and American schools; therefore it has come to seem natural among these peoples that "real" schooling rests on a foundation of conventional literate practices and assumptions. But this is a result of custom backed by political and economic domination, not of the cognitive requirements for learning to read and write (Conklin 1949). Sometimes African American schooling in the antebellum era did parallel the European model, as in the pit schools. But there are also African and African American precedents for learning phonological script informally and for using nonphonological signs as markers of deep knowledge and teaching *them*, not alphabetic literacy, in a formal manner.[26]

In suggesting that the signs, ideologies, and modes of instruction just sketched serve as transatlantic resources, I am interested in plausibility, not proof. I am primarily interested in illustrating the kinds of material that scholars of African American expressive culture and literacy should take into account, particularly before they venture deficit accounts of African American literacy, couched in polarized terms: preliteracy versus literacy, orality versus literacy, and so on. The problems with these polarities become even clearer in the material that follows.

Keep your head to the sky.
(Grave marker epitaph,
south central Virginia)

4

Diaspora of Signs

A

Transatlantic

Network

*I*n chapter 3 I reviewed a number of potential resources for the interaction of conventional literacy and vernacular African American expressive practices. In this chapter I take a narrower view, focusing on one network of signs, mainly the in United States, but with additional illustrations from the Caribbean: the interrelated four-eyes, crossmark, and four moments of the sun signs. This chapter shows that semantic coherence as well as geographic and temporal links obtain among these African American graphic signs and their contexts of use. I explore only a few of many possibilities here. This chapter deals with a vernacular graphic complex, not a "writing" system; the signs I discuss are semantic rather than phonological in orientation.

The illustrations in the chapter come mainly from my fieldwork, often from sites that I visited and photographed before I realized what I was seeing. Later I returned to test my conclusions. But testing conclusions about the meaning of particular signs is not a straightforward business. Often African Americans themselves do not notice or translate the signs, even when neighbors they know well use them. And the signs themselves are deeply implicated in ambiguity and indirection. Those who use the signs consider interpretation self-evident. Persons whose business it is to read the signs already know them; for those who don't already know, it is rude, even dangerous, to ask too many questions because drawing attention haphazardly to certain signs may bring negative aspects of powers they represent down on oneself.

Even with these limitations, the

FIGURE 4.1. Four eyes variations.

signs are not difficult to investigate. Often, sign users who avoid direct statements give indirect and oblique explanations willingly. In addition, sometimes what seems indiscreet when spoken aloud can be written or coded in objects without offense. Sometimes a written paraphrase accompanies a graphic sign. When this happens, vernacular graphic and object signs interact with an alphabetic text to clarify and double-voice the meanings of both. These signs are ubiquitous in areas with African American populations throughout the United States, the West Indies, and, presumably, further afield. Anyone who cares to check on my interpretations should have no trouble doing so.

The signs in this chapter have definite, though usually complex, relations with an African past. The nsibidi system, mentioned in chapter 3, includes a specific graph for spiritual sight across the boundary between worlds: the four-eyes sign, a Greek cross with a circle in each quadrant. Worn on a disk tied to the back of the heads of Ngbe maskers, the sign asserts that spirits can see in more directions than humans (Thompson 1974:182; Ottenberg and Knudsen 1985:37–38). Nsibidi originated in the Cross River area where Nigeria borders Cameroon; the four-eyes sign, however, came to the attention of outsiders in Cuba some years before Europeans in Africa became aware of the nsibidi system. "[I]n 1839, a black worker on the docks of Havana, Cuba, was writing signs in a creolized form of the same Nigerian script, one of which, symbolizing the fusion of ordinary and mystic vision, was a circle quartered with four eyes" (Thompson 1978:29). The four-eyes sign also appears in the United States (fig. 4.1) and other parts of the West Indies, where it also connotes double vision, especially the protection of home and property through insight into the hidden motives of potential enemies. At the extreme end of the protective spectrum, four darkened holes—signifying poison, death, or extreme danger in nsibidi and anaforuana (Thompson 1983:251)—signify death in the United States as well. For example, in New Orleans of the 1930s (a city in touch with Cuba and Haiti) a sure sign of impending voodoo death was an acorn pierced by four holes and stuffed with human hair (Hammond 1930, quoted in Bodin 1990:50). The pierced acorn container also resembles Kongo funerary vessels pierced with "mediatory scripture written around the void": *maboondo* designs connoting death, inversion, and release of the spirit from the physical body (Thompson and Cornet 1981:76–94). In the diaspora, the four-eyes sign has also become bound up with other signs with different histories, and with a wide assortment of materials—including found objects, from flower pots to stuffed animals, furniture, and auto parts. The various signs and materials have become so entwined in use that it can be distorting and misleading to focus on any one sign alone without understanding the others. By tracing the signs across varied settings I hope to convey some of the associations that spin off from any single sign in use. Like the graphic signs on buildings and the body that I mentioned earlier, four-eyes and four-moments signs involve multilayered associations that overload linear notions of transatlantic continuity.

The various signs that interact with the four-eyes sign in African America have sometimes overlapping, sometimes divergent meanings and functions. These signs have emerged from European and American popular culture and folklore and from at least four graphic and culture complexes in Africa: (1) the Cross River area; (2) Congo-Angola, via Kongo cosmographic signs; (3) southwestern Nigeria and Dahomey; and (4) Senegambia.

Associations that recur in all these areas involve crossroads as ambivalent, even dangerous places, and the protective qualities of the number four, especially as a marker of completeness, of mastery in all the cardinal directions. From the United States, Mary Alicia Owen quoted a traveling conjurer from Missouri: "debbils is 'fraid o' fo' time fo' time fo'" (1893:176). In Christian tradition, the sacredness of four traces to Revelation, which is by far the most cited book of the Bible in esoteric and creolized black religious tradition (Rev. 7:1): "I saw four angels standing on the four corners of the earth, holding the four winds of the earth."

In the following spiritual, the reference to a horse probably derives from Rev. 6:2, a verse in which the Lamb rides forth to conquer on a white horse.

> Jesus rides a milk-white hoss,
> No man can hindah!
> *He rides him up an' down de cross,*
> No man can hindah!
>   (chorus)
>
> Ride along, Jesus,
> No man can hindah!
> Ride along, Jesus,
> No man can hindah.
>   (Bales 1928:84, my emphasis)

The cross in this spiritual is not straightforwardly Christian or biblical. Instead, the spiritual realigns the cross to the four directions and sets Jesus in motion along a mediatory boundary comparable to the horizontal Kalunga line of the Kongo cosmogram and the vertical center post (*poteau mitan*) of Haitian Vodou.

The subtle reshading of associations in this spiritual is fairly typical of how African American art forms reinterpret European and African resources. But the significance of the reinterpretation was apparently lost on the collector and publisher of the spiritual. A footnote on the transcription states that other versions of the spiritual differ from the one just quoted and claims, "The line 'He rides him up and down de cross,' illustrates the hazards of oral transmission. In the earlier transcript the line runs 'The River Jordan he did cross.'" While oral transmission and literate transcription both have their drawbacks, this variation is entirely consistent with how spirituals varied from one performance to another. Although the words change, important associations remain stable. If one interprets the Jordan River as a river boundary analogous to the Kalunga line, the "African" sense of the spiritual remains intact in both versions, while the "European" sense changes.[1]

In any case, the cross, the four cardinal points, and the crossroads are important in the Cross River, Kongo, and so many other areas that there can be no single "origin" or meaning for an unadorned X or + crossmark, based on appearance alone.

In contrast to the X, it seems quite possible to track four-eyes signs and some of the more visually elaborate cosmograms in the Americas (spiral shells and crossed circles as well as the four moments of the sun sign) back to particular regions in Africa, for not only do these signs often look identical on both sides of the Atlantic, but they occur in similar contexts of use as well.

Nevertheless, focusing on origins leaves out other factors that contribute to the signs' durability: how disparate signs reinforce each other, how one sign can substitute for another, and how they vary in accessibility and interpretation. Despite differences in graphic form, important philosophical, conceptual, and graphic overlaps between four-eyes and four moments of the sun signs become evident as African Americans use and interpret them. Even more important, as Antonio Benitez-Rojo has written of the Virgen de la Caridad del Cobre, this Cuban figure—whose personas include the Arawak great mother Atabey, the Roman Catholic Nuestra Senora, and Oshun, a Yoruba deity whose own multiple personas encompass the lover, the sorceress, and the sweet waters—the cosmogram and crossmark are *"not 'original' but rather 'originating'"* (1992:13, my emphasis). So it is with the signs in this chapter.

In addition to biblical associations, European folk traditions and American popular culture contribute other materials and imagery to the four-eyes-four-moments network. For example, the Halloween jack-o'-lantern pumpkin, with its cutout eyes (recall the acorn and the Kongo maboondo) stands guard over certain homes from Virginia to Louisiana throughout the year. So far I have not encountered comparable double-visual signs in European American settings, except the signs and symbols of fraternal organizations, like the Masonic all-seeing eye, which even appears on dollar bills.[2]

This exploration of the four-eyes-four-moments signs is divided into five sections: (1) first, examples of the four-eyes sign, other signs of sight, and redoubled powers of sensory awareness; (2) variations of the Kongo cosmogram four moments of the sun sign; (3) crossmarks; (4) diamonds and stars; and finally, (5) a composite mojo sign. Although these signs relate to each other, they are not parts of a single whole; nor are they simply "the same" sign in different guises across groups. They draw on several traditions, but on the African continent prior to the Atlantic slave trade, and later in the Americas, they came to owe something to each other, and to contribute to an African American graphic repertoire that is readable, knowable, but not by any means homogeneous in either content or accessibility. Although some signs *can* mean more or less the same thing despite differences in appearance and setting, each use demands contextual attention.

The Four-Eyes Sign

Sometimes the four-eyes sign appears in an abstract form, but on other occasions it depicts eyes representationally; either way, the overall message of the sign is that its surroundings are under continual observation. Most of the people using this sign whom I have visited put their belief in Christian terms: God sees all—including personal property. A passage from the Rev. C. L. Franklin's famous sermon "The Eagle Stirreth Her Nest" expresses this conviction in a vivid and visual way that promotes permeable boundaries between verbal and visual art forms.

> Another thing about the eagle is that he has extraordinary sight. Somewhere it is said that he can rise to a lofty height in the air and look in the distance and see a storm hours away. That's extraordinary sight. And sometimes he can stand and gaze right in the sun because he has extraordinary sight. I want to tell you my God has extraordinary sight. He can see every ditch that you have dug for me and guide me around them. God has extraordinary sight. He can look behind that smile on your face and see that frown in your heart. God has extraordinary sight. (Franklin 1989:48)

God's sight gives believers guidance and protection from the traps and obstructions that human beings lay for each other.

The sight of the eagle is part of the rationale for placing eagles over the door of the home (fig. 4.2). Special sight is an African American "coded" aspect of the patriotic American eagle, an especially apt double voicing, given the vigilance required for the exercise of black citizenship.[3]

Variations on the theme of extraordinary sight take many forms. A metal disk, penetrated by four circular holes that form a square, lies on a slight angle facing the road in the yard of Willie Deloatch, a man in his sixties who lives on the Eastern Shore peninsula of Virginia (fig. 4.3). When I visited him in October 1990, Mr. Deloatch confirmed that the disk was one of several objects on the property that he placed in highly visible locations to remind "people of my watchdogs," an explanation that satisfied him but would communicate little to anyone unfamiliar with a double-sighted approach to objects.

Mrs. Annie Sturgill of northeast Georgia placed beside her door an overturned flowerpot with four holes in its bottom (fig. 4.4).

On the ambiguous edge between decoration and protective observation, Mrs. Sturgill also edged the screened porch in front of her home with birds turned in profile, one eye to the street (fig. 4.5).

Mrs. Sturgill's pierced, overturned flowerpot and bird arrangements

FIGURE 4.2. Eagles surround the thresholds of a Virginia home.

cross-reference African American traditions of grave decoration, and imply permeable boundaries between spiritual and material worlds.[4] Like Willie Deloatch, Annie Sturgill also combined an abstract rendering of the four-eyes sign with a reference to watchdogs in another arrangement by placing a large dog with another small dog on its head in front of her house (fig. 4.6). This action not only doubled the number of watchdogs, it doubled the number of eyes to four.

Compare Mrs. Sturgill's arrangement to Robert Farris Thompson's summary of the dog motif in Kongo art:

A dog scents more than game in the forest, according to Kongo mystical belief. Dogs see and hear otherworldly presences, and for this reason the theme of the dog is important in Bakongo art. Numerous *zinkondi* (blade images) are carved in the shape of double dogs, linked to make the point about double vision, about powers of clairvoyance. *Banganga* [ritual experts] also have "four eyes." (Thompson 1989:41)

Another stuffed Snoopy accompanied a Keep Out sign on the roof of the carport of Ruby Gilmore in southeastern Mississippi, until neighborhood children climbed up and stole it (fig. 4.7). This watchdog was only one of the protective signs in Mrs. Gilmore's yard.

A house that also has far-sighted eyes on the roof, this time in human form, belongs to a retired couple near Chattanooga, Tennessee, who placed cast concrete heads of Beethoven, Benjamin Franklin, and Michelangelo's *David* so that they gaze unblinking from peaks and intersections on the roof (fig. 4.8). These sculptures and Annie Sturgill's double dogs suggest not only sensory and extrasensory awareness but also, of course, popular and not-so-popular styles of home ornamentation and the expressive incli-

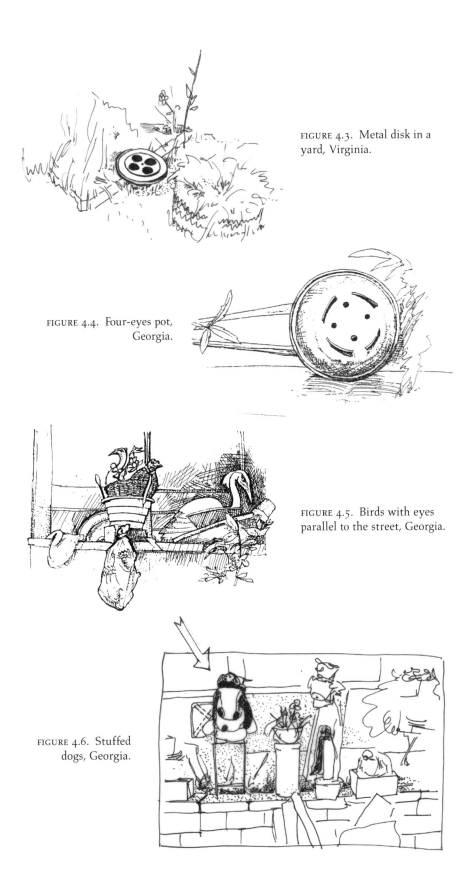

FIGURE 4.3. Metal disk in a yard, Virginia.

FIGURE 4.4. Four-eyes pot, Georgia.

FIGURE 4.5. Birds with eyes parallel to the street, Georgia.

FIGURE 4.6. Stuffed dogs, Georgia.

FIGURE 4.7. Watchdog and Keep Out sign, Mississippi.

FIGURE 4.8. House with sculpted heads on the roof, Chattanooga, Tennessee.

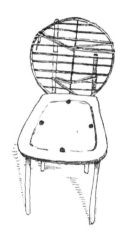

FIGURE 4.9. Chair with four-eyes seat, Georgia.

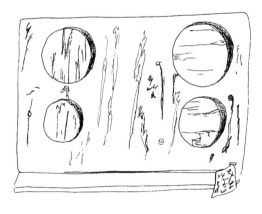

FIGURE 4.10. Stove top painted with writing in an unknown tongue by J. B. Murray, Georgia (after photograph by Judith McWillie).

nations of the homeowner. Returning to more abstract versions of the four-eyes sign: the basic circle-in-quadrant motif is repeated in the seat of a chair belonging to Elijah Davenport in northeast Georgia (fig. 4.9). He replaced the back of the chair with a barbecue grill that in context recalls an antenna. He placed the chair beside a tall tree near other emblems of spiritual communication, cross-referenced with grave decoration: a white quartz cosmogram around the base of the tree, a vessel, a stone, and a pipe.

A stove top in Georgia is covered with "writing in the unknown tongue" by J. B. Murray surrounding the four eyes (fig. 4.10). According to Judith McWillie, who also provided me with the photo on which this drawing is based, some black households have stove tops with four eye-holes propped protectively against their fences (personal communication, 1991). The design of the four eyes of the stove resembles that of a quilt made by Mississippi quilter Pecolia Warner (see Wahlman 1986:72−73).

The Four Moments of the Sun

The examples so far all allude to extra powers of sight. But other graphs in the network of four-eyes and four-moments signs emphasize cyclical movement and persistence over time: the four moments of the sun. In the United States, as in Kongo, the renderings in figure 4.11 emphasize, respectively, (a) the solar cycle and (b) the Kalunga division between worlds. Variations of this sign appear most often in the United States in settings concerned with spiritual matters, especially near homes, churches, and graveyards (Thompson and Cornet 1981; Fenn 1985). The four moments of the sun sign also interplays conceptually with wheels, and with wheeling and motion motifs (see the extensive discussion in Thompson 1988:29−37.)

About thirty miles north of Willie Deloatch's home, the lower panel of a stained-glass side window from a Baptist church on the Virginia Eastern Shore (fig. 4.12) virtually duplicates the Kongo four moments of the sun sign as it appears on the title page of Robert Farris Thompson and Joseph Cornet's *Four Moments of the Sun* (1981). The designs on windows along the sides of the church are abstract diamonds and eyes. Those in front combine diamond shapes with representational designs of the rising/setting sun (fig. 4.13). The church building is aligned on a precise east-west axis so that the sun rises each morning directly over the steeple. According to the chairman of the board of elders, (personal communication, October 1990), the church was designed and built at the turn of the century by the elder's grandfather and other forebears of the present congregation. In addition to the cosmogram motifs in the church design, vessels, pipes, and mirrorlike objects on graves in the churchyard indicate a historically durable African American religious outlook vested in material form.

The elongated diamond with discs at the four points in the church window in figure 4.12 is virtually identical to the transit of the sun around a diamond-coffin that Harriet Powers appliqued for the top left (first) panel (fig. 4.14) of her remarkable narrative quilt (ca. 1895−98).[5]

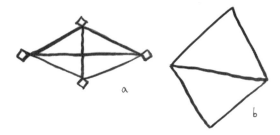

FIGURE 4.11. Graphs emphasizing (a) the counter-clockwise solar cycle and (b) two mirror-image worlds (mountains) separated by water.

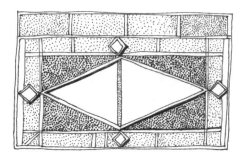

FIGURE 4.12. Church window, Virginia.

FIGURE 4.13. Church with sun motifs, Virginia.

In the final panel of the quilt (fig. 4.15), another rendering of the sun's motion appears, this time oriented from east to west, dark to light, indicating the darkness that fell at noon over the crucifixion of Jesus. A small radiant sun in the center beneath the cross shines at the point of high noon in the spirit zone, perhaps signaling that Jesus has "crossed over." This sun is literally cut from the same cloth as the four small suns/stars in the first panel of the quilt. These identical suns make the entire design of the quilt into a cycle incorporating the movements of the sun and stars, signs of sight and growth of knowledge drawn from a Masonic vocabulary, events from Mrs. Powers's lifetime and the recollections of her forebears, and events from the Bible.

Designs like Harriet Powers's use of double suns at the ends of the arms of the cross recur in other settings. A locally crafted grave marker from southeast Mississippi also explicitly suggests the sun's transit (fig. 4.16). In the same Mississippi cemetery, other markers also use the sun motif. On the marker in figure 4.17 and several others like it, stamped hands point to the sun.[6] Although the rising sun symbolizes resurrection in European American Christian tradition, the African American sun motif often, though not always, differs in one important particular: it depicts the sun *in motion* or the path of the sun through the day (fig. 4.18).

One of the two grave markers from this Mississippi cemetery includes a cross; the other does not. The markers are located in a Baptist cemetery, and the cross is certainly a Christian symbol, as the sun is a Christian symbol of resurrection. But it is also well to remember that in Dahomey and in Kongo, symbolic use of the cross predates Christianity.

FIGURE 4.14. (*left*) "Job's coffins" star constellation or solar transit (after Bible quilt square by Harriet Powers, collection of the Museum of Fine Arts, Boston); FIGURE 4.15. (*right*) Crucifixion (after quilt square by Harriet Powers, collection of the Museum of Fine Arts, Boston).

FIGURE 4.16. Grave marker, Mississippi.

FIGURE 4.17. Grave marker with stamped hands and suns, Mississippi.

FIGURE 4.18. Double suns/wheels near Ninety-six, South Carolina

Johnson Smith (of the stereoscopic viewer in chapter 2) interpreted the designs on this group of markers through an analogy between the passage of a day and a human lifespan: "God is with you from sunrise to sunset, till the sun comes up again, and from the East to the West all over the world" (interview, June 10, 1991).

His interpretation also resembles the theme of the famous sermon by the nineteenth-century preacher John Jasper, called "The Sun Do Move," mentioned earlier, and a powerful prayer that the novelist Julia Peterkin, a white planter's daughter, included in a camp meeting scene in her novel *Green Thursday* (1924).

> O Gawd,
> I know de time ain' long
> When my room gwine be lak a public hall
> My face gwine be lak a lookin'-glass,
> And my teeth'll be shet 'gainst a silence.
> No mo' breat'll heave in my breas',
> My hans'll be col' an' empty,
> An' be layin' fole puntop 'em.
> Dese ol' feet'll be tu'n todes sunrise-side,
> An dis head'll be tu'n toes de wes'.
> Tain no use den fo' my eyes to crack ey-se'f open.
> De life ob a man is same lak e pat' ob de sun.
> Een 'e mawnin 'e rise up bright een de east . . .
> But de time haffer come we'en 'e strengt' gwine fail.
> 'E ceasted f'om climbin' higher.
> 'E sta't fo' drap todes de wes'.
>
> (Peterkin 1924:71–73)

In African American grave decorations, certain handmade headstones contain inset mirrors, tile chips, glass, and other shiny objects. Silver paint and wavy lines cover grave slabs in Southern black cemeteries, and silvery foil—often reversed for maximum reflection—covers flowerpots (Thompson 1983:142). All these mirrorlike surfaces create a watery effect and a composed, deep stillness, like the *looking-glass* face in the prayer just quoted.

The X and Crossmark

Crossmarks on graves and personal property have other connotations besides four eyes and the cycle of the sun. All these signs and connotations share a kind of layered double voicing: one level articulating European-derived and African-rooted concepts that probably are invisible to outsiders, sometimes even as Christian symbols; and a deeper level, *cross*-referencing the intersection of worlds.

Newbell Niles Puckett mentions the following associations with the crossmark:

> The use of the cross symbol is closely akin to conjuration. If you want to stop a path across your field, make crossmarks in it. . . . Negroes will step around the "X" marks, but they won't step over them. . . . [The

crossmark's] effectiveness probably . . . [came from] the fact that it pointed toward all four cardinal points; hence allowing nothing to get by it. The spirit is supposed to get into the angle of the cross and, not having the intelligence of a human being, have difficulty in extricating himself. The crossroad also figures considerably in Negro and European lore. (1926:319–321)

Trapping spirits in the angles of a graphic crossmark also relates to trapping spirits three-dimensionally in folds of paper and cloth; crosswise folds figure in numerous recipes for charms and power objects. "Quincunx" is a term for this figure in European magic. Roland Steiner (1899:262) and J. E. McTeer (1970:21) report that the X or Greek cross effectively blocks a path, entrance, or exit because it is dangerous to step on or in a crossmark. The African-oriented prohibition against stepping on the cross double-voices with Christian themes in a spiritual that Joanna Thompson Isom of Lafayette County, Mississippi, recalled singing to children:

> I know, I know dese bones gwine rize agin
> Dese bone gwine rize agin
> *Mind my brothers how you step on de cross*
> *Yo' rite foot's slippin' an yo' soul will be los'*
> Dese bones gwine rize agin.
> Dese bones gwine rize agin.
>   (Rawick 1977 vol. 8:1098,
>   my emphasis)

A variant of the line about the cross appears in *American Negro Spirituals* preceding a reference to conjure:

> Sister, you better mind how you walk on de cross,
> Yo' foot might slip an' yo' soul git loss'.
> De devil is a liar an' a conjurer too,
> Ef you don't look out he'll conjure you.
>   (Johnson and Johnson 1925:41)

Harry Middleton Hyatt's interviews (1970–78) with hoodoo specialists and root doctors in the 1930s mention the crossmark countless times, linking it to the crossroads, site of offerings, pacts, and the parting of the ways. The following formula from Fayetteville, North Carolina, combines the crossmark with Roman script. (I have eliminated Hyatt's underlining but the questions in parentheses and comments in brackets are his.)

> Well, if yo' wants tuh be lucky an' draw de influence of people . . . yo' would sharpen yo' a piece of stake of a fence 'bout dat long . . . An yo' would trim it smooth on each side wit a knife an' sharpen de end of it . . . Den yo' kin write wit ink on it: make R, make a cross mark [an "X"]; Z, 'nothah cross mark; S; A, 'nothah cross mark; D.R. [A cross mark is probably made after each of the letters—"X" the 7th letter.] An yo' drive dat stick down right out in front of yore do' where no one will see it, turn it out from the house, tuh draw the influence of who may come by an' dey come in.
> Den yo' write de 72nd psalm on yo' papah an' hang it right up behin' yore do' an' den hang a pichure of any kind ovah it [to hide it].

(Up over the top of the door?)

Yessuh. An' hit'll be incorp'rated wit dis peg what chew drove down by de do'.

(What did you say? Read the 76th psalm?)

Write it.

(Write it and put it over the door?)

Yassuh, but readin' it will be incorp'rated wit dis peg whut chew drove down by de do'.

A more commonplace rite, crossing a room, ensures that unwelcome visitors or tenants vacate the premises:

Well, if you are in dis room. . . . Take yo' a white crayola.

(A white what?)

Crayola—dats a crayon dat dey use on blackboards. Yo' makes a cross . . ."

(Like an "X".)

Uh-huh, jes like an "X"—see. An den yo' put dat dere yo' have dis saltpetah an' yo' take dis devil's snuff an mix it togethah an yo' throw it . . . at de setting of de sun, jes' cross it. . . . No one in de world will nevah have no good luck in dat room nor de house. (Hyatt 1970–78, vol.2:1613)

Crossmark rites like this probably emerge from a confluence of Dahomean groundpainting—into Haitian Vodou (Brown 1975)—with the Kongo cosmogram. Laman reports that children in Kongo were routinely forbidden from making crossmarks:[7]

The lines in the palm of the hand, and even more the deep groove of the spine, are known as Nzambi's [God's] roads (nzila), by which he enters man's body, or as Nzambi's writing (wasona). Parents impress this on their children at an early age, and forbid them to draw lines on the ground that cross each other, punishing them severely if they disobey and threatening them with Nzambi's disapproval. He has created heaven and earth and he has not drawn any crosses on it. To draw crosses was by the old people considered trifling with Nzambi's writing on the human body. The old people sang: "Let us leave drawing to Nzambi." They believed Nzambi would be moved to punish those who drew crosses. (Laman 1962:56)

Kongo (and other African) crossmarks differ from the Christian cross in being relational, diagramming the interplay of material and spiritual worlds, rather than being an integral symbol like the Christian cross (MacGaffey 1986:119).

The tomb in figure 4.19 is one of many at St. Louis Cemetery Number One in New Orleans on which devotees have scratched crossmarks to seal requests made to the spirits, especially (in that cemetery) those of Marie Laveau and other Voodoo priestesses. A circle around an X indicates that a wish has come true. Offerings of flowers, oils, and coins accompany the marks. In New Orleans, there seems to be fairly general agreement about the significance of crossmarks on tombs (see, for example, Teish 1985: 187–188). An X also appears on a grave slab near Sunbury, Georgia (fig. 4.20). However, this X is of a kind that local people prefer not to talk about,

FIGURE 4.19. Tomb with crossmarks and offerings, New Orleans.

at least not directly. Discussing the X mark in her own country, a Trinidadian woman summed up the reasons for this reticence: if you understand the X there is no reason to talk about it; and "[I]f you don't already know what's behind that X, then you better not talk about it. You might bring what's behind it down on you. Everybody knows that" (Ann Thomas, personal communication, October 1989).

The X on the grave in Sunbury may seal a request, or a promise to the deceased. It may also enjoin the spirit to stay in the grave and not roam abroad to disturb the living.[8] The X may warn away thieves, for it is a common complaint that nowadays even a simple "love offering" of flowers or the favorite possessions of the deceased is liable to be stolen right off the grave.[9] Or it may encompass all these themes by marking a point of contact between two worlds (see Desmangles 1977:20). Consistent with the open-endedness of African American signs, and the X in particular, the

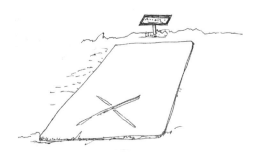

FIGURE 4.20. Grave slab with crossmark, Georgia.

intentions of the reader help to index the appropriate reading—to a potential thief the X is a warning, but it may have other meanings as well. In
some cases, as in figures 4.21–25, tighter conventions apply and contextual cues strongly favor a particular reading. Occasionally such signs accompany and interact with a Roman script message. These five examples
from the West Indies as well as the United States illustrate crossmarks
drawn on or embedded in objects. The crossmarks appear (1) beside a front
door in Dominica, to protect the house while the owners are away (fig.
4.21); (2) on an electric powerhouse near Nassau, Bahamas, as a sign of
danger on a construction site where some of the workers are Haitians who
cannot read the English warning poster (fig. 4.22); (3) on containers of re-
cyclable cans in a yard in Mississippi belonging to a woman who has been
robbed many times (fig. 4.23); (4) on a pile of goods in a yard in Louisiana
(fig. 4.24); (5) in the design of carrier flats for milk propped in front of a
home in northeast Georgia (fig. 4.25).

Blue is the color of choice for crossmarks, although it is not essential
that they be blue. The preference for blue almost certainly derives from
the same protective associations that made blue a popular color for the
window frames of the homes of black southerners for generations (Crum
1940:40; Cooley 1926:53; Thompson 1989:118, 140). Sky blue persists on
the front porch ceilings of white and black southerners today. It was a
readily accessible color even to residents who used whitewash instead of
store-bought paint, requiring only a little laundry blueing to mix with the
lime in the whitewash (Sister Shirley Dailey, personal communication,
April 1989). Crossmarks scratched in the dirt or forming part of found objects can be any color. But figures 4.21–25 are all blue.[10] In Haiti the blue
cross on the door of the house is said to be one of the signs of Legba, the
Vodou lwa of the crossroads who is the messenger and mediator of the
gods and guardian of thresholds (Pierre 1977:31; Desmangles 1977).

European American signs that almost certainly did not start out as part
of the African American crossmark network, like the Blue Cross–Blue
Shield insurance logo, can also be recruited into it, and a local interpretation of the sign need contain no reference to the African American history
of crossmarks, for—from the interpreter's point of view—the logo simply uses the sign properly: to symbolize protection and therapy.

Figure 4.26 is a detail of a large sculpture in the yard of Bennie Lusane
in northeast Georgia. Throughout his yard, Mr. Lusane uses corporate
trademarks and bits of commercial packaging to label ideas in sculptures that
he has been building from found objects since his retirement (McWillie
1992; Szwed 1992).

The phrase "4-way" on the hair pomade jar restates the crossmark
theme in Roman script, while the logo for Lucky Heart cosmetics does so
graphically by combining heart shapes to form a lucky four-leaf clover.[11]

Sold door to door, Lucky Heart cosmetics have led a double life that fits
aptly with other doubling patterns. Lucky Heart—like Avon products and
cosmetic lines designed especially for black consumers—provides hair and
skin care products, toothpaste, and so forth, delivered conveniently to the
client's home; for over fifty years the line has also included oils, colognes,

FIGURE 4.21. House with cross-mark beside the door, Dominica.

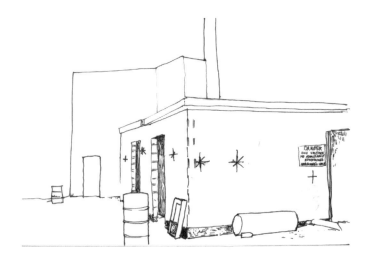

FIGURE 4.22. Powerhouse with warning, explosive crossmarks, Nassau, Bahamas.

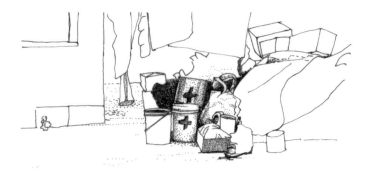

FIGURE 4.23. Crossmarks on containers of recyclables, Mississippi.

FIGURE 4.24. Crossmark on a pile of tires stored in a yard, Louisiana.

FIGURE 4.25. Crossmark milk flats, Georgia.

FIGURE 4.26. Crossmark
and inscribed trademark in yard
assemblage, Georgia.

and powders suited to magical purposes at the client's discretion. Hearts
Cologne figures in an especially large number of formulae for dressing
and feeding charms, magical drawings, and seals. (See the interview with a
Lucky Heart saleslady in Hyatt 1970–78, vol. 2:1075–1085.) The term
"4-way" on the jar alludes to a crossmark and the four directions, but of
course primarily refers to the multiple benefits of the hair dressing—control, nourishment, and manageability.

The Xs and Os in figure 4.27 are painted in blue inside the window of
the home of Mary T. Smith, whose writing-tied fence appeared in figure
2.4. On homes and thresholds in the United States, an O often accompanies the X (see Yolles 1989 for a wall painted by Tyree Guyton of Detroit).
This O has several connotations: full coverage of a situation (each I dotted
and T crossed); an all-seeing eye; and a conduit like the open end of a
pipe.[12] The intriguing grave marker in figure 4.28, from a cemetery near
Sunbury, Georgia, has a sheet of paper with typewritten X's and O's
mounted in cement under a piece of glass. Water damage has made the text
illegible, but the list seems to be taken from a book or pamphlet and resembles a tally (perhaps counted against Judgment Day—compare it with
the calendrical sculpture of Z. B. Armstrong, fig. 6.5). Because of the nature of the marks and their location on a grave, these signs seem to fit into
the four-eyes four-moments network, and to relate to the network's broad
range of meanings concerning protection, guidance, healing, and rebirth.

Seeing the signs from this perspective can help outsiders appreciate
that these X's and O's are not a game like tick-tack-toe, as the superficial
reading of an outsider might suggest. They almost certainly are not even
idiosyncratic; stars and Xs mark other graves in the same cemetery. All
these signs are deeply personal, and they intentionally communicate in an

FIGURE 4.27. Xs and Os in a window and crossmark on a porch, Mississippi.

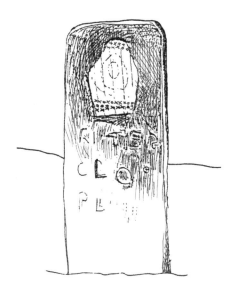

FIGURE 4.28. Grave marker with typed X's and O's, Georgia.

indirect way, so that we can never know exactly what they meant to the person who put them there.

Diamonds and Stars

Just as the X is a tilted cross, the diamond is a tilted square. But some African American speakers also refer to this shape as a "star"; as I will try to show, this term (which, to date, I have not heard white speakers use for straight-edged, four-sided shapes) cues especially rich and durable associations.

Judith McWillie (1987, 1990; personal communication, 1987) first pointed out to me that diamonds decorate homes in black neighborhoods more often than in white neighborhoods. For most homeowners, the diamond is simply an ornamental shape, one manifestation of the broader aesthetic principle that a home should bear material witness to the owner's attention to every detail of the building and yard.[13] In this respect, diamonds on shutters and porch posts resemble blue trim on porch ceilings and window frames: older, more explicit rationales for selecting these embellishments have largely subsided into general ideas about what looks pleasing and what type of decoration is appropriate in a particular location (figures 4.29–32).

Occasionally, a homeowner still chooses to place a diamond/star outside his or her home for other reasons. Figure 4.33 shows a metal weight with a diamond/square embossed in the center surrounded by the words "Super Star." The weight is yellow with a white inner circle and belongs to Victor Melancon of southeastern Louisiana, who found it in the woods. In the following excerpt from a conversation I had with Mr. Melancon, he tells in an oblique way how he determines the identity and proper placements of objects that he finds. It is also clear from these remarks that conventional literate skills assist Mr. Melancon in his use of vernacular signs.

GG: Do some of the things you find in the woods have a message for you?

VM: I kinda wonder. I read books—I try to see—I wouldn't say message—I try to place them in the right line of direction and see—Say: everything have a purpose, you know. And you try to figure out—if it's not dirt, it's not grass, it's not sand, now, but everything have a purpose. It's not there just to be there. So I try to—to /provelate/, /provelate/ the purpose. Books and things help you, help find it. It might not be exact, but it puts you in the right line of direction. Find, just, you know, what's what.

GG: Then you arrange—you rearrange—to fit—

VM: —accordingly.

GG: Accordingly.

VM: Right.
    Then I say—It looks straight, but everything is supposed to be *set* straight. Everything is not level and square. You understand that? Everything's not built straight. The Leaning Tower of Pisa, you say, what about it? Is it level? Or is it straight? It's built on an angle.

(June 6, 1991)

In June 1991 the Super Star weight from the woods leaned against the front porch of the house; earlier that year it occupied a table closer to the other objects arranged across the front of the house (fig. 4.34). By association with the cemetery, the forest, and special events in Mr. Melancon's life, many of these objects complement the Super Star weight.

One day when Mr. Melancon and I were sitting on his porch talking about other things, he pointed to the weight and said, "See that. Super Star. See that star in the middle. That's the super star: God is watching. He's watching this house" (June 16, 1991). Mr. Melancon's statement

FIGURE 4.29. Church with red double star/ diamond door, New Orleans.

FIGURE 4.30. Diamond/star and crossmarks on house, New Orleans.

FIGURE 4.31. Diamond/star and crossmarks on house, Alabama.

FIGURE 4.32. Diamond decoration on window panels, Virginia.

might be taken to imply that the Super Star not only represents God but also God's eye—the all-seeing eye that watches everything in the world. Figure 4.35 shows one of several eyes Mr. Melancon drew and mounted on the interior walls of his house next to the windows. He placed these eyes inside the house just through the wall from where many of the diamonds on the outside of the house appear. Inside or out, the signs guard a threshold where the house is especially vulnerable to intrusion. The interplay of eye and diamond also appears in the stained-glass window (fig. 4.36) that is located directly across the church nave from the window in figure 4.13.

In Memphis, Tennessee, Felix Virgous used signs that include four-sided stars and mural panels to decorate a personal clubhouse in his backyard (fig. 4.37). Edward Houston of northwest Alabama wove a diamond/star/eye/cross from strips of blue and white cloth that he wrapped around iron pipes at the end of his driveway (fig. 4.38). The star/diamond/eye here combines with blue crossmarks Houston made by crisscrossing and wrapping the cloth strips, and with pipes and stones associated with burials. (Mr. Houston had died before my visit to his yard, so I am unable to confirm this interpretation.)[14]

It seems likely that these interconnections—diamond, star, eye, God —lie somewhere in the not-very-far-distant history of many of the diamonds and stars that decorate porch posts, window frames, and shutters in black neighborhoods in the United States. Although they have not been formally surveyed, these designs certainly are not limited to the continental United States. For example, a beautifully illustrated survey of Puerto Rican houses by Carol Jopling includes two photographs of a house exterior decorated with large red diamonds on either side of a threshold, a five-pointed star outlined in light bulbs, and a small yard shrine (1988:150).

An additional association relates the diamond/star full circle to the four moments of the sun. This association hinges on the star/diamond as a sign for the human soul. As I have already mentioned, the spiraling cycle of the soul through material and spiritual worlds parallels that of the sun in Kongo cosmology, and the same (or a similar) cycle emerges in signs and narratives in the United States.[15] Therefore, it is not surprising that the

FIGURE 4.33. Super Star weight
beside porch, Louisiana.

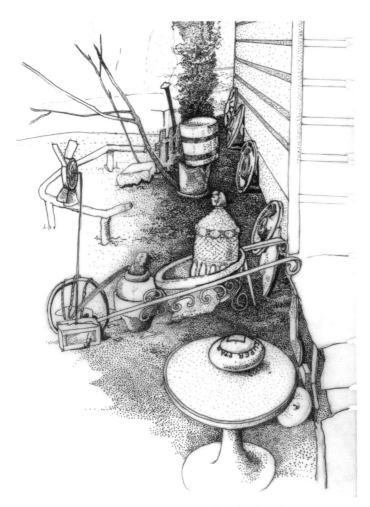

FIGURE 4.34. Super Star weight arranged with other objects,
Louisiana.

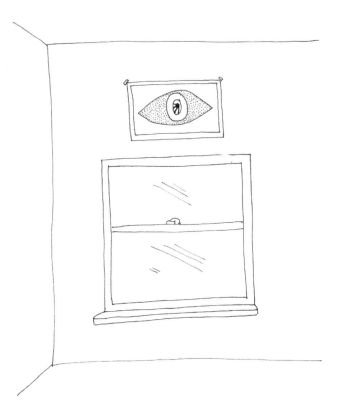

FIGURE 4.35. Drawing of eye mounted over window, Louisiana.

FIGURE 4.36. Eye/diamond church window, Virginia.

FIGURE 4.37. Clubhouse, Memphis, Tennessee.

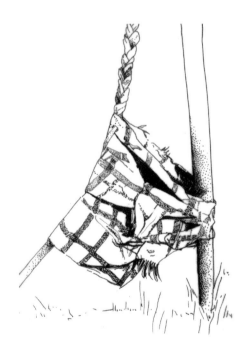

FIGURE 4.38. Diamond/star construction,
Center Star, Alabama.

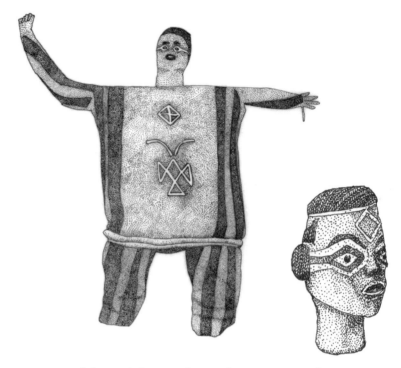

FIGURE 4.39. (*left*) Sundi funerary figure (after Laman 1957: plate 1);
FIGURE 4.40. (*right*) Forehead star (after Laman 1962:196).

star/diamond sometimes connotes the soul itself—especially the essential
and distinguishing qualities of a particular individual—in certain contexts
on both sides of the Atlantic.

Figure 4.39 is a drawing of a Nyombo figure from the Sundi people of
what is now Zaire, as reported in the extensive documentation of Kongo
peoples compiled by the Swedish missionary Karl Laman. The Sundi are
KiKongo speakers. Nyombo figures represent and sometimes actually enclose the body of a deceased leader. They are made from dense layers of
wrapped red blankets, marked with white kaolin and sometimes with black
paint. The sign on the chest of the figure indicates the continuing life of
the soul. Note the white marks of spiritual sight around the eyes (fig.
4.40).[16] In Kongo art, reports Wyatt MacGaffey,

> [s]ince the soul (ndunzi) is thought to be located in the head, more par-
> ticularly the forehead (ndunzi), it is sometimes represented on statues
> as a circular or rectangular metopic spot (Thompson 1974 plate 98).
> Such shapes are also called "stars," and the soul is said to be like a shin-
> ing star. Cruciform and helioform heads occur in cave drawings of oth-
> erwise realistic human figures. . . . On old gravestones and elsewhere,
> the soul in transit may be represented as a Greek cross or a stylized rec-
> tangular reptile. (1986:124)

In the United States, the word "star" is, of course, a common designa-
tion for a lead player or person of stellar success, especially in the per-

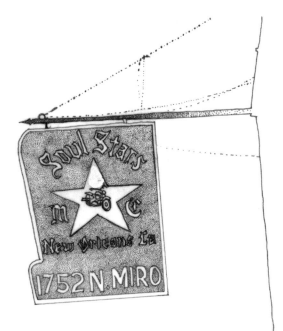

FIGURE 4.41. Soul Stars sign, New Orleans.

forming arts. In African American parlance, these masters of expression are sometimes also said to have soul, and the two terms "star" and "soul" cross paths in suggestive ways. For example, the sacred black dance form, the ring shout (which dates to the antebellum era but is still performed) also had secular variants that included "breaks" when dancers moved to the center of the ring to show off their personal style and best moves.[17] Dancing in the center of the ring was called "star dancing" (Emmons 1969). This term calls to mind that Kongo children learned astronomy by dancing in a large circle and taking turns moving into the center of the ring to dance the constellations of stars and their relative positions (Robert Farris Thompson, lecture at Yale University, September 20, 1990).

Both concepts, star and soul, inform figure 4.41, the emblem of a black motorcycle club in New Orleans. On one level the club's name combines star, as "person with stardom," and soul, as "person with soul," into a statement about the fame and roots loyalty of the members. Here, as in the Jes-Us church sign, double voicing underscores the deeply personal and transcendent qualities of soul and *the* soul.

The five-pointed star, the pentangle, also has a long and well-documented history among Freemasons and other secret societies, and in European and cabalistic magic. The following procedure combines the cross/crossroads with two aspects of the star: first, the moment of the sun's circuit most auspicious for magic, the eastern extremity when the sun is rising through the spirit world to meet the horizon just before dawn; second, a lucky "directional star" in the mind of the individual—a kind of interior metopic spot.

If they had an idea of traveling, like if they wanted tuh go north or wanted tuh go to California or Oklahoma—well, they haven't got the money to go with. So they . . . walk out tuh the forks of the road an turn dere face eastwards and pray for the Lord to give them that *directional star* in their mind that they might be able to get ahold of the luck that would . . . give them that trip. An' Ah've had them to say that . . . shortly after doing that . . . they would meet up with some rich person who would wish for them to go as a chauffeur or cook . . . to such a place, to such a state. And they would go . . . make them a trip jest by going to the cross of the road an' looking eastward [toward sunrise] and making that prayer. (Hyatt 1970–78, vol.1:360)

The interplay of star, God, sun, eye, and soul in the cases I have discussed is far too complex to trace to a single source. Still, I have drawn freely on African source material, especially from the Kongo culture area. This reflects my position toward possible transatlantic resources: contextual use of any one sign is not reducible to the influence of any one source. But ignoring historical African and African American resources is folly, whether African American and European American practices differ or seem similar, because similarity of appearance need not mean similarity in meaning, or vice versa.

A Mojo Sign

The final illustration in this section is known in the area around Memphis, Tennessee, and probably throughout the Mississippi delta, as a *mojo sign*.[18] It appears on the cardboard box pictured in figure 4.42, which occupied a side table near the oil, charm, and candle department of Schwab's drug and dry goods store on Beale Street in Memphis in April 1988. The box contained bottles of special-purpose oils (Squint, Come Back) waiting to be shelved. The other signs and numbers on the box also have magical associations: 33, 44. Thus the varied signs on the box and its location make it a kind of Rosetta stone for outsiders. (Clerks at Schwab's almost certainly decorated the box with tourists in mind; they eyed me with obvious amusement when I noticed it).

The mojo sign illustrates the importance of knowing how different ideas contribute to the 4 × 4 sign network. The sign resembles a squared-off version of the elongated diamond-and-disk design in the church window from Virginia in figure 4.12 and the appliqued constellation in Harriet Powers's quilt (fig. 4.14). Its open holes also resemble the nsibidi four-eyes sign (nsibidi for poison), and the use of open loops to indicate that a script is of the magical, mystical variety (see Dalby 1968:171n, Ibn Washiya 1977:138, 178). Considered geographically and (inter)ethnically, the sign leaves many interpretations open. Memphis is a great crossroads city in African America. While one can usually pin discussion down to a few major groups in, say, the Georgia and South Carolina Sea Islands—especially to peoples from the Guinea Coast and Congo-Angola—along the Mississippi River between delta and New Orleans, all the diaspora's cross-currents coexist in unpredictable flux.

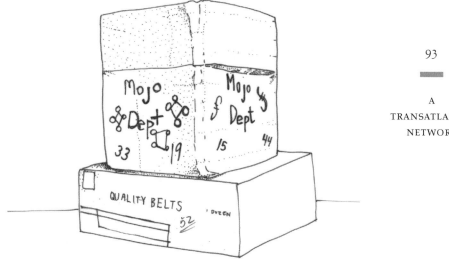

FIGURE 4.42. Cardboard box, Schwab's drug store, Memphis, Tennessee.

The key idea that unites the mojo sign with four-eyes and four-moments signs and knits the network of signs together is, of course, the pairing of double vision and double worlds.[19] Other than physical appearance, what differentiates these signs, and contributes to their identities and contextual appropriateness, is that different signs indicate different *modes of mediation* across physical, social, and spiritual boundaries. Phrased in That Talk, the signs illuminate different ways to *get over*, ranging from protection of hard-earned personal property to acquisition of deep knowledge.

These modes of mediation and differentiation along spiritual-material lines also point toward certain ways that the signs vary in *semiotic mediation*. From a semiotic perspective, signs are packages that differ from each other not only in appearance and semantics but in iconic, indexical, and symbolic function. African American four-eyes and four-moments signs mark a point where academic notions such as these intersect indigenous concepts. In this way, African American graphic signs play into the interaction of vernacular graphic practice with conventional literacy not only in certain physical settings, but in matters of interpretive negotiation: they draw attention to difficulties in translation across different graphic, social, and cultural orientations and to the adequacy of signs to say some things but not others.

But if the signs in the four-eyes-four-moments network point up the difficulties of translation, they also expand the range of vernacular expression, providing means to tie negativity inside the crossmark, invoke the divinity through found emblems like the Super Star, and add complementary dimensions of surveillance and protection to the printed message Keep Out. Signs that tie, wrap, invoke, and project identities expand the media of inscription into the realm of objects. The Super Star weight, the double-eyed Snoopies, and the head of David on the roof map serious concerns onto new and recycled consumer products in ways their designers and marketers never imagined. With its flexible vocabulary of signs, the African American graphic repertoire is well equipped to tie popular American objects of consumption into the reinterpreted terms of the black vernacular.

From the conventional standpoint, the signs in this chapter are too loosely engaged with each other, with precise denotation, and, most important, with the sound system of a spoken language to serve as a "script." They also do not fall under the rubric "writing" for people who use them. During fieldwork, when I suggested that the crossmark related to writing, people looked perplexed—as if I could not distinguish a cow from a goose. Nevertheless, the continuing use of the signs in this chapter alongside writing in Roman script shows that these signs can reframe conventional literacy through resources from the history of African scripts, graphic practices, and ideologies.

Some Kongo traditionalists associate break-patterning with the potency of the other world. As Fu-Kiau Bunseki remarked to me . . . "every time there is a break in pattern that is the rebirth of [ancestral] power in you." Break-patterning suggests spirit-possession. Break-drumming directly occasions it.

(Thompson 1987:21)

ʃ

Narratives of Literacy Acquisition and Use

My daddy told me I was born for a writer so I am going to wheel a pen [see fig. 5-1].
(Byrl Anderson, quoted in Perdue et al. 1976:10)

*T*his chapter draws on autobiographical narratives and historical accounts in which African Americans describe how they learned to read and write outside school settings in the eighteenth, nineteenth, and twentieth centuries.[1] I will not survey the history of African American literacy or literacy as a theme in African American autobiography; others have already done so.[2] However, I will look at several scholars' interpretations of the role of literacy in particular narratives.

The purpose of this chapter is to trace one pattern that emerges from the interaction of conventional and vernacular approaches to reading and writing in these accounts: the relationship of reading and writing to pointedly *not* reading or writing in circumstances that the narrator deems greatly significant for his or her life.

Although the terms "subversion" and "subordination" could describe the moral and aesthetic outcomes of interactions of conventional and vernacular practices in the accounts, the sort of lay-out-the-Euro-and-swamp-it imagery that these terms suggest is misleading. Instead, African and African

FIGURE 5.1. Motif on graves from Delaware to South Carolina to Texas: a broken wheel.

American style-shifting, break-patterning, and cross-rhythms offer better ways to conceptualize the dynamics of reading and not-reading, writing and not-writing in the narratives that follow. In break-patterned interaction, conventional literate values and practices do not diminish in value as they become swamped in/swapped for black alternatives. Rather, African American alternatives cut across the escalating beat of literate European ascendancy, challenging seemingly fixed relations between top and bottom, high and low, foreground and background, and the framing of events themselves. This strategy shifts emphasis to performance. It also amounts to the claim that real mastery—as the four eyes, four moments and cross-mark signs in chapter 4 asserted—means knowledge and movement in *all* directions—down, around, under, and through, not just up and over, not merely in the ruler lines of alphabetic text.

Conventional Literacy, African American History, and Ideologies of Literacy and Freedom

Ascendancy through conventional literate skill—through encoding and decoding alphabetic script—is a recurring theme in African American history, a symbol of reason imposed by European notions of the Great Chain of Being (Gates 1985–86:8), an adjunct of slave revolt, a means of achieving and asserting personal identity, and a practical tool for escape from slavery, and for social advancement.

When slaves like Phillis Wheatley showed that they could not only read and write but compose works of artistic merit, they undercut claims about racial differences in rationality that whites used to legitimate slavery (Gates 1985–86:7–11). One sign that planters took abolitionists seriously in the South was an escalating stream of restrictions, beginning in the eighteenth century, limiting instruction in reading and writing for enslaved people in some states. At first the restrictions were piecemeal, but between 1829 and 1834 in southern states extensive legislation was passed to limit the rights of enslaved as well as free blacks.

This was not the whole story. Janet Cornelius, who has studied slave literacy extensively, has pointed out that because many white southerners believed that all people should have access to the Bible, there was not a total ban on teaching slaves to read (1991:12). We also cannot assume that slaves did not read and write just because doing so was forbidden by a particular state government or planter. Collections of interviews and narratives contain considerable evidence to the contrary (Cornelius 1991:153, 163–164; Blassingame 1977; Rawick 1972, 1977, 1979). Cornelius has argued convincingly that because of the habit of hiding literacy from whites, which probably carried over into the postbellum period, and because interview questions were skewed by gender, the percentage of literate slaves on U.S. plantations was closer to 10 percent than the 5 percent usually claimed (Cornelius 1991:8–9).[3]

Despite restrictions and laws, enslaved people sometimes displayed literacy overtly when it did not threaten the planters. Literate slaves kept records and corresponded with absentee planters (see letters in Starobin

1974; Miller 1978:139–263).[4] Writing sometimes aesthetically enhanced the work of skilled artisans. For example, a famous enslaved potter named Dave, who also worked for a newspaper, inscribed rhymed couplets on ceramic vessels in South Carolina in the 1830s–1850s at a time when teaching blacks to read was illegal.[5] Orville Burton has shown that Dave (the) Potter's verses convey cryptic messages.

> For example . . . "this jar is made cross / if you don't repent you may be lost," may have reflected his feelings about slavery, religion, or both. . . . Dave probably was reflecting on freedom when he wrote, "The Fourth of July is surely come / to sound the fife and beat the drum." (Blacks were prohibited from beating drums after the Stono Rebellion of 1739.) (Burton 1985:152)

I would argue that the first couplet refers to the Black Atlantic crossmark as well as the Christian cross, warning against stealing from the jar.

Dave also wrote this poignant couplet on a large storage jar: "I wonder where is all my relation. . . . Friendship to all—and every nation" (Burton 1985:148).[6]

In the North autobiographers wrote eloquent narratives describing their former enslavement, and from this base an African American literary tradition gradually developed. Henry Louis Gates Jr.'s introduction to a collection of narratives by formerly enslaved authors illustrates the values that became associated with conventional literacy in this process.

> In the long history of human bondage, it is only the black slaves in the United States who . . . created a *genre* of literature that at once testified against their captors and bore witness to the urge of every black slave to be free and literate. . . . As several scholars have shown, there is an inextricable link in Afro-American tradition between literacy and freedom. . . . As Ishmael Reed put the matter in his fictional slave narrative, *Flight to Canada* (1976), the slave who learned to read and write was the first to run away. (Gates 1987:ix)

In real life, one such person was C. L. Hall, interviewed in Canada by the American Freedman's Inquiry Commission in 1863, after his successful escape from bondage in Maryland. "[T]he more I read," he said "the more I fought against slavery. Finally, I thought I would make an attempt to get free, and have liberty or death" (Blassingame 1977:417).

However, as William L. Andrews has pointed out, more than escape was involved in these autobiographical narratives. Even in the so-called free states, writing an autobiography was in itself a liberating activity: "a very public way of declaring oneself free, of redefining freedom, and then assigning it to oneself" (1986:xi).

While conventional literacy provided the foundation for a literary tradition in the North, it also had practical benefits in the South. Literate skill allowed African Americans to write passes and transit documents to gain freer movement on the roads and better opportunities to escape slavery altogether. So it was for the Rev. Emperor Williams, interviewed in 1879.

> While a slave Williams sometimes carried a pass, written by himself, which read as follows: "Permit the boy Emperor to pass and repass, and

oblige Mr. Williams." His master, whose name was Williams, saw it, and the following colloquy took place:

"Where did you learn to write like that?"

"While I was collecting your rent, sir."

"My name, is that?"

"No, sir; that is not your name, but mine. I would not commit a forgery." (Blassingame 1977:621)

Thus, though difficult for many to achieve, the practical possibilities that reading and writing afforded forged the link between personal liberty and literacy in a day-to-day plantation world bounded by gangs of slave-catching patrollers close to home and the Ohio and Rio Grande rivers farther away.

The process by which the narrator acquired literacy formed an important part of escaped-slave autobiographies. As I mentioned in chapter 3, white children relayed information from school to the slaves or bartered bits of education for apples, oranges, or marbles.[7] White adults sometimes traded instruction for liquor or cash. James Fisher told an interviewer in 1843:

> I . . . thought it wise to learn to write, in case opportunity should offer to write myself a pass. I copied every scrap of writing I could find, and thus learned to write a tolerable hand before I knew what the words were that I was copying. At last I met with an old man who, for the sake of money to buy whiskey, agreed to teach me the writing alphabet. . . . I spent a good deal of time trying to improve myself; secretly, of course. One day, my mistress happened to come into my room, when my materials were about; and she told her father . . . that I was learning to write. He replied, that if I belonged to him, he would cut my right hand off. (Blassingame 1977:234)[8]

The seriousness of the threatened punishment indicates that by the nineteenth century masters needed less and less convincing of slave humanity. In fact, they seemed quite willing to enslave people they did realize were fellow human beings, for profit. Planter attitudes toward literacy changed as planters recognized that they were dealing with intelligent people, profoundly dissatisfied with their enslavement, who needed little more than opportunities for covert communication and concerted action to move against the slaveholders.

Trading marbles for letters indicates that conventional alphabetic literacy was, and is, a form of cultural capital and a marketable commodity. Writing was also a means of protecting commodities, so long as slaves could not write themselves. Ellen Butler, enslaved in Louisiana, told her interviewer:

> When the white folks go off they writes on the meal and flour with they fingers. Then they know if us steals meal. Sometime they take a stick and write in front of the door so if anybody go out they step on that writin' and massa know. That the way us larn how to write. (Rawick 1972 vol. 4, pt. 1:177).[9]

Thus writing and learning were enmeshed in duplicity. One recurring element in stories of literacy acquisition is the sheer mother wit involved in using the limited means at hand to learn to read and write against great odds. However, although subterfuge and parodic undercutting of white master-race smugness abound, many narratives contain no renunciation of the hard-won goal, no mystery, no double-sided, double-voiced view of literacy as a dubious good. Many narrators muster literacy forthrightly toward the goal of freedom for themselves and others still enslaved.

Reading and Not-Reading, Learning and Not-Learning

Yet some autobiographies and narratives of former slaves do approach reading and writing ambiguously and double-voicedly, whether they foreground mysticism or the mystifyingly oppressive powers of European Americans, whose literate skills the narrators eventually make their own. Cornelius has drawn attention to stories of miraculous literacy acquisition and their relationship to African traditions of spirit possession, reinterpreted in a Christian context, excerpting a remarkable passage from the Federal Writers Project (FWP) Alabama narratives (1991:93–94). Young Bartley Hamburg Townsley, who had been a "waitman" for a planter in Pike County, Georgia, told his story in the third person:

> One night, when he had gone to bed and had fallen to sleep, he dreamed that he was in a white room, and its walls were the whitest he ever saw. He dreamed that some one came in and wrote the alphabet on the wall in large printed letters, and began to teach him every letter, and when he awoke he had learned every letter, and as early as he could get a book, he obtained one and went hard to work. (Rawick 1979 vol.6:300)

Similar accounts are not uncommon. In some autobiographies the ease with which the narrator learns reading and writing, with or without divine aid, heralds a special destiny.

Perhaps the most famous slave narrative involving the theme of rapid literacy acquisition is Nat Turner's confession, dictated to Thomas R. Gray (and possibly extensively edited by him) while Turner awaited execution for leading the slave revolt of 1831 in Southampton County, Virginia. Looking back over his life, Turner recalled signs that led him to believe that he was marked for a special destiny, beginning with the ease with which he learned to read.

> To a mind like mine, restless, inquisitive and observant . . . it is easy to suppose that religion was the subject to which it would be directed, and . . . this subject principally occupied my thoughts . . . The manner in which I learned to read and write, not only had great influence on my own mind, as I acquired it with the most perfect ease, so much so, that I have no recollection whatever of learning the alphabet—but to the astonishment of the family, one day, when a book was shewn to me to keep me from crying, I began spelling the names of different objects— this was a source of wonder to all in the neighborhood, particularly the blacks—and this learning was constantly improved at all opportunities. (Gray 1968:100)

Turner also told Gray that his precocity caused his master to say that "I had too much sense to be raised, and if I was, I would never be of any service to anyone as a slave" (Gray 1968:100). Nevertheless, Turner was forced to remain in bondage.

F. Roy Johnson, a publisher and resident of Murfreesboro, North Carolina, which adjoins Southampton County, Virginia, investigated Nat Turner's rebellion and its legacy in the folklore of the area from the 1950s to the early 1970s. He found local memory remarkably alive on the subject, and he collected a number of stories about Turner. The following story from Maggie Artis and Persie Claud of Boykins, Virginia, expands on Turner's autobiographical account of learning to read.

> The blacks must have been greatly impressed by his claim [that he started spelling without instruction] for there has survived to this day a folk story which explains how Nat learned his letters:
> One day while Nat was at play in the back of his mother's garden . . . a voice spoke to him, "Son, the time has come for you to begin your learning." At first Nat thought it was his master speaking to him, but he looked and saw no one. Then the voice spoke again, "Look at the fig tree and the holly tree and you will see."
> A fig tree and a holly tree were near at hand, and Nat gathered some leaves from each of them, spread these on the ground and sat down to play. Then he knew that voice came not from one of this earth, for upon the leaves which lay before him were plainly inscribed certain lines and forms. And as he looked at them his tongue was unloosened and he called aloud the meaning of what he saw.
> "Here is an 'A.'"
> "Here is a 'B.'"
> "There is a 'T.'"
> At this time his mother came into the garden and heard him talking. She asked him, "Son, what are you doing?"
> "Learning my letters."
> "But there is no one here to help you."
> "They were on the leaves, and that man is teaching me."
> His mother saw no one and heard no one, and so her belief that her son was directed by some patron spirit was strengthened. So she said, "Come into the house and I will help you."
> When Nancy got the book and started to teach her son, she was more amazed than before. He recited to her the whole alphabet through when but a short time before he did not know a single letter. (Johnson 1970:37)

This story hints at the power of the ABCs (not so distant from abracadabra) as keys to knowledge. It also moves forward in Turner's childhood an event that Turner himself placed later: reading signs written on the leaves of trees. (I return to the alphabet and Turner's autobiography in the discussion of scripts in chapter 7.)[10]

Accounts of rapid or miraculous reading acquisition persist to the present, usually coupling this event to a singular destiny. The case of Ma Sue Atcherson is fairly representative. A respected healer from La Grange, Georgia, Ma Sue received the call to heal and teach when she was about forty years old. Reportedly, the call came in the middle of a family crisis. A group of white people were chasing Ma Sue's father with guns and bloodhounds, and Ma Sue was chasing them. Suddenly, a voice called Ma Sue's name, telling her to " 'Go home and minister to God's people.' On returning home Ma Sue picked up a Bible and easily read it. Until that time she had been illiterate" (Noll 1991:127). A student from West Georgia College met Ma Sue when the healer was 102 years old. The student took some of her textbooks to Ma Sue and found that she could read them "like an educated person" although she never attended school (Noll 1991:128).

Another account in which ease of literacy acquisition foreshadowed an unusual future occurred at a considerable spatial and temporal distance from Turner and Ma Sue. Norman Paul was a Grenada-born religious leader whom the anthropologist M. G. Smith interviewed during the 1950s.

> I liked reading, all different books, I liked singing; reading and singing that was the only thing I favored. A set of children playing hoop or so, spinning top, I didn't worry with them. . . . I read the ABC book, when I were reading the ABC book I could have read in the Royal Reader, sometimes in the Second Standard book I could read something in it. If you are reading in a book, I would remain alongside of you and listen to everything, and when you put down the book I would take it and read the very place which you had read. I read the Bible when I was at school in the Seventh Day Adventist, just a couple of days after Mr. Sweeney told me to buy a Bible. My brother brought a Bible for 6 d. and from the time they started to read the first chapter of Genesis for me, I come home, I could have read the first chapter of Genesis—whatsoever they told me at school I could repeat the same things in the house. (Smith 1963:17–18)

Norman Paul's recollections illustrate the wide distribution of such accounts around the diaspora. Paul later founded his own religious sect, combining Afro-Caribbean religions and Christianity.

Like Nat Turner's narrative, Norman Paul's account of not-learning to read displays a sort of retroactive double vision through which the narrator uses his or her current interests and accomplishments to illuminate past events. Norman Paul's story seems mysterious if one expects that learning requires schoollike instructional procedures, but his description is quite consistent with ethnographic accounts of literacy acquisition by informal methods from other parts of the world (Conklin 1949; Scribner and Cole 1981). Other parts of Paul's narrative situate books and reading in visionary experience.

Although the theme of divine aid in learning to read is fairly common in African American narratives, neither Nat Turner nor Norman Paul explicitly attributed ease of reading Roman script to divine intervention. The folk account of Turner reading the ABCs on leaves implies such intervention, but the narrative remains focused on the prodigiousness of the reader himself, whenever Turner used Roman script and conventional literate skills. This focus reverses when Turner encounters non-Roman script (discussed later).

John Jea

102

▬▬▬

SIGNS OF
DIASPORA
•
DIASPORA
OF SIGNS

Other narratives place more weight on divine assistance and attribute powerful qualities to Roman script and books, especially the Bible.

Henry Louis Gates Jr. discusses one such motif: a book that speaks aloud (1988:127–169). "The trope of the Talking Book is the ur-trope of the Anglo-African tradition," he says, because it indicates intertextuality even in the early stages of the tradition, and because it reveals the "curious tension between black vernacular and the literate white text, between the spoken and the written word, between the oral and the printed forms of literary discourse" (1988:131). Gates sees the trope of the Talking Book as double-voiced discourse in Bakhtin's sense; that is, as a parodic intervention of one voice into another, forcing the first voice to serve the oppositional aims of an inner, hidden polemic (Gates 1988:110; Bakhtin 1981:185–186).

Gates traces the trope of the Talking Book through five eighteenth-century narratives: James Albert Ukawsaw Gronniosaw, who put his ear to a book belonging to his white master but heard nothing; John Marrant, whose copy of the Bible would not speak to the daughter of a Cherokee chief; Ottobah Cugoano, who retold a story of Atahualpa, the last Inca of Peru, who lifted the breviary of a fanatical monk to his ear but heard nothing; Olaudah Equiano, who, as a slave, a mere object among other objects, also heard nothing when he put one of his master's books to his ear; and John Jea, enslaved in New York state, whom an angel taught to read the Gospel of John aloud in English and Dutch.

Gates shows that these autobiographers successively play off the others' handling of the trope of the Talking Book, using black vernacular oral strategies of signifying, capping, and naming. While the first four autobiographers treat the trope of the Talking Book figuratively, in order to represent "a truly cultural or metaphysical manumission," John Jea, the fifth, "erases this received trope by literalizing it to a degree that most narrators would not dream of attempting before Jea's usage and especially afterward" (1988:163).

What Gates terms "Jea's literalizing erasure" consists of incorporating the trope of the Talking Book into an ostensibly straightforward account of a miracle in which an angel of God taught Jea to read. Gates quotes most of the five pages in which the trope of the Talking Book unfolds.[11] Early in the passage that Gates excerpts, Jea is taunted by his master and the master's sons, who claim that the Bible talks to them but not to him. "[S]o . . . every opportunity when they were out of the way, I took the book, and held it up to my ears, to try whether the book would talk with me or not, but it proved to be all in vain, for I could not hear it speak one word" (Jea 1815?:33, Gates 1988:160). The miracle that eventually follows this period of frustration is the culmination of five or six weeks of intensive prayer during which Jea begged "earnestly of the Lord to give me the knowledge of his word, that I might be enabled to understand it in its pure light, and be able to speak it in the Dutch and English languages, that I might convince my master that he and his sons had not spoken to me as they ought, when I was their slave" (Jea 1815?:34; Gates 1988:160).

The following excerpt condenses parts of Jea's account of the miracle that are especially relevant in the interaction of conventional literacy and vernacular practices.

> The Lord heard my groans and cries at the end of six weeks, and sent the blessed angel of the covenant . . . in a vision, in shining raiment, and his countenance shining as the sun, with a large Bible in his hands . . . and said, "I am come to bless thee and to grant thee thy request." . . . Thus my eyes were opened at the end of six weeks. . . . I awoke as the Scripture saith, and found . . . the angel standing by me, with the large book open, which was the Holy Bible, and said unto me, "Thou has desired to read and understand this book, and to speak the language of it both in English and in Dutch; I will therefore teach thee, and now read"; and then he taught me to read the first chapter of the gospel according to St. John; and when I had read the whole chapter, the angel and the book were both gone in the twinkling of an eye. (Jea 1815?:34–38)

Jea's master did not believe that Jea could read, but a minister tested him with a Bible.

> The minister then brought the Bible to me, in order that I should read; and as he opened the Bible for me to read, it appeared unto me, that a person said, "That is the place, read it." Which was the first chapter of St. John, the same that the Lord had taught me to read. So I read to the minister; and he said to me, "You read very well and very distinct"; and asked me who had learnt me. I said the Lord had learnt me last night. He said that it was impossible; but if it were so, he should find it out. On saying this he went and got other books, to see whether I could read them; I tried, but I could not. He brought a spelling book, to see if I could spell; but he found to his great astonishment, that I could not. This convinced him and his wife that it was the Lord's work, and it was marvellous in their eyes. (Jea 1815?:34–38)

Later Jea repeated this feat. Once again, this time for the magistrates, he read the Gospel of John "very well and very distinct." But still he could not spell or read other texts. Both repetitions of the reading test end with the same display of not-reading. Among the magistrates, where the essential issue was proving that Jea knew the "the word of the Lord on his soul," opponents "said that it was not right that I should have my liberty. The magistrates said it was right and just . . . for they were persuaded that no man could read in such a manner, unless he was taught of God." The episode closes with Jea saying that from the hour the Lord taught him to read onward, "I have not been able to read any book, nor any reading whatever, but such as contain the word of God" (Jea 1815?:38, Gates 1988:161–163).

Gates analyzes Jea's account at length, pointing out that with all other avenues closed to him by slavery, God was the only means Jea had to learn to read (1988:164). Throughout, Gates stresses that reading was essential to freedom and to proving one's humanity.

> Jea shows us that the trope of the Talking Book figures the difference that obtains in Western culture between slave and free, between African

and European, between Christian and non-Christian. His revision tells us that true freedom, in the life of the slave, turns upon the mastery of Western letters or, more properly, upon the mastery inherent in the communion of the subject with the logos, in the most literal and figurative forms. He tells us that in literacy was to be found the sole sign of difference that separates chattel property from human being. (1988:165)

I am less sure that this is what Jea is telling us. But more of that in a moment.

Gates also sees in Jea's narrative "the distance that separates the oral from the written" (1988:165), for from the conventional literacy standpoint, it seems unlikely that Jea could read at all. His reading aloud was confined to the Gospel of John, and at the close of his account Jea mentions that he was unable to write down his autobiography himself. Gates suggests that Jea's was the "oral reading" of memorization that prevailed in his birthplace, " 'Old Callabar' " (in the Cross River area of southeastern Nigeria), at the time of his birth in 1773: memorization that, according to Gates, resembled that of Yoruba *babalawo* when they prepare to perform Ifa divination. Thus, says Gates, "Jea's is at best an ironic mode of reading" (1988:166): by introducing the supernatural, the narrative becomes the *reductio ad absurdum* and end of the line for the trope of the Talking Book in the tradition of slave narration. Subsequent narrators, like Frederick Douglass, could not afford "Jea's luxury of appealing . . . primarily to the Christian converted." Instead, according to Gates, post-Jea narrators from the turn of the nineteenth century through the Civil War refigure the trope of the Talking Book by the "secular equation of the mastery of slavery through the 'simple' mastery of letters" without reference to supernatural agency (1988:167).

This progression is certainly one pattern in African American autobiographical narrative, but it is not the only one. My focus on interaction among various settings, texts, and codes differs from Gates's focus on the history and characteristics of African American literary tradition. This difference in orientation leads to different questions, particularly concerning cases where reading and not-reading, or Roman script and vernacular signs, combine or contrast within a single narrative. From this point of view, Jea's narrative may mark the end of the trope of the Talking Book, but it may also mark a point in another tradition that reconfigures again and again up to the present: a *break* pattern that cuts across the ascendancy of conventional literacy.

As I have already mentioned, this tradition/pattern reconfigures the implications of reading and not-reading so that African American values subsume conventional literacy. This reconfiguration can take a number of forms. Some narrators, like the ones I focus on in this chapter, align special, personally and spiritually valued reading and writing—like the non-European reading of "Old Callabar"—with direct, often visionary communication with God. Not infrequently the narrator claims that God taught him or her to read. Other narrators, who previously learned to read and write by the practical strategies we've already seen—trading marbles for letters, learning from planter's wives or at school after emancipation—contrast appropriate occasions for using conventional literacy with important occasions in which conventional literacy is *not* appropriate and vernacular priorities predominate. The "dream of freedom" expressed by the "mastery of letters" (Gates 1988:166) is certainly present, but it is present as part of a larger dynamic. Literacy makes a worthy foil for different personal and cultural priorities precisely because it is so important, and so difficult to attain.

Scholars of literature may or may not notice that conventional literacy and vernacular practices interact in recurring and patterned ways across narratives. If they do notice, like Gates, they tend to privilege one side of the interaction, the literacy, freedom, and social-advancement side, instead of the larger relationship. Given the importance of conventional literacy for literature, this tendency is understandable; yet it has consequences. One is the tacit and uncritical application of European-oriented folk rubrics of literacy—mythic literate ideology—to the activities of people who probably do not share them, or who share them in double-voiced fashion alongside other values. Perhaps the most commonplace recruiting mechanism for the European mythic literate ideology in scholarly discourse is application of the keywords "oral" and "literate" as if they refer to objective phenomena "out there" in the world. Given the scripts, signs, and practices reviewed in chapter 3, it is clear that Africans and their descendants had ample resources to draw on that call these keywords into question, and draw on them they did. And do.

A second consequence is that comparisons among various approaches to reading, writing, and literacy-associated artifacts arise nonetheless. And when comparisons arise on a tacit footing, the outcome is usually predictable. Instead of pulling their own cultural weight—whatever that might be—vernacular practices end up looking merely deviant in relation to conventional literacy, and fall into preordained places at the backward end of the continuum of progress. Thus, according to Gates, in the intertextual, "[s]ignifyin(g)" chain of tropes, "Jea is the third-term resolution between the illiterate slave and the fully literate European."

Even if Jea's narrative is an "exception," and "simple," conventional literacy and freedom go together in African American literature and personal narrative, it remains true that mastery of conventional literacy often parallels mastery of "standard," literacy-backed English. Literacy is thus part of the process that makes black vernacular speech optional instead of inevitable when spoken narrating figures in printed authoring. Black vernacular oral strategies such as signifying, marking, and naming, therefore, enter literary tradition as the conscious, double-voiced strategies of conventionally literate authors. But a second look at Jea's narrative suggests that a different level of double voicing is embedded in its narrative structure.

As Gates points out, authorial double voicing in African American literature accords with Bakhtin's notion of polemical polyphony. Authorial double voicing is especially salient in texts when vernacular oral strategies, like signifying, signify *on* other authors intertextually, and on aspects of European literary tradition that are alien to the author's experience yet also implicated in writing in English. To signify one's way through this situation is to co-opt literacy for the cause of freedom. But double voicing in Jea's narrative operates on a different level: it relates to his claims to double sight. Jea presents himself as one whose eyes have been opened and who has "come through" a watershed experience. When he contrasts reading with not-reading, conventional with vernacular approaches to literacy, he also expands the scope of participation with text in narrative in new directions. The narrower communicative channel of print expands toward multichannel, multisensory involvement: toward performance. For example, Jea's reading test before the magistrates is a performance complete with audience. Literary terms like "figurative" and "literal" derive from true/false, is/isn't assessments of textual credibility under the one-sided rubric of conventional literacy. They are unequal to the task of describing Jea's narrative, or other performance-oriented accounts involving interaction between the conventional and the vernacular, because what may seem "literal" and "superstitious" on one level may be a metaphoric and liberating expansion of the participants' frame of reference on another. Put another way: which is the foreground and which is the background—Jea's other-side world of visionary learning, or the everyday world of repression and legalistic machination that visionary learning crosscuts?

There is a third consequence as well. A one-sided view that privileges conventional literate assumptions, automatically "erases" (to borrow a term from Gates) the personal significance of visionary experience, rendering it mere "irony" in relation to literacy.

This view also relegates claims of spiritual insight to the realms of superstition. However, such experiences and claims have cultural as well as personal significance. They play an enduring part in black folk religious belief and in rituals of conversion and personal testimony in black worship. Because they accord with enduring tenets of folk and vernacular belief and modes of participation with text and script, narratives such as Jea's indicate the persistence of an interaction of vernacular precedents with literate conventions in which the vernacular precedents *shape* narratives in an integral fashion. Because this interaction crosses participatory contexts, it is more encompassing than literary intertextuality or recurring tropes. It is an organizing, cross-cutting impulse that embeds narrative within contexts of participation, and vice versa.

Jea's narrative may depart from earlier versions of the trope of the Talking Book, but it is consistent with other visionary and conversion narratives in its broad contours. As Jea tells his story, visionary experience in fact contributed more toward his gaining freedom than did conventional literacy. As the story progresses, Jea recasts the role of God from the last resort of the slave to the inscriber of the word "on his soul." It was evidence of this divine inscription, not literal reading, that ensured Jea's freedom. This fact becomes clear when one takes into account the passages in the narrative that fall before and after the portion that Gates quotes. These passages do not deal with the Talking Book, but they do deal with freedom.

Some years before the Talking Book episode, Jea's master sent him to church as a punishment. Jea tells us that this was the biggest mistake his master ever made. Although at first Jea disliked church intensely, he was also fascinated with the power of this entity, God—the only force that seemed stronger than the masters in his circumscribed world. When the master attempted to make his farm more productive, "God, who doeth not as man pleaseth, sent the caterpillar, the canker-worm . . . and his fond hopes were blasted. . . . Thus [the master] was . . . disappointed but still remained ignorant of the hand of God being in these judgements" (1815?:6).

After the master forbad Jea from attending church, he continued to go in secret and, eventually, at about age fifteen, experienced a profound conversion: "I became regenerated and born again of the water and of the Spirit, and . . . began to speak the language of Canaan to my master and mistress, and to my own friends, but it seemed to them as if I was mad" (Jea 1815?:25). About two years later, when he was seventeen, Jea underwent another intense religious experience "and began to speak boldly in the name of the living God" (1815?:31). At this point Jea

> ran to the house of God and was baptized, unknown to [the master]; and when the minister made it known to him, he was like a man that has lost his reason, and swore that I should not belong to any society; but the minister informed him it was too late, for the work was already finished, and according to spiritual law, I was considered a worthy member of the society. (1815?:32)

This spiritual law underpinned the secular law that freed Jea.

Under the laws of New York, Jea obtained his freedom through his conversion to Christianity and worthy membership in "a society"—the congregation of the Presbyterian minister who performed the baptism. It was just after Jea's baptism and declaration of freedom by the magistrates that his former master claimed that the Bible talked to him but not to Jea. Given its timing, the master's claim appears to be a last-ditch effort to make Jea doubt God, question the efficacy of his conversion, and ultimately lose his freedom. As we have already seen, after five to six weeks of prayer—which Jea compares with "Jacob of old" but which also echoes the forty days Jesus spent praying in the wilderness—an angel appears, and Jea receives his miracle.

Immediately following his second appearance before the magistrates to verify the miracle of instruction by an angel, Jea began his second career: "to proclaim the glad tidings of salvation by Jesus Christ" (1815?:39). From then on he served as an itinerant preacher with a dual mission: saving sinners *and* obtaining freedom for others still enslaved.

> I was now enabled by the assistance of the Holy Spirit, to go from house to house, and from plantation to plantation, warning sinners, in the name of Jesus. . . . Sometimes after I had been preaching in a house, and was leaving it, some of the people . . . would beat me and use me in a very cruel manner.
> But, forever blessed be the Lord, he was pleased to give me one soul for my hire, and one seal to my ministry. . . . This poor soul . . . was a

poor black slave, the same as I had been; the Lord in infinite mercy, was pleased to liberate his soul from the bondage of sin and Satan, and afterwards from his cruel master.

It was a law of the state and the city of New York that if any slave could give a satisfactory account of what he knew of the work of the Lord on his soul, he was free from slavery, by the act of Congress. . . .

After this poor man had received his liberty from slavery he joined me in hand and heart. . . . His employment while with his master, was sweeping chimnies; but now his master, who was God, had given him his labour to endeavor to sweep the evils out of the hearts of poor slaves. (1815?:39)

For those whom Jea helped to free, as for Jea himself, achieving freedom depended on demonstrating conversion. It was also conversion, not literacy, that freed Jea's chimney-sweep companion. This fact does not mean that literacy was irrelevant to freedom or proving the humanity of African captives, but it does mean that the means that will actually gain freedom for the slave is what becomes strongly associated with freedom in a given time and place.

Turning back, then, to Jea himself, it seems reasonable to take him at his word and take the trope of the Talking Book as yet another instance of duplicity involving literacy. From the master's side, this duplicity involved mythic, not practical aspects of conventional literacy. The notion of the Talking Book assumes that written text communicates in a direct, unmediated fashion from sender to receiver. When the sender is God and the receiver is a slaveholder hellbent on regaining chattel, this assumption is clouded by revulsion at the master's perversion of legal statute and religious belief and by skeptism that the Bible talks to anyone. However, from another perspective, the notion of a book talking also echoes the Western myth of alphabetic script as a clear and neutral medium that decontextualizes the voice and permits perfectly precise communication from mind to mind across time and space. The master thus claims unmediated communication with God. Jea in due course trumps this claim with a miracle. The angel verifies not only Jea's faith, but God's power over masters as well as slaves, prefigured earlier by the destruction of the master's crops.[12]

For the cause of freedom, mediating agents, not communicative media, matter in Jea's narrative. The key text that these agents mediate is the legal code of New York, not the Bible.

In the narrative, the white people—master, mistress, minister, magistrates—mediate the slave's relationship to the legal code. They determine whether or not the slave is "of God" and therefore deserving of liberty under law. The angel and the miracle of *partial* reading thwarted the master's attempt to regain his slave. Reading the Gospel of John helped to solidify Jea's claim that an angel visited him. But it was through pointedly not-reading "other books" and "a spelling book" that Jea showed that his "eyes" were indeed "opened at the end of six weeks" and that his reading was of the soul-deep variety required for freedom (1815?:37). The overall result of all these realignments was that God through his angel now spoke and read for Jea, and that Jea, not the whites, gained the moral upper hand, despite their legal dominance. God, in effect, had "crossed over" to Jea's side. God, Bible, freedom, Jea, and the "oral reading" of Old Callabar were now ideologically aligned.[13]

Elder Green

The following excerpt comes from a religious conversion narrative collected for Fisk University in the 1920s. It crystalized for me the idea that a dynamic relationship between pointedly reading and not-reading recurred in narratives of literacy acquisition that in other ways were richly varied, and that this recurring pattern involved reconfiguring conventional literacy relative to African American vernacular cultural values. The narrator, formerly enslaved, now a preacher, describes his efforts to read and write and the emphasis that black adults placed on literacy for children in the community where he worked as a teacher. When the topic changes to oratorical mastery and devotion to God, the theme of literacy spills over. But in spite of (or because of?) his great investment in reading and writing, the preacher makes "running without parse of script"—without decoding or analysis of written words—his key metaphor for acting in the Spirit.

> My father was a good man but I didn't see much of him because he belonged to different people. They let him come once a week to see us. I was always glad for him to come because he could read a little and he taught me about all I ever learned out of the Blue Back Speller. I was anxious to learn and I wouldn't hesitate about asking anybody to tell me something. Once in a while my mistress would let me and my cousin go over to the adjoining plantation where my father was. This gave me a chance to learn more, for the slave children over there knew more than we did. . . . Whenever I went over there wasn't much playing for me. I got around them and asked so many questions they had to stop and tell me something. In this way I learned a little something and by the time I was sold I had covered fifteen pages in the Blue Back Speller. (Rawick 1972 vol. 19:147)

> When my father's mistress found out that I couldn't read she called my father and told him that he would have to buy me a book. He promised to do it and he did. One of the last things he said to me was, "Son, here is a blue-back spelling book. Keep it with you as long as it lasts and when it wears out buy another one." I kept it for years and years.
>   I never went to school a day in my life but once while I was in Texas—this was after the war—I taught some children how to read and spell. There wasn't no schools and teachers but many of the old people that got freed and had children wanted them to learn something. So anybody that could read and write a little would take a few children and teach them. (Rawick 1972 vol. 19:166–167)

> I wore out my spelling book and bought another one. About this time I was beginning to feel myself much of a man. I was preaching the gospel and praising God every day. One day a white man that had heard me

preach came to me and after we had talked a long time he noticed my thirst for knowledge. . . . When he was ready to leave he took a piece of paper and wrote this sentence: "George Washington was the first president of the United States." He then read it to me and told me to copy it over and over until I could write it as good as he had written it. I copied it and studied on it until I could do fairly well. My biggest trouble came in trying to join the letters together. After I caught on to the knack of it I went sailing. It was hard to find anybody that could do much reading and writing back in them days.

The old folks couldn't read and write but they wanted their children to get some little education. I didn't teach long because of my ministerial duties. I started to travelling then and I swept the country as I went. All over the South, West, and as far North as Kansas, the name of Green got to be a by-word. Whenever I stood up before a congregation there was some preaching done. I was so full of fire. I just went running without parse of script and I was filled with the Holy Ghost. (Rawick 1972 vol.19:168)

Unlike in the case of John Jea of New York City, God did not teach Elder Green. Much like many other young people in the plantation South, he learned to read and write piecemeal, taking advantage of the slightest opportunity for new information and honing his prior attainments all the while. During the postwar era, when black communities were founding new schools of their own, Elder Green—like many others with skills to share—became a teacher. But preaching was plainly his main calling.

The fact that Elder Green was a Baptist preacher fits with the shift in emphasis from written text to direct spiritual communication in the narrative. This transition parallels the shift in emphasis from biblical text to group participation and spiritual communion characteristic of African American sung sermon style. What makes the shift especially interesting in a narrative of literacy acquisition is that the *same* values that shift *away* from textuality to direct spiritual communication in sermon and narrative also, in the narrator's view, embue him with the fortitude to learn to read and write in the first place. In this way the narrative establishes a mutually enhancing reciprocity between outsider, conventional literacy, and secular-freedom associations and insider knowledge, vernacular, not-reading associations. Thus, as emphasis moves toward deeper, more "African" patterns, the narrative forms an interactive loop that recursively incorporates mastery of a "European" form, then subsumes it to Elder Green's quest for omnidirectional mastery.

This pattern of transition and (call-and-response) reciprocity is obscured if one approaches Elder Green's narrative from the standpoint of literacy theories that presuppose great (or even relatively modest) divides between the categories literate and illiterate, literate and oral. While any cultural translation involves slippage and loss, and while distinctions such as these may reemerge in some form in the course of inquiry from an ideological, values-oriented perspective, my perspective does not presuppose what form the distinctions take in "real life" and what work they do in "real world" participation. In Elder Green's case a moderate-divide-driven approach would probably theorize his narrative and African American sung sermon style as shifting from a European American literate orientation back to traditional black orality.[14]

There are several problems with this perspective. As de Certeau says of writing versus orality,

> I assume that plurality is originary; that difference is constitutive of its terms; and that language must continually conceal the structuring work of division beneath a symbolic order.
>
> In the perspective of cultural anthropology we must moreover not forget that:
>
> 1) These "unities" (e.g., writing and orality) are the result of reciprocal distinctions within successive and interconnected historical configurations. For this reason, they cannot be isolated from these historical determinations or raised to the status of general categories.
>
> 2) Since these distinctions present themselves as the relation between the delimitation of a field (e.g., language) or a system (e.g., writing) and what it constitutes as its outside or its remainder (speech or orality), the two terms are not equivalent or comparable, either with respect to their coherence . . . or with respect to their operativity. . . . It is thus impossible to assume that they would function in homologous ways if only the signs were reversed. They are incommensurable; the difference between them is qualitative. (1984:133)

In other words, lump-sum notions of orality derive from the same premises as lump-sum notions of literacy. Presuppositions still generate the explanation.

In addition to problems that arise from treating orality and literacy as comparable terms or entities, specific African American considerations prompt a second set of objections. These center on the fact that African Americans shift emphasis from European to African orientations in settings like carnival, which usually do not give top priority to oral channels but instead combine voice, gesture, dance, costume, music, and so forth, in complex performance. I therefore suggest that a more appropriate characterization of Elder Green's narrative—like John Jea's narrative, the sung sermon, and other cases to which I turn shortly—means shifting from the European, sender-receiver, write-read model to multivalent performance, including aspects of African American performance style such as breaking, offbeat phrasing, staggered entry, dominance of percussion (see Waterman 1952) and also, on occasion, spoken, written, visual, and tactile work with text.

Rebecca Cox Jackson

Visionary reading and not-reading also cut across conventional literacy in the journals of Rebecca Cox Jackson. Jackson was an early-nineteenth-century black Shaker elder who originally came from Philadelphia. Her collected writings, *Gifts of Power* (1981), document her visions and spirit journeys.

Jackson considered learning to read one of the greatest gifts of her life. She wrote that God eventually taught her, but only after she struggled to persuade her brother to teach her.

After I received the blessing of God, I had a great desire to read the Bible. I am the only child of my mother that had not learning. And now, having the charge of my brother and his six children to see to, and my husband, and taking in sewing for a living, I saw no way that I could now get learning without my brother would give me one hour's lesson at night after supper or before he went to bed. His time was taken up as well as mine. . . .

So I went to get my brother to write my letters and to read them. So he was awriting a letter in answer to one he had just read. I told him what to put in. Then I asked him to read. He did. I said, "Thee has put in more than I told thee." This he done several times. I then said, "I don't want thee to *word* my letter. I only want thee to *write* it." Then he said, "Sister, thee is the hardest one I ever wrote for!" These words, together with the manner that he wrote my letter, pierced my soul like a sword. . . . I could not keep from crying. And these words were spoken in my heart, "Be faithful and the time shall come when you can write." (1981:107)

In this passage, Jackson insisted on an exact rendering of her messages in the letters that her brother wrote; she had obviously already absorbed considerable information about conventions of literacy, even though she could not yet read or write herself. She had expectations about the accuracy of the written word and about how conventional sequences of reading and interpretation unfold: that one first decides what to say, then encodes the communication in writing, reads it back, and interprets the message. She also knew from the difficulties she had with her brother that being able to read and write for oneself provides better control over the communicative channel and the interpretive process.

Jackson's expectations about conventional literacy are important because in other parts of her journal she pointedly reversed them to construct a double life for reading and writing. Like John Jea and Elder Green, Jackson went through a long ordeal in order to learn to read, then conditionally renounced this skill in favor of direct spiritual communication. She centered this renunciation around an interpretive reversal. In passages of her journal concerned with conventional literacy, learning how to read is a prerequisite for interpreting the text. In passages concerned with visionary experience, knowing the "interpretation" of the text—God's intended message—is a prerequisite for knowing how to read.

Scholars have called behavior of the latter sort "compensation" for "illiteracy," "residual preliteracy," or what-have-you; the assumption is that "learning" proceeds unilineally from not-having to having certain predetermined skills. These skills constitute a putative core of literacy, and whatever falls outside the core is liable to be labeled deviant or compensatory. On the contrary, John Jea, Elder Green, and Rebecca Cox Jackson's accounts suggest that such behavior is part of a wider dynamic in which conditions for acquiring and renouncing literacy mutually play into and against each other in an evolving relationship.

From the perspective of her identity as an African American woman, Rebecca Cox Jackson's case is also troublesome. Her ways of engaging with literacy and literature have raised questions about the extent to which her voice was co-opted to a European American point of view. Was this woman the mouthpiece of alien forces that dominated her life? Henry Louis Gates Jr. discussed Jackson in *The Signifying Monkey* (1988) as a singular exception to the demise of the trope of the Talking Book. In an earlier essay, he suggested that the following passage from Jackson's writings was emblematic of what he termed the black literary critic's "indenture" to the "great white Western literary tradition" (1985–6:13).

> Jackson . . . claimed . . . to have been taught to read by the Lord. She writes in her autobiography that she dreamed a white man came to her house to teach her how to *interpret* and understand the word of God, now that God had taught her to read:

> [Jackson wrote:] A white man took me by my right hand and led me on the north side of the room, where sat a square table. On it lay a book open. And he said to me, "Thou shall be instructed in this book, from Genesis to Revelations." And he took me on the west side, where stood a table. And it looked like the first. And said, "Yea, thou shall be instructed from the beginning of creation to the end of time." And he took me on the east side of the room also, where stood a table and a book like the first two, and said, "I will instruct thee—yea, thou shall be instructed from the beginning of all things to the end of all things. Yea, thou shall be well instructed. I will instruct."

> And then I awoke, and I saw him as plain as I did in my dream. And after that he taught me daily. And when I would be reading and come to a hard word, I would see him standing by my side and he would teach me the word right. And often, when I would be in meditation and looking into things which was hard to understand, I would find him by me, teaching and giving me understanding. And oh, his labor and care which he had with me often caused me to weep bitterly, when I would see my great ignorance and the great trouble he had to make me understand eternal things. For I was so buried in the tradition of my forefathers, that it did seem as if I never could be dug up. (Jackson 1981, quoted in Gates 1985–6:14)

For Gates, Jackson's role as an emblem of critical indenture derives from the presence in her vision of a white spiritual guide who taught her how to read and interpret a holy book. My argument is rather that this passage operates in a pattern of double-voiced narration that Jackson herself articulated. Rather than confining her interpretive horizons to limits defined exclusively by whites, Jackson complemented Shaker discourses with an African American vernacular discourse in which assertions of deep, double-sighted knowledge cut across practical accomplishments, and emphasis shifts from narrow mastery of a skill to broader, multichannelled performance. In this way Jackson places visionary matters in a sphere where combined African American and Shaker values predominate, and places day-to-day (though often still spiritually inflected) matters in the sphere of conventional literacy that orients toward "European" values. Given this, I am also arguing that passages of Jackson's journal like the one just quoted reflect the down-shifted, deeper, and more "African" of Jackson's several approaches to reading and writing.

Proceeding from what I take to be Gates's assumptions, resolving our difference of opinion would involve determining whether Jackson's narrative contains any African continuities or distinctive African American features, and then deciding if these are weighty enough to countervail against white Western literary critical indenture. This approach, however, could neglect the fact that the determination that a shift to a "more African" emphasis in performance style has taken place can emerge from actual transatlantic connections; from discourses on Africanity that draw referents from Swahili and other sources beyond the scope of the Atlantic slave trade; from comparison with the contemporary alternatives to or appropriations of European-associated styles that continually emerge in black youth subcultures; or from a mixture of these—with or without participants invoking Africa or even viewing their activities as explicitly linked to their African descent. What is more essential, and more difficult, is to determine what was deep and what was "African" for Jackson.

This question also creates problems. For one thing, Jackson worried about being "buried so deep in the tradition of [her] forefathers"—which hardly evinces an approving attitude toward her African ancestors. In keeping with Christian doctrine, she also implied that spiritual growth involves rebirth and a break with the past. Furthermore, whether it makes her an emblem or not, she did look to a white man as a spiritual guide in her dream. So what could possibly be "more African" about this passage?

The short answer is: nothing. The passage contains no explicit references to African or specifically African American practices. Its religious outlook and Jackson's writing in general accord well with experiences described by white Christian visionaries.

A more involved answer is the persistent, almost certainly purposeful ambiguity in the narrative. There may be no clearcut answers, but there are other ways to read—and read into—Jackson's account of the vision of the Holy Book. Did Jackson definitely "hide" clues to alternative readings along the way? I cannot say. Her text is like the signs in contemporary homes and yards I described in chapter 4, and it raises some of the same questions: When is a stove top a stove top? When is it a four-eyes sign? Such signs are not so much hidden as masked from outsider view by being at once ordinary to the point of invisibility and subject to multiple interpretation. Yet in all probability, carefully selected and created objects along with variations on key recurring themes, such as the crossmark, have marked the American landscape since the first African captives arrived. Is Jackson's text such a mark on the landscape? Given the prevalence of ambiguity and indirection as expressive strategies, it seems likely. Certainly, several aspects of the passage and Jackson's life lend themselves to double-sighted reading.

First, there is Jackson's personal history. Jackson did not grow up among Shakers. Her family contributed to the formation of African American Protestant denominational churches. Her brother—the same brother from whom she sought reading instruction—was responsible for changing the order of worship in the African Methodist Episcopal (A.M.E.) Church where he was pastor (Brown 1984:52). Like several of his up-to-date contemporaries, he viewed much black worship as excessively emotional, even hysterical. This style of worship built upon and arose out of the dynamic call-and-response of preachers and congregation during prayers, sermons, and spirituals. As with the sung sermon today, the culmination of such worship was visitation by the Spirit. Jackson's brother and others sharing his views put a stop to such practices in their churches by making written texts and written hymns from books the central elements of the service. This change was profoundly upsetting to many churchgoers who viewed manifestations of the Spirit as the centerpiece of the service and who asserted that the Old Time Religion was good enough for Peter, Paul, the saints, and themselves. Many members of the older generation left the A.M.E. Church during this period. Joseph A. Brown points out that the book-based, "literate" style of hymn singing changed worship in some black Methodist churches to virtually preclude spirit possession (1984). For older members this preclusion amounted to taking religion out of the church altogether.[15]

Jackson aligned herself with this older group, at first arguing for retention of spiritual enthusiasm as an integral part of Methodist worship, later leaving the church over this issue and her call to preach, a role closed to women in most Christian denominations (Brown 1984:53–60). Eventually she joined the Shakers because they not only allowed women to preach but also espoused the doctrine of spiritual gifts, and also engaged in vigorous liturgical dance, whence came the name "Shaker."[16] Although membership in the Shakers was mostly white, the Shaker worship style, by at least some criteria, was "blacker" than that of other sects at the time, especially during the founding decades.[17] Furthermore, during the final years of her life Jackson left the Shakers to return to Philadelphia's black community (Connor 1994:100).

A second aspect of Jackson's narratives that opens up alternative readings is her preoccupation with the four cardinal points—important in Shaker as well as African and African American cosmologies. Jean McMahon Humez, editor of Jackson's writings, has discussed the orientation theme.

> Jackson carefully locates the scene and describes movements by their geographical orientation—she finds herself in a room with a door in the north, she takes a road to the west, then sees a cloud in the northeast, and so on. Why the points of the compass are so essential in setting the scene in dreams we can only guess—is she thinking of the arms of a cross, the twelve gates of the City, the four winds of the earth? Her insistence on specifying directionality has the quality of a ritual. . . . But what ritual? Is this part of a private mental world or part of a once public, though now obscure, cultural inheritance? . . . There is also the possibility that Jackson worked with some kind of esoteric "code" or private language to convey a message that she did not want "outsiders" such as whites to understand. (1981:47–48, 48n).

Shifts from conventional to African American vernacular approaches to literacy often involve multisensory and multidirectional dimensions of performance—movement, rhythm, proxemics, taste, hearing—not just vision. Jackson's narratives especially expand into performance when activity in visions realigns the body and important objects in space. Participants orient toward and circumambulate the four cardinal points in numerous African American expressive and religious activities. Certain performances, like the counterclockwise ring shout, culminate in spirit possession (Stuckey 1987). Cosmographic orientation to the four cardinal points also appears in various other contexts: the design and use of traditional healing centers such as Jamaican balmyards (Barrett 1976); Vodou ritual (Rigaud 1969; Deren 1953; Metraux 1959); the construction of power objects (Owen 1893); rootwork (Hyatt 1970–78); and the ritual cleansing of houses (Teish 1985). Orientating creates a break with the secular world, setting events in motion in the proper direction and entraining behavior on the proper course.[18]

The use of circling movements to cleanse and differentiate insiders from outsiders persists in African American ritual practice to the present. For example, as an outsider visiting African American places of worship, I have been instructed to walk around the four corners of the room before viewing consecrated objects. I have also been told to pass through each corner of the room on the way out, so that my exit would be complete, leaving behind no negative influences. (This clean sweep around the square and out the door recalls the properties of the crossmark and folded charm packages, but reverses the process, diffusing influences rather than tying them together.)

The white spiritual guide is a third complicating aspect of Jackson's vision of the Holy Book. On the surface the guide obviously seems to be a white male Shaker. But African and African American associations also attach to white guide figures in dreams and visions. Some involve writing systems and books; others involve initiation and religious conversion; all these figure in Jackson's narrative.

As I mentioned in the review of African scripts in chapter 3, white messengers in dreams and visions revealed several scripts to their mortal inventors. Dalby (1970:116–118) points out that white need not mean Caucasian in such cases because the outsiders whose linear scripts prompted development of indigenous scripts were mostly dark-skinned people of African descent. North American freedpeople resettling in Liberia brought Roman script literacy with them; Arabic literacy mainly moved into the area with African Mande-speaking peoples. In many West and Central African belief systems, whiteness signifies the spirit world and spirit visitors (Hauenstein 1984:570, 572). Therefore, interpreting a white messenger as a spirit rather than, say, a colonial administrator fits the theme of revelation in script origin stories. This interpretation may even be better because the administrator is a secular intruder, whereas the white messenger bypasses the colonial regime, bringing the signs themselves or inspiration for the script directly from the spirit world to the inventor or the leader of a cooperative script design team. It is also possible that in such narratives Caucasian whiteness is a double-visual mask to hide the spirit messenger or ancestral whiteness from outsider comprehension.

Whiteness is also a prevalent sign in other settings. Throughout West and Central Africa masqueraders use white clay body paint to construct spirit identities. Participants in initiation rituals wear white to show that they are not of the everyday world but set apart by processes of rebirth that place them temporarily in the spirit world. In Kongo white skin is but one of the spirit world's inversions; as the cosmogram illustrates, times of day are also reversed. Wyatt MacGaffey reports a Kongo belief that souls of the dead cross the ocean to America and Europe, where they turn white (1988a).

In African diaspora religious practice, whiteness has similar connotations. White guides appear in dreams and visions relating to initiation, conversion, and *mourning*, which in the United States usually means seeking a conversion experience, and in the West Indies may include a prolonged period of isolation. Norman Paul, the Grenadan religious leader, received guidance from Oshun, a Yoruba deity who has many devotees, and a New World double in the guise of a Roman Catholic saint. Paul says of a visitation of Oshun:

> So this *white lady*, I questioned her one time and she told me she is Saint Philomena. . . . [S]he told me to build the altar, I don't know where the person came from, but they put a book on the altar, The Life of Saint Philomena, so when I took the book and read it, the very things that I am doing is the very things I read. . . . So that get me to believe that she is the same as Oshun. . . . I say, "That is African Powers that is with me." (Smith 1963:79, my emphasis)

In a similar vein, according to Jeannette Hillman Henney, a white gentleman in white clothes is an important element in visions when Spiritual Baptists in St. Vincent seek Baptism (1968:72).

Whiteness is also one of the most frequently recurring themes in accounts of seeking conversion in the United States. Samuel Miller Lawton carried out an exceptionally thorough investigation of black religious practice in the Sea Islands during the 1930s. Reporting on visions of seekers, he says, "A total of sixty-eight different kinds of objects was reported as having been seen by eighty-two individuals during their visionary experiences. The object most frequently reported as having been seen was 'white man,' reported by twenty-five individuals" (1939:153). In culminating visions that signified that the seeker had "come through the wilderness"— been assured salvation—"fifty-seven of the eighty-two individuals reported having either seen something white or a bright light" (1939:154).[19]

The Fisk University collection of conversion visions, *God Struck Me Dead*, (reprinted as Rawick 1972 vol. 19), has received considerable attention from scholars. (Elder Green's account comes from one of the autobiographies in that collection.) The visions in the Fisk collection weave together repetitious elements and distinctive personal experiences. Mechal Sobel analyzed these visions and those of whites.

> In both [black and white converts' visions], the individual begins in a low state and is saved by a cry for mercy to God in his Glory to be reborn. The black visions have four unique aspects: (1) The concept of the two selves, the "little me" in the "big me" permeating the vision struc-

ture; 2) detailed journey or travel of the soul from Hell to Heaven; (3) appearance of a little (white) man as guide on this journey; (4) the visual description of Heaven and God, with its emphasis on whiteness. In each case, these differences . . . can be attributed to an African ethos. Sobel 1979:109)

For Sobel, then, whiteness is an attribute of those aspects of visionary experience that orient toward Africa rather than Europe.

Sobel and Lawton both also point out that conversion is not a one-time-only event. Often several visions confirm sanctification and salvation, and religious instruction by a spiritual mother or father guides the process. Other authors have also discussed multistage forms of African American religious conversion involving prayer, isolation and special spatial positioning during rituals, spiritual guidance, visionary travel, and oral testimony (Henney 1968; Simpson 1970; Simpson 1985; Glazier 1985; Williams 1982). In essence, African American traditions of conversion resemble African initiation in their practices of extending conversion over time and building in multiple stagings along the way.

This recognition brings us to another aspect of Jackson's narrative that warrants consideration: her persistence in interpreting and reinterpreting the dream of the Holy Book throughout her lifetime—at least four times over a span of nearly thirty years.

> In 1847, I received *The Holy Sacred and Divine Roll and Book*, which was printed in 1843. . . . As I said that, it was spoken in my heart, "This is the book you saw laying on the west table, in 1836." . . . Saturday, June 4, 1864, the mystery of the three books was made known to me by revelation. The book that lay on the north table, was the Bible . . . being told that I should be instructed in it . . . meant that I should have the spiritual meaning of the letter in my soul by the manifestation of God. This revelation, then being in Heaven, was the true book which must come to give us the true meaning of the letter—as "the letter killeth, but the spirit maketh alive."
>
> The book that lay on the west table was the *Sacred Roll*. The book that lay on the east table was the *Divine Book of Holy Wisdom*. . . . These two last books, which I saw in 1836, were not written by mortal hands till 1840, '41, '42, and '43. And these two books contained the mystery of God. . . . The ministers of God are busy in the spirit world, preaching the Gospel of full salvation to *souls out of the body*. (1981:291)

Jackson's account of this dream and her persistence in refining her interpretations of it as she passed through various stages of her life suggest that the dream of the Holy Book was roughly analogous, for her, to that culminating vision that proves that a seeker has "come through."

The dream of 1864 resembles earlier her accounts that also emphasized orientation to the four directions. It also has several other provocative features: the concept that revelation in heaven gives true meaning to the written word, which without revelation "killeth," and that "the ministers of God are busy in the spirit world, preaching . . . to souls out of the body." While the notion that the letter kills was expressed in the Bible by the

Apostle Paul (II Cor. 3:6), the latter point seems strikingly nonbiblical. If Jackson uses "soul" in the usual Christian sense, for that aspect of the person that persists after death, then she certainly departs from orthodox Christian doctrine if she is implying that souls can be converted, apparently *after* death. Yet what this departure from orthodoxy does accomplish is that it offers the prospect of conversion to the forefathers Jackson had mentioned years earlier. And it does so as part of an active interchange with the spirits of the forefathers that differs from orthodox European conceptualizations.

In Christianity, there are two basic versions of what happens when the soul leaves the body at death: (1) dead people stay dead until the general resurrection at the Second Coming, and then on Judgment Day emerge from the grave to be sent to heaven or hell; (2) when people die they face judgment immediately and go straight to heaven or hell (or purgatory, if Roman Catholic). Jackson's strong emphasis on continuing exchange with souls out of the body does not fit either of these schemas. From a European perspective, it resembles Spiritualism, a belief system that has contributed to creole religions like Umbanda in Brazil. From a more African orientation, it recalls a belief that ancestors in the spirit world affect the lives of the living and vice versa. The idea of a soul that can be acted upon by others ("ministers") also recalls African and African American concepts of multiple souls, such as the Ti Bon Ange and Gros Bon Ange of Haiti.

The point I am trying to make is that Jackson's narrative is ambiguous. Its "heritage," or "cultural" loading, is unclear and probably inevitably so, for symbols like whiteness, guide figures, and the four cardinal points appear in European, African, and European- and African American settings. Indeed, this historical and associative overlap may help to account for the importance of such imagery to Jackson. Therefore—especially given the strong-minded way she addressed her brother—it seems only fair to keep an open mind about whether or not the imagery in Jackson's narrative reflects her indenture to white critical traditions. While this issue cannot be definitively resolved one way or the other—nor should it be—what is clear about the narrative is that there is a shift in emphasis from nonvisionary to visionary concerns, and that this shift is constructed in a way that highlights Jackson's deep knowledge and access to spiritual communication, and thus her worth as a person. While from Jackson's point of view this emphasis may have established her as the humble superior of both black and white noninitiates, from the broader perspective of conventional and vernacular approaches to literacy, it fits an African American performance orientation that reconfigures and subordinates conventional literate skill.

The key dynamic that this chapter has described arises from the tension between reading and not-reading. I have shown that this dynamic cuts across narratives as well as other African American expressive images and practices. I have suggested that not-reading is itself a vernacular African American expressive "tradition." This idea is new—I, at least, have not encountered it elsewhere—but outsiders in other parts of the diaspora have also noticed that participants in various African American be-lief systems distance reading, writing, and artifacts of literacy from certain types of knowledge. These participants claim that the Spirit of God teaches directly and does not require an intermediary such as the Bible; indeed, the Bible could actually hinder communication with the Spirit (Stewart 1992:143). For example, the Rev. Benjamin Franklin wrote, from Morant Bay, Jamaica, in the late 1830s, of one of the area's leading "faith" or "angel men" named Pennock:

> He told me that if he laid down to sleep, and put the prayerbook or Bible on his breast, the Spirit would not speak to him, but if these were not there, he would have dreams, visions, voices, etc., and that when he had the Spirit, if he opened either of the above books, the paper would ap-pear perfectly white and clean—no print could be seen. Pennock ac-knowledged that the Bible would teach him many good things, but he was firm in his doctrine, "That God by his Spirit taught him many things which could not be found in the Bible." (London Missionary So-ciety correspondence, quoted in Stewart 1992:143)

These remarks also mention *doctrine*: epistemology cemented in conven-tion and practice—if not encoded in alphabetic script. Yet most profes-sional outsiders, whether travelers, missionaries or folklorists, seem in-clined to notice only bits and pieces of doctrine, not a knowledge system, and to attribute these bits and pieces to psychological "needs" that liter-acy, science, or both would eventually satisfy.

Newbell Niles Puckett, a sociologist and white southerner who amassed a vast compendium of African American lore during the first quarter of this century, regarded much of the material he collected as superstition and wondered how to "cure" black Americans of their benighted inclinations.

> [M]ere training in reading and writing will not do to remove supersti-tion. Many of the conjurers whom I know could read and write, and some turn this knowledge into direct use in sorcery, as where the Bible is used for purposes of divination. In New Orleans the "Secrets of Al-bertus Magnus" and the "Sixth and Seventh Books of Moses," compila-tions of old medieval magic, printed on very cheap paper with paper bindings, are retailed to the Negroes at a dollar each, though they cost, I am informed, only about ten cents each. The sale is enormous and their use by literate Negroes very widespread. . . . This is reversion with a vengeance and shows the futility of a certain kind of education. Super-stitions even gather around the seat of learning itself. . . . It is said, for example, that if you part your hair in the middle on examination day, or sleep with your books under your pillow, you will surely know your lesson. (1926:579)

In Puckett's view, literacy was not a cure for superstition, although it was a start. He regarded training in biology, chemistry, physics, and other sci-ences as a better remedy than the Three Rs because sciences reveal the logic of natural processes and stifle the notion that chance and luck can be ma-nipulated (1926:580). The sciences, taught to impressionable youth, also help to "break up" conjure because it is "more often passed from mature man to mature man outside of the household" (1926:578).

What African American not-reading and reading of esoteric texts suggests to me, however, is that such pro—or con or how—arguments about
education and literacy will forever miss the point. As Benitez-Rojo puts it:
"In the Caribbean"—and here I would add "and in the Black Atlantic
world"—"epistemological transparency has not displaced the dregs and
sediments of the cosmological arcana, the spatterings of sacrificial blood
. . . but rather, unlike what happens in the West, scientific knowledge and
traditional knowledge coexist as differences within the same system"
(1992:17).

Not-reading, then, as we have encountered it in this chapter, is a coex-
isting difference, a cosmological break-pattern that cuts across literacy, not
devaluing reading, writing, or alphabetic script but momentarily illumi-
nating and provisionally displacing them.

An object never serves the same
function as its image—or its name.
René Magritte

6

Alternative Modes of Participation with Text and Artifacts of Literacy

*T*his chapter explores vernacular practices that involve texts and artifacts of literacy and fall outside the rubric of conventional literacy, focusing on four overlapping modes: (1) expression through metaphors; (2) performances and rituals; (3) the use of talismans and power-objects; and (4) acts of divination and revelation. These modes certainly do not exhaust the list of such practices, but they do exemplify some of the ways that African Americans incorporate reading, writing, and literate artifacts into preexisting patterns of activity through emergent events in which values and resources from both sides of the Atlantic cross-fertilize each other. Americans have approached reading, writing, and related artifacts quite diversely, as they have shaped the contours of a vernacular repertoire. This chapter shows that the interaction of conventional literacy with vernacular practices, expressed in pointedly reading and not-reading as well as other arrangements, is significant in these four modes of participation. This significance only becomes apparent when inquiry attends to relationships instead of isolated objects, and to performance, broadly construed, instead of mere mimicry. (Whites have been prone to such interpretations when they assume that any sensible person, given a chance, would want to be just like them.)

These four modes of participation often involve religious beliefs and material forms of mediation at a juncture between physical and spirit worlds. Some are stigmatized by other black and white members of society.[1] In other words, these modes often involve the kinds of practices that exemplify superstition and preliteracy or illiteracy in conventional literate ideology. Indeed, the guiding premises of this ideology provide such strong license for marginalizing these practices that adjectives like "primitive" and "superstitious" persist even though scholars have abandoned them with reference to nearly everything else. For example, the *Cambridge Encyclopedia of Language* contains a section entitled "The Magic of Language" (Crystal 1987:8–9). It begins with the following paragraph:

> The magical influence of language is a theme which reverberates throughout the literatures and legends of the world. Language, especially its written form, is thought to contain special powers, which only the initiated are allowed to understand or control. The beliefs are often linked to a myth about the divine origins of language, but they extend beyond this, to influence religious activities of all kinds, and to reflect widespread primitive superstition about objects and events which have a symbolic meaning and use. (1987:8)

This kind of assessment forecloses inquiry before it begins. As a result, we have too little information on the social-culture work that participants accomplish with these practices. Participation in such activities, in and of itself, gives no fair indication of whether or how the participants use reading and writing in other settings.

One less pejorative phrasing labels such practices and beliefs "nonliterate syncretism" because, although they often involve reading and writing in some form, they tend to emerge in contact among different segments of society, if not different societies altogether. As "syncretism" implies, such practices seem to render pure, autonomous literacy impure because they use literacy-related materials in ways that deviate from the "proper" functions of writing and reading: encoding and decoding messages in alphabetic script.

But rumblings about impurity and superstition also hint at creolization, albeit in negative terms. Creolizing processes often mix and reconfigure practices that scholars habitually treat as distinct. This situation recalls a point Drummond made: "we shall have to pay particularly close attention to material too often dismissed as fragmentary or in some way 'spoiled'"(1980:372). The issue here, though, is essentially epistemological: if mixing equals spoiling, and spoiling warrants dismissal, what is left? In the practices described in this chapter, alphabetic literacy interacts with African American folk religious beliefs. The latter creolize Christianity and West and Central African belief systems.[2] This activity in turn brings into contact different traditions that probably also crossed paths in the distant past, when early Christianity incorporated philosophies and beliefs in circulation around the Mediterranean rim.

Metaphor, Creolization, Word, Text, and Artifact

One might say that what creolization is to cultural contact, metaphor is to semantic contact, via figures of speech and material juxtapositions. Creolization and metaphor both cross-reference things, activities, and categories that formerly seemed to have little in common. Metaphors pull together cues to disparate contexts, make new associations between unlike domains, and help to stabilize old associations, sometimes in a habitual, almost formulaic manner. Some metaphors have become conventions for describing creolization: pull together, mix, entwine, and so on—as if culture really consists of palpable strands.

Talk moves through networks of metaphor, like love-is-a-journey and argument-is-war; metaphor is built into language-in-use (Lakoff and Johnson 1980). Metaphors do not make or entrain understandings in and of themselves, but because they are based on cultural understandings shared by some, if not all, of a population (Quinn 1991). Metaphors thus provide a kind of shorthand for the sociocultural relationships that frame how we see events and each other. This shorthand is one of the ways that expression organizes experience from the outside in, rather than the other way round, constraining what can be said and understood across persons (Volosinov 1986:85). The notion of "shared understandings" refers to something that is said according to a *rule* and not "actual events," for telling what "actually happened" is also a cultural process. The appropriate image of shared understanding is therefore "an *operation*—a sequence of activities—rather than a common intersection of overlapping sets" (Garfinkel 1986:320). Furthermore,

> [W]e do not decide that a word is used metaphorically because we know what a person is thinking; rather we know what he is thinking because we see that a word is used metaphorically. Taking poetry for his case, [Monroe Beardsley] points out that "the clues to this fact must somehow be in the poem itself, or we should seldom be able to read poetry." (Garfinkel 1986:321)

Poems and lived situations encode cues to their own interpretation, and metaphor is one of the ways that cues are arranged. But the mere fact that a given metaphor becomes a conventionalized interpretive frame does not mean that it is static or eternal. Perspectives shift along with definitions of the situation, including perspectives on metaphor itself. Scholars approach metaphor in two main ways, orienting primarily toward either the nouns/things/symbols or the verbs/activities/relationships in metaphoric constructions. No firm line divides these approaches, but—like the metaphors they attempt to characterize—they entrain different interpretations.

The more widespread noun/thing/symbol orientation characterizes metaphor as seeing one thing in terms of another: for example, argument is war.[3] Sometimes the things that metaphors relate also lend themselves to contrastive constructions: as a bloodless form of conflict, argument contrasts with the bloodshed of war.

Just as metaphors have a cultural basis, realignments among metaphors have cultural implications. For example, several standard metaphors such as "read" and "reading" anchor relationships between literacy and divination. Calling divination sessions readings makes an analogy between two or more interpretive domains. In some Gypsy, European, European American and African American traditions a recurring analogy links reading lines on the palm of the client's hand with reading lines of script on the page of a book. If one assumes that the driving force of metaphor is resemblance among things or symbols, then reducing the analogy to its component parts—wrinkled palm and written page—permits the relation between the components to shift easily from an assertion of likeness to an equally forceful contrast. In this case the contrast pits a spurious code against an authentic one: mimetic, superstitious palm reading versus authentic, rational book reading. As de Certeau has pointed out, mythic notions that link literacy with Western identity thrive on just such conventions and divisions.

A verb/activity/relationship orientation to metaphor foregrounds relations among complexes of action rather than similarities among things. According to Gregory Bateson's definition, metaphor retains unchanged the relations that it "illustrates" while substituting other persons and things for the relata. From this perspective, then, domains are constituted through activity and modes of participating.[4] When metaphors involve named things or categories or symbols, they do so because the things serve as *clues* to the persisting relationship that grounds the metaphor, and as indexical *cues* to the kinds of participation that keep the relationship stable. This perspective on metaphor does not "redeem" palm reading as a form of literacy or a good way to learn about the future. But it does highlight what palm reading and book reading share; both practices bring experience to bear on systems of marks that are open to multiple functions and interpretations.[5]

Interest in metaphor thus complements interest in creolization. Although the term *metaphor* rarely appears in discussions of creolization, metaphor is one of the mechanisms through which creolization unfolds.[6] For example, in the African American yards and buildings illustrated in chapter 4, all sorts of objects, from stuffed dogs to chair seats, hubcaps to flowerpots sustain in material form the metaphor of double sight, with its implication of different, interpenetrating realities. At the same time that these materials creolize an enduring transatlantic concept, they also attest to the systematic relationship of different cultural orientations: the "mainstream" orientation of buying flowerpots for geraniums, and the "insider" orientation of upending the pot so that the four holes on the bottom point toward passersby. The key to visual metaphors like four holes that can also be read as four-eye signs by insiders is simply that one feature (or occasionally two) serves as a contextual and interpretive cue, while others fade into the background. This selectivity, and the background required to recognize cues, is the groundwork for masking and double sight.

This kind of selective cuing has been very important in the material culture of African diaspora religions—Shango in Trinidad, Vodou in Haiti, Santeria in Cuba, Candomblé and Umbanda in Brazil, and the offshoots of all of them that thrive in ethnic enclaves in the United States. Michel Leiris wrote an especially clear account of cuing mechanisms and visual puns in the use of Roman Catholic religious chromolithographs by practitioners of Vodou in Haiti (1960:84–94). He stresses the tenuousness of the connections between Catholic saints and Vodou lwa. Devotees purchase prints in local markets and place them on altars at home or in peri-styles, the temples of Vodou. Usually only one or two details in an image act as pivots, linking the European-oriented aspects of the print with Vodou's values and activities; and while the tenuousness of connections based on one detail creates only weak relationships between particular saints and lwa, this same tenuousness ultimately strengthens the Vodou belief system by ensuring its flexibility. If merchants run out of one chro-molithograph, another will do.

> [O]ften the connection between *loa* and saint is established because of some purely circumstantial detail and through what might be called a pun, not on words but on objects (as, for example, the lowered visor of the helmet identified as the chin-cloth of corpse). In order to establish such a connection, there need not exist an analogy in the content of the symbol: a superficial resemblance, fragmentary and generally acciden-tal, seems to suffice in most cases. . . . A plurality of attributes and names for the same divinity or the same saint (from which arises an ex-tremely extended and complex play of elements between which identi-fication can be made), extreme elasticity in the possibilities of identi-fication (which can be made . . . outside any community of attributes), variability in the representation of the same divinity, variability in in-terpretation of forms—all tend to the conclusion that one can expect lit-erally anything, from the moment that historical circumstances and so-cial conditions are such as to favor the process of syncretism. (Leiris 1960:91–92)

Leiris does not use the term "metaphor"—and in any case "synechdoche" is the technical term for the part-for-whole punning he describes. He also states that connections between saints and lwa do not involve the content of symbols so much as chance resemblances, thus ruling out the noun/thing/symbol approach to metaphor. However, the notion of metaphor as a particular, sustained *relationship* underlies the "complex play of elements," the changeable material relata, "between which identification can be made." Thus, in a sense what Leiris describes is a visual analogue to lin-guistic and cultural ambiguities, standing much as double vision does to double voicing.

When African American vernacular participation with literacy-associ-ated texts, artifacts, and activities involves metaphor, the situation is much like the Haitian Vodou use of chromolithographs as Leiris describes it. Al-though texts, artifacts, and activities play out their roles in written or ver-bal accounts, the primary appeal seems directed toward the visual sense, and the metaphors are the material or visual pivots on which different systems of values and activity open and close.

The visionary recollections of a Jamaican spiritual healer reported by Leonard Barrett are a case in point. Barrett reported that the healer, Mother Rita, shortly before her mother's death, dreamed that a white woman came to her and pointed out her mother's "books packed up for heaven." In the vision Mother Rita also saw pairs of eyeglasses, which the angel instructed her to try on. With the first two pairs, Mother Rita's vi-sion was blurry. But when the third pair enabled her to see clearly, the angel instructed her to take over her mother's healing practice. Although Mother Rita protested that she was too young for such responsibility, she eventually gave in. "I myself cannot explain how this gift of healing comes about. . . . I have studied no books; I only read through the spirit" (Barrett 1976:61–62).

Like Rebecca Cox Jackson, Mother Rita received information of a spiritual nature from a "white" person; like Jackson, too, she was concerned with coexistent realities and double sight, trying on glasses until she found a pair that fit: that enabled her to read/divine the causes of illness as her mother before her had done. Like Jackson, she also questioned her own abilities but nevertheless heeded the instructions of a persistent spirit guide.

Despite these similarities, the nature of participation with the tools of literacy is obviously quite different here. Jackson actually used her conventional literate skill to *write* a journal of dreams, although spiritual communication takes priority over reading and writing in the content of the narrative. For Mother Rita, literacy-related activities and artifacts — eyeglasses, books, reading — provide metaphors for talking *about* spiritual experience and the process of gaining knowledge during healing.

The relationship that knits together the various metaphors and changing relata in Mother Rita's narrative is one of mediation. In folklore and African American religious accounts, metaphors resembling Mother Rita's occur quite often: metaphoric reading, writing, and artifacts mediate between matter and spirit, temporality and eternity. Sometimes even God writes and reads. Author and eraser of the world, God is the all-seeing, all-knowing recordkeeper. In the Fisk University collection of conversion narratives, a convert described the following vision in which God keeps up with earthly events.

> I was dressed up and I went on east I saw a lot of people and I wanted to go with them but something seemed to tell me that I had to ask God. I came to some winding steps and began to climb them and came into the presence of God. He had His hair like lamb's wool and He was sitting there reading something like a newspaper." (Rawick 1972 vol. 19:36)

The reference to "hair like lambs's wool" probably derives from Revelation 1:14 in the New Testament. Other metaphors (to which I turn later) of God reading and writing involve creation, revelation, and the Book of Revelation.

In the cases described so far, literacy lends vocabulary to vernacular imagery. The flexibility that Leiris stresses allows for variations in the visual and material attributes of special knowledge and mediatory vision across the border between coexistent realities. This flexibility is more than verbal and visual artistry; it is a manifestation of the elasticity on which creolization thrives and which people in creole societies deploy with consummate skill.

The interpretative ambiguity and bridging possibilities of metaphor are bound up with the integral contextuality of metaphoric communication, the cultural basis of metaphor. African Americans have coined numerous proverbs and truisms that make a point about who gets the point and who does not; for example, the sayings You have to walk the walk and You have to wear the shoe.[7] Metaphors are integral to such truisms, cuing action-relationships like the gradual shaping of a shoe in lived experience.

One category of truisms is sometimes called "control-signs" (Puckett 1926:311–438). These signs preserve a central relationship but change the relata that cue it. Control-signs warn young people to avoid dangerous behavior and offer stock after-the-fact explanations for why something has gone wrong. Some control-signs from the plantation era pull together domestic objects, writing, and marking. Puckett recorded several.

> "The Trail of a Whipping." It is a sign of trouble to mark on the back of a chimney. Some say that your back will be marked the same way by whipping; one old slave negro says this applies to marking on any parts of the house and adds that "in *slavery* times" (in a tone of reproach as regards the modern generation) the mothers would actually whip their children for doing anything of that sort. Another informant adds that if you write on the back of a dish someone in your family will die. (1926:413)[8]

It is unfortunate that Puckett did not elicit more details from his consultants. The metaphoric relationship that seems to govern these control-signs is the idea that writing and trouble, even violence, go hand in hand. This idea is a familiar one in critical theories of writing, particularly Jacques Derrida's chapter, "The Violence of the Letter" in *Of Grammatology* (1976:97–140), and Jonathan Goldberg's account of violence and the physical act of writing, based on English Renaissance writing manual instructions for the use of quills, knives, and other tools (1990:56–107). Recent literary studies also offer apt, though incomplete, conceptualizations of cases dating back to the plantation memories of the formerly enslaved. Like the control-signs Puckett recorded, plantation memories involve not only the violence of the letter, but the notion of inscription on the body-as-object, as the whip in the hand of the white overseer, mistress, master, or his henchman, the black driver, incises marks on the torso of the slave. Some planters ordered cuts from the whip salted and peppered to slow healing and raise permanent welts.[9] If the slave was later sold, prospective buyers could "read" these welts as signs of rebelliousness.

The prospect of violence at the hands of whites certainly informs control-signs. But as so often happens, new and old concerns seem to cross-reference each other. The control-signs, especially the injunction against children marking the house, call to mind the Kongo prohibition against children marking on the ground because they might inadvertently make a crossmark, and because writing is the prerogative of Nzambi (chapter 4). The main idea is that writing and marking are not lighthearted undertakings; they require maturity and instruction. Writing and marking open doors to the unknown, so their consequences are unpredictable.

In addition to discouraging vandalism, the prohibition against marking on the chimney probably pertains to the chimney as a conduit for spirit communication. This connection is fairly clear in the following excerpt from an interview by Ruby Pickens Tartt with a man who described himself as a "regular conjure doctor in the full." In the excerpt, he is recounting his cure of a woman who claimed her husband had placed a scorpion in her chest.

> And that night and every night for seven nights I give her this here powder. . . . So she started to get better, but she say she still could feel the scorpion. . . . so I make her get down on the floor and turn toward the fireplace. Then I makes a letter L inside the chimney and I puts my left hand on the chest where she say the scorpion is at. Then I jerks her up off the floor and hits her on the back so hard she hollers . . . and there I's got Bre'er Scorpion by the tail! . . .
> Then I took her out in the yard and showed her the smoke where it made the letter L when it riz out of the chimney, I told her that was the hoodoo leavin her for good. So was I. (Brown and Owens 1981:116–117)

The chimney in this account resembles the pipes placed on graves in traditional African American grave decoration in shape and function. Smoke also gives material form to spiritual presence; for example, to ritually cleanse a house, blow smoke from a cigar into the four corners of each room. Tobacco pipes can function the same way as the chimney on a smaller scale. The danger of marking on the back of a plate recalls the perforation of plates and other vessels in Kongo and African American grave decoration (Thompson and Cornet 1981; Fenn 1985), as well as crossmarks on the surfaces of ritual vessels (Ferguson 1989, 1992).

As the century turned, the rope joined the whip in metaphors of inscription. The rope, the instrument of lynching, is the "rope of wind" written in the dust clouds of a passing carload of white men in a story by Henry Dumas (1988:213–229). Over the years, metaphors involving whips, ropes, and writing have retained the notion of disproportionate violence brought on by small acts or accidents. Note also that the looping ropes and whips echo the gesture of tying and wrapping, as well as the growth of vines.

"Mark" has other associations in African America involving the violence one person can do to another, especially to another person's good name. Verbal artistry, humor, and the contextual message "this is play," blunt the edge of violence but retain and stylize some of its forms (Bateson 1972:177–227).

In black vernacular speech, there is a persisting interplay between the words conventionally spelled "mark" and "mock" (Mitchell-Kernan 1972:176). The distinguished African American folklorist J. Mason Brewer recalled:

> as a child . . . one of the most unpleasant feelings that my playmates and I experienced was to be mocked. We would always say "Don't mark me!" or "Stop marking me!" childishly unaware of the correct pronunciation or spelling. It was a long time before I realized that what we were really trying to say was "mock" rather than "mark." (Spalding 1990:ix)

By the mid–twentieth century, and perhaps long before, marking was also an established a term in its own right, referring to a form of verbal art.

> Marking is essentially a mode of characterization. . . . Rather than introducing personality or character traits in some summary form, such information is conveyed by reproducing or sometimes inserting aspects of speech, ranging from phonological features to particular content. . . . The kind of context most likely to elicit marking is one in which the marker assumes his hearers are sufficiently like himself to be able to interpret this metaphoric communication. (Mitchell-Kernan 1972:176–177)

Interdependence or reciprocity of a sort therefore obtains between marking/mocking, the figure of speech, and marking/writing, the graphic inscription. In a sense the mocked person is a marked person; it is as if marking/mocking affixes the substance of mockery to the person. Furthermore, the marker mimics aspects of speech and behavior in a heightened way that undercuts the speaker's "impression management" (Goffman 1973: 238). Urban markers often mimic southern regional speech because it is a class marker, stereotypically associated with backwardness and credulity.

The conflation of "mark" and "mock" that Brewer recalled thus involves not only a spelling "error" but a potential occasion for marking as well. Not to know that "mark" is misspelled "mock" (and vice versa) is to open oneself to status belittlement by revealing ignorance of conventional literate criteria, the schooled standard of higher social classes. But at the same time, according to vernacular criteria, the distinctive artistry in the performance of *marking* enhances the marker's status among peers and follows a loose formula that is quite familiar to insiders. Between them, Brewer's recollections and Mitchell-Kernan's definition delineate two different modes of participation. Both are African American, and both are accessible to many of the same participants via style-shifting, but it is also virtually impossible to participate in both modes—the "conventional" and the "vernacular"—at once.

This situation reflects both the sociocultural tensions articulated in double voicing and the interaction between conventional literacy and vernacular practices. It resembles the situation of the student who said she didn't "talk that talk" in chapter 2. Like the "Jes-us" church sign in the same chapter, the convergence of mark/mock in one composite soundpackage ambiguates the relation between the two words and leaves interpretation open-ended. Ambiguated words like mark/mock occur fairly often in African American vernacular speech; another example occurs in the account from Frederick Law Olmsted's travels in the nineteenth century that is quoted hereafter. Emerging not quite by accident, not quite by design, composite words echo other forms of African American improvisation in which the move that breaks the pattern is just what the situation calls for.

The practical skills conventionally associated with literacy seem quite distant from vernacular control-signs, double-voiced words, metaphors of reading, and the like. This distance is not limited to African American cases and probably emerges wherever people know of reading and writing, where society at large is divided and stratified, and where the idea "literacy" carries ideological weight.

Metaphors involving text and activities and artifacts associated with reading and writing cue and help to stabilize systematic relations that inform the interaction of conventional literacy and vernacular practices. Similar issues arise in ritual and performance.

Text and Artifact in Ritual and Performance

Books, the Bible, gestures of reading—the relata of spoken and written metaphors—appear in concrete form in ritual and performance. I use these two terms in broad and sometimes overlapping senses, conceiving ritual as a recognizably repetitive and usually named sequence of actions, and performance as concerted activity in which "one or more persons *assumes responsibility* for presentation" (Hymes 1981:79, my emphasis). I am especially interested how the assumption of responsibility includes purposefully selecting literacy-associated gestures, verbal forms, and artifacts that help to constitute what a given performance "is."

A stereotyped view of such practices, which occur in intercultural situations throughout the world, is that they are poor imitations of real literacy and civilized behavior. As the story goes, illiterate participants use artifacts of literacy in order to imitate literacy and, more importantly, to imitate more affluent members of society because literacy is a badge of status. Inevitably, glaring flaws betray the imitation. The ways in which participants "betray their ignorance" and are "caught in the act" by their "betters" are, of course, precisely the uses of conventional literate material that appear anomalous to outside observers (and just what one might expect anthropologists to leap on as "cultural").

In the nineteenth century, uses of books and gestures that seemed anomalous or exotic attracted the attention of northerners and Europeans who wrote accounts of touring the antebellum South. William Cullen Bryant (1850:87, quoted in Abrahams 1992:225) observed a speechmaking scene after a plantation cornshucking at which the speaker demanded a piece of paper to hold during his performance. (I will quote this passage later.) Another famous traveler, Frederick Law Olmsted, described an African American funeral near Richmond, Virginia, shortly before the Civil War, at which the preacher held a handkerchief across his hands as if it were a book.

> Most of the company were of a very poor appearance, rude and unintelligent, but there were several neatly-dressed and very good-looking men. One of these now stepped to the head of the grave, and, after a few sentences of prayer, held a handkerchief before him as if it were a book, and pronounced a short exhortation, as if he were reading from it. His manner was earnest, and the tone of his voice solemn and impressive, except that, occasionally, it would break into a shout or kind of howl at the close of a long sentence. I noticed several women near him, weeping, and one sobbing intensely. I was deeply influenced myself by the unaf-

fected feeling, in connection with the simplicity, natural, rude truthful-
ness, and absence of all attempt at formal decorum in the crowd. (Olmsted 1861:44)

The piece of paper at the cornshucking and the handkerchief at the funeral
seem clearly to have been badges of authority for the men who held them.
Both men performed theatrical "readings" that were in fact extemporized
speeches. Although one may reject the nineteenth-century view that these
performances were poor imitations of civilized behavior, the ideology of
conventional literacy makes available a number of other plausible explanations: the speakers were illiterate; they inhabited an oral culture; they
were compensating for illiteracy through gestures that "enhanced self-
esteem." These explanations also verge on stereotype in that they seem to
provide adequate accounts of what the speakers were doing based on only
a few flexible cues. As they did in the nineteenth century, these cues continue to consist of virtually anything that deviates from the literate expectations of the observer.

In this respect, conventional literate ideology is flexible in roughly the
same way as Vodou and other belief systems. A brief experiment illustrates this point: visualize the scene that Olmsted described—say, in black
ink, in the style of a nineteenth-century illustration in *Scribner's* magazine. Now place this image next to a chromolithograph of St. Patrick driving the snakes from Ireland. In effect, the handkerchief held like a book is
analogous to the snakes or the visor of a helmet in a chromolithograph.
For participants in the Vodou belief system, the snakes cue the existence of
the lwa Damballah somewhere "behind" the surface image of St. Patrick.
For participants in conventional literate ideology—a belief system that
organizes common-sense explanations—the handkerchief cues interpretations that orient toward deficit and deviance: lack of literacy and failure to
accede to schooled expectations.

Unhelpful as they are, the issue is not whether explanations that ascribe deficit and deviance are true or false; it is that they foreclose the
outcome of inquiry almost before it has begun. What, beyond apparent
mimicry, is the nature of the performances involving the piece of paper
and the handkerchief? We need to know this before we make inferences
about literacy.

I cannot answer that question definitively, but I can address three of the
many possibilities that Bryant and Olmsted's observations open up. First,
leadership. The piece of paper at the cornshucking and the handkerchief at
the funeral indexed the special roles of the performers who held them.
Moreover, cornshucking speeches and funeral preaching contributed to
the development of two avenues of black community leadership that have
endured from the plantation era to the present: the work crew and the
black church (Abrahams 1992:107–130).[10] The black church and the leadership of preachers and elders have been especially influential. As Booker
T. Washington noted, the call to preach often came just as a person was
first learning to read. Narratives like that of Elder Green, the preacher in
chapter 5 who "went running without parse of script" and also taught
school, show that both vernacular and conventional approaches to literacy

have their places in the leadership roles of the preacher as teacher and performer.

Thus, although the linking relationship is a loose one extending over a long period of time, *there is a mutually enhancing reciprocity between the vernacular forms that scholars have tended to write off*—like the emblematic use of paper and handkerchief to signify leadership—*and the emergence of conventional forms of literacy in black communities.*

Janet Cornelius's history of literacy and religion among antebellum African Americans in the South repeatedly mentions the reciprocal relationship between emerging leadership roles and literacy (1991). In the tense political climate of the soon-to-be-disunited States, it was a relationship that cut both ways. Leadership opportunities for blacks paralleled opportunities to learn to read and write, especially in the northern urban churches of the early nineteenth century. But when African American leaders called for an end to slavery, the rights of free blacks to work for themselves, preach, assemble, and learn to read and write were curtailed in both the North and the South (Cornelius 1991:29).

The handkerchief itself also deserves consideration. Why did the preacher choose this object to hold in his hands? What resources might inform the choice, and what associations might it entrain? The stereotyped answer is the deficit/deviance formula that the slaves were not permitted to own Bibles or were too poor to buy them; therefore, they "compensated" with an object that was readily available, white like paper, and shaped approximately like the page of a book.

The alternative is that the handkerchief is an object with associations that are familiar to the African American participants but not to outsiders like Olmsted. Although we can only speculate about the handkerchief that Olmsted observed, handkerchiefs in African America do have special associations, particularly in private and public religious practice. For example, blessed handkerchiefs called prayer cloths are available in churches and by mail order. Usually they help to focus private prayers for specific goals, but they may also be carried to attract good fortune. Sunday morning radio worship programs routinely advertise prayer cloths.

In public worship, participants in certain African American church services wave white handkerchiefs in visual counterpart to the verbal call-and-response that culminates in manifestations of the Spirit. This practice dates back to the plantation era and probably earlier. Following Robert Farris Thompson, I understand it to be a creole variation "on a fundamental Kongo theme—*nikusa minpa*—the ritual agitation or unfurling or 'dancing' of squares of cloth to open the door to the other world" (1983:185). Handkerchiefs in this connection have much in common with the umbrellas carried en masse at New Orleans funerals and raised high into the air at the moment called "cutting the body loose" (Thompson and Cornet 1981:203; Smith 1984: photos at 80, 105).[11] Simultaneously, pallbearers elevate the casket, raising it with only one arm to emphasize the lightness of the spirit in flight. Given these associations—and more could be mentioned—the setting in which Olmsted observed the handkerchief is precisely what one might expect: a funeral, a sacred occasion to commemorate and satisfy the spirit of the dead.

The handkerchief is potentially multivalent in much the same way as the overturned flowerpot with four-eyed holes beside the gate to an African American home, and the details in chromolithographs that link the Catholic saints to the lwa of Vodou. For participants, instead of (or beyond) cuing interpretations generated by literate conventions, the handkerchief indexes a different interpretive domain, the sacred cosmos and worldview of African American vernacular religion (Sobel 1979). For participants in the funeral, the handkerchief may have made the following double references. First, it may have referred to the Holy Spirit, which lent authority to the preacher's words—inspired words, *like* the voices of the biblical authors of the book the preacher alluded to, through gesture, but pointedly *did not read*. Second, the handkerchief may have referred to the spirit of the deceased, by covering the preacher's hands in the white color of spirit and death—like a miniature shroud but also, in African American tradition, like a flag or umbrella. The handkerchief and objects like it therefore function as double-visual analogues to the ambiguous double voicing of composite terms like "mock/mark."

Read as emblems of leadership, the piece of paper and the handkerchief cue interpretations that orient toward conventional literacy and political and economic opportunity. Read as an emblem of the spirit, the handkerchief cues interpretations that orient toward vernacular practices and insider knowledge.

The copresence of these two orientations, pivoting on one object-cue, opens another matter that deserves consideration before deciding how literacy figures in the scenes that Bryant and Olmsted described: both the cornshucking and the funeral sermon are occasions that seem to call for pointedly not-reading. Not-reading and not-writing may be just as important, perhaps more important, than reading or writing in some African American performance contexts, because of the overall dynamic of the performance. Not-reading at the cornshucking and the funeral foregrounds the eloquence of the speaker and the contribution of the Spirit to the sermon. Even a schooled reader might elect not to read in similar circumstances.

I base this claim on references to literacy in African American performance style. Earlier I suggested that conventional literacy is a prime exemplar of—or cue that indexes—a European American orientation. As performance intensifies, participants often display mastery of, and stylistically shift away from European oriented forms, moving toward forms that are more "African" in orientation, more deeply attuned to African American precedents and values. This shift can involve display and subsequent subordination of conventional literate forms or forms *signified on as if* they were literate—for example, the shift from text to utterance in the sung sermon, or from reading instruction to pointedly not-reading in the narratives of John Jea, Rebecca Cox Jackson, and Elder Green.

This realignment is obscured when the use of literacy-related artifacts at the cornshucking and the funeral is construed as imperfect mimicry of whites and conventional literacy. However, again, the vernacular practice is by no means irrelevant to literacy; notions of literate behavior inform both the content of the speeches and the outside observers' critiques. This is apparent in subsequent portions of Bryant's and Olmsted's accounts. Note the striking similarities when these two travelers describe African American verbal art. The remainder of both accounts supports the claim that the cornshucking speech and the funeral sermon are the kind of vernacular performance that involves purposefully not-reading, not failed imitation of European American literate behavior or Standard English (Dillard 1972: 246). Nor are such performances simply "oral," for this characterization also obscures how the speakers selectively draw on conventional literate forms.

Following is William Cullen Bryant's brief description of the speech at the cornshucking.

> [The commander of the cornshucking work crew] called upon a huge black man named Toby to address the company in his stead. Toby, a man of powerful frame . . . his face ornamented with a beard of fashionable cut, had hitherto stood leaning against the wall, looking upon the frolic with an air of superiority. He consented, came forward, demanded a piece of paper to hold in his hand, and harangued the soldiery. It was evident that Toby had listened to stump-speeches in his day. He spoke of "de majority of Sous Carolina," "de interests of de state," "de honor of ole Ba'nwell district," and these phrases he connected by various expletives, and sounds of which we could make nothing. (Bryant quoted in Abrahams 1992:225)

This speech was only one part of an event that included dancing, singing, joking, and of course shucking great heaps of corn. The remainder of Olmsted's account of the funeral helps to put some of Bryant's comments in perspective:

> I never in my life . . . heard such ludicrous language as was sometimes uttered by the speaker. Frequently I could not guess the idea he was intending to express. Sometimes it was evident that he was trying to repeat phrases that he had heard used before, on similar occasions, but which he made absurd by some interpolation or distortion of a word, thus: "We do not see the end here! oh no my friends! there will be a *putrefication* of this body!" the context failing to indicate whether he meant purification or putrefaction, and leaving it doubtful if he attached any definite meaning to the words himself. He quoted from the Bible several times, several times from hymns, always introducing the latter with, "In the words of the poet my brethren;" he once used the same form, before a verse from the New Testament, and once qualified his citation by saying, "I believe the Bible said that." (Olmsted 1861:45)

Several aspects of these passages are salient: both speakers display prowess as "men of words" (Abrahams 1972, 1983); both engage in forms of verbal performance that draw on and refer to literate forms; and another double-voiced analogue to mark/mock appears in Olmsted's account—the composite word "putrefication." These elements mutually contextualize each other.

The cornshucking speech and the funeral sermon fit well in the African

American tradition of eloquence that Roger Abrahams has summed up as "good talking." "'Good talkers' rely on elevated diction and elaborate grammar and syntax, and speak in the local version of Standard English" (Abrahams 1983:21), a version that may vary considerably from BBC standard and from the standard in other locales. Dillard calls such speech Fancy Talk (1972:245–257), and locates it in a broader "elegantizing tradition" that also includes elaborate dress and is often sustained by purposeful instruction (Abrahams 1983:109–121).[12] These traditions of eloquence and elegance evince recognized expressive continuities with African styles of oratory (Abrahams 1983:21–22). Formal, even opulent speechmaking sways public opinion, renders moral judgments, and furthers social status.

In the anglophone New World, many observers have noticed the phenomenon that Olmsted points to in "putrefication." Dillard mentions several cases, noting that narrow-minded whites label such words malapropisms and misunderstand the "free-wheeling" and improvisational African American approach to eloquence (1972:247–255). He points out that so-called malapropisms "may be either morphological (like . . . *revorse*) . . . or phonological (like the Washington Negro Non-Standard homophony of *fairy* and *furry*), producing forms which might be interpreted by a speaker of Standard English as *Cinderella's furry godmother*" (1972:254).

Morphological and phonological double voicing is not elucidated by terms like "malapropism" that impute simple error. Rather, double-voiced improvised composites like mark/mock that build multivalent associations into one sound package are a serviceable form of language use. The art of composite wordmaking is alive and well today, a small part of the repertoire of the man-of-words. For example, Johnson Smith, the elderly man who taught me about double vision with a stereoscopic viewer, asked me to drive him along the Mississippi gulf coast highway so that he could watch the young ladies in their "butt-teenie" bathing suits on the beach. Clearly, composite words may be used in secular as well as sacred settings. Similarities of organization link composite words with parallel visual and material assemblages and objects across domains—from "Jes-Us" to "puzzle-gut" to the double-visual handkerchief/book in the hands of the preacher at the funeral. All these verbal and material assemblages retain old associations but also open new tangents; in this way they contribute to creolization and language change. Adapted to immediate circumstance, but not random or arbitrary, composite words like "putrefication" ambiguate conventional literate dictionary definitions and spelling and reticulate competing voices with great economy. They are minimal units in the interaction of conventional literacy and vernacular practices.

Traditions of eloquence extend into writing as well as speech. The assumption of personal responsibility for elegant performance overshadows the medium and referential details. How one speaks outweighs what one says, or, better, actually is what one says, in the broadest sense. Eloquence reflects well on the performer but also honors the addressee. This tradition is especially apparent in traditional courtship letters (Dillard 1972:250–252; Jackson 1967:280–281; Abrahams and Szwed 1983:95–100; Rampini

1873:103–110). A letter of thanks that dates from the early twentieth century exemplifies the kind of language that Olmsted found ludicrous:

> A secretary of a Negro church in a letter to a friend of mine, thanking her for an organ she presented to the congregation, regrets "to note that your affectionating act found me in an unequipped attitude to express to you our gratitude." Nevertheless he takes "this probability" to thank you, saying, "if my letter was made to elongate a mile in distance" it could contain but a small portion of his "countless gratitude." (Puckett 1926:29)

Literacy does nothing to stem the flow of eloquence, although the rude opinions of whites surely motivated many performers to focus on the more likeminded and appreciative audiences of their home communities.

Abrahams points out that "good talking," and African American verbal skills in general, have received nearly diametrically opposed assessments from outside observers (1983:28). Ironically, these assessments impute cultural and communicative deviance and deficit to African Americans regardless of their slant. During the mid–twentieth century, and again, disconcertingly, in the 1980s and 1990s, some African American speakers have been characterized as barely able to talk at all (Heath 1990). During the eighteenth and nineteenth centuries, the opposite view prevailed. Observers of good talkers described them as verbose, even verbally talented, but given to *misusing* language through blatant disregard for dictionary definitions and elaborate phrasing (Abrahams 1983:28). One contemporary theory attributes this reversal to the notion that African Americans formerly had rich traditions of oral performance, but are now losing them because of the socially pathological conditions in which they live, especially in inner-city neighborhoods and housing projects (Heath 1990). Given the emergence of the Hip Hop subculture and rap music from this environment, this theory seems groundless.

The theme of literacy crisscrosses these assessments in links between reading, writing, and standard language. Literacy is thought to stabilize the standard and distribute it across time, space, and social distance. In the nineteenth century, lack of literacy and its reputed cultural and cognitive benefits explained the "misuse" of language by slaves and their descendants. Conversely, in the most recent version, the lack or loss of verbal performance traditions supposedly explains why some children have difficulty in school—the argument being that inner-city children find literacy instruction difficult because they have been deprived of appropriate verbal interaction at home.

In light of these attitudes, a further irony is the stress on orality that arises in connection with performances like those that Bryant and Olmsted described. The obvious importance of men-of-words and good talking among Africans and African Americans has provided a warrant for the divide between oral and literate and, more recently, a kind of "yes, but" attitude that questions the descriptive adequacy of polar divides in literacy theory but falls into them in practice all the same. Frequently scholars substitute one divide for another; for example, replacing a cognitive divide—preliterate versus postliterate—with a communicative one: orality versus literacy. Since the idea of evolutionary progress is built into those aspects of literate ideology most concerned with identity, this tendency is difficult to avoid; orality and literacy remain poles between which much purported cultural relativism oscillates.

In this respect progress, according to conventional literate ideology, relates to the supposed disappearance of African American verbal performance skills via what Alan Dundes has called the "devolutionary-evolutionary premise" in folklore studies. This premise, which Dundes rejects, states that "the folk" constitute the illiterate portion of a literate society and lose their folklore when they become literate (Dundes 1969:14). The interaction between conventional literacy and vernacular practices calls this premise into question, for it has persisted in varied forms for at least two centuries, although African American access to literacy has gradually changed—until recently, at least—for the better.

Some African American performances seem at odds with literate conventions in another way that we have already encountered: they reverse the conventional sequence that begins in reading/decoding a text and then moves on to reading/interpreting it. This reversal often accompanies pointedly not-reading. For example, Rebecca Cox Jackson followed the conventional sequence when she expressed her desire to learn to read and her concern about the accuracy of the letters her brother wrote for her. But she reversed the sequence when she described dreaming of books in heaven before the books appeared on earth (see page 118). A passage that Albert Raboteau compiled includes other examples; Raboteau summarizes ways that several enslaved and recently liberated African American women used the Bible.

> Because they were unable to read the Bible, some slaves believed that God revealed his word to them directly, in their hearts. "De Master teaches we poor colored folk in dat way," claimed one elderly freedwoman, "for we hasn't education, and we can't read his bressed word for ourselves." A missionary to the contrabands (fugitive slaves behind Union lines) at Beaufort, South Carolina, heard the same belief expressed by another freedwoman: "Oh! I don't know nothing! I can't read a word. But, oh! I read Jesus in my heart, just as you read him in de book," and drawing her forefinger across the other palm, as tracing a line: "I read and read him there in my heart just as you read him in the Bible. O—...my God! I got Him! I hold him here all de time! He stay with me!" Several ex-slaves claimed they recognized verses read to them from the Bible because they had already heard them before in visions they had experienced during slavery. Some slaves apparently espoused a doctrine of enthusiasm which stresses direct revelation from God rather than revelation contained in the pages of the Bible. Susan H. Clark noticed this emphasis on personal revelation among the freedmen with whom she worked at Fortress Monroe. "The Bible being so long a sealed book to them, they believed that God revealed everything that pertained to their salvation, without reference to the Bible or its teaching. They think no one should read the Bible until after conversion— that it is then a guide." (Raboteau 1978:242)

Like Rebecca Cox Jackson and Mother Rita, these women made reading contingent on spiritual guidance and knowledge. Again, the conventional view is that the behavior of the freedpeople was compensatory, something they did *because* they could not read. But Rebecca Jackson could read, and others who share her outlook can read also. Therefore, perhaps a better way to look at the freedpeople's behavior would be to explore connections between the multistaged conversion process and African secret society initiation.

Margaret Washington Creel suggests that the Poro and Sande secret societies of Liberia and Sierra Leone may have profoundly influenced the development of social organization and folk religion among the Gullah of coastal South Carolina (1988). Joining other scholars, she asserts that captives from the Congo-Angola region also contributed to these developments (Stuckey 1987; Thompson 1983).

A good bit of information about the coastal area in the mid–nineteenth century exists because of the so-called Port Royal experiment (Rachal 1986; Pearson 1906; Botume 1893; Rose 1964). Union forces captured Southeastern coastal islands early in the Civil War. During the early 1860s, while the war continued inland, northern missionaries arrived to work with refugee freedpeople called contrabands behind the Union lines. The missionaries established schools and taught adults and children to read and write. The memoirs of these teachers describe a number of non-conventional (from the European American point of view) literate practices and performances involving text, books, and other artifacts.[13] The Port Royal missionaries also wrote the accounts from which Raboteau selected the preceding excerpts. The following passage does not mention reading or writing, but it supports the claim that procedures like those of secret societies became part of folk religion in the coastal region.

> Religion contributes a large part of life's interest to the inhabitants of Port Royal. . . . The prevailing belief is that of the Close-Communion Baptists, and nearly the whole church management is now in the hands of the blacks, who have their regular deacons and preachers. Subsidiary to the church are local "societies," to which "raw souls" are admitted after they have proved the reality of their "striving." This "striving" is a long process of self-examination and solitary prayer "in the bush," so unremitting must be the devotion that even attendance at school is thought to interfere with the action of the Spirit. (*North American Review* 1865:9)

The process of "striving" relates to "seeking," the extended period of instruction and prayer that culminates in baptism and church membership. Often this process also involves visionary experience, special dreams, and spirit possession. Although they did not use the terms "striving" and "seeking," John Jea and Rebecca Cox Jackson seem to have undertaken extended steps toward conversion as well. Striving and seeking may help us to understand another account that Raboteau cites as an example of reverence for the Bible (1978:240). A Scottish traveller and Presbyterian minister, David MacRae, observed:

[One] case was that of a poor black woman—a nurse in a planter's family—who had become a Christian, and was never weary hearing the children reading the Bible and telling her about Jesus. To her great delight, the little girl one day showed her the name of Jesus, and made her spell letter after letter, and look at the word until she knew it, and was able to point out when she saw it. After that it was a favorite employment with her to take the Bible and search for the name that was so precious to her. She had no idea in what parts of the Bible it was to be found; and so, opening it anywhere, she would travel with her finger along line after line, and page after page, through the wilderness of words that were all unintelligible signs to her, till she found the name of which she was in quest.

"And oh!" she said, in narrating her experience, "how dat name started up like a light in the dark, and I say, 'Dere's e name of my Jesus!' It was de on'y one word I knew," she added, "but dat one word made me hunger for more!" (1870:112–113)

Although this woman probably invented her own devotion, she did so in a way that also miniaturized and encapsulated the processes of striving and seeking. Such encapsulations of the process of salvation appear in other, closely related areas of expression, such as Gospel music (Marks 1971).

This woman also lived in the right place and time to have known of and perhaps even participated in a religious ritual known as Seeking Jesus. A Georgia planter who observed the ritual wrote that in the evening participants gathered in a darkened cabin. First, one member called out "Where is Jesus?"

Some one would answer: "Here is Jesus." They would rush to the part of the cabin where the answer was given, and, of course, not finding him there, would say, "He ain't here." Then another voice would cry out in the darkness from another part of the cabin: "Here is Jesus." Another rush would be made, when the statement, "He is not here," would again be made. The calls and answers would be repeated for hours, sometimes all night. The women and men would become excited and frantic, would tear their hair, and scream and pray until the meeting was broken up in a frenzy. (Steiner 1901:172).

"Seeking Jesus" seems to have been a full-fledged ritual performance brought to culmination on escalating waves of rhythm. In this aspect it was analogous to the ring shout, speechmaking at cornshuckings, and the call-and-response of congregation and preacher in church. Seeking Jesus combined the visionary "traveling" of seeking and striving with the call-and-response of the ring shout tradition (Ahlo 1976:124; Spaulding 1863).

The Seeking Jesus ritual also compressed and miniaturized seeking. Participants reenacted the process leading up to salvation in a relatively short period of time and a circumscribed space: the cabin or Praise/Prays House, where shouts also were held.

Seeking Jesus thus offers another way to look at the woman's search for J-E-S-U-S in the Bible. The existence of this and similar performance traditions in the coastal region suggests that the woman's travels with her finger through the Bible remodelled familiar activities. Like the Prays House but on a smaller scale, the pages of the Bible framed a space or field for ritualized transitions from ordinary to deeper, spiritually charged states.

The scene below occurred in Virginia.

> As Aunt Deborah talked, her eyes were fixed covetously upon an old pair of spectacles which lay upon the table. "Would you like to have those spectacles, mammy?" said Dorothy. "Thankee, honey, dey's jes' what yo' mammy want; now I specs I kin read meh Bible." We handed her an open Bible, and the delighted old woman, with the book upside down, mumbled over and over again, "In meh father's house are many mansions." Then, when encouraged to read more, she began to move up and down, swaying from side to side, shouting fashion, her beaming black face bent over the book, and half said, half chanted, "I thank de Lord, he took meh feet out'n de miry clay, long wid Mary, Shadrach, an' 'Bednego." She evidently thought she was reading, and 't would have been folly indeed to enlighten such blissful ignorance. (Newton 1891:356)[14]

This account, rendered in the condescending tones of a white Missy observing a black Mammy, implies a similar approach to the Bible as a space/field for religious practice in the Shout tradition.[15]

Practices of this sort do not point back directly to any African graphic system. Nor do they trace to any single ethnic group or region: aspects of seeking seem influenced by both Upper Guinea secret societies and white Baptists, while the ring shout is usually linked to Kongo precedents (Stuckey 1987). But these interconnected practices nevertheless help to contextualize practices that all too often are written off as aberrations along a unidirectional continuum from "orality" to "literacy."

An alternative to calling such practices oral—clearly inappropriate, since the book-as-artifact is essential to the performance—would be to term them responsorial (see Tallmadge 1968). Seeking Jesus by looking for the word "Jesus" in the Bible makes the Bible a ritual tool rather than a source of "information." The book is *for* something, not merely *about* something; it is a space. The marks on the page move rhythmically through the searching gaze of the beholder, becoming a surrogate congregation to call-and-respond with in order to meet the cultural conditions that call forth manifestations of the Spirit.

There are other connections in ritual and performance between reading, writing, trance, possession, and spiritual communication in the South Carolina and Georgia coastal region. The following spiritual in the repertoire of the Sea Island Singers originated in the ring shout.[16]

Read Em John

John brought the letter and laid em on the table
No one can read em quite like John
Read it let it go

Read em John
Read em John
Read em John
Read it let it go!

O Read em John
Read em
(repeat)

One by one
Two by two
Three by three
Four by four
No one can read it
Quite like John
Read it
Let it go!
    (Sea Island
  Singers 1994)

As the performance escalates in tension and enthusiasm, the injunction "Read em" passes through several interpretive inflections. Early on, "read it" seems to refer to decoding the "letter" on the "table." But we quickly learn that John has special gifts as a reader: "No one can read it quite like John." From this point on, heavy, percussive exhalations—Huh!—punctuate repetitions of "Read em." Now, reading becomes a metaphor for working-in-the-spirit. Opening one's own person to the Spirit and to 1×1, 2×2, 3×3, 4×4—omnidirectional mastery in the circling shout—creates an ensemble of movement, music, words, and breath that supports manifestations of the Spirit upon all the participants.

To summarize, then, the piece of paper at the cornshucking, the handkerchief at the funeral, the bookish references in grandiloquent speeches, the search for Jesus' name, and the Read Em John shout all occur at a border where African and European orientations cross-reference but do not merge. Such practices relexify aspects of conventional literacy so that they acquire new cultural significance oriented toward African America. Although it seems unlikely that many, or any, of the participants in the nineteenth-century cornshucking or funeral could read or write, because there were few opportunities for them to learn, it also seems unwise to infer a lack of literacy from the kind of description of expressive performance that observers like Olmsted, Bryant, or the Port Royal missionaries provide. This caution is appropriate not because these observers were unreliable, or because they expressed racist views, though they often did so, but because African Americans who can read and write and those who cannot have organized interactions between conventional literacy and vernacular practices in very similar ways, incorporating them into larger repertoires of activity.[17]

Text and Artifact as Charm, Power-object, Talisman

Writing is a common ingredient in African American charms and power-objects. For example, good luck charms include seals with inscriptions from the *Sixth and Seventh Books of Moses*, rings with Chinese characters, and black stones bearing *natural* writing (Puckett 1926:314–315). The most potent talisman of all, the Bible, has been explored as a conjurational foundation for Black American religion and culture by Theophus Smith (1994). Folklorists have noted the use of the Bible to ward off ghosts and negative influences of all sorts (Puckett 1926:141). Overall, written text seems to function in three overlapping ways in charms, talismans, and power-objects: as (1) a form of filter; (2) a conduit or conductor for spiritual power; and (3) a substitute for the human body (see Hyatt 1970–78, vol.3:3589–3610).

FILTER

African American traditions include a wide variety of counting charms and protective filters: benne seeds, brooms and broom straws, raffia, rice, pepper, fine mesh sieves, and cloth with sievelike patterns such as checked gingham. These substances force witches and spirits to count every seed, fiber, or hole in the mesh before they can cause harm.[18] Sieves and gingham protect doubly because of the myriad small crossmarks in their weave.[19]

Perhaps because it seems too obvious, folklore accounts rarely mention that these materials do not protect automatically; rice in a jar is usually a staple and nothing more, unless it is activated in use. Someone must assume responsibility for selecting the proper material and placing it appropriately. Thus counting charms and filters have a low-key ritual performance aspect, much like setting a trap, and, like certain traps, they often fade into the background, becoming almost invisible. This process promotes ambiguity; ordinary objects entrain divergent associations, are now this, now that. Through this dynamic, I have been arguing, African Americans have attuned the interactions among literacy-associated material, vernacular expression, and events to their own circumstances.

The function of writing and print as a filter has at least three aspects: first, the density of discrete marks upon the page; second, the offbeat, break-patterned irregularities of columns and margins, especially in newspaper and magazine formats; and third, the widespread association of writing with secular and spiritual efficacy. The latter association links printed and written filters with other methods of protection such as tying property with script. Patterned irregularities echo the polyrhythms of African American music, the visual improvisations of black quilters (Fry 1990; Leon 1987; Thompson 1983, 1987; Wahlman and Scully 1983), and the offbeat phrased design of some painted home exteriors.[20] Fine print makes a superb counting charm because the marks are denser than most patterns in the everyday environment.

One protective practice using print is lining the inside of shoes with newspapers.[21] Another is surrounding the human body with print. A nineteenth-century observer noted that some of the "colored ladies of New Orleans command notice" with laced petticoats "decorated with a fringe of quack advertisements" (Sala quoted in Abrahams and Szwed 1983:408). Letha Golson, interviewed in the Mississippi narratives of the FWP, said that she was tormented in bed and "jes wouldn' be let alone" until she got up and spread newspaper around the bed. "Ah'll stay in dese sposed to be hainted houses if I'm paid and I can git plenty newspaper" (Rawick 1977 vol. 8:814).[22] Proximity to the human body also neutralizes negative messages in print. Robert Farris Thompson (personal communication, April 1987) observed a Haitian man who had sewed disastrous newspaper headlines onto his shirt, thereby canceling their negative affects.

All these examples relate to the best-known practice: protecting a home by covering the interior walls with newspapers (fig. 6.1) so that intrusive spirits must read every word before they can harm the occupants (Bass 1973:393). If a spirit is unable to read, it still must count every letter (Puckett 1926:142). When Lydia Parrish restored a cabin headquarters for the Sea Island Singers, she recalled:

> [I took a] precaution which has afforded the singers much amusement. The walls of many small cabins are covered with newsprint, because the prevailing idea in the old days was that a hag had to read every word before she could work evil on you. I used the financial section of *The New York Times* for good measure. (1942:11)

But newspaper also created a fragile buffer against the drafts that poured through the cracks of shoddy slave quarter and tenant cabins, and this explanation for papered walls appears in the literature at least as often as protection from spirits.[23] Newspapers on the walls of African American homes had other associations as well. Writing at the turn of the century, W. E. B. Du Bois draws a vivid and unromantic image of the conditions that southern Black Belt sharecroppers and tenants endured.

> The size and arrangements of a people's homes are no fair index of their condition. . . . All over the face of the land is the one-room cabin. . . . It is nearly always old and bare, built of rough boards, and neither plastered nor ceiled. Light and ventilation are supplied by the simple door and by the square hole in the wall with its wooden shutter. There is no glass, porch, or ornamentation without. . . . Within . . . A bed or two, a table, a wooden chest, and a few chairs compose the furniture; while a stray showbill or newspaper makes up the decorations for the walls. (Quoted in Stepto 1979a:88)

Robert B. Stepto pushes beyond the glimpse at past pleasures that newspaper and playbill decorations suggest and interprets Du Bois's passage as a variation on the thematic quest for literacy and freedom.

> The very idea of a newspaper tacked to a rough dark wall is not only true to life but, in this context, a poignant reminder of the Afro-American quest for literacy. It is difficult to envision a lithograph, daguerreotype, photograph, embroidered homily or other wall decoration that better expresses the dawn of freedom. (Stepto 1979a:88)

Stepto's literacy-freedom interpretation, placed alongside accounts of newspaper as filter, echoes the interacting of the conventional and the vernacular in the double voicing of narratives like those of John Jea, Rebecca Cox Jackson, and Elder Green. For Stepto and Du Bois, whose primary concerns link literacy with economic and educational advancement, the newspaper and playbill are documents to be *read*; whereas newspaper functioning as filter does not rule out reading, but also does not require it.

FIGURE 6.1. Newspapered walls, Alabama (after photograph by Arthur Rothstein, 1937; Library of Congress).

Differing interpretations are thus not mutually exclusive. The practical and decorative functions of newsprint align with "mainstream" functions of the sort that sometimes hide or mask the "deeper" aspects of activities from whites. Clearly, there is no general rule here. Sometimes the protective function of newspapers is hidden, sometimes it is widely known, and sometimes outsiders are simply unaware. Access to information varies as well. For example, Lydia Parrish knew enough about protective newspaper to confuse hags by papering walls with the extra dense print of the financial pages, to the amusement of her black acquaintances. But this fact does not mean that all the practices familiar to the singers were equally accessible to the white outsider; Parrish remarked that she had lived in her Sea Island home over a decade before learning that a member of her own household could perform certain songs and dances like the buzzard lope, which Parrish especially wished to witness.

Protective newspapers depend on the qualities of printed marks, not text. But textual content can also be relevant to the protective possibilities of print. Judith McWillie described the exterior walls of a house in Augusta, Georgia, on which the owner had varnished photocopies of his arrest records, government documents, and paper money (personal communication, February 18, 1988). His photograph was superimposed wherever pictures appeared in the documents. (See Houlberg 1992 for comparable practices in Nigeria and Haiti.) This device adapts the traditional newspaper filter into a warning to visitors and potential intruders. The placement of the documents also seems to deflect and redirect the institutional powers that the documents represent—the police, court, IRS—away from the house and toward the outside world.

Biblical and inspirational messages on the walls of some African American homes also have a protective aspect, but one that involves textual content rather than the marks of print, especially since the print used for inspirational messages is often quite large. Examples are the interior walls in the homes of Mrs. Olivia Humphrey, Chattanooga, Tennessee (fig. 6.2); and Mr. Harvey Low, a resident of the Mississippi delta (fig. 6.3). In both these homes, inspirational messages fit into the design of decorations on the wall and room as a whole. Note that the overall design contains characteristic break-patterns on a large scale similar to those that newspapers contain on a small scale. As I have already mentioned, break-patterning also appears in home exteriors, landscaping, quilts, and even narratives. Photographs of family and friends also contribute to the protection of the home through positive associations and, implicitly, through the mediation that human and animal images provide (see Thompson 1990). In a few homes the crossmark also figures in the decoration of interior walls. Mrs. Annie Sturghill placed blue-and-green handtowels with cross and diamond patterns at intervals around the circumference of her living room in Athens, Georgia (fig. 6.4).[24]

A repertoire of possibilities ranging from crossmark, to print, to text begins to cohere when we look at vernacular uses of newspapers and inspirational messages alongside other materials like the handtowels above. Questions arise like: When is Roman alphabetic writing or print essential to a given practice, and when does it occupy a slot that another kind of mark or material function could fit just as well? Together, the illustrations in this section all fall into the broad functional grouping "tying with writing." Aspects of inspirational messages seem to fall into all three groupings; they encode text alphabetically; they join other items on the walls of the room to enclose those inside in the safety of irregular patterns; and they invoke the presence of God through crossmarks and his name.

In the preceding examples, print and text that tie a space, object, or person block undesirable entry and deflect negative energy back to its source. When artifacts of literacy, text, and print serve as conduits, the reverse is true: they focus positive energy and facilitate its flow. In this respect, conduits combine the spatial extension of tying with the focusing quality of invocation.

In the following passage, writing mediates the relationship between a living numbers player and the dead.

> When a person speak about dey write de dead, yo' know fo' de numbers. . . .
>   (Just how do they do that?)
>   Well, dey just write 'em—jes' yo' write some yo' peoples, says, 'Dear Fren', I would like tuh hear from yo'. I am writin' yo' few lines to

ALTERNATIVE
MODES &
ARTIFACTS
OF LITERACY

FIGURE 6.2. Wall design composed of objects and printed messages by Olivia Humphrey, Chattanooga, Tennessee.

FIGURE 6.3. Wall design of objects, images, and printed signs, Harvey Low, Mississippi.

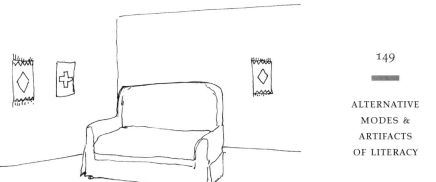

FIGURE 6.4. Cross and diamond towels, Athens, Georgia.

let chew know I am well. I wants dis number. I wants chew will please send hit to me tonight while ah'm sleep.'

An' yo' set chew a glass of water [also a conduit—G.G.] an' fold de letter up—set de glass of water on top de letter, an' dis ghost will come an' bring yo' de number in yo' sleep. He might come in de form of a cow or a dog or a horse but he'll bring yo' de number. (Hyatt 1970–78, vol. 1:545–546)

The writer hopes that the dead will communicate a winning number in the game.

In healing, restorative spiritual energy moves through writing or artifact of literacy to the body of the recipient. The following passages from Arthur Huff Fauset's *Black Gods of the Metropolis* (1944) treat magazines as conduits for healing. (*Black Gods* is a study of religious groups in northern U.S. cities.) Fauset wrote that the case materials that follow "seem typical" of what participants told him (1944:107). "Daddy," an honorific term (Abrahams and Szwed 1983:2) refers to the influential religious figure Daddy Grace (see Washington 1972:127).

Mrs. F: Daddy is the Savior. I found the mission, and through the power of the Savior was healed . . . and too I want to say that there is healing power in the *Grace Magazine,* and the products is my doctor. I use them for medicine, and they healed both soul and body. Thank God for that, and for Daddy Grace, for he is the cause of it all. He caused me to live holy.

Mrs. M.G.: I wish to testify of the wonderful healing power which is in the *Grace Magazine.* I am not a member of House of Prayer, but Elder Bush was the one that gave me the *Grace Magazine.* I suffered a long time with a pain in my side. The *Grace Magazine* was the only thing that healed me. Pray for me that I will soon have more faith and be a member of the House of Prayer.

Mrs. R.W.: For five years I suffered with the agonizing pains of the rheumatism. I tried different remedies but they did not help me. At last

150

▬▬▬

SIGNS OF

DIASPORA

•

DIASPORA

OF SIGNS

when all hopes were gone, Elder Bush, a minister of the House of Prayer, gave me a magazine and I applied it to my body and I was healed. I am not a member but I thank God for such a wonderful prayer. Pray for me that I will become a member. (Fauset 1944:112)

The three women testified to the healing power of *Grace Magazine* applied directly to the body, testimony in which the function of the magazine as a conduit for healing power took precedence over its conventional literate message content.

This testimony echos forms of initiation and conversion. Two of the women, Mrs. G. and Mrs. R. W., were not members of the House of Prayer; they expected to undergo further preparation before they could become members. Although they benefited from the conduit function of the magazine, they were not yet prepared to interpret its messages. Thus the content of the magazine, beyond mere words and apart from its role as a healing conduit, derived from a spiritual domain made accessible by initiation. The freedpeople from Fortress Monroe (quoted earlier) who believed that the Bible should not be read until after conversion shared this approach to the written word, as did Rebecca Jackson. This correspondence suggests cultural precedents for shifting the emphasis of interpretations from those cued by *Grace Magazine's* conventional orthography and publication format to those in which encoding and decoding are secondary or largely irrelevant.

In the following formula, message content is important, but so is the procedure that transforms literate material into a conduit to the spirit world, independent of decoding.

> Take a *lightnin'-struck tree*. Yo' git a splinter offa dat jest about as long as you han' an be sure it's kinda broad—jes' prob'bly about a inch broad. Yo' write on it—yo' take yo' *an ink pencil usin' black ink* an' yo' inscribe on dat jes' de kinda luck dat yo' want to be in yore home. Yo' want peace—seems like yo' always gittin' tough, yo' want peace. Yo' want tuh gain mo' money or yo' wants to be lucky in yore undertakings. An' den when yo' git dat wrote down wit dat black ink—be sure it's black ink—yo' conceal dat above yore do' where no one won't interfere wit it at all. Dat brings good luck. (Hyatt 1970–78, vol. 2:1490–1491)

Folklorist Harry Middleton Hyatt recorded this passage, along with many others that I have quoted. Altogether he published close to five thousand pages of hoodoo and conjure interviews and formulas, including hundreds of references to reading, writing, the Bible, graphic signs, special inks, pens, and other tools. I chose to quote this formula because it calls to mind specific West African Muslim magical procedures.

These procedures may help us interpret the African American formula and its conduit function, because the specialist's insistence on black ink compares with formulas for good luck in contemporary Mende *mori* magic, which substitutes written charms for traditional magic and sorcery (Bledsoe and Robey 1986:209).

> A moriman uses his command over Arabic writing, which is widely regarded as the literal word of God, to obtain God's assistance. A moriman

evokes a verse's power by writing it on paper, rolling it and tying it with string or putting it in an amulet pouch. Alternatively, he may write the verse on a special length of board (*wala*) with a piece of burnt wood from the *luba* tree and wash off the words with water to make a black potion (*nesi*, "holy water"). The moriman blesses the amulet or liquid and gives his client instructions for its use. The client may wear the amulet or bury it, or he may drink the *nesi* or rub it on himself. Sewing up the Arabic writing in a leather pouch or dissolving it in water lends an air of secrecy to the event by concealing the letters. . . . [M]orimen work their most powerful magic at night in dim candlelight and prefer black ink for writing charms and making *nesi*, which then appears as a black liquid. (Bledsoe and Robey 1986:210).

There are discrepancies between the formula in Hyatt's interview and Bledsoe and Robey's description. However, lightning-struck wood is certainly burnt, both accounts stress black ink, and Waycross, Georgia, where the American interview took place, is as promising a site to look for Muslim threads in creolized practices as any in the United States (see the maps in Austin 1984:11, 13).

More to the point than the possibility of transatlantic connection, Bledsoe and Robey further our understanding of practices that fall outside European American literate conventions by showing that Arabic literacy and secrecy serve important social functions among the Mende. This point is a reminder that the same considerations apply to African American approaches to literacy, both vernacular and conventional. Whatever the touted benefits, it is naive to expect uniform adoption of technologies with as murky a history in forced contact, dominance and subordination as alphabetic reading and writing. Many of the narrators I have quoted highlight precisely this process of "knowledge management," and culturally appropriate functions for literate skills and artifacts.

SUBSTITUTE FOR THE BODY

The best-known function of writing in charms and talismans is to serve as a substitute for the person upon whom the magic is supposed to act.[25] Writing can also substitute for the person directing the magic, either the specialist or the client, or both. Such writing is usually of one or two overlapping kinds. Either it serves as a residue of the body—for example, a letter, which is roughly analogous to hair, excreta, footprints, fingernails and toenails, semen, menstrual blood, and clothing or other objects—such as a tool or dishrag—closely identified with the person. Or writing is a proxy for the person, analogous to a photograph or candle or doll. The *name* is by far the most common form of writing in magic.

Writing that substitutes for the body in African America resembles sympathetic magic around the world, including European witchcraft. Writing in spells and potions in African America has been extensively documented. The popular how-to literature and instructions for "miracle" products, oils, and novelties are a ubiquitous source; Hyatt (1970–78, vol. 3:3497–3610) quotes over one hundred pages of formulas involving names and writing, transcribed from his interviews in the 1930s. My impression is that such activity has diminished only slightly, if at all, in the past fifty years.[26]

Divination and Revelation

Many peoples throughout the world assign special relevance to written communication with supernatural powers in revelation and divination (Perrin 1986:216; Levy-Bruhl 1923:424–433). According to Victor Turner, among the central African Ndembu, divination discloses what has previously been concealed; revelation is the manifestation of that which resists conceptualization in linguistic terms. These distinctions also bear usefully upon African American uses of writing, text, and artifact.

DIVINATION

> [D]ivination is a mode of analysis and a taxonomic system, while revelation is a prehension of experience taken as a whole. . . . Divination proceeds by a process of binary oppositions, moving stepwise from classes to elements. Revelation, on the contrary, begins with authoritative images or root metaphors, manifested as sets of connected symbols, and is culturally contrived to give those exposed to it a sense of what Walt Whitman might have called "the rondure, the cohesion of all." Divination is dualistic, revelation is nondualistic. (Turner 1975:15–16)

Like communication by conduit, divination transmits messages from higher powers and the spirit world. But divination differs from direct conduits because divination techniques usually interject a degree of randomness or unpredictability into the ritual, and a specially trained or "called" diviner usually interprets randomized elements. Divinatory reading may be an intuitive and sensory search for clues to a person's problems through appearance, temperature, skin texture, and demeanor. It may also involve special tools: cowrie shells and sections of coconut shell, divining chains, and sediments in liquids. Dream Books have a long history in African American numerology; policy players especially favor them to select lucky numbers (see McCall 1963).

Some methods of divination also involve actually reading and writing texts and books. One method uses the Bible for what the Spiritual Baptists of St. Vincent call "taking a prove." This method occurs across the diaspora (a healer in Mississippi used it to advise me). The spiritual leader uses scissors tied to a ribbon to point to a passage or permits a Bible to fall open at random and finds a relevant message in the verses nearest the thumbs (Henney 1968:58).[27] In Roman Catholic areas, *The Imitation of Christ* by Thomas à Kempis may be put to similar use. The following procedure from the southern United States falls into the category of hoodoo because it uses the Bible for personal gain.

> To *find de lucky numbahs* [in gambling] take de Bible. Now, ah want chew to read de ninth chapter of Psalms—reads it ovah three times befo' goin' tuh bed. When yo' read it ovah three times befo' goin' tuh

bed, *open de Bible an' sleep wit it*—sleep wit dat Bible right under yore pillah an' yo'll dream of dat lucky numbah. When yo' git up de next morning, yo' kin tell a person exactly about dat numbah. An if yo' throw dat numbah den dey'll ketch it. (Hyatt 1970–78, vol. 2:1488)

Like most of those described in this chapter, Hyatt recorded this procedure during the 1930s.

Hyatt also recalled participating in an episode of suspect divination (1970–78, vol. 2:1323). The spiritual doctor-informant whom Hyatt consulted used the Bible as a kind of incubator for messages that the Spirit supposedly wrote for a particular individual. The spiritual doctor removed a piece of paper from between the pages of the Bible and read aloud to Hyatt, "you are crossed," that is, someone has put a spell on you. Undaunted by the message, Hyatt said, "I saw without his telling me that he wrote with invisible ink answers upon slips of paper and chose one suitable for any of the problems he mentions. The answer becoming visible he calls an *illustration*."[28]

The following passage is one of the most detailed instructions for performing divination that Hyatt recorded:

> You go to running water or a stream. This heah—ah know yo've seen these streams like this slick greenish-looking moss [algae]. Yo' cut chew out seven . . . small pieces of paper. Yo' lay dat paper into dat runnin' water an' block it where it can't go no further dat's right on dat moss. An' every one those pieces whirl an' come to de top. Yo' have yo' something there an' yo' dip under all dat paper an' moss an' bring it to de house. Now, let's see, sech-an'sech-a one was in heah an' ah believe dat dey stole sech-an-sech-a thing from me—ah believe dat. An' ah want it brought back. Well, yo' set dat glass of water befo' yo'—dat paper an' all is in dere with dat moss-slime. An' de next morning when yo' get up dat person's name—take up dat piece of paper right carefully to keep from tearin' it an yo'll see his name written on at paper. Dat moss will write it during dat night. Yo' know 'zackly who stole it from yo' an which direction dat dey went in, because yo'll see a white streak dat goes off from dat piece of paper. . . . Dat light of day will tell yo' an yo'll see de whole name wrote on dere plainly jest like somebody printed it wit typewriter. (Hyatt 1970–78, vol. 2:1478–1479)

This form of divination uses paper as a bounded field to contain marks made by nonhuman agency. The emergent character of the marks resembles several of the forms of writing discussed in chapter 7. African American healers often use a glass of water as an aid in diagnosing illness and spiritual distress. Like so many other artifacts in African American vernacular practice, the glass of water has multivalent associations. Some are practical—a glass of water is a convenient magnifying glass—and some are esoteric; water is the habitat of spirits in many parts of the world. In west and central Africa and the diaspora, bodies of water often symbolically divide the material from the spirit world. Along with frogs, snakes, other amphibians, and certain insects, fish, and birds (see MacGaffey 1986:52), the moss and slime mediate the relation between worlds and make the action of the transparent water visible.

Although it is an unusual approach, divination with water and moss shares several features with other methods of divination. The action of the water injects randomness into the process of writing but also leaves ample room for interpretations that validate prior assumptions; moss-writing surely requires considerable reading-in on the part of diviner if it is to resemble letters at all! Steps and stages like carefully positioning the glass and leaving it overnight invest commonplace actions with ritual significance. The outcome, a written name, emerges in a form suitable for further action; hoodoo abounds with come-back powders, potions, and recitations that bring escaping thieves to justice and recover their booty. The white streak sets the static proxy for the person—the name—in motion and "sheds light" on the direction of the thief.

Divination with water and moss is an analogic process: interpretation, itself a recursive, nonsegmentable activity, proceeds on the basis of prior nonsegmentable assumptions *about* some data. The marks written by water and moss are preinterpreted *as* writing prior to their being interpreted as the name of a thief. Virtually all the African American divinatory practices involving reading, writing and literate artifacts that I have so far encountered are comparable in this respect; they allude to but do not actually depend on a stable code. Thus they differ from the more "digital" systems, such as Ifà in Cuba and West Africa. Ifà involves much interpretive skill, in addition to memorization, yet it is Ifà, with its mathematical permutations, that scholars have suggested compares in complexity to Western literate forms. But this assessment seems only to reconstitute familiar divides like that between science and the humanities.

REVELATION

In Victor Turner's characterization, revelation is holistic in orientation and broadly metaphoric in expression. Numerous African American artists have explored themes from the Bible in their work. Minnie Evans and, as we shall see, James Hampton used imagery of the Second Coming and revealed writing, but did so in a way that also alluded to revelations that God made personally to them. Even without personal revelation, the arrival of the Better Day can be a major preoccupation. For example, in a humorous eschatological account of childhood in Mississippi, Clifton Taulbert's "Poppa, Black Buddha of the South" (as the chapter is called) encounters Preacher Hurn, a jackleg preacher who lacked a congregation but never missed an opportunity to discuss Scripture, and who pointed to "the advent of the skywriting airplane as an example that the end of time was fast approaching" (1989:14–15).[29] This episode thus connects writing, technology, revelation, and the end of the world.

Writing and reading, especially by God and the chosen representatives of God, are recurring metaphors in African American expressive culture. We have already encountered John the Revelator, a representative of God closely associated with writing, in the earlier section on performance. John, to whom God revealed the future and who in turn revealed his vision to human beings, was frequently named in the ring shout. Personal and apocalyptic revelations provide goals and subject matter for ritual performances, like the shout.

In Vodou, Santeria, and other diaspora religions, spirits and deities who possess participants reveal information to individuals about their health, families, and future prospects. Possession by individual deities and spirits is uncommon in the United States, except in the wake of Caribbean and Latino migration. But it does occur in certain Spiritual churches, especially in the less "European" and more "African" rites like the Black Hawk service (see Jacobs and Kaslow 1991).

Although individual spirits—as opposed to the Holy Spirit—rarely manifest in the contemporary United States, there is at least a hint that such may not always have been the case. For example—and such examples are extremely rare—John Matthews of Pike County, Mississippi, told an FWP interviewer in the 1930s, "I believe in spirits. I is seed many one, but it is against my religion to tell about dem; dat is a sacred thing. In fact I have acted de part of de spirit, but dat was a long time ago. I don't belong to dat sect any more an' can't tells deir secrets" (Rawick 1977 vol. 9:1459).

John the Revelator was a figure of exceptional power in black biblical mythologizing. It has been said of John that the Romans were forced to exile him to the Isle of Patmos because when they tried to boil him to death in oil, "the fire and oil were subjects of John" (Boyd 1924:208). When John saw Christ in a vision sixty-three years after the Ascension, Christ's hair was white like wool as an emblem of maturity and authority (Boyd 1924:209).

John was also a messenger and mediator not unlike the African and diaspora trickster-messenger Eshu-Ellegua/Papa Legba.[30] Sometimes he has been conflated with or related to John the Baptist. The Baptist's association with ritual waters, particularly the water of rivers, the traditional site of Afro-Christian baptism, implies mediation across worlds in a manner that parallels John the Revelator's writing at the dictates of God. But John the Revelator also has less visible non-Christian associations; he has sometimes been linked to John the Conqueror, the mythical African king celebrated in John Canoe/Junkanoo masquerades, who lent his name to the most potent charm root in North American black spiritual healing and hoodoo. Moreover, there is also an occasional hinted connection with John, the trickster, of plantation tales (see the John stories in Courlander 1976:419–442). Boyd's statement that oil and fire were "subject" to John the Revelator parallels the plantation John's extraordinary ability to get out of hot water. There are a number of connections among John the Revelator and other Johns.

> John the Conqueror is sometimes associated with St. John, Christ's apostle. The similarity between the words "conjurer" and "conqueror" is too close to ignore, and Dr. John was one of New Orleans' most famous Voodooists, who allegedly conducted rites with Marie Laveau on Bayou St. John on June 23rd, St. John's Eve. (Jacobs and Kaslow 1991:91)

Conqueror/conjurer is a composite word pair—with double-voiced potentialities. Here again, as in mark/mock and Jesus/Jes-us, some "hearings" are more "European," others more "African," while within the pair oscillates the multiply redoubled voices of a complex America. Although Jacobs and Kaslow focus on the Spiritual churches of New Orleans, the connections they make are quite widespread.

156

━━━

SIGNS OF
DIASPORA
•
DIASPORA
OF SIGNS

A spiritual doctor in New Orleans told Hyatt that Unkas, the spirit he invoked for his work, was the son of John the Revelator. "He one of the greatest lawgivers on land. You gotta feed him with blood" (1970–78, vol. 2:1296–1298). I do not know how widespread the idea of the Revelator's son is, but the connection between Unkas and John is suggestive, and makes a parallel between Legba and John the Revelator in the United States a degree more explicit. In Haiti, Legba is associated with St. Peter (Pelton 1972:79), but also with Sts. Lazarus and Anthony (Metraux 1959:325); clearly—and appropriately, given his changeable character—Legba's links to various Roman Catholic saints are relatively loose and flexible.

Other features that also suggest connections, some tenuous, among Unkas, Legba, and John include the candles on the altar of Unkas, son of the Revelator. These are blue and, as I mentioned in chapter 4, blue cross-marks can refer specifically to Legba, although many do not (Hyatt 1970–78, vol. 1:773). The blues is Legba's music; he represents the "bad" side of deep knowledge, the volatile devil's double to whom bluespeople supposedly barter their souls with midnight offerings at the crossroad.

Associations like these seem quite remote from the persona of John, apostle of Jesus. They are less remote from the ambivalence of Fon and Yoruba deities. If the negative side of Legba's changeable nature overlaps the devil in the Americas, it seems reasonable that his more positive side could overlap a figure like John.

In any case, the distance between good and evil in Judeo-Christian tradition may help to account for the intermediate Unkas. This spirit whose powers can serve for good or ill preserves the two-sidedness of much African and African American philosophy. Feeding the spirits with blood is also characteristically African. Although blood sacrifice endures in Vodou and Santeria, feeding blood to Unkas is one of the few examples of such a practice in the twentieth-century United States, and it is located, not surprisingly, in New Orleans on the Caribbean rim.[31]

The preceding associations are fragmentary and open-ended, but in one respect Legba and John the Revelator resonate strongly: both are writers and messengers of God. As Metraux has said of Legba, "Only He can translate into human language the messages of the gods and express their will" (1959:319, quoted in Pierre 1977:31). Since African deities are not polarized in the Christian sense, from the human point of view they can be either extremely dangerous, extremely benevolent, or both. What I am suggesting, then, is that if the devil attached to Legba's trickster side—transformed from sober Calvinism into the exuberant artistry of the Signifying Monkey and Stagolee (see Gates 1988)—then the Revelator attached to, renamed, and fed on the positive energy of Legba's role as mediator and master of language and writing.[32]

The story of John the Revelator and the Book of the Seven Seals in the New Testament Book of Revelation has fired African American religious imagination.

And I saw another mighty angel come down from heaven, clothed with a cloud: and a rainbow was upon his head, and his face was as it were the sun, and his feet as pillars of fire. And he had in his hand a little book open: and he set his right foot upon the sea, and his left foot on the earth, and cried in a loud voice, as when a lion roareth: and when he had cried, seven thunders uttered their voices. And when the seven thunders had uttered their voices, I was about to write: and I heard a voice from heaven saying unto me, Seal up those things which the seven thunders uttered and write them not. And the angel . . . lifted up his hand to heaven, and sware by him that liveth for ever and ever . . . that there should be time no longer. . . . And the voice which I heard from heaven spake to me again, and said, Go and take the little book which is open in the hand of the angel. . . . And I went unto the angel and said unto him, Give me the little book. And he said unto me, Take it, and eat it up; and it shall make thy belly bitter, but shall be in thy mouth as sweet as honey. And I took the little book out of the angel's hand and ate it up; and it was in my mouth sweet as honey: and as soon as I had eaten it, my belly was bitter. (Rev. 10:1–11, King James version)

Images and symbols from this passage recur in countless spirituals and sermons. Some of these—the rainbow, the sun, the feet of fire—fit aptly with African symbols like the rainbow of Dahomean Damballah, the central sun of Kongo, and the fiery, lightning step of Shango. The passage is also interesting because it is a revelatory episode involving writing that dates from ancient times. The passage closes with John eating the book that the angel gave him, and with a contrast between the sweetness of simply tasting—reading—and the bitterness of digesting—understanding—the book that revealed the end of earthly existence.

An African American preacher in Chattanooga, Tennessee, whose New Year's Day sermon I heard on WNOO radio in 1988, presented John eating the book in a somewhat different way.

John, John, that book you wrote, I want you to put it in your mouth and eat part of it because I don't want man to know too much, but I got a new home—

John retains his position as a chosen intermediary in this sermon, but the focus shifts to the prerogative of God to conceal as well as reveal. The chorus of the following spiritual also emphasizes partial knowledge.

John the Revelator

My Lord called John while he was a-writin'
My Lord called John while he was a-writin'
My Lord called John while he was a-writin'
Oh John, John

   (chorus)
Seal up your book,
and John don't you write no more
Oh John, John
And don't you write no more

He wrote the book of Revelation while he was a-writin'
etc

(chorus)

He wrote the book of Seven Seals while he was a-writin'

(chorus)

(Lomax 1968:480)

A related aspect of the theme of revelation is the preoccupation with time, and writing as mediator between temporality and timelessness, between the linear and the cyclical. Thus the spiritual:

Come down, come down, my Lord, come down,
My Lord's writing all the time;
And take me up to wear the crown,
My Lord's writing all the time.

Oh, He sees all you do and hears all you say,
My Lord's writing all the time;

When I was down in Egypt land,
My Lord's writing all the time,
I heard some talk of the promised land,
My Lord's writing all the time.

(Suggs 1963:257)

In this chorus the Lord is writing *all* the time. In other versions and other references to divine omniscience, God is writing *down* the time. A man interviewed for the Fisk University collection of conversion narratives stated, "I tried to live in the sight of God like I expect to meet him, for he sees all we do and hears all we say. *He is writing down the time*" (Rawick 1972 vol. 19:143, my emphasis).

This phrase has an auditory partner that creates a sound package like mark/mock, conquer/conjure in which the different "hearings" ambiguate the words yet reinforce certain interpretations. Thus "God *writing* down the time" partners with "God *riding* down the time": an apocalyptic horseman figure in which Jesus rides *up and down* the cross, the Kalunga border between this world and the world of the spirits and ancestors (chapter 4). Another Fisk narrator, whose phrase "God struck me dead" gave the collection its name, recalled an experience that suggests parallels between exceptional, omnidirectional sight and time:

Some people pray and call on God as if they think He is ignorant of their needs or else asleep. But God is a time-God. I know this for He told me so. I remember one morning I was on my way home with a bundle of clothes to wash. . . . I felt awfully burdened down so I commenced to talk to God. . . . I said, "Lord, it looks like You come to everybody's house but mine . . . looks like I have a harder time than anybody." When I said this something told me to turn around and look. I put my bundle down and looked towards the east part of the world. A voice spoke to me as plain as day but inward and said, "I am a time-God working after the counsel of my own will. In due time I will bring all

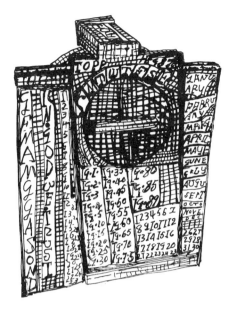

FIGURE 6.5. Timekeeper by
Z. B. Armstrong.

things to you. Remember and cause your heart to sing." (Rawick 1972
vol. 19:20).

Although this mission has not to my knowledge been discussed as such, it
is not uncommon for African Americans, especially in late middle age and
older, to assume personal responsibility for *marking time*: keeping track of
time in preparation for time to end, as prophesied in Revelations and
Matthew 25.13: "Watch therefore, for ye know neither the day nor the
hour wherein the Son of man cometh."[33]

The late Z. B. Armstrong of Thomson, Georgia, assumed this responsibility by making sculptures covered in timelines and clock faces with
which he literally marked time (fig. 6.5).[34]

Armstrong wrapped his sculptures with a tying motion that he called
"taping," a concept perhaps owed partly to one of his jobs, as foreman in
a box factory (McWillie 1987, 1990). More significantly, taping carried
through Armstrong's preoccupation with encirclement and precise location. Carefully indicating top and bottom, front and back, he oriented
found objects, predominantly circular, within each sculpture, enclosing
them in calendrical inscriptions, while repeating themes and colors pro-
pelled multiple works forward in series. Many of the sculptures have slots
to peg down each day, month, and year as it passes. In this way Armstrong
constantly calibrated the here-and-now in relation to the unknown apocalyptic moment when the beginning and end meet.

Z. B. Armstrong's work is a visual exposition of the interlocking
themes—vision, time, clocks, history, and Revelations—that Rev. C. L.
Franklin also expounded in his sermon *"Watchman, What of the Night?"*

> *Isaiah . . . stood upon the lofty wall of vision,* and in vision he heard the
> cry of frustration, the cry of oppression . . . and that cry was an inquir-

ing cry: *"Watchman, what of the night? What of the times? What time of history is this? What time of trouble is this?" For after all, history is God's big clock.* For a day is but a thousand years in terms of eternity. (I wish somebody here would pray with me.) . . .

For to us, it is like it was with John; for John said, he saw an angel standing with a scroll rolled in his hand, and it was sealed on all sides, and nobody could break the seals or read the writing therein, but the lambs. So we know that history is God's scroll, already sealed, written within and without; and we cannot read the writing; and we cannot break the seal; only God can reveal it to us, or reveal it to his men of mystery. And so . . . we inquire to the men of vision . . . "Watchman, what of the night?" (Franklin 1989:166–167, my emphasis)

While others inquire, the men of vision, like Z. B. Armstrong, C. L. Franklin, and James Hampton, assume the responsibility as best they can for—if not answering—at least displaying accountability to the question put to the watchman (the walker on the wall of vision): Where in history are we? The same elements—writing, time, cycles, revelation—recur again and again.

Assuming responsibility for keeping time, marking time, and "writing down time" also may relate to other African American concerns about recordkeeping, the passage of time, and European timekeeping instruments that extend back to the plantation era.[35] Mechal Sobel, describing the worldviews of Virginians of African and English descent in the eighteenth century, has pointed out that although many slaves reckoned time in the African way, according to the cycle of the seasons and major events, they resented the fact that whites kept records of black births and deaths, thus "'stealing' their birthdates as well as their birthrights," and even going so far as to burn the family Bibles where this information was recorded in order to avoid sharing it with their former slaves at Emancipation (1987:16). Taking charge of time and recordkeeping thus in a very real sense can represent taking charge of one's destiny.

Images that show an individual taking charge of timekeeping have been part of black visual culture at least since the civil rights movement and probably long before. In the late 1980s, Hip Hop fashion included oversized watches. Rappers were and are occasionally photographed holding watches or stopwatches (see Beckman and Adler 1991). At first glance these not very oblique references to approaching revolution seem secular compared with sacred traditions that connect timekeeping and Revelation. However, as with so much African American expressive imagery and performance, the distinction between sacred and secular is fluid. Whether they express their concerns in a vocabulary of revelation or revolution, the Bible or Black Power, individuals who display their responsibility as timekeepers—*Watch Men*—do so under the rubrics of justice and judgment.

Another artist with these concerns is Robert (Boot Roots) Montgomery, now of Chattanooga, Tennessee, who was born on Bimini Island in the Bahamas in the mid-1930s. The sketch (fig. 6.6) shows a combination shoeshine stand and judgment seat that Boot Roots and a colleague built and parked across from the former railroad station—now a tourist

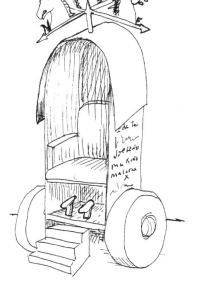

FIGURE 6.6. Bumper sticker and judgment seat shoe shine stand by Robert (Boot Roots) Montgomery.

attraction, the Chattanooga Choo Choo Holiday Inn. The shoeshine stand was Boot Roots's response to the racist popular songs "The Chattanooga Choo Choo" ("Pardon me, boy, is that the . . .") and "The Chattanooga Shoe Shine Boy." The stand–judgment seat—also throne for Boot Roots—was covered with writing about African American heroes. African American history is Boot Roots's revelation to the people of Chattanooga. By making the Four Horses into a revolving whirligig, Boot Roots has also invoked the cosmogram and crossmark through circling mastery of the four directions. The reference to Judgment Day, according to Boot Roots (interview, May 23, 1988), warns that the day of reckoning is at hand for racists and the human race alike. Boot Roots also made a bumper sticker commemorating the space shuttle Challenger, another reminder of life's transitoriness.

Recurring configurations that involve writing, writing down time, watches, watching, vision, clocks, eternity, revelation, the cross, the crossmark, and the cosmogram cannot explain the behavior or intentions of particular individuals, but they do suggest cultural grounds for appreciating ventures that might otherwise seem idiosyncratic. This account comes from the FWP interviews with people formerly enslaved in Washington County, Mississippi.

A copper-colored man was an interesting study. . . . His . . . curious tastes [were] not to be explained.
This man was an amusement to both whites and blacks on the plan-

tation, yet without resentment toward those who laughed at him he continued with his dreams undaunted. . . . A very striking figure was John and his standards of honor would have been suited to a white man of breeding; his word was accepted without question by his master.

He was plantation blacksmith and peg-leg carpenter during the day, but at night he turned his attention to efforts to discover perpetual motion. . . . All kinds of absurd machines sat about the blacksmith shop made of discarded pieces of iron and with them John would tinker until the small hours of the morning, hoping at any moment to discover the everlasting movement.

Defunct clocks interested this strange man and he would take them to pieces but was never able to get all the wheels back. The poor old clocks would run at ridiculous speed, but John, unperturbed, said they were all right. . . . Along with John Martin's childish mistakes, there was a strange taste for good pictures. His cabin walls were hung with newspaper copies of paintings by the masters. There was not a trashy picture among them, and if asked why he liked them, he would answer, "I don't know. When I'm 'sleep I knows why, but when I wakes up, I done forgot." (Rawick 1977 vol. 9:1445–1447)

This passage does not explicitly mention revelation or writing and describes John Martin as a childlike crank with aberrant good taste. Nevertheless, Martin's preoccupation with perpetual motion and clocks begins to make sense when placed alongside the other accounts in this chapter.[36] Like so many other African Americans, Martin seems to have conducted his activities in plain sight, yet his real work remained virtually invisible to outsiders behind the mask of their prior expectations.

I . . . crossed a great river. . . . I looked in the water and thought came to me: If all this water was ink, it wouldn't hold 'nough ink to write out the mysteries of God.
Preacher from Macon County, Georgia, quoted by William H. Pipes (1951:17)

There is no such thing as white ink.
B. *Culture* magazine masthead

7

Contrasting and Complementary Scripts and Graphic Signs

This chapter explores the interaction of conventional literacy and vernacular practices when Roman script shares a context with another kind of script or graphic system. It also looks at how inscriptions disrupt and reconfigure the Roman alphabet and orthodox punctuation. These conjunctions and disruptions accomplish what neither conventional Roman script nor the vernacular alternative could do alone. They make double voicing an inherent property of the acts of writing and reading. Some interactions foreground a contrast between different sets of values, much as Elder Green did in his narrative. Sometimes an alternative sign system simply fulfills a function to which Roman script is less well suited, because of its phonological and linear properties or its cultural history.

Alternative graphic signs may function indexically like marks that point to a change of state or context. Or, more rarely, they may compose a linear script.

Emblematic signs are similar to names or logos. Emblems and other semantic signs relate only loosely to the sound system of a language, if at all. For this reason, schemas of the evolution of writing put such signs at the bottom of the branching tree of scripts, and some theorists rule them out of the story of writing systems altogether (for example, DeFrancis 1989:20–64).

A common-sense attribute of conventional literacy, according to Eric Havelock, David Olson, and others, is a monologic reduction of ambiguity and an increase in clarity, which is construed as consistent and dependable referentiality. Not only does this view depend on treating codes like the alphabet as neutral media, it also implies sufficient ideological homogeneity so that senders and receivers of messages can say, "We all know what we mean."

But what if we don't? Or won't?

Given the contacts and conflicts among media and histories in African America, in order to be clear it may be necessary to say two (or more) things at once: the paradox of double consciousness. But oppression and conflict are only part of the story. Given that indirection is, and has been, a valued African and African American accomplishment that eases the flow of interpersonal life, the impulse to ambiguate redoubles. Ambiguity and doubling are venerable tools for political resistance, but artfully generating these qualities in interaction also commands respect for the performer. Conversely, explicitness can be undesirable. Along these lines, James Bullock, an African American teacher and father of three, proposed the following theory of why some black children have trouble in school:

> Black people get the point quickly. It's essential to their survival. Once they see something or once it's been said they assume everybody gets it. They don't like to repeat it. They don't see any reason to spell things out. The kids I coach hate the drill and practice routine. They hate getting information in sections. They want the whole thing. If you keep repeating something back to them it's like telling them they're stupid. But in school they want you to spell it out. That's what they grade you for. That's how you show you are smart. Black kids show they're smart by showing how far they can go playing all around the point but they consider it stupid to spell out what everybody gets. (personal communication, April 1994)

Bullock's observation is as relevant to writing and print as it is to the spoken word. The "whole thing" depends on contextual, cultural expertise to "get." Thus "wholes" are multivalent, ambiguous—and being able deal with them, play with them, not only opens up opportunities for creative maneuver and resistance but also signifies intelligence. Many young people do use in-group gestural and speech codes as well as graphic emblems in this way. The appropriation of football and baseball team logos by youth is a case in point.

The same openness to ambiguity that makes semantic signs imprecise in comparison with phonetic scripts makes them useful for in-group communication. This openness also suits them to expressing global concepts and broad identities.[1] We have already looked at one such case—the network of four-eyes and four-moments signs in chapter 4. These signs communicate with great economy, yet their indirection is well suited to warning and protective functions in the home and yard—potential intruders can read the message at a glance, but no one who approaches in goodwill need suffer unjust accusation. The open-endedness of the signs allows for double-sided, double-sighted readings. Thus, a diamond/square/"star" interacting with the Roman script phrase "Super Star" may read as an accusation to a trespasser and a welcome to a guest, all under the broader rubric God Sees Everything (fig. 4.34).

Signs for Group Purposes

From a sociocultural standpoint, African American uses of non-Roman graphic signs divide loosely into signs that mainly serve the purposes of groups and those that mainly serve personal purposes.

Regardless of whether signs primarily serve groups or individuals, they have cultural dimensions and are not idiosyncratic. Though limited, access to signs is culturally organized. Often in African American practices a message becomes available, if at all, only after one or more special procedures have been carried out. These procedures may take the form of instruction, initiation, or progressive personal cultivation. They prepare recipients to receive messages from higher powers that have intrinsic value and confer special status.

This pattern reflects a key dimension along which sign systems reconfigure from Africa to the Americas, for in Africa indigenous scripts and graphic systems, though by no means confined to secret societies and specialized activities like divination, are often bound up with them. This connection affects public display of script knowledge because what can be displayed indicates the degree of access to which participants are privy, while hinting at private knowledge that cannot be shown to noninitiates (chapters 3 and 5).

Of signs serving mainly group purposes, several of the better-known graphic systems are associated with religions and fraternal organizations. The vèvè of Haitian Vodou are emblematic signs that devotees draw with kaolin, flour, or cornstarch at the outset of rituals to call the lwa (Deren 1953; Rigaud 1969; Metraux 1959; Brown 1975). More permanent vèvè adorn the walls of temples. The designs sum up the attributes of the lwa who possess the devotees, and are composites spreading out from central crossmarks—the crossmark itself being the intersection of worlds mediated by the lwa Legba, the master of thresholds, uncertainty, and writing.

In order to give readers unfamiliar with vèvè an introduction to their appearance, I have reproduced three vèvè for the lwa Simbi (figs. 7.1, 7.2, 7.3). A lwa in the Petro ritual family, Simbi's Kongo antecedents are local spirits, associated with enduring features of landscape, twins, eddies of water, whiteness, kaolin clay, and unusual formations of wood, root, and liana: twisted forms that bear witness to divine power and the action of water.[2] I leave the history and significance of vèvè and Simbi in Haiti to those better qualified to tell it;[3] rather, I have included these vèvè because of several design features that parallel other African American graphic practices: the double presence of Roman script with non-Roman signs, the directional orientation of vèvè, and the pwe, points, at the extremities of the most strongly directional lines.

Another well-known and well-documented system is anaforuana, the graphic system of the Cuban secret society Abakua (Cabrera 1970, 1975;

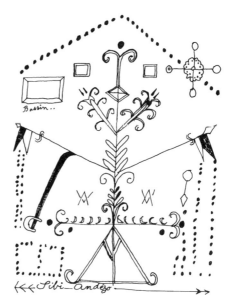

FIGURE 7.1. Vèvè of the lwa Simbi-Yandezo (after Metraux 1959:106).

FIGURE 7.2. Vèvè of Simbi (after Brown 1975:412).

FIGURE 7.3. Vèvè of Simbi (after Rigaud 1969:105).

Thompson 1983:228–229, 248–268). Anaforuana has direct links to an African system, the nsibidi signs of the Cross River Ejagham, Efik, and neighboring peoples (see chapter 3). Anaforuana graphs can be combined sequentially and are used during rituals of initiation, of investiture of ascending ranks of membership, and of enforcement of society policies. As with vèvè, I am concerned here only with illustrating anaforuana for those unfamiliar with their appearance. Particular signs acquire meanings from the interplay of several basic elements, including the four-eyes motif; allusions to the sacrifice and transformation of the princess Sikan into a powerful spirit; leaves—forest things with the potential to heal or kill; the darkening of parts of the sign to indicate extreme danger; and directional arrows that signal the purposeful movement of the powers that the sign illustrates and helps to sustain. All these elements orient in relation to the four cardinal points.

The signs in figure 7.4 are anaforuana emblems of dignitaries who officiate for the Powers of the Efik: the *nation* of Abakua that traces its origin to the Efik of Calabar. According to Lydia Cabrera, who collected these signs and wrote extensively on Abakua, the use of the circle and cross in this way is characteristic of the Efik.

I have included these illustrations of vèvè with pwe and anaforuana with arrows and crossmarks—marks of power and enforcement—to highlight the striking similarities between these signs and the gang signs in Vicksburg, Mississippi, painted at a crossroad in a residential neighborhood, that I photographed in 1989 (fig. 7.5). The signs not only resemble vèvè and other African and African American forms of ground writing, but their location at a crossroads positions the painted signs inside a larger sign. The resemblance of these gang signs to vèvè and anaforuana need not result from direct visual connection, because components like the crown are a logical extension of values and terminology familiar to gang members and of recurring principles of design like orientation to the four cardinal points, directionality, and emblemizing. All these visual qualities, alluding as they do to powerful backing and enforcement, underscore the territorial claims that the signs assert and seem on the surface to arise from local circumstances. Nevertheless, it would also be unwise to rule direct connections out; the signs of major gangs diffuse to Vicksburg and other small cities from urban centers like New Orleans, which has had continuous contact with Haiti and the West Indies for four centuries.

Signs for Personal Purposes

Signs like vèvè spill over from ritual settings into daily life where, sometimes incorporated in seals, they play roles in obeah and hoodoo. These magical complexes are culturally organized and operate through individual initiative and through the interaction of a client with a specialist practitioner. Personal religious experience may also be expressed in a distinctive script that contrasts with conventional writing in appearance and function.

The following quotation from Norman Paul illustrates the slippage between group and personal use of signs and texts.

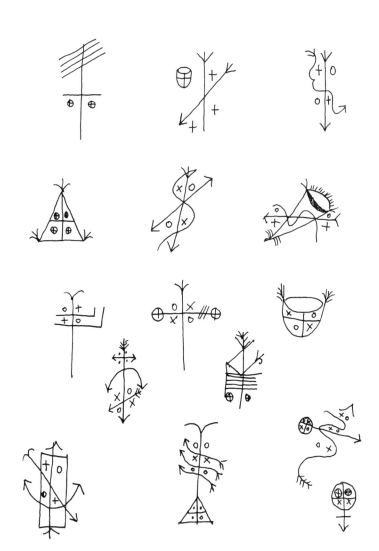

FIGURE 7.4. Anaforuana for Dignitaries of the Efik Powers (after Cabrera 1975: fig. 191)

If the Baptists have a love for you, they use some signs that when they put you on the mourning ground you will travel far by them, and you will see things in a better way. If they does not care about you, they does it through mischief, because these books they have teach you both good and evil; the Sixth and Seventh Books of Moses, or the Titalbeh, or the Book of Black Arts.

They make the sort of things that hurt people by using this same book, and that is how the people who make obeah does. (Smith 1963:88–89)

Note that both Roman script and special Spiritual Baptist signs appear in the inscription.[4] This was also true of the Spiritual Baptist inscription I discussed in the preface (fig. P. 4).

FIGURE 7.5. Gang signs in a crossroads, Vicksburg, Mississippi, 1989.

Like magic around the world, obeah, hoodoo, and sorcery often involve conventional literate practices and sometimes non-Roman, special scripts and other graphic signs.[5] Rootworkers and spiritual advisers do a thriving business by mail. The weekly tabloid *The Star* contains a full column or more of ads from practitioners soliciting contact with clients through letters that describe a problem and enclose money for a special prayer, an amulet, even a duppy (spirit) in a bottle. (I recall that an ad for a mail-order duppy from the Bahamas also ran in the classified section of the *Saturday Review* in 1965–66.) Apparently, such ventures have gone forward through print and word-of-mouth for a century or more, even in areas where obeah was or is considered a serious crime. A British civil servant, S. Udall, described a complicated case brought to trial in Nevis, West Indies, in October 1904. The accused obeah specialist covered letters from clients in conventional writing with superimposed "hieroglyphics."

> Theophilus Dasent . . . was charged . . . [and a] considerable number of
> letters were found by the police in the defendant's possession—a cir-

cumstance which obeah men seldom allow to occur—and formed a very
important feature in the proceedings.

The usual "instruments of obeah" were discovered. . . . A keg containing white lime and hair. Bottles containing carbolic oil, and something white like—but not—a fruit salt. Kerosine oil and quicksilver. In
a locked-up room were found phials of Florida water, turpentine oil, and
parcels of Epsom salts, and of sulphur. . . . In a trunk in that room were
found the letters, of which several were made "exhibits" in the case. . . .

Nearly all the letters were covered with hieroglyphics in pencil, very
similar in character, representing plain short strokes in regular lines, as
if scoring a cricket score-book, and finishing up each line with a couple
of o's; thus: /////////////oo. They extend over a period of four years.
Some asked for protection against the machinations of other persons,
and for means of attacking or injuring them in return. . . .

Several applicants for assistance evidently looked upon Dasent as a
doctor. Indeed, there was evidence in the case that he was commonly
known in Nevis as "Dr. Dasent." There is one letter . . . from a woman,
complaining that she had been sick for over a year with a sore on her
foot and had done everything he advised without success, and appealed
to him to send her something to cure it, promising to give him a little
barrow pig. . . .

The effect of the letters was no doubt reflected in the magistrate's de-
cision, for he found the defendant guilty. (1915:277–279)

Thus, writing in obeah is a means of acting upon situations. Here, using
one type of sign on top of another seems to index a change of situation.
The specialist's marks—dashes "sealed" at the ends of lines by circles (a
variant of pwe?)—cancel out particulars of the client's problem one character at a time, while the contrasting marks that totally cover the client's
letter impose the specialist's will on the situation globally. Put another
way, the obeah specialist *ties* the client's problem in his own crossmarks.

Frequently outsiders to the belief system label such practices imitations
of "real" writing.

> As an outward and visible sign of his power, the obeah-man sometimes
> carries about with him a long staff or wand, with twisted serpents, or
> the rude likeness of a human head carved round the handle. He has his
> cabalistic book, too, full of strange characters, which he pretends to con-
> sult in the exercise of his calling. One of these is now in my possession.
> It is an old child's copy-book, well-thumbed and very dirty. Each page is
> covered with rude delineations of the human figure, and roughly-traced
> diagrams and devices. Between each line there runs a rugged scrawl, in-
> tended to imitate writing. The moral precepts engraved at the head of
> each page seem strangely out of place with the meaningless signs and
> symbols which occupy the remainder of the page. (Rampini 1873,
> quoted in Abrahams and Szwed 1983:212)

Since the marks described in this passage differ markedly from conventional Roman script, it seems fair to wonder why the "imitation" is so unlike its supposed source. One explanation is that the obeahman used contrasting scripts for obfuscation and mystification to enhance his reputation
for esoteric power. This explanation has two sides: first, the implication of

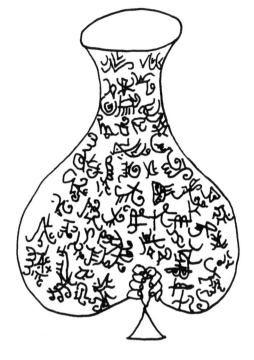

FIGURE 7.6. Detail
of signs, Minnie Evans
(after Kahan 1986:
fig. 9).

fraud—which may well be justified; second, the shift of emphasis from using writing for encoding to displaying special knowledge.

This style-shift parallels the contrast between practical, communicative speech and Fancy Talk in anglophone black communities, as well as the shift in narratives from the monologic communicative orientation of conventional literacy to multichannel performance in which writing plays one part among many.[6] Some obeah specialists and hoodoo doctors have reputations for Fancy Talk; furthermore, the convoluted language in Fancy Talk turns over itself, nonlineal fashion, much as convoluted lines of writing unfold in graphic practices like the "rugged scrawl" just described.

When sign systems interact through contact between previously separate groups, the values that become attached to different marks, signs, and scripts reveal a great deal about the groups themselves and their relations. These relations also affect the way graphic signs are used and interpreted. Some authors argue that geographic distance and power are complementary.[7] Scribner and Cole claim that because few West Africans understand Arabic, spoken and written Arabic appear powerful, magical (1981). The same claim has been made about the Latin language and the Catholic Church: that the remoteness of the Latin Mass enhanced the authority of the Church, while the vernacular Mass made the Church more accessible.

Some African Americans also use scripts and signs that allude to distant places. The artist Minnie Evans developed a repertoire of personal signs that resemble Chinese in some of her drawings (fig. 7.6).[8] The signs reflect her interest in a film, *Fu Manchu*, and probably testify to travel to distant places in the spirit (Kahan 1986:24, 37).

Nevertheless, in African America the assumption that distant origins and conquest enhance the power associated with scripts like the Roman alphabet is complicated by a number of factors—the same factors that underpin creolization, double voicing, and double vision. The African American modes of inscription that interact with conventional Roman script rarely are mere mystifying signs that serve only to obfuscate. For example, once one recognizes that tying with script is a recurring vernacular function for writing and marking in African America, then the obeahman's marks on the client's letter make sense on their own terms. Nor are the signs that African Americans use in vernacular practices primarily those of the alien captors who forced Africans to labor on plantations. Like Minnie Evans's Chinese, whether these signs orient toward group or personal purposes, they are rooted in the cultural resources of insiders—in Evans's case, in practices of spiritual travel and writing in unknown tongues, a topic I turn to later. Thus, while they may imply distance, the signs simultaneously index African American social worlds and the performance orientation of black expressive culture.

Writing in the Spirit

Writing in unknown tongues, writing in the spirit: these practices occur in a number of settings around the diaspora and also resemble mediumistic writing in other parts of the world.[9] They have been likened to glossalalia, the talk in tongues of ecstatic worship. However, writing in unknown tongues often differs from speech in unknown tongues in one significant particular: in all the cases I have learned of so far, only one writer at a time in the setting serves as a channel for spirit script; however, verbal glossalalia often involves several speakers talking or shouting at once, as in Pentacostal worship.

Judith McWillie has researched and discussed the African American tradition of writing in unknown tongues in detail (1991); and several instances of what the author Joyce Elaine Noll refers to as "spirit writing" appear in her *Company of Prophets: African American Psychics, Healers, and Visionaries* (1991:216, 153–154), a compilation from secondary and primary sources. Noll and McWillie concur that spirit writing relates to divination and meditation; often it accompanies other mediumistic activities that elicit information from spirit guides about the causes and cures of clients' problems.[10]

Peter James Brown Jr., pastor of Cathedral Temple of Divine Love in Chicago, followed instructions that he received in the form of spirit writing to diagnose and treat cases of epilepsy, family conflict, and "a girl who had sixteen entities in her" (Noll 1991:153). The accounts in *Company of Prophets* give few details about spirit writing, but it seems reasonable to infer some connection to the automatic writing that European and American Spiritualists have practiced from the turn of the century to the present, as well as the automatic writing that figured in late-nineteenth- and early-twentieth-century studies of the stream of consciousness conducted by the psychologist and philosopher William James.[11]

The African American healers in Noll's book usually work through churches and use the Bible extensively, both artifactually, as a tool in the healing process, and textually, as a source of religious doctrine, information—read and divined—and inspiration. This orientation is similar to that of African American Spiritual churches where elements of spiritualism combine with African, Roman Catholic, and innovative components. The liturgy of these churches, found throughout the country but most densely in New Orleans, incorporates and creolizes biblical teaching, elements of Roman Catholic ritual, ecstatic worship, anointing with sacred oil, spirit possession, and communication with a host of spirit guides. Although many Spiritual church pastors and participants are reluctant to talk about it, there is a longstanding relationship between Spiritual church activities and hoodoo/voodoo.[12] Central to this relationship is the use of oils blessed in the church and candles whose colors represent saints and African Powers (Shango, Legba, et al.), and correspond to goals like domestic peace, love, and financial gain. Arguably, Spiritual churches, spiritual healing and counseling practices, and hoodoo are the most "African" of the African American participatory networks emerging on U.S. soil. Cross-fertilized by Afro-Caribbean emigration, this network resembles Spiritual Baptist worship, Shango, and obeah in Trinidad and other West Indian islands.

Some, but by no means all, African American spirit writing is part of the graphic economy of Spiritual churches, overlapping into hoodoo. Rituals that use oils and candle-burning frequently involve writing names to place beneath the candles and enclose in amulets.

A larger number of writers, however, most of them unknown outside their families and communities, began to write in the spirit through an intensely personal, yet culturally grounded, form of visionary experience. Documentation for this approach to writing dates back at least to Emancipation. For example, on July 30, 1936, J. Ralph Jones interviewed the former slave Mary Gladdy, who had grown up on the Holt plantation in Muskogee County near Columbus, Georgia.[13] Jones wrote:

> [I] was impressed by her intelligence and utter sincerity. She claims never to have attended school or been privately taught in her life, and she cannot write or even form the letters of the alphabet; but she gave me a convincing demonstration of her ability to read. When I asked her how she mastered this skill, she replied: "The Lord revealed it to me."
>
> And indeed for more than thirty years the Lord has been revealing His Holy Word and many other things to Mary Gladdy. For over twenty years she has been experiencing "visitations of the spirit." These do not occur with any degree of regularity, but they do always come in "the dead hours of the night" after she has retired, and she is invariably impelled to rise and write in an unknown hand. Her strange writings now cover eight pages of letter paper and bear a marked resemblance to crude shorthand notes. Offhand she can "cipher" about half of these strange writings; the other half, however, she can make neither heads nor tails, except when the spirit is upon her. When the spirit eases off,

she again becomes totally ignorant of the significance of the mysterious half of her spirit-directed writings. (Rawick 1977 vol. 3:257)

From the standpoint of conventional literacy, one might argue that Mary Gladdy wrote in an "unknown hand" to compensate for the fact that she could not write in the Roman alphabet. From this standpoint, Gladdy's deficits and strategies to remedy them parallel the freedpeople at Fortress Monroe who could not read but believed that they received the word of God directly in their hearts. In their case and Mary Gladdy's, divine intervention overshadows conventional literacy with something far more valuable. In both cases, however, the activities of reading and writing also fall into place among preexisting practices and beliefs, and it is surely this connection, not compensation for supposed deficits, that has made writing in the spirit an enduring option, especially in concert with visionary experience and healing.[14]

J. B. Murray of Sparta, Georgia, told Judith McWillie, during one of several audio and video tapings that she made of this healer and artist at work, that he began writing after a time of illness and family turmoil when the sun came down in his yard and an eagle crossed in front of his eye, giving him special powers of sight. Murray incorporated writing like that in figure 7.7 into a prayer service in which he chanted as God guided his hand. He then read the writing through a bottle of water from the well on his property, holding it much as healers in Jamaica and other parts of the diaspora hold water in a bottle through which to "read" as they divine the cause and treatment of illness. Like the not-readers of Fortress Monroe, Rebecca Cox Jackson, and so many others, J. B. Murray invested activities related to reading and writing with spatial and temporal dimensions in performance. And like the freedwoman who searched for J-E-S-U-S along the lines of print in the Bible, Murray's writing served in call-and-response with the writer's own words and breathing to call the Spirit and to focus special insight on visitors and their problems. In some of his works made in the process of healing prayer, Murray's writing seems to tie up problems and draw them forth from the visitor, depositing them on the page in angry shapes and bundles.[15]

J. B. Murray was undoubtedly an unusual man. His writings and drawings attracted favor in the art world, and Murray himself has been labeled an outsider artist, a singularly inappropriate label given the social and personal ills he sought to heal. Murray's writing in the spirit not only aligns with the work and spiritual concerns of other African American healers and artists, but appears to have numerous historical precedents, in writing like Mary Gladdy's writing in an unknown hand and in reading that calls-and-responds with text to culminate in a visitation of the Spirit.

Double Sight, Double Script

Mary Gladdy and J. B. Murray wrote only in revealed scripts, but they did so in ways framed both by aspects of conventional literacy tools and formats and the expectation that their writing could be read under the right conditions. Other writers in the diaspora couple writing in the spirit with

FIGURE 7.7. Writing in the Spirit, J. B. Murray (after photograph by Judith McWillie).

conventional alphabetic writing or other vernacular signs in the same event
or document. When Roman script and another kind of writing (four-eyes
signs, emblems, writing by or in the spirit, wildstyle graffiti, etc.) interact
in a single setting or event, they do so in ways that parallel the relationship
between reading and not-reading in the narratives in chapter 5.[16] The shift
from Roman to another kind of writing is a means of signaling a change in
orientation: from wider world to home ground, from outsider to insider
communication, from uplift to omnidirectional mastery, from one reality
or register of a multifaceted cultural repertoire to another.

Winti Writing

In a famous case from Surinam, Melville and Frances Herskovits describe
a change in script that parallels change in an informant's state through
spirit possession (fig. 7.8).

> One of the things [our informant] does under possession, and which he
> did when he was possessed in our hotel room, is to write in the language
> of his *winti* [familiar spirit]. We reproduce a sample written in a state of
> possession. Since leaving Suriname, we have had several letters from

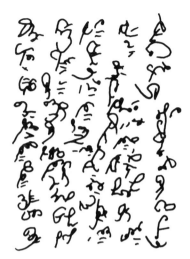

FIGURE 7.8. Writing by an individual (a) during spirit possession and (b) in a letter (after Herskovits and Herskovits 1936:84).

him which contained this writing, included, he explained, as a greeting from his *winti* to us. Objectively considered, the symbols he employs are consistent, and we have seen him write them with ease. He has not yet solved for himself the meaning of this writing . . . though he assures us that once the *winti* is pacified, it will make known to him the meaning of the symbols and their origin. This man's difficulties in getting his *winti* pacified are many. Most important of all is getting the money to engage a *wintiman* to do the pacifying, and to provide for the essentials of a ceremony. (1936:83)

The letter from the Herskovitses' informant contains conventional writing and spirit writing in one document creating a contrast between two bodies of knowledge in one double-voiced, double-visual document. At the same time, the combination supplies a metacommentary on how these bodies of knowledge relate to each other culturally and interpersonally. The informant's Roman script is clear and well crafted. It could easily pass through the Post Office—a test self-taught African Americans sometimes set themselves to learn whether their writing was clear enough to pass muster in the world at large (see Blassingame 1977:588). The writing of the winti, which the informant himself could not decode, suggests that winti possessed literate skill even greater than that of humans.[17] Humans could read the winti's script, but only after ritual pacification, an expensive procedure that required several steps and specialist help.[18]

Double-Sighted Inscription and Revolt

References to double-sighted inscription appear in historical accounts and autobiographies in the United States dating back nearly two hundred years. Above and beyond freedom from slavery and economic hardship for particular individuals, literacy has long been associated with collective resistance and slave revolts. According to Michael Craton, in 1683 enslaved members of different African ethnic groups in Barbados used English as a lingua franca and circulated plans to revolt in Roman script (1982:110–111). This strategy proved their undoing when a document in English came into the hands of the British authorities.

The great leader of Haiti's victory over France, Toussaint l'Ouverture, in some popular legends is regarded as literate in French and even Latin and Greek, having mastered these languages while serving as coachman for a French planter. However, according to C. L. R. James, Toussaint could hardly speak French and "to the end of his days could not write three words without the grossest errors in spelling and grammar" and dictated his correspondence in Creole, which his secretaries then wrote and rewrote in French until "he got the exact meaning he wanted" (1963:104).

However, in addition to his roles as leader, lawmaker, and writer of letters to his adversaries in Europe, Toussaint has another persona. At least one scholar, Edward Kamau Brathwaite (lecture, April 1988), has argued that Toussaint was also a Vodou priest and healer. While all the facts are unlikely ever to be known, in both personae Toussaint's legacy of liberation endures for Haitians and other African descendants in the Americas.

The issue of literacy versus not-literacy in accounts of Toussaint's life bears witness to the conflicts and cultural ambiguity that also figure in many other Caribbean biographies. Although the issue of whether or how Toussaint read and wrote is peripheral to the success of the Haitian revolt, the *standing* of writing in Toussaint's story is another matter. In accounts of his life, the pattern that takes shape is a dialogic relation between reading and not-reading, writing and not-writing, "European" and "African" oriented versions of leadership.

A similar pattern emerges from other accounts of revolt. In the Bahia revolts of the early nineteenth century, Hausa and Yoruba rebels combined Arabic talismans—*tied* script—with instruction in Arabic literacy prior to the revolt (Reis 1982). Possibly they also wrote documents in Arabic as organizational aids in planning. Thus there is some indication that participants in the revolts in Bahia routinely style-shifted among message, tying, and emblemizing functions as situations warranted.

In other circumstances, rather than two scripts or two knowledge systems converging on one person, two leaders come to the fore who embody two different masteries. So it was in the Vesey revolt of 1822 in Charleston. Denmark Vesey, the leader, was a literate craftsman and preacher, well-spoken and well-mannered. From the European American perspective, therefore, Vesey was the kind of man who had benefited from "civilizing" contact with whites and literacy. Like Sam Sharpe of Jamaica, Vesey was an "ingrate." After the revolt, his literacy served as a rationale for restricting African American reading and writing in South Carolina until Emancipation.

> [T]he Vesey plot embodied an extraordinarily rich ideology. Beyond a general antiwhite attitude, Vesey combined the Old Testament's harsh morality and the story of the Israelites with African religious customs, knowledge of the Haitian Revolution, and readings of antislavery speeches from the Missouri controversy. . . . While Gullah Jack provided recruits with African religious symbols to guarantee victory, Monday Gell [an Ibo by birth] may have written to the Haitians in order to obtain assistance. (Starobin 1971:3)

If Vesey was ungrateful, his coconspirator Gullah Jack was incorrigible. Originally from Angola, Jack was a conjurer who called himself a "Doctor Negro" and boldly claimed that the amulets he prepared would render the rebels inviolate and invisible. So great were his powers of persuasion that at least one member of the plot claimed to have joined because of Jack's coercive magic, and witnesses against Jack feared for their lives (Starobin 1971:43–45). Jack himself claimed that no white man could capture or harm him. On this account the white population set great store in his capture and execution, using Jack's vulnerability to torment surviving black South Carolinians with their own precarious situation.[19]

The Vesey revolt shows that, side by side with conventional literacy, accounts of revolts also refer to folk beliefs and vernacular expressive practices that reciprocally supported overt and covert acts of resistance (Brathwaite 1977; Levine 1977; Creel 1988).

Nat Turner

Contrasting Roman and revealed scripts play significant roles in the story of the famed insurrection leader Nat Turner. Like the Vesey revolt, the Southampton, Virginia, revolt prompted antiliteracy sentiments that reversed more moderate attitudes toward slave education and continued to escalate until the Civil War. After the revolt, literacy became a symbol for whites of the consequences of allowing so-called liberties for blacks to a degree that far outweighed its actual importance in the revolt. Many whites blamed Turner's master for teaching him to read and write and assumed that this was the only way Turner could have learned.

These concerns were probably misdirected.[20] According to Turner's autobiography, just as not-reading ultimately secured the liberation of John Jea in magistrate's court, it was not-writing—more precisely, engagement with non-Roman, non-European, indeed nonearthly script that ultimately certified Turner's worthiness for his mission.

In chapter 5 I discussed some of the ways that conventional literacy aligns with political and economic power in Turner's education. Within this frame, Turner's rapid mastery of the ABCs and reading and writing signified to him and those close to him that he was born to fulfill a special destiny, linked to the practical and political matters that conventional literacy represented. In short, Turner's literacy served as a sign of his entitlement to freedom—not surprisingly, given the long association of literacy with freedom among black Americans in the antebellum period and later. Turner recalled growing up with the conviction that he would be freed, but as the years passed and the prospect grew more remote, his anger grew and fueled his belief in a special mission given to him by God. Following instructions from the Spirit, which spoke to him as he worked in the fields, Turner launched a preaching career and began preparing his followers, telling them that "something was about to happen that would terminate in fulfilling the great promise that had been made to me" (Gray 1968:103).

In an apocalyptic vision in 1825, Turner saw black and white spirits engaged in battle, a darkened sun, and streams flowing with blood. He engaged in seeking "more than ever to receive the true holiness" (Gray 1968:103) and was rewarded by visions of lights in the sky that were Christ's hands "stretched from east to west . . . on the cross . . . for the redemption of sinners" (Gray 1968:103).

> And I wondered greatly at these miracles, and prayed to be informed of a certainty of the meaning thereof—and shortly afterwards, while laboring in the fields, I discovered drops of blood on the corn as though it were dew from heaven—and I communicated it to many, both black and white, in the neighborhood—and then I found on the leaves in the woods hieroglyphic characters, and numbers, with the forms of men in different attitudes, portrayed in the heavens. And now the Holy Ghost had revealed itself to me—For as the blood of Christ had been shed on this earth, and was now ascending to heaven for the salvation of sinners, and as the leaves on the trees bore the impression of the figures I had seen in the heavens, it was plain to me that the Savior was about to lay down the yoke he had borne for the sins of men, and that the day of judgment was at hand. (Gray 1968:103)

These "hieroglyphic" characters, numbers, and forms of men in the heavens inscribed Turner's visionary mandate onto a concrete world of action. Special not-of-this-world writing confirmed Turner's reading of his mission and his readiness to lead.[21]

The interaction of conventional literacy and vernacular signs in Turner's story enacts doubling parallel to that of Roman script and indecipherable winti script side by side in the Herskovitses' letter from Surinam. In both cases, the recipient of a message in revealed writing had to undergo special instruction. Although the Spirit, who instructed Turner, did not have to be pacified, comprehension of the message did depend on a long sequence of preparatory visions and meditations. This sequence contrasts pointedly with Turner's description of almost instantly mastering conventional reading and writing—skills that attested to his intellectual capabilities and right to full social participation as a free man, but not to the spiritual worthiness that the Spirit certified through hieroglyphic and heavenly signs.

A more speculative interpretation of Turner's narrative would link it more closely to Kongo iconography. Consider the following passage.

> And from the first steps of righteousness until the last, I was made perfect; and the Holy Ghost was with me, and said, "Behold me as I stand in the Heavens"—and I looked and saw the forms of men in different

FIGURE 7.9. Possible form of Nat Turner's vision of the Holy Ghost.

attitudes—and there were lights in the sky to which the children of
darkness gave other names than what they really were—for they were
the lights of the Savior's hands, stretched forth from east to west, even
as they extended from the cross on Calvary for the redemption of sinners. (Gray 1968:103)

Stripped to visual essentials, the image of the Holy Ghost standing in the
Heavens might look something like figure 7.9—a cruciform that overlays
the Christian cross with the cosmogram that encapsulates the cycle of life
and the sun. The "lights of the Savior's hands" fall on the Kalunga line,
the horizon and water line that divides spirit and living worlds. Indeed,
the term "Kalunga" is sometimes used by Bakongo synonymously with
"spirit" (Thompson 1983; Thompson and Cornet 1981; MacGaffey 1986,
1988a; Torday 1928). Furthermore, the hieroglyphic characters in Turner's
narrative appeared not on just any convenient natural object but on leaves,
the traditional sign of the healer and spiritual doctor.[22] Turner's next remarks expand the theme of healing.

> I told these things to a white man . . . on whom it had a wonderful ef-
> fect—and he ceased from his wickedness, and was attacked immediately
> with a cutaneous eruption, and blood oozed from the pores of his skin,
> and after praying and fasting for nine days, he was healed, and the
> Spirit appeared to me again. (Gray 1968:103)

In other words, Turner served as a spiritual guide to a white man who was
healed of terrible sores.

Turner's entire narrative is organized around the interplay between
two modes of inscription and two kinds of criteria for leadership. Rapid
mastery of conventional literacy—something even a child can do, albeit a
special one—underwrites Turner's assertion of secular leadership. Prolonged instruction in lessons of the Spirit—something only a mature

adult could grasp—confirms Turner's role as spiritual leader and healer.[23] The picture of Turner that emerges in the interaction of these two modes of inscription is at odds with much that has been written about him; it suggests a disciplined person undertaking responsibilities at the culmination of long preparation. This picture is as much at variance with the image of Turner as a pathological slave bent on murder and rape as with accounts that focus only on his secular and political goals, emphasizing his conventional literacy but attributing his religious visions to an interviewer bent on painting Turner as an unbalanced fanatic.[24]

From the perspective of interaction among scripts, the item-by-item veracity of Turner's narrative is not the issue. Rather, the narrative indicates important cultural resources for transforming, improving, or opting out of an intolerable situation of forced contact and oppression. In processes of creolization, cultural dualities or even more complex cultural dynamics articulate imbalances in the society at large. These in turn organize the functions of different kinds of graphic and material signs.

Interaction between conventional literacy and vernacular signs persisted in stories about Turner long after his death.

> An 1831 report states that Nat's papers were extracted from his wife, a slave of Giles Reese, by whipping her. The Jerusalem man into whose hands these fell said, "they are filled with *hieroglyphic characters* on the oldest paper, apparently [sic] appear to have been traced in blood; and on each paper, a *crucifix and the sun is distinctly visible*; with the figures 6,000, 30,000, 80,000 &c.—There is likewise a piece of paper, of late date, which all agree, is a list of his men. (Johnson 1970:70–71, my emphasis; also see Tragle 1971).

The Two Scripts of James Hampton

Style-shifting among sign systems, imagery that creolizes European and African precedents, double voicing, and double vision all converge on the interaction of conventional literacy with personal script in the monumental accomplishments of James Hampton. Hampton built the Throne of the Third Heaven of the Nations Millennium General Assembly in a rented garage in Washington, D.C., over a twenty-year period from the late 1940s until 1964, when he died of cancer before finishing his work. Composed of materials like castoff furniture, light bulbs, construction paper, and carefully collected silver and gold gum wrappers, a portion of the Throne complex is now permanently on view in the National Museum of American Art, Smithsonian Institution.[25] Many of the Throne's components bear double labels, one in Roman printing and the other in Hampton's personal, revealed script (fig. 7.10).

It is not clear whether Hampton intended anyone but himself to read his script or whether it can be decoded in the conventional sense. Government cryptographers could not decipher it, but their assumptions about the design of scripts probably differed radically from Hampton's (Horwitz 1975:131). My speculation is that the signs are logographs that correspond to words that Hampton chanted in call-and-response with the Spirit as

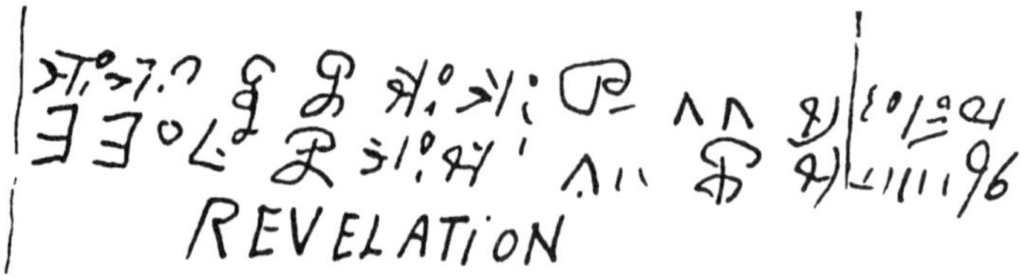

FIGURE 7.10. The two scripts of James Hampton.

he wrote. I base this hypothesis on the performance-oriented African American approach to reading and writing that I have already described and on repetitions that resemble visual chanting in Hampton's one surviving notebook. The pages in this notebook are laid out in ledger format, and most lines of Hampton's writing conform to this format by breaking their rhythmic flow across the page at the margin that would mark a tally of several figures in a ledger. This break, the word "Revelation" printed at the foot of each page, and Hampton's preoccupation with time and eternal cycles in the iconography of the throne, leads me to speculate further that at least one of Hampton's concerns, like Z. B. Armstrong's (chapter 6), was that of marking time until the onset of the millennium, when the throne that he had prepared would be occupied.

In any case, Hampton employed consistent characters for at least twenty years in notebooks and on the parts of the Throne. Otelia Whitehead, who visited Hampton several times in the garage where he worked, observed "more than twenty" notebooks (McWillie 1991:104). Parallel placement of Roman letters and Hampton's revelatory script appeared on a blackboard found in the garage where Hampton worked on the Throne at night (fig. 7.11), Smithsonian curator Lynda Hartigan (1977) has suggested that this blackboard is a kind of master plan. Roman numerals and script on a Ten Commandments–type tablet labeled "BC" suggest revelations of past law, while a contrasting "AD" tablet in Hampton's own script implies revelations concerning the future given to St. James: Hampton himself. Unfortunately, because Hampton's work was not documented during his lifetime, little can be said about the origins of his script without renewed efforts to find people who remember him and to understand his one surviving notebook.

To compare James Hampton and Nat Turner, both men undertook great responsibility as a result of visionary encounters with the Spirit. Both used two scripts to claim double sight and to position themselves as mediators and translators between worlds. Both established a contrast between Roman and revealed script to indicate a great change coming in the future and a revelation of the end of an era that it is the writer's destiny to help to bring about.

The use of two scripts—one open to general readers, the other closed to them, one socially dominant and the other spiritually revealed—accents the writer's passage toward deeper knowledge, and at the same time emphasizes to would-be readers the knowledge that they must master before they can

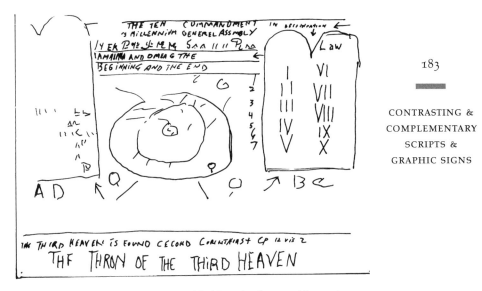

FIGURE 7.11. James Hampton's blackboard (after Gould: 1987).

comprehend the script. This pattern echoes the revealed origins of West African syllabaries, the Djuka script of Surinam (Dalby 1967, 1968), and Arabic occult scripts (Ibn Wahshiya 1977). The esoteric reading and writing of Hampton and Turner and the indigenous West African syllabaries all combine personal and social aspects. In all these cases, the personal aspect asserts a claim to deep knowledge, and the social asserts a changed world, whether apocalyptically altered or simply revised for the better.

James Hampton and Nat Turner were outstanding personages. But doubling like that in their work also recurs in less dramatic circumstances. Several African American artists whose work and biographies appear in the *Encyclopedia of Twentieth-Century American Folk Art* (Rosenak and Rosenak 1990) place a personal script alongside conventional Roman script in the same work. For example, Henry Ray Clark, incarcerated in Texas, began to paint in 1977, using futuristic designs, hieroglyphs, and a superwoman figure (Rosenak and Rosenak 1990:74). One painting (illustrated in Rosenak and Rosenak 1990:74) shows this spacewoman with the Roman block caption "I AM BIRDBEAM FROM THE PLANET SKYBEAM." On either side of this image are graphic signs enclosed in blocks in what appears to be an otherwise decorative border. In Clark's work, as in Hampton's, an unknown script aligns with events in the future.[26]

Transforming the Ordinary

When special or doubled signs appear in a drawing or painting, they are tacitly (and sometimes actually) framed in a way that separates them from

FIGURE 7.12. Grave with
messages and handprint,
Hattiesburg, Mississippi.

the visible fabric of everyday life. The graphic signs and practices I turn to now are part of that visible fabric; ironically, some of them are nearly *invisible* because they are so commonplace. Yet it is the commonplace world of things/actions—the T-shirts, the named cars, graffiti, church signs, and burial marking—that offers the richest array of expression.

The grave of a beloved mother and grandmother in Hattiesburg, Mississippi (fig. 7.12) exemplifies how vernacular practices and conventional literacy interact in ordinary yet deeply felt circumstances. Here, Roman script is realigned from an outside-oriented, school-taught skill to an inside-oriented mode of communication and expression.

Two kinds of Roman script appeared on the grave when I sketched it in September 1991: one on a marker from the funeral home at the foot, another in two poems on pages laminated in plastic at the head under a wreath on a stand. The page of one of the poems is also imprinted with purple handprints, like those children make in school art classes. But the handprint also numbers among important African American emblematic signs, recalling Harriet Powers's quilt as well as other quilts and grave markers. The hand is a familiar motif on black and white graves; however, the flat, open handprint—as opposed to a sculpted or incised image of a closed hand pointing heavenward—seems more strongly African American in orientation. (A well-known open handprint appears on a marker in the Bowens family plot at Sunbury, Georgia; it has a piece of mirror embedded in the palm.) Other traditional components of the grave in Hattiesburg include arrangements of flowers at head and foot, the empty pot inset over the heart that also echoes a conduit pipe, and the "good" burial mound: that is, a carefully shaped mound clean of grass that rises crisply from the ground in a long oval.[27]

Although they also accord with European American literate conventions, the poems on the grave relate to African American commemorative practices that bestow honor and create material traces for toasts and orations, reinterpreting longstanding verbal art in the form of durable keepsakes. As the singer Bessie Jones says, writing formal keepsakes shows that a community is a sociable place where things are done right, not slapped down crudely or blurted out in haste. She recalled that before her conversion to Christianity, when she was "in the world,"

> Toasting was my business; I didn't want anybody to say a better toast than I said. I was writing up papers on them in those days. When you were living in a place where people were civilized and sociable and liked God's ways, sometimes they would come . . . and ask me to write a paper. Anything in this world that a person could name or say, I could make a paper for them and draw it out. Just like you'd say making a poem, I call it writing a paper. . . . And I'd want it to rhyme. (Jones 1983:136–137)

Also part of the ordinary visible fabric of street and community, yet also ambitiously transformative, is the sign on the facade of a storefront church in Memphis, Tennessee (fig. 7.13). The Roman print of the sign has been modified into pictographic narration. On the facade of a white church, wheels would probably seem out of place, evoking, if anything, thoughts of good barbecue. Here they recall wheels at the thresholds of residences, the Prayer Wheel turning in gospel songs, the ring shout, and the importance of omnidirectional knowledge, to name only a few of many possible associations.

Naming traditions are among the best-documented aspects of African American expressive culture. The everyday and the extraordinary intersect in well-chosen names. Nicknames and given names move through everyday events with their bearer, simultaneously endowing him or her with roots in the community and specialness, especially if the name is an unusual one.[28]

In recent decades, naming traditions have proliferated into diverse forms, with graffiti and car names among the most visible and graphic.[29]

> [C]hildren make constant use of symbols and marks which proclaim and are often part of their activities. When a gang writes: "Defenders Turf —Junkies keep out" on a supermarket wall, they are not merely labeling a wall that is already theirs, but actually claiming that wall as a boundary of their territory through the act of making a mark on it. (Kohl and Hinton 1972:116–117)

Both car naming and graffiti redistribute conventional literate-alphabetic message-bearing among the three functional groupings (see fig. 1.1); messages; tying or marking off places and spaces; and projecting identities on situations through emblems.

Graffiti has been reasonably well documented as a form of popular culture and of youth subcultural resistance, especially in urban areas since the late 1960s. Although stationary buildings and the intersections of gang zones and thoroughfares attract writers, the mobile venues of public trans-

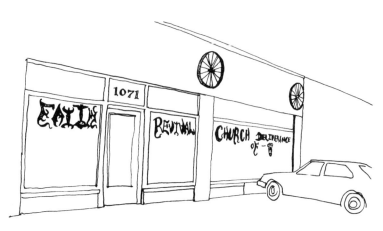

FIGURE 7.13. Church signs, Memphis, Tennessee.

portation were where writers perfected the daring, speed, and visibility that is their claim to fame. Since the flowering and demise of subway graffiti in New York as a darling of the art world has been discussed at length, I will look more closely at car names than at graffiti.[30] But two points about urban graffiti of the 1970s and 1980s, and what graffiti writing has in common with the naming of cars, are important. First, both sorts of writing are coded—they involve double voicing and double sight in that they purposefully address outsiders and insiders differently. Like nsibidi, vèvè, anaforuana, Arabic and esoteric Islamic scripts, and the indirection and double-entendre of African and African American verbal art, graffiti and car names promote multiple layers and sort readers according to the depth of their knowledge. This multiplicity does not mean that appeal to a broad audience is unimportant for graffiti writers. As researchers Martha Cooper and Henry Chalfont have pointed out, many writers dislike wildstyle lettering because it is difficult to read. For others, the illegibility reinforces their sense of having a secret society that is inaccessible to outsiders. A writer will therefore make a piece deliberately hard to read (fig. 7.14). There is pressure on him to make his style more complex, partly to enhance his reputation as a virtuoso and partly to discourage other writers from "biting" or stealing it (Cooper and Chalfont 1984:70–71).

Second, subway graffiti and car naming exemplify the vernacular principle that writing is *mobile*, and that ideally an individual should encompass as many important places with his or her mark as possible. Such writing, as well as preprinted logos from desirable products like Mercedes cars, fulfills the emblematic function of projecting identity: if the writer's

FIGURE 7.14. My tag "GrāZ" from plain to wildstyle (after Hager 1984:28–29).

reputation is not yet as great as the Mercedes, the logo asserts that it will be soon. In this aspect, car naming more closely resembles graffiti writers' *tags* than their more elaborate work on subway trains: both spread the writer's reputation though a name/emblem that is well chosen, recognizable to cognoscenti, and disruptive of staid social order. A recent trend involving named cars is cruising public streets with a megabase sound system.

Vehicle naming is widespread throughout the diaspora and is by no means limited to people of African descent. For example, James Kus researched Peruvian religious truck names (1979), a category that grew steadily in popularity from the 1950s to the late 1970s, with religious names like San Martin de Porres gradually displacing some of the names based on pop culture, greetings, and good luck wishes that had prevailed in the 1950s.[31] In Jamaica, David DeCamp found that naming vehicles was part of a more general pleasure in naming.

> Jamaicans enjoy naming things. The place names of Jamaica are a source of onomastic delight: e.g., *Maggoty Pen, Look Behind, Corn Puss Gap.* . . . Houses, trucks, sometimes bicycles are named. Most Jamaicans give a *"nom de plume"* when buying sweepstakes tickets, not primarily (as some have supposed) to avoid their creditors if they should win, but because they hope an original and appropriate *nom de plume* will bring

them luck and because thinking up a good name is part of the fun of the sweepstakes. Similarly the Jamaican cart owners explain their motives in naming are not only to identify their property, but also to bring good luck, to catch the eye of a prospective employer with a bright and unusual name, and to personalize the relationship between cart and owner. As one man put it, "I wouldn't paint only a number on a cart. I'd never get to know the cart then. A good cart deserves more." (1960:17)

Note that it takes an original and appropriate name to attract prospective customers, not just a description of the cart's service. DeCamp found that only seven out of ninety-three carts bore names describing their function (1960:16).

Some Jamaican handtrucks, handcarts, and snowball carts have fleet names (e.g., *Star of the East No. 5*) even though the fleet consists of only one cart. Others are political: *Martin Luther King* and *Lucy*, a black woman who applied to the University of Alabama (1960:19). Some allude to sweepstake winnings and place names, like *Detroit* and *New York*; and some voice proverbs and complaints: *I am Lonely, Lonely Boy, Leave Me Alone, Black and Hungry, Little Hero's Daily Bread* (1960:22).

The consistency of these names over time and distance is striking. The names of popular figures honored by name may change, but the basic sentiments do not. Jamaican hand carters are near the bottom of the economic scale; ownership of other kinds of vehicles is a mark of prosperity, at least of upward mobility. I recorded the names of transports on the roads in St. Lucia in July 1987:

Momma Wede	Honesty	Isaiah 45:22
Brown	By Grace	High Class
Brother B	Let Them Say the Eighth	Victor
Nations	Black Bullit	Smash
Fame	Lips Stict	Saltibus
St. Cristophe	Dr. Kay's True Colors	Cute
Hot Line	Praises	Phoenix
Surprise	Simple	Beatitude
St. Anthony	Red Angel	Get Inside
Interlect	T Son	Rough
Panic	Night Nurse	Soca
Get Through	Suger Daddy	Look at You
Let Me Be Me	Poe yie	D D Boy
Sugar Cock	Kit	Charlo
Fresh	Hardest Hard	Roots
Song of Angels	Papa Washn	Don't Panic
Safeway	Rejoice	Flash
Tete	Good News	Victory
Desert Hawk	Greetings	
Mr. Fox	Call on Me	

Transports are fixed-route vans that hold fourteen to sixteen people; they are privately owned by an individual or collective, and owning a transport is sign of financial well-being.

Many of these stylish names promote double readings through composite words, puns, and rhymes. Snapping with black style, they help to make transport travel a performance, a traveling road show that strives to tie up an islandwide reputation, aided by a big sound system, high speed, and good brakes.

Vehicle naming in the United States goes in and out of vogue. Names for cars proliferated in the 1950s during the heyday of the hotrod, and Jan Harold Brunvand collected a sizable list of teenagers' car names in Indiana and southern Michigan (1962). Brunvand does not report driver ethnicity, but some names on his list seem almost surely European American: for example, Constipated, Can't Pass a Thing; there is a notable lack of bathroom humor in African American naming and graffiti, though sexual innuendo abounds. However, other names hint at African American inspiration: Why Not, Snow Cone, Mo-Ta-Tion, Half Fast. Most are indeterminate: Tempest, Pink Dream, Six Pack, Moon Beam, One in a Million.

Something of the coded, layered side of car naming became apparent in my own neighborhood. In the fall of 1988 I noticed an increase of named cars with black drivers on the streets of New Haven, Connecticut. Most names were mounted on the car's front bumper on European-style license plates. Some cars also had names painted on the side on a racing stripe. VW Jettas, BMWs, Hyundais, and Volvos were popular, but many other kinds also had names. Usually the named cars were also customized (dressed) with features like skirts (enhancing solidity and closeness of the car body to the ground), clip-on wiper attachments, dark tinted glass, car bras (a black vinyl covering on the front of the hood), bubble window vents, and sometimes fancy paint.

Johnny Townsend, of Checkered Flag, Ltd., a customizing shop on my block, told me that he introduced current naming of cars to New Haven approximately two years before, after the manufacturer of custom plates sent his firm order forms. Checkered Flag was the only place in New Haven that sold the name plates. The order form offered several styles based on the shapes, sizes, and number of characters and numbers on various foreign license plates. German-style plates proved most popular, perhaps because they have twelve horizontal places for characters. English, Japanese, and other styles were also available. Most plates were white with black lettering, but some had red-and-black and some other two-color schemes.

Mr. Townsend also reported that people dressed to match each other and the car. "And that gold they're wearing is real; don't ask where it comes from." Many of the names came from rap music. Customers were *glad* when they came up with names someone else had used; they did not mind duplication. Instead, this seemed to confirm the name's high quality. Sometimes the duplication was not complete; spellings varied.

Although cars had never ceased having names altogether, the practice had slowed down considerably with the passing of the hotrod. But in the late 1980s car names were back, and this time the fashion clearly prevailed among young, affluent black drivers. As Johnny Townsend implied, the affluence that funded many of these four-wheel-drive vehicles, Volvos, and BMWs was widely attributed to a burgeoning market in crack cocaine.

By 1990 the style in automobile attire had changed; naming was out, except for vanity license plates. I compiled the following names in 1988 from cars I observed and those that obtained plates from Checkered Flag.

Dollar-Bill	Tee's Sentra	Antoinete
Fel's 224	Poison	Lisa-Lisa
Encst	Love-Bones 4	Iron Mike
I'm Blazzin	Beanie	Just Chillin
Cressida	Who's 1200	##/H-Mal
I Love Rose	Jus Me I	L8T 4-Diane
Beme II Cool	Baby Lincln	Yeah Boyee
2 Damn Hype	Ree-Se	Yo Wiz
Dee & Delisa	They Caught	Polo
True Rican	Don Man	Booes-Booes
Blue Room	1 Tuf Jet	(3) Rock Possie
Mad! Max!	Wise	Nike Edition
Shave 1	Goldn Looks	Nice-N-Slow
Power Move	Seekin' Who?	Guy-Swift
Redbone	Ms. Peach	Her-Volvo
Zoom X I Mark	Suave'	Bankroll
Tonya Gerl	Sim N Effect	Flack 9
Rippen Rebel	The Hard Way	No Static
What Ever	Juicy	Reach-Tree
446-FTE	Raggamuffin	China-Rabbit
Hardbody	Get Busy CB	Stupid Deff
Diamond Boys	Dark & Lovely	Eizotic
Um Um Um	Ask Ya Girl	I-Love-It
Val's Ville	L.A.'s Baby Toy	The Strength
Mike Nice	U Got 2 Chill	Chief Rocker
Mika-Jr-Toy	Keisha's Mom	Jazzy Jay
Why-You-Looking	Unique I	Fatal Beauty
Big Mel-15	Red Hot	Sweet Red
(2) Excel-Ent	Bad News	Larry-Love
Tyrell's 5-10	Ojetula	Mr. Irie
3-Dollars	Why You Looken	Black Flag
Too Sweet	The Vapors	Special-K
Just Got Paid	One And Only	Ezol-E
Quiet Cool	Jonesy 1	Gail-Sewell
The Vapor's	Don't Be Cruel	Mr. Scorpio
The Toy	Respect It	Red Alert
Chaka Zulu	Raw	Ruthless
Exclusive	Loverboy Ken	Lady-G
Lady Dee	Big Daddy-G	On The Run
Illusion	Kkaos	Lethal
Ms. Hamilt N	Black-Out	Doxxy G
Zulu Witch	Blazin'	Lonely Heart
Starr's Bmer	Night Nurse	On A Mission ++
Kelley-Girl	Dark-Lovely	Damage-Inc
Giddy Up Pony	Blazing One	Living Large
Moe Loves Toy	Respect	Ms. Pulsar
Blue Angel	I.N. 1000000	Right Stuff
Dope-Aint It	Move Dammit	Red-Alert

Ant Love	Ina 1000000	777 B-MI
Nite-N-Day	Spectrum	(2) Raw Attitude
Mythological	Nasty Jetta	Strictly Biz
Valerie	Cupie-J No. 1	World-Wide
Raga-Muffin	Co-In Effect	
The Queen	Squeaky	

Although they are rooted in black vernacular relationships with personal names, car names are *written*, and they depend on visibility for effectiveness. They are *not* "oral" (even "residually"), despite the fact that conventional literate ideology urges the label "oral" on any inscribing activity that so boisterously overruns straightforward explicitness and one-to-one referentiality. Vehicle naming shares the aptness of good talk but roves with the vehicle across space, foregrounding the namer-driver's skill along the way. Vehicle names appeal primarily to the eye, for by choice they are usually more succinct than spoken wordplay. This succinctness falls as close to emblems and logos in function as it does to message-bearing script, and may draw as much on west and central African resources in the form of emblems as on linear scripts. David Dalby has written suggestively:

> [A] vestige of the earlier tradition [of graphic symbols] appears to be preserved in the painting of propitiary and aphoristic "slogans" on motor vehicles and canoes in West Africa: to-day the Roman script is normally used for this purpose, in contrast to the indigenous symbols which have been traditionally carved on canoes. (1968:196n)

Certainly the succinctness of the names occupies the same border zone between proverbs and graphic and material signs that also comes into play in the names and phrases associated with of African textile motifs, like those of the Fon and Ashanti (see Nketia 1972).

The relationship between names, slogans, and emblems is obvious. But there are other ways of using inscription to regularize and seal a certain set of important relationships; for example, by diagramming the attributes of a lwa around a centerpost or by projecting territorial ambitions through graffiti tags. Most important, one can demonstrate a regularized relationship or given state of being by *shaping* writing, especially into a square or circle. This procedure is central in the construction of Islamic talismans, but it also occurs in North America in settings that have not attracted much attention. Charles Williams of Arkansas wrote an autobiography, which was included with his own spelling and punctuation among the FWP narratives.

My Education

> My mother carried me to six grade and turned me loose. One month before she did, she carried me to Teacher. . . . Sooner we got reddy Mama say: "Jump up, Chas., behimb me on this horse and lets get going. She had those 6 readers in her purse. Started toward ol school howse. I jump down first and help Mama down. I hitch her horse while she was gone in to teach right now. I burges in with a smile. Mama then mence (com-

mence) tell teach the cause of her errance (errand). . . . She hand teach those six book. Continue: I carry my onliest boy to sixth grade. I got a job to attend to and must get to it; raily got to carry own." . . . I want to see you start on him and carry him through his six book." They set me tween them and started. Went through first just like taking candy from infant. Started in alferbits from A B C. Me, I tell her I on't know them that way, No Mam. "Well", speake up the teach, "lest see ef you cin say them back words (backword). I started them A B C back words and went strait ahead. When finish she say: "Throught you couln say them stright erlong." I told her it ent no telling about me, what I do next, teacher. "Bleeve that, Chas.," she reply. (Rawick 1979 vol. 1:191–192)

In his life story Charles Williams repeatedly refers to his mother's strong character and her cowhide whip. Eventually, as if to sum up his parents' influence and take its measure, Williams creates a package that encompasses these formative relationships, a kind of talisman of letters and punctuation.[32]

> One woman did not born the only sharp child.
> M. M. W. M. C.
> M. F. W. M. S.
> C. H. W. M. C.
> My Mother Was My Captain
> My Father Was My Sergeant
> Cow Hide Was My Corrector-C
> (Rawick 1979, vol. 1:198)

In addition, Williams seems to have used periods percussively, as does Claude Davis, whose work I discuss shortly. A similar squaring occurs in an inscription I photographed on the wall of an abandoned building in Hattiesburg, Mississippi, amid gang signs: "two strong, two be, four gotten"; and recall the four-square Shaker movements of Rebecca Cox Jackson. Tying and circumambulation delimit emblematic boundaries. One part of the African American vernacular repertoire of inscription ties into the next, full circle.

Wordplay and double-entendre through reconfigured punctuation and spelling most often occur in texts composed by African Americans in connection with cultural and personal identities. Reconfigured punctuation and spelling create a visual contrast with other parts of the text, differentiating ideas and portions of text that the author identifies as markedly African American and playing with the reader's conventional expectations. Examples are the spellings AFRICA, AFRIKA, AFREEKA, and AFREEKID, a retailer in New York City that sells children's clothing from AFREELAND.

Like the Jes-Us church sign and objects assemblages, these reconfigurations result in a both/and doubling, not an either/or dichotomy. Like car names and tags, this type of wordplay depends on the visual channel and involves double sight in the same way that other visual puns do, through oscillating meanings.

Script and Signs on Home Ground

In closing this chapter and this book on African American vernacular signs and writing, I turn to two residences and extend the discussion in chapter 4, which dealt with one network of signs across a number of different sites. Here, I want to indicate some of the ways that individuals attune conventional literacy and vernacular practices to particular circumstances. Neither of the people whose surroundings I discuss are typical or representative of African Americans. What they share with each other, and many other African Americans, is a thorough, tacit understanding of a traditional material and graphic repertoire of signs, and the aesthetic and philosophical background necessary to render these signs fresh and emergent yet readable to passersby.

Both sites combine Roman script messages with vernacular signs, an advantage because passersby, and would-be visitors and intruders, are not all equally well grounded in both systems. Like many other cases I have discussed, the two systems complement each other, but the vernacular signs are broader in scope in that they classify and metacomment on the Roman script messages.

CLAUDE DAVIS

Claude Davis grew up in an orphanage in southern Alabama and was homeless and about fifty years old when I met him in November 1989. The meeting came about because an article appeared in the *Chattanooga Times* reporting that "mysterious hieroglyphics" were appearing along the Ridge Cut, the cleft where Interstate 24 crosses Missionary Ridge, an Appalachian foothill that bisects Chattanooga. I called the reporter, and he took me to see Mr. Davis. What the reporter took for mysterious hieroglyphics were initials that Mr. Davis had worked into an emblem and painted on trees around the site below the overpass that Mr. Davis had selected as his home. Although this area backed onto a residential neighborhood, no one noticed Mr. Davis's camp until November when the leaves fell off the thick vines that had hidden it from view. At last a neighbor noticed Mr. Davis and called the police, who called social services. Soon afterward Mr. Davis disappeared.

In common with many other writers, Mr. Davis felt called to a special mission. He planned to construct a jail under the highway, round up Chattanooga's criminals, and keep the peace. To this end he had laid a foundation and accumulated lumber, a wheelbarrow, and heaps of aluminum cans that netted several hundred dollars when Mr. Davis and a social worker later sold them at a recycling center.

Claude Davis's uses of script illustrate the interplay of narrative, tying, and emblemizing functions in the voice of one person. As I have already mentioned, Mr. Davis tied/enclosed his site with signs, deploying his mark as an assertion over territory, much as graffiti writers make spaces their own through tags. He also labeled all items on the site with his emblem and occasionally with a few lines about the item's future use (fig. 7.15).

FIGURE 7.15. Wheelbarrow, Claude Davis.

In addition, Mr. Davis painted longer narratives along the sides and
supporting beams of the highway overpass (fig. 7.16). He explained to me
that the dots he painted between words and letters do not mark the end of
a sentence. Instead, they are like this: he struck his fist into the palm of his
other hand—Whomp! Dots between letters show that the passage is important and that it should be read in a measured, percussive way, stressing
each sound in turn.

The longest piece Claude Davis wrote was his autobiography (fig.
7.17). He used red and blue enamel on the back of a road sign that measured about four feet square. Because Mr. Davis did not use conventional
spacing and punctuation, this sign contributed to the mistaken impression
that his writing was mysterious. But Davis was not writing in an unknown tongue, nor did he mention God, or supernatural agency, or special
or deep knowledge of any kind. He was an easy figure to exoticize; one
photo in the newspaper showed Mr. Davis with a paintbrush inserted in
his mouth, handle extended. My overwrought interpretation of this behavior was that Mr. Davis was showing the camera that the paintbrush

FIGURE 7.16. Writing on highway overpass, Claude Davis.

was an extension of his tongue. Later, when I asked him if my interpretation was correct, he was clearly amused. He replied, "You can say that if you want to, but all I was trying to do was keep the brush from getting rain and dirt on it. It's muddy out here. There's no place to put the brush down while I'm working."

Although most people would probably find him peculiar at first encounter, Mr. Davis presented himself as a practical man with a social mission, albeit one who was understandably leery of the police and the helping professions. He read his autobiography aloud matter-of-factly, without difficulty, beginning with his childhood, the orphanage, his operation for a digestive complaint, and his plans for the jail. When he vacated his camp beneath the underpass he made it clear that he did not want to be followed.

RUBY GILMORE

Ruby Gilmore is a retired city employee and a widow who lives in a small city in southeastern Mississippi. She reads the newspaper every day; she attended school through the eighth grade. Her home, a bungalow fully paid for by herself and her husband, formerly had a well-tended lawn and flowerbeds. But in the decade since her husband's death it has become the home base for her recycling business and is filled with building supplies, scrap metal, tools, and countless odds and ends.

Although she receives social security payments and a small pension, Mrs. Gilmore arises at four o'clock in the morning, rain or shine, to drive through her city's residential neighborhoods ahead of the official garbage

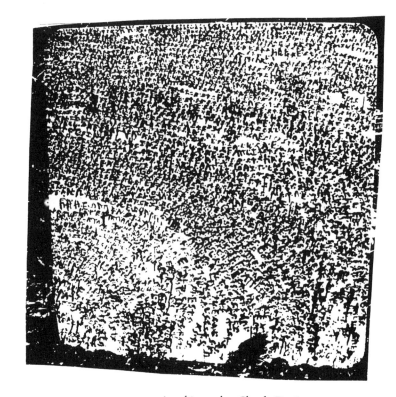

FIGURE 7.17. Autobiography, Claude Davis.

truck. She gathers up aluminum, glass, plastic, and sometimes whole bags of refuse if they look promising. When her white Pinto is loaded to capacity, with bags tied to hood, trunk, and roof, she returns to her front yard to sort what she has collected and sell it to a scrap dealer a few blocks from her home. This routine places a great strain on her arthritic joints, but she refuses to rest until she has paid off the medical bills accumulated by her late grandson.

Ruby Gilmore worries a great deal about thieves. Her collectibles have tempted neighborhood children and teens. On Sunday, Mrs. Gilmore breaks her cycle of work with a day in church, and it is on Sunday that she especially worries about thieves, because on that day the bootlegger who lives a few doors down her block does his best business, and he has been known to take objects like tools and lumber in trade for liquor.

After her live watchdog was poisoned, Mrs. Gilmore built her fence to greater height and began to protect her property against intruders. She mounted a stuffed watchdog (chapter 4) on the roof of her carport, and placed other material signs at intervals: plastic red peppers and an orange, scowling jack o'lantern beside the front porch, a mirror on the back wall of the house, and several ensembles that combined found objects with found writing.

The particular ensembles around Mrs. Gilmore's home change fairly

FIGURE 7.18. Arrangement in window, Ruby Gilmore.

often, depending on what she finds, what she sells, and what she decides to shift to a different location. Regardless of their changing content, though, the ensembles always seem to have one thing in common: they combine a negative admonition in Roman print—No Trespassing, No Hustling, Keep Out, No Parking—with a positive message that God and his deputies are watching the house. This latter message comes through a variety of material signs: the stuffed dog, a china collie on the ground beside the mailbox, shells shaped like ears, white things that recall grave decorations, a plastic duck with its eye on the street, pipes, twine tied around the mailbox and gate even in places that do not need shoring up, red wheels, an open wheel on a fencepost.

The sketches show three of Mrs. Gilmore's arrangements. In figure 7.18, a coat hanger—a proxy for the shoulders of a person—hangs alongside a No Hustling sign on a window of her house. At other times Mrs. Gilmore has used a rubber Frankenstein mask and a paper skeleton in the same location.

In the posted sign arrangement (fig. 7.19), Mrs. Gilmore shows that her house is posted. She striped the post with the warning/sight color, blue, and inserted a four-eyes clock at the base. Mrs. Gilmore also cut a curved sword with a crosslike hilt out of plywood and fixed it to the post. This ensemble faces the street.

The path to Gilmore's door has a sign that reads "Danger Do Not Enter" and warns that "treadles damage tires" (fig. 7.20). However, the door is

FIGURE 7.19. (*left*) Posted sign, Ruby Gilmore.
FIGURE 7.20. (*right*) No Parking and other warning signs, Ruby Gilmore.

many feet away from the street, there is nowhere nearby to park, and certainly the street and yard contain no treadles. This seeming anomaly points up one of the most interesting things about Mrs. Gilmore's use of Roman script signs: she does not demand an exact fit between the literal message on the sign and its reading in context; in other words, she uses the Roman alphabet in an almost *semasiographic* manner, leaving ample room for interpretation and indirection. The key word and idea in all these signs is *No!*: Mrs. Gilmore is worried about thieves, not hustling, or speeding cars, or illegal parking. The signs are emblems as much as messages, and together they protectively seal or tie the house.

I asked Mrs. Gilmore if she thought her post and dogs would really deter thieves. "No," she said, "but the most important thing about these signs is that they tell the thief what kind of person's house they are breaking into. Then they know they better watch out."

*T*he work of Claude Davis and Ruby Gilmore is not unique; many homeowners make similar arrangements. Efforts like these are part of the everyday visible fabric of script and graphic practice that crests from time to time in the more elaborate vision of a James Hampton or Z. B. Armstrong. But even when vernacular values and practices do not extend to script itself, they still can organize approaches to reading, the artifacts of literacy, and narratives.

As I mentioned in the preface, I initially planned to focus narrowly on literacy and graphic practice in one community or among a cohesive group of people. However, I soon realized that some of the practices I was encountering seemed disjointed and ahistorical unless they were placed against a larger background. As I began to explore this background it, in turn, began to expand. I therefore selected one interaction—one kind of interference pattern—and attempted to trace it wherever it led across time, terrain, and topic. I hope this work will provide a beginning for more detailed research on specific cases in the future.

Along the way I have pursued three aims. First, I have sought to explore a way of investigating African and African American culture and history that responds to vast resources and recurring patterns without imposing false closure or ruling out profound disjunctures. Second, my intent has been to provide a context for better understanding of certain African American activities, particularly protective, therapeutic, and performance-oriented approaches to reading, writing, and the artifacts of literacy; and to call into question the descriptive adequacy of the terms "oral" and "literate" in accounts of these and other African American activities. Finally, I have tried to comment on the study of literacies and graphic systems by showing a willingness to look at signs and practices that fall outside conventional rubrics of literacy. I think this flexible attitude is essential, given the hierarchical assumptions built into the very tools with which we do our work.

Notes

1 INTRODUCTION

1. One might call this combined registering and generating an instance of both/and as opposed to either/or organization. Robert Farris Thompson views the both/and form of organization as a crucial aesthetic principle in African and African American expressive culture. Both/and organization allows for, even encourages, the unexpected. It characterizes repetitions and differentiations of motifs in the paintings of Mbute women in Zaire (Thompson 1983), rhythmized Mande and Afro-Brazilian strip textiles (Thompson 1983:195–222), African American traditional quilts (Thompson 1983, Wahlman and Scully 1983, Leon 1987), as well as offbeat phrasing and staggered entry in music (Waterman 1952). On a broader level of abstraction, Bateson (1972:61–72) proposed that both/and complementarity among unlike elements is one of two main patterns of relationship that emerge from sustained intercultural or internal differentiation. Complementary relations emerge when relatively evenly matched parties contribute in different but ultimately balanced ways to a dynamic equilibrium that neither party could sustain independently. The other pattern, either/or organization, Bateson calls schismogenesis: a divisive trajectory that can escalate indefinitely if parties are evenly matched. Schismogenesis patterns characterize global arms races as well as interpersonal disputes. Aesthetically and philosophically, therefore, the both/and form of organization is a diagram for livability and mutually enhancing differences-that-make-a-difference.

2. The interplay between graphic and literate practices takes place within a vastly complicated network that includes such events themselves and their subsequent "sinking" into various socially and culturally organized accounts.

My focus should not be confused with symbolic accounts that treat recurring contrasts (black/white, male/female) as keys to explaining a culture as a whole.

3. See Volosinov's critique of the Romantic "individual subjectivist" theory of expression as "something which, having . . . taken shape in the psyche of an individual, is outwardly objectified for others with the help of external signs of some kind" (1986:84). This statement implies that "all the creative and organizing forces of expression are within. Everything outer is merely passive material for manipulation by the inner element" (1986:85). Literate ideology has tended to follow the subjectivist paradigm in assuming that script and print are passive materials that merely represent the individualistic expressions of inner psyches. The alternative that Volosinov espouses—and I depend on here—begins with the recognition that the idea of a gap between a lively inner psyche and an outside world of passive material is untenable.

4. The nonconventional or exceptional nature of these practices is of course recognized, constituted, and sustained by the practitioners. The practices' extraordinary status serves to foreground them, making them forceful components of the contexts in which they occur.

5. For the history of and critical thinking about African American community education, schooling, and literacy, see Du Bois (1973), Morris (1982), Bullock (1970), Webber (1978), Woodson (1915), and Anderson (1988).

There is, of course, an extensive literature on literacy education throughout the diaspora, much of it in the form of UNESCO reports. There is also a large literature on literacy as a tool for political empowerment, notably works by Paulo Freire (1970) and his followers. In the United States, literacy among African Americans is usually approached from one or more of five perspectives: (1) as part of the general commentary on adult American illiteracy and remediation (Hunter & Harmon 1979); (2) the history of African American education and differential access to schooling (Morris 1981; Webber 1978; Anderson 1988; Cornelius 1983, 1991); (3) explanations of minority school failure (Ogbu 1978, 1991; Heath 1984); (4) studies of the effects of Black English Vernacular (BEV) speech patterns on student efforts to learn to read (see note 9); and (5) literary studies. Only the latter two perspectives begin with premises about what African Americans *have*, rather than what they lack. Even so, the issue of BEV rarely arises in relation to literacy unless reading difficulties are also at issue. And literary criticism usually treats reading and writing as way stations on the road to artistry.

Missing are investigations of the relation of literacy to African American knowledge systems. An excellent study of literacy in this vein is Joanne Rappaport's account of literacy, myth, and history among the Paez of Colombia (1987). Also missing—probably because of the assumption that literacy automatically eclipses or indelibly alters modes of communication that predate its incursion—are studies that attend to interactions of alternative graphic practices with conventional literacy, my focus in this book.

Jack Goody's paper on the role of literacy in the 1835 Bahia slave revolt (1986) is one exception. He theorizes that the way a group of Yoruba Muslim slaves organized the revolt stemmed in large part from their familiarity with alphabetic Arabic literacy and participation in a "religion of the book." According to him, this feature of their Muslim background endowed the rebels with communicative and organizational abilities that slaves captured from "preliterate" societies lacked. However, as João José Reis has shown, the 1835 revolt was not a novel event spurred by literacy but one of a series of slave revolts and food riots extending over a twenty-year period (1982, 1993). Reis, Victor

Monteil (1967 a and b), and Rolf Reichart (1967) discuss literate skills and paraphernalia in the revolt without ascribing a causal role to them.

6. I agree with Vé Vé Clark's assessment summarized in the passage quoted in this note. (For present purposes, read "Black Atlantic" in place of "Third World.")

> Euro-American measurements of African culture conspicuously start without the Third World. On a scale that mixes classical Greece and the Industrial Revolution in one grand, illogical shock, Third World cultures are omitted from the yardstick, labeled "pre-logical," "pre-industrial," "pre-literate" in one breath. This situation will not do for an informed international readership; this type of ignorance makes a mockery of Euro-American advances and destroys the possibilities of transmitting African and Afro-American knowledge to others. (Clark 1984:15)

7. Among scholars, no easy strategies seem to exist to get on with the study of literacy as a clearly bounded topic. The major debate of the 1980s in literacy research concerned whether or not any autonomous attributes or cognitive consequences of literacy exist (cf. Olson 1977), independent of specific cultural conditions. Eric Havelock (1963, 1986) has been the major proponent of the argument that writing "restructures consciousness" and was responsible for the rise of civilization in Greece and ultimately in western Europe. Havelock's opinions provide the foundation of the "autonomous model" (Street 1984, 1993) of literacy, propounded by Ong (1982), Goody and Watt (1963), Goody (1977, 1987), and Olson (1989). See Andersen (1989) and Halverson (1992) for searching critiques of Havelock's views on literacy and his interpretation of Greek sources. A strong case can be made that literacy played a negligible role in setting the Greek course toward democracy and speculative thought—the qualities upon which the case for autonomous literacy and predictable cognitive consequences rests, and the qualities that predicate claims for Western superiority.

To assume that literacy comprises a stable and autonomous set of properties consistent with evolutionary progression (see critiques in Frake 1983 and Street 1984) also implies referencing cultures and persons as voids that reading and writing fill up like water in a bucket. The fact that people so labeled may share this deficit view of themselves does not validate the assumption, but underscores the fact that ideas about literacy are socially organized and culturally potent, carrying with them (like other sociocultural assumptions) the potential to continually reconstitute their own putative "naturalness," while undermining conditions in which participants in the process can be articulate about its dynamics (McDermott 1987; Foucault 1971, 1973; Haraway 1989).

One response to recent debates has been increasing particularism in literacy research. A growing literature describes particular literacies and examines relations among literacies, special-purpose scripts, and local value systems around the world (Basso and Anderson 1973; Janzen 1985; Kulick and Stroud 1990; Rappaport 1987; Bledsoe and Robey 1986; Perrin 1986). However, there have been few studies of literate and graphic traditions among people of African descent or their encounters with European and European American assumptions about alphabetic literacy.

8. For alternative views, see Bernal (1987), James (1954), Snowden (1983, 1970), and Diop (1974, 1978). Martin Bernal's picture of mobility in the an-

cient Mediterranean accords with the views of a number of scholars of writing systems who reject the simplistic idea of a "pure" Greek "invention" of the alphabet; they propose instead complex relations among Phoenician script, which was consonantal and Semitic, Egyptian syllabaries, from which the Phoenicians adopted some structural features, and Greek syllabaries, which may have been largely moribund when Greek traders brought knowlege of Phoenician script home with them. For critical assessments and nontechnical summaries of this literature, see DeFrancis (1989:174 181) and Coulmas 1989:158–167).

9. The underlying premise of interference, as I use the term, is Gregory Bateson's claim that in social interaction "longer cycles will always be enlarged or repeated reflections of pattern contained in the fine detail" (1971:33; see also Bredo et al. 1990). In this sense interference is a jagged edge of systemic conflict, bridged or left hanging, that is disclosed in details that unfold in feed-back-feedforward relation to longer temporal cycles.

I also draw on linguistic research on interference between European American Standard and Black English Vernacular (Dillard 1972; Piestrup 1973; Melmed 1973; Stewart 1975). Most of this research is part of the effort to describe and remediate difficulties that some black children, often from inner cities, experience in learning to read in school. In school reading lessons, interference is said to occur when children stumble over sounds, grammar, and school-prescribed semantic interpretations. Linguistic interference thus has physical symptoms—hesitation, repetition and reformulation, stuttering, silence—that may even be inaccurately labeled learning disabilities (McDermott 1987).

Such symptoms of interference mark a moment in which conflict between two (or more) linguistic and cultural knowledge systems comes to the cognitive surface and to the foreground of a contextual event. This characterization does not mean that the knowledge systems involved are totally different or discordant, merely that they differ *in some ways* that *become relevant* at particular moments. The competitive setting of reading instruction in U.S. schools spotlights just such symptoms and moments, inserting tensions into operations of literate coding and decoding that, demonstrably, learners in other sociocultural settings can master readily, even when the writing system they are learning bears a more complex relation to spoken sound than the Roman alphabet does (see Conklin 1949; McDermott n.d.; Scribner and Cole 1981).

In African American history, schooling is one of the more recent sites where linguistic interference has emerged from cultural and communicative conflicts. John Szwed has drawn my attention to two more instances. Stuttering signals interference in African American sung sermon performance— when the voice of the Spirit interfers with and takes over the ordinary speaking voice of the preacher. More akin to conflicts in classrooms are the accounts of "speech defects" in antebellum advertisements for escaped slaves and reports of master-slave communication; see the survey of slave resistance in eighteenth-century Virginia by Gerald W. Mullin (1972:98–103). Szwed suggests (personal communication June 1988) that this stuttering could be interference between the master's speech and the slave's, adding weight to the evidence for some form of creole language on the plantations (see Dillard 1972:73–113). More broadly, such moments of interference (in)articulated the larger circuits of interpersonal conflict, power imbalance, and cultural tension that pressed in on master-slave encounters. Resolving such systemic pathology involves lifting the deep grounds of paradox to consciousness and the surfaces of discourse (Bateson 1972:309–339). Thus one wonders if during the plantation era there might not have been more stutterers among the group of slaves who were not resigned, who struggled to contain the impulse to speak out, and who actively contemplated rebellion or flight. One wonders, too, whether some found a cure for stuttering in successful escape. Double consciousness and double voicing arose as concepts that describe such articulations of cultural and interpersonal tensions, and thus work toward transforming interference into a new order.

10. See Vygotsky (1978,1986), Wertsch (1991), Lave (1988), Scribner and Cole (1981), Street (1984), and Varenne and McDermott (1986).

11. For example, see Lehiste (1988) and Hagège (1990:16–26).

12. The main primary sources I use are Rawick (1972, 1977), Hyatt (1970–1978), and autobiographies and memoirs cited as they occur. For critical guidance to these sources, see Yetman (1967), Blassingame (1975), and Perdue (1976:xi–xiv).

2 CREOLIZATION, DOUBLE VOICING, DOUBLE VISION

1. See Loretto Todd (1974) for an introduction to creole languages and linguistics. Important anthologies and surveys include Hymes (1971), Holm (1988, 1989), and Mufwene (1993).

2. Drummond's influential article (1980), "The Cultural Continuum: A Theory of Intersystems," is based on the multiethnic situation in Guyana and aspects of the linguist Derek Bickerton's *Dynamics of a Creole System* (1975). I find the term "intersystems" helpful, but "continuum" seems too rigid to fit the phenomena that Drummond describes. Williams (1991) has also critiqued the political weaknesses that render this model inadequate to explain power imbalances. The four most important implications of this model for this book are: (1) that there are cognitive and social limits on the modes of participation available to people at any given time; (2) that participants oscillate within a given set of limits or, as cues and conditions change, shift to a different context of participation entirely; (3) that participants understand a wider range of intersystemic behavior than they personally command (i.e., they can understand but not necessarily speak most of the range of creole language in the society); and (4) that this variability and adaptability is not exceptional, or a characteristic of atypical societies, but an underlying uniformity that crosscuts ethnic and cultural typologies. These implications leave us with culture theorized not as an entity (or singular system of "symbols and meanings" packaged by one of the various ethnic groups in a plural society) but as "the universal cultural formulation of systems of essential similarity and difference" (Drummond 1980:355). Since Drummond's article appeared, other anthropologists, including Hannerz (1987), have begun to see creolization across a broad front of change and multicultural juxtapositions as the economic world system closes in on particular locales throughout the so-called Third World.

3. These issues, especially that of "the border"—racial, linguistic, gendered, cultural, economic, geographic—are crucial in reconceptualizing classifications like "minority" and "the Other" that have become incorporated into marginalizing discourses (see Spillers 1991 and Gilroy 1991, among many others). Creolization represents only one of a number of vocabularies for talking about border-crossing and cultural process. Overall it may not even be the best. Nevertheless, it is especially appropriate here for three reasons: 1) much of my ethnographic data comes from portions of the southern United States

that have had long-term relationships to Africa and the West Indies; (2) interviews with former slaves also focus on this region, thus permitting a discussion with greater temporal depth; and (3) creolization offers concepts such as the linguistic calque and loan-translation that fit some of the specific cases I discuss later.

A contextual account of literacies needs to be accountable to situations like those that creolization addresses. Part of this shift of outlook means seeing humans as engaged in a battle to render livable stabilities against a background of constant motion, rather than taking the view, prevalent in anthropology, that "cultures" are stable and discrete entities that change from time to time or disappear.

4. A few African Americanist ethnographers and historians who mention double systems are Herskovits (1941), Abrahams (1983), Abrahams and Szwed (1983), Bastide (1978), Reisman (1970), Wilson (1969), Wilson (1973), and Brathwaite (1971). These authors differ among themselves, but it is worth noting that none are preoccupied with double systems in the semiotic sense of Barthes (1983:290–292) and other investigators concerned with social and linguistic "codes," following Saussure (1983). Saussure's distinction between *langue* and *parole* implies incommensurable "logical" and "natural" systems, *langue* and *parole*, context-independence and context-dependence. In contrast, these authors discuss double systems that are contextual on both "sides" of ascribed pairings and emerge in particular conditions of cultural contact. What seems "European" in one context may seem "African" in another. The African Americanist perspective is perhaps more akin to Bateson's notion of "double description" (taken up by the French theorists Deleuze and Guattari as the ever-mobile "nomadology" of "power word" and "rhisome" [1987]) in which map and territory, abstraction and actual event are heuristically distinguishable yet at the same time intimately intertwined.

5. This interpretation is based on the detailed account of the Jombee Dance in Dobbin (1986).

6. On style and subculture, see Hebdige (1978) and Willis (1977). Of course African Americans have contributed richly to the history of fashion, including twentieth-century apparel such as the swinging beaded Charleston flapper dress, the zoot suit, and the Ivy League look of the 1950s (Schwartz 1963). Clothing styles such as these often have linguistic correlatives: rap music terms and intonation patterns for the young man at the mall, hipster jive for the zoot suit wearers of an earlier generation (see Mezzrow and Wolfe 1946:215–223, 354–360; Burley 1944, 1973). From time to time someone points out that these verbal styles, which have been emanating from black neighborhoods into mainstream popular culture throughout the century, contrast with "bookish" literacy-associated language just as the clothing of the speakers has tested the patience of school authorities.

7. These aesthetic contributions may include high affect color, offbeat phrasing (R. F. Thompson, lectures, Yale University, 1986–91) and use of cloth as "text" or message-bearing medium (see Borgatti 1983).

8. See Mitchell-Kernan (1972), among others.

9. A classic novel of double voicing and double consciousness is Ralph Ellison's *Invisible Man*. Many authors refer to double-voiced strategies to hide meanings from whites. In literature, see Petesch (1989); in spirituals, see Fisher (1953), Ahlo (1976:118–121), and Walker (1979); regarding sex, see Guy Johnson (1927–28) on double meaning in the blues. On the other hand, as the singer Bessie Jones points out, whites have often failed to understand

what blacks considered obvious. For example, white audiences did not grasp the pointed message in the refrain of a song performed by the Sea Island Singers, "Throw em/me anywhere Lord in that old field." Jones explains in her autobiography (1983:48–49) that this line refers to the disrespectful treatment that deceased slaves received from masters who cast their bodies aside like trash and refused to give survivors the time and land required for proper funerals. Albert Raboteau stresses that it would be odd if spirituals did not communicate on more than one level of meaning, for, after all, veiled comment and social criticism are important aspects of West African, Central African, and African American verbal art (1978:249). Roger Abrahams reminds us that African American performers know and plan for the fact that they may be playing to two audiences simultaneously (Abrahams 1992:155–157).

Recently, efforts to found an African American literary theory based in black vernacular have included double voicing and other doubling patterns; see Gates (1988) and Baker (1987). Two fertile essays by Vé Vé Clark (1984, 1991) look to graphic practices and ritual for vernacular models, rather than—or in addition to—the oral-literary and musical forms (toasts, blues) that Gates and Baker use to ground their theories. Urging "diaspora literacy" that includes double- structures but moves beyond them, Clark outlines a "mythical theory of textual relationships" called "*marasa* consciousness," based on the Haitian Vodou vèvè for the divine twins who created the world in the Fon/Ewe tradition of Dahomey.

10. For example, on Du Bois's ideas of double consciousness, see Bruce (1989:204–217).

11. For example, on indirection, see Herskovits (1958:154–158) for comparisons with African behavior; see also Reisman (1970) and Williams (1987).

The Rev. I. E. Lowery's *Life on the Old Plantation in Ante-Bellum Days or A Story Based on Facts* is one of the most interesting instances that I have encountered of a black author infusing double-entendre throughout a text addressed primarily to white readers (1911).

12. See Robert Hemenway's comments on the visualness of Hurston's writing in his introduction to the second edition of *Dust Tracks on a Road*: "In short, one *sees* Hurston's prose. One also hears it, smells it, and touches it, but primarily one sees it. As she put it, 'I am so visual minded that all the other senses induce pictures in me'"(1984:xxxvi).

13. The "party line" of conventional literacy theorizing would probably be that Brathwaite recounts and Hurston recreates "orality." I assess this viewpoint in subsequent chapters.

14. The following spell is one example of conjuring with a foot track.

Whut tuh do wit chure foot track? . . . Yo' take dat left foot track up an' yo' take an' seal it up in a envelope. An . . . writ de person's name on dat envelope an' jes' below it chew take [write] de Lord's Prayer. . . An' yo' go tuh de rivah an' yo' take it . . . turn backwards an' throw it ovah yore [left] shoulder . . . an' dey will go in de direction dat gone. (Hyatt 1970–78, vol. 2:1721)

15. Four-eyed and two-headed (or even three-headed, for a reputedly top-notch clairvoyant) are recurring attributes around the diaspora. Robert W. Pelton says a master houngan in Haitian Vodou must be "quattre yeux" (1972:70, 109). In Jamaica, the term is *foyeyed* (Williams 1934:160). In Guyana an obeah-related treatment for male genital disorders involves beating the afflicted part with a live "four-eyes fish (*anableps tetrophthalmus*)

until the fish dies" (Campbell n.d.: 17). Four-eyes is also the name of a string figure in Sierra Leone (Hornell 1928:8). By crossover association, Gemini, the twins, doubling heads and eyes, are also linked to special powers of perception (Riva 1974:14). The idea of special sight is also common, even without mention of extra eyes. Sometimes blue or gray eyes signal this capacity (Puckett 1926:456). A New Orleans spiritual doctor told Harry Middleton Hyatt in the 1930s, "[Y]ou must have the *spiritual sight* and know what the *immaterial sight* is—you gotta use the *immaterial sight* for these things, just like a motorcar engine have to use oil" (1970–78, vol. 2:1297).

Extra eyes, clairvoyance, deep vision—these attributes are also commonplace among African diviners. Writing about art from Zaire, Frere Joseph Cornet draws attention to a diviner's staff shaped like a man's body and featuring double pupils signifying clairvoyance (1975:46, plate 23). Among the Batammiliba of Togo, diviners "are believed to have an additional set of eyes through which they can view the goings on of both the mind and the world beyond" (Blier 1991:77). In Sierra Leone, among the Temne (Senegambians preyed on for the slave trade), "Certain categories of people can penetrate the darkness and can see and participate in these worlds by virtue of possessing 'four-eyed' vision, in which the two visible eyes of ordinary people are supplemented by two invisible eyes" (Shaw 1991:143). Divination and spiritual counseling also involve the "re-vision" of problems in revealing solutions (Peek 1991:200).

16. Eric De Rosny, studying *nganga* (magical healers) near the southern Cameroon coast, mentions four-eyed sight and points out that the double sight of nganga also finds a parallel in their verbal style—nganga always seem to say less than they know (1985:180, 284).

17. All the objects listed can play special protective and communicative roles in African American yards (see Thompson 1983:147–158, 1988, 1989; Gundaker 1993).

18. Smith behaves rather like a diviner. He alludes to a misapprehension on my part and an appropriate revision, but his therapeutic approach only works for those who willingly collaborate with him. Diviners in some cultures are trickster figures or are associated with them (Peek 1991:204). Trickster speech characteristically is disruptive and ambiguous (Pelton 1980).

19. Studies of sermon style include Pipes (1951), Rosenberg (1988), Mitchell (1978), Davis (1985), and Maultsby (1986/87). See especially the critical review of the literature on African American sermon performance in Pitts (1986:16–39).

20. For an account of the ways in which literacy, scholarship, and African American performance traditions interweave in the career of one distinguished preacher, see also Titon's lucid preface and introduction (Franklin 1989:ix-x, 41–45).

21. In some African religions such as Yoruba Orisha belief, devotees and dieties or spirits have a reciprocal relationship, expressed on the divine side through intervention in human affairs and on the devotee side by offerings, sacrifices, and praise. Without active devotees the Orisha themselves fade away or retreat from contact with humans. There is thus a sense in which humans "make" the gods and vice versa. The intense call-and-response in some African American churches seems to partake of this dynamic as well, subtly "Africanizing" by shifting toward more direct forms of reciprocity between the worshippers and God.

22. Opening the eyes is a recurring metaphor for conversion and initiation. See the quotation from John Jea in chapter 5, which includes this phrase. If

there is truth to the generalization that rhythmic, oral, and aural modes of participation characterize African American spiritual *expression*, there should also be a parallel generalization that visual modes and metaphors characterize spiritual *knowledge*. To my knowledge no one has made this point in general terms, although several detailed case studies seem to support it. One of the most important studies is that of Samuel Miller Lawton, a blind scholar who—perhaps because he did not take the visible world for granted—elicited marvelously detailed descriptions from others (1939).

Occasions combining vision and knowledge include visions in conversion experiences, dreams involving culturally coded and symbolic objects and attributes, visionary travel, and four-eyed sight. Knowledge claims are also expressed through ocular signs such as the all-seeing eye and four-eyes signs discussed in chapter 4, and the shifts from one type of script to another discussed in chapter 7.

23. Pitts sees a parallel between changing performance frames in Afro-Baptist church ritual and in African initiation (1986, 1989, 1991). The key transition, in his view, is the change from rather monotonous praying and singing of lined-out hymns in the first part of the service to energetic participation and improvisation in the second part. He aligns the initial frame with the repetitious chants that prepare participants in African initiations for trance. The rapid change of pace when frames shift signals the arrival of the Holy Spirit. Pitts also points out that performance frames differ among various church denominations and sects; sometimes parallels with initiation are entirely absent.

24. B. Hardy, pastor of Holiness churches in Stamford and Waterbury, Connecticut, explained to me that hats were so important to many women that fine hats could threaten the solidarity of the church members by inspiring competition and jealousy. In an effort to remedy this problem, Pastor Hardy began making hats and opened her own hat salon to make fine hats available to all women at a reasonable price (interview, September 23, 1991).

For a broader view, see Gibson and McGurk (1977). One (of many) descriptions of status differentiation reflected in headgear is the following recollection of the early-nineteenth-century Ijebu of Nigeria:

> Headdress is highly variable. The common people go bareheaded, or at the most content themselves with the *botiboti,* a simple cap made in the country. The more well-to-do prefer the *akode* or brimless hat, or the straw hat, called *akoro,* both of them native to the country. Distinguished men require a red wool hat; and the rich, a felt hat with a wide brim imported from Europe. The chief priest wears a kind of brimless cloth hat similar to our toque. As for the king, his headdress is raised up in the form of a tiara of great richness. It is made of coral beads mounted close together on a background of crimson leather; at a crest is a tuft or tassel of gold. (Curtin 1967:265–6)

25. Without wholehearted point-by-point agreement, I am indebted to Melville J. Herskovits (1958, 1966). Herskovits's most serious shortcomings are his lack of fieldwork in the United States, a limitation shared by others who have also spoken broadly to the "birth" or "origins" of African American culture, and his underestimation of connections between the material life of African Americans in the United States and in the rest of diaspora. Nonetheless, I find Herskovits's broad outlook, as well as his concepts of reinterpretation, syncretism, cultural focus, and cultural imponderables, very helpful. His

goal was to deflate the "myth of the Negro past," the dominant notion that African Americans were cultural ciphers whose past had been erased and whose future was driven by efforts, and failures, to imitate the behavior of whites. The following quotation from Ruth Benedict's *Race, Science, and Politics* is a typical articulation of the "myth":

> Their patterns of political, economic, and artistic behavior were forgotten —even the languages they had spoken in Africa. Like the poor whites of the South, they gathered together instead for fervent Christian revivalistic camp meetings; they sang the hymns the poor whites sang, and if they sang them better and invented countless variations of great poignancy, nevertheless the old forms which they had achieved in Africa were forgotten. Conditions of slavery in America were so drastic that this loss is not to be wondered at. The tribes on any one plantation had come from tribes speaking mutually unintelligible languages, with mutually unfamiliar arts of life. . . . They worked hard on the plantations. It is no wonder that their owners remarked on their lack of any cultural achievements; the mistake they made was to interpret the degradation of the slave trade as if it were an innate and all-time characteristic of the Negro. (1945:86–87)

The key components of the myth were (1) that African "tribes" were separate and distinct, lacking cognate customs and languages; (2) that the harshness of the Middle Passage and slavery erased all significant African influences, and (3), for Benedict and like-minded theorists, the notion that even on this side of the Atlantic, African Americans formed no significant culture of their own.

Anthropologists in the second quarter of this century were preoccupied with variables that could be isolated; then, as now, additive, positivistic arguments, amenable to statistical representation, were hallmarks of "real science." Thus Herskovits attempted to construct a diaspora-wide sliding scale of "Africanisms" and "survivals," using isolated traits—a virtual necessity for additive arguments. However, this scale is by no means *all* that Herskovits did, for he was also an on-the-ground ethnographer, continually challenged by the complexities of culture contact and change. His views were much more attuned to the fluidity and indirections of transatlantic connections than some of his critics have recognized (cf. Mintz 1992). It is clear in his writings that he struggled with the limitations of his own vocabulary.

A subsequent generation of theorists, more sociological and Marxist in orientation than Benedict and Herskovits, have also asserted that there are few, if any, significant continuities between Africa and African America. Their argument has retained components 1 and 2 of the myth more or less intact but developed a revised version of component 3. For these theorists, institutions— the mainstays of sociological analysis—were essential to the development of culture. New World Africans, they posited, brought no institutions with them, thus no culture; however, African Americans did begin to forge a new culture from the time of their enslavement onward, and this culture, lacking African precedents to build on, was primarily European and European American in institutional orientation; however, some resemblances to African precedents do occur, made anew on the foundation of "deep structure," an abstract grammar that is supposedly capable of generating new forms, discontinuous with, but strikingly like, those found in African cultures. For elaborations of this point of view, see Smith (1965), Mintz (1970), and Mintz and Price

(1976). (A somewhat confusing new preface by Mintz and Price (1992) to a reprint of their earlier publication attempts to align their position with that of creolists, while leaving the earlier text unchanged.)

Historian John Thornton has developed one of the most plausible and concise pictures of the transformation of African culture in the Americas (1992:152–234). Thornton critiques both Herskovits's emphasis on survivals and traits and Mintz and Price's argument that ethnic and linguistic diversity among African captives overshadowed similarities and resulted in the formation of new culture without significant African contributions. Thornton proposes that coastal West and Central Africa contain three major zones: Upper Guinea, Lower Guinea, and Angola. Not only did Africans communicate with each other across these zones, but members of cultural groups within each zone had sufficient cognate customs and languages to reach common understandings and found institutions based on familiar African precedents. Moreover, it was commonplace for Africans to be bilingual or multilingual (Mufwene 1993:193). However, Africans in the Americas did not rigidly attempt to preserve the past; rather, they responded flexibly to the diverse conditions they encountered. Various institutional and noninstitutional aspects of culture, such as language and family structure and religious belief, did not form a cohesive whole at any one time or change at the same rates. Out of a "mass of interactions" with people of similar backgrounds, as well as with Europeans and Africans from distant groups "would gradually emerge an Afro-Atlantic culture, not necessarily homogeneous throughout the Atlantic, in fact, displaying substantial regional variations, but shaped by these new forces into a new creation" (1992:211).

In short, then, African America is not a direct descendant of Africa, but it is not a direct descendant of Europe either. Nor can any aspect of the past be ignored a priori as potentially relevant to American history.

26. *Tie* has enough specialized African American uses that it should be treated as a "native term." Its meanings require careful ethnographic investigation; we should also be alert to the possibility that it functions as a loan-translation for terms in one or more African languages for sealing vows, cementing resolutions, or binding together diverse elements into a power-object. With reference to linkages to particular African societies, associations between tying/wrapping, speaking, and sealing intentions are too widespread to attribute to the influence of a single ethnic group. See Williams (1934:42) for an Ashanti-Jamaica linkage; MacGaffey (1991) for relevant Kongo texts and illustrations of tied *nkisi*; Thompson (1983:117–131) on Kongo *minkisi* in old world and new; and Hyatt (1970–78, vol. 1:389, 597–8) for several instances from the southeastern United States. My fieldwork indicates that the practice of tying gardens and personal property is alive and well in United States; bright blue surveyors' tape seems to be the late-twentieth-century twine of choice. Martha Beckwith describes *writing* that "ties" a field in Jamaica against theft of the crop (1929). Falconer, an independent Jamaican cultivator, told Beckwith that he

> saw a field of corn guarded by a cloth "written over in a strange language." An old man at the field warned him and the white man with him "if you go into the ground to steal corn you will never pass out until the master of the ground comes." (Beckwith 1929:127)

In addition to tying *with* writing, certain thresholds at which a household is vulnerable to negative messages conveyed in writing are also tied. For example, a resident might tie twine around the mailbox. An interesting resemblance to the contemporary practice of tying property with writing may be seen in Effie Graham's novel, *Aunt Liza's Praisin' Gate* (1914).

27. Consider the ramifications if one began with a single study—say, Lorenzo Dow Turner's *Africanisms in the Gullah Dialect* (1949)—and, building out from the names and terms he lists, pursued all possible linguistic and cultural connections in ethnographic detail. Quite soon the number of languages and ethnic groups would exceed any one anthropogist's lifetime expertise. Eventually, working down the West and Central African coasts, taking all groups touched by the slave trade into account, the material could approximate or exceed the number of excerpted items on African peoples in the Human Relations Area Files. It seems reasonable, then, to follow up what promising leads we can, expecting slow, accretive revision of our understanding of the African American past. Some of the most promising leads lie in the areas of visual and material culture, where comparisons can be reasonably concrete.

28. M. G. Smith argues that in order to claim that continuities or connections exist, one must isolate discrete "items" of culture and trace them back to specific ethnic groups (1965:18–74). This argument assumes that culturally "pure" items and groups can be isolated. However, West and Central Africans exchanged goods and ideas among themselves before and during the slave trade.

3 AFRICAN SCRIPTS, GRAPHIC PRACTICES, AND CONTEXTS OF LEARNING AND USE

1. A commonplace—and dubious—assumption is that because one or more discrete graphic signs in two different scripts resemble each other, this means that one script has historically influenced the other. Thus if both ancient Egyptian hieroglyphics and a West African pictographic system include signs for such commonplace things as a duck or a sun, then the Egyptian system must have influenced the West African system. This assumption ignores the ease with which signs involving common objects like the duck and sun might arise independently and seems likely to underestimate the intelligence of peoples who could easily design their own graphic systems, should an occasion to use one arise.

2. An alternative approach could characterize African and African American graphic systems on the scale of communication systems that Owen devised: a continuum from "sequential" to "presentational"(1986). Sequential systems are those encoded linearly from a single starting point; presentational systems may be decoded from more than one starting point.

See Gelb on semasiographic signs (1963:11). I use the term "semasiographic" to refer to signs that do not correspond to any particular language. Such signs include the color-coded octagon of the STOP sign and pictographic representations on restroom doors. The terms "morphosemantic" and "logogram" refer to signs that have a relatively stable relationship to one morpheme or group of synonyms in a given language. There is thus an overlap between semasiographic and morphosemantic signs. A sign that is semasiographic across lingistic borders may be morphosemantic within one speech community. For example, in practice for English speakers in the United States, the red octagon is a logogram for the word /stop/, not /cesar (de)/ or /parar (se)/.

Looking across the range of African American signs in use in the United

States and Caribbean, I believe that the best way to view the relationships of these signs to the alphabetic messages that sometimes accompany them is as *determinatives*. Determinatives are morphosemantic signs that sum up the value of, or classify, the phonological signs that they accompany. Thus in Egyptian hieroglyphics the word *ra* includes phonological signs, the solar disk determinative, and a vertical bar that indicates that in this context the disk is a determinative and not what many scholars have called an ideograph.

(I would prefer to call signs such as this disk logographs: thus, here, a one-part symbol for ra, as "1" is a logograph for "one." "Ideograph" is a misleading term because it implies a platonic ideal in the head, and also unmediated, pure communication from sign to mind and mind to sign. Because "ideograph" implies an abstract something in the head prior to what signs express, the term is bound up with the linguistic ideology of Romantic Individualism that Volosinov has criticized [1986]. Romantic Individualism assumes that pure ideas come first; expressive systems come later; identity is given rather than achieved; the relationship between signifier and signified is arbitrary; and individuals and society are fundamentally opposed. African and African American vernacular forms do not seem particularly compatible with this ideology. They are exquisitely sensitive to the varieties of motivation and mediation that operate among sign systems, and the possibilities for clarity and ambiguity that various sign systems offer.)

3. In addition to references cited in this chapter, sources on the Vai script include Hair (1963); Goody, Cole, and Scribner (1977); Scribner and Cole (1981); Smith (1978); Stewart (1967); Johnston (1906); Spence (1979); and the bibliography compiled and annotated by Stewart and Hair (1969). On the Bamum script, see Delafosse (1922), Schmidtt (1963, 1967), and Dugast and Jeffreys (1950).

4. Michael Smith found that among the three writing systems—Roman, Vai, and Arabic—available to contemporary Vai, Arabic script was favored for writing on walls and in talismans. Most Vai living quarters are rectilinear, sometimes with attached passages and verandas.

> Some houses have Arabic inscriptions on the walls. Practically everyone has the opening sentence of the Qur'an, chalked or inked over the lintel of the front door, while on the inside just above it hangs a talisman—a Qur'anic scripture bound up in a little packet. (1978:5)

5. Although a comprehensive account of the subject remains to be written, there is hardly a place in the diaspora or an era in African American history without some form or fashion of message-bearing headgear; see chapter 2, n. 24. Regarding bands around the head: a photograph from the Civil War era shows missionary teacher Laura Towne behind Union lines on St. Helena Island with three of her pupils. The smallest of the three wears light-colored clothing (probably as much white as the child's family could provide) and has a white cloth seeker's band tied around her head (Rose 1964:after 142). In Trinidad, Spiritual Baptist mourners also wear bands tied about the head and eyes. Markings on the bands help to direct travel in the Spirit, and in the opinion of one Spiritual mother, it is the writing on the bands that sets the Spiritual Baptist faith apart from all others (Alma Woodward, personal communication, July 1990). In the "crowning" ritual of Spiritual Baptists in St. Vincent and the ordination of Bishop Lydia Gilford in New Orleans, Spiritual mothers surround the candidate and place the Bible on his or her head (Henney 1968:86; Smith 1984:53).

6. For comparison, see Gundaker (1993) and Jopling on houses in Puerto Rico (1988, especially figs. 109a, 118, 122a, 122b, 142b, 198a) and consider the following passage from an Alejo Carpentier essay (1966:55–56), translated and quoted by Antonio Benitez-Rojo in *The Repeating Island*, who calls it essential reading on "polyrhythmic space that is Cuban, Caribbean, African, and European at once" (1992:81).

We would have to make an immense inventory of gratings, an endless catalog of ironwork, to define fully the baroque features that are always implicit and present in the Cuban town. There is . . . the white and intricate grating, almost plantlike in its abundance and in the tangles of its metal ribbons, with pictures of lyres, flowers, vaguely Roman vases, and infinite spirals that form, in general, the letters of the woman's name that was also given to the villa over which she rules, or a date, a succession of historically significant numbers. (Carpentier, quoted in Benitez-Rojo 1992:80)

7. Sources in English include Gonggrijp (1960), Kahn (1931), and Price (1976:61).

8. On object coding, see Thompson and Cornet 1981; Thompson 1983, 1988, 1989; McWillie 1987; Gundaker 1993.

9. See Griaule and Dieterlen (1951), Calame-Graule and Lacroix (1969), Zahan (1950), and de Ganay (1950).

10. See Thompson (1978, 1983:227–268), Talbot (1912), Kalu (1978), MacGregor (1909), Dayrell (1910, 1911), and Spence (1979).

11. Nsibidi is the only African graphic system known to have traveled to the Americas virtually intact. It forms the basis for anaforuana, the sign system of the Afro-Cuban Abaqua secret society (see Thompson 1983:248–266).

12. Ground writing and object coding with a healing orientation are recurring themes in the dressing of African American yards; some contain personal history narratives. Some Spiritual, Holiness, and other pastors have created therapeutic environments in their pastoral counseling rooms. For example, Sister Shirley Dailey of St. Jude Freewill Holiness Crusade, Inc., Hattiesburg, Mississippi, made two therapeutic environments. One is a former bus refitted with a clean white interior and cool cotton bunks. It can be used as a prayer retreat or temporary home for displaced persons. The other is a counseling chamber adjacent to the worship area of the church. It is furnished with red and white satin furniture and cushions, with Bible verses and poems on the walls, and several vases of red and white artificial roses on end tables. Sister Shirley explained that she planned all facets of the room to soothe troubled spirits—white—yet give a sense of spiritual energy and purpose—red (personal communication, April 1989).

13. Holloway provides a summary of quantitative and archival information on the ethnic heritage of African Americans (1990). See also Rawley 1981. Predominant ethnicity varied regionally and historically. Charles Joyner's summary of the origins of captives brought to South Carolina between 1730 and the end of the slave trade states that nearly 40 percent came from Congo-Angola, 20 percent from Senegambia, and the remaining 40 percent from various other regions, including the Gold and Windward coasts, and Sierra Leone (1984:205–206). Colonial Virginia received the largest portion of its slaves from the Bight of Biafra, a sizable number from the Gold Coast, and a smaller group from Angola (Sobel 1987:5). Through sale and planter migration, South

Carolina and Virginia were sources of slaves for plantations in Alabama, Mississippi, and the states farther west. Additional complexity came with the influx of slaves brought from Santa Domingo through the port of New Orleans during the wars for Haitian independence near the turn of the nineteenth century; by the ongoing smuggling of illegally captured slaves through southern ports such as Mobile and Charleston; and by the resale of African and Creole slaves from West Indian islands, especially Barbados and Trinidad. Far from obliterating the slaves' culture(s), this situation forced them (and also free African Americans) to emphasize similarities in their heritages and to achieve adaptations that interleaved diverse traditions without necessarily obscuring all traces of their origins.

14. See also Raboteau 1978:327.

15. Obviously, slaveholder attitudes were riddled with contradictions, since scruples about enslaving persons with Caucasian blood did not deter whites who begat and then bought and sold the children of black women.

16. Planter zeal in actual (as opposed to rhetorical) suppression of literacy varied, as did legislation and enforcement of legislation that banned black literacy. Janet Cornelius provides an excellent summary on this issue (1991: 18, 33–34, 37–42, 63–64).

17. "Brass ankles" and "Turks" are derogatory terms for people who live in south central South Carolina and have ambiguous racial status. One common last name among them is Benenhaley (Berry 1963:186–188), which sounds remarkably like Benali and Bilali, versions of Ben Ali, a common Muslim name. Since West African day names persist to the present in the United States (see Dillard 1972:123–135), perhaps African Muslim names also endured in some form. Numerous other groups of this kind were and are spread across the eastern half of the continent, including the Moors of central Indiana. Peter Lamborne Wilson and others have begun to explore links between these groups and the emergence of the Moorish Brotherhood and the Nation of Islam in Chicago and Detroit (1993).

18. See also Prussin's thorough overview (1986) of the relationship between talismans and textile design, architecture, and landscape.

19. For example, Sydney Omarr's horoscope column reported, "Of all things: Mike Tyson, Cancer, youngest heavyweight boxing champion in history who also claims he will be the oldest, has what he terms a 'Jewish charm' attached to one of his boxing shoes" (Omarr 1990).

20. See Mommersteen on the role of numerical equivalents in fabrication of a love charm in Djenne, Mali (1988) and Prussin (1986:67–68, 74–75).

21. On Masonic signs in vèvè, see Brown (1975:241–242). According to Maya Deren, Vodou houngans who serve Ogoun are especially likely to be members of Masonic orders and, since Vodou is a decentralized religion, to use Masonic lodges as meeting places (1953:134–5).

22. For a detailed investigation of layered speech in relation to a layered graphic system, see Calame-Griaule's *Words and the Dogon World* (1986). Miller goes on to point out that the Mande griots, who occupy a socially marginal position because they are artful speakers, are nonetheless necessary to society as a whole. Silence or brevity is the marker of the noble class's speech, and the status of secret society initiates who know deep, silent secrets. Yet speech is also necessary for ruling others; the griot is an essential intermediary who releases nyama but is also a member of a special caste that is equipped to deal with nyama. Based on the critique of writing offered by cetain Mande griots, Miller concludes: *"Writing is to speech as speech is to si-*

lence; in both cases there is movement *from authenticity to alterity, from truth to tropes"* (1990:95). The Mande critics said of the kind of Western-style literacy used for recordkeeping that it "kills memory and lacks warmth" (Miller 1990:94). This attitude has its appeal but also promotes the nostalgic view of orality as a state of precolonial innocence and wholeness.

23. This Salih Bilali is not to be confused with Ben Ali/Bilali of Sapelo Island whose book is pictured in figure 3.11. However, Salih Bilali (known also among whites as "Tom") is one of the Muslim forebears whom depression-era black Georgians recalled for FWP interviers (Georgia Writers Project 1940).

24. Ishmael Reed has a different and satirical take on the blue-back speller in *Mumbo Jumbo*: "Charlotte goes into the bedroom and returns with a tattered blue-covered book. This is PaPa LaBas' *Blue Back: A Speller*, required reading at Mumbo Jumbo Kathedral." (1972:104–105).

25. Akinnaso seems basically to accept the oral/literate distinction as discriptively adequate, with certain qualifications. As should be clear by now, I do not.

26. We need to be alert to overlaps between both formal and informal learning and practical and esoteric knowledge, and to possibilities for remodelling African forms. Although the esoteric use of scripts has been excluded from the scope of conventional literacy since the Enlightment, such uses did not disappear altogether. Rather, magic fell from its former academic (semi)respectability and its former position as a challenge to the Church rooted in ancient writings (see Yates 1964). A legacy of the Euro-Egyptian Hermetic tradition is a repository of nonphonological signs that meld with African graphic and object sign systems. These cross-fertilize in the South among the black Masons, Knights of Pythias, and Knights of Tabor and other fraternal organizations.

4 DIASPORA OF SIGNS

1. The following is another variant of African American reinterpretation of the cross: Theodore Ford points out that the spirituals often use the metaphoric "tree" for the cross as a symbol of the crucifixion (1939:67). For Ford, this is an Egyptian retention referring to the death of Osiris. However, it is not necessary to go so far back in time to see that the tree metaphor accords with European American Christian symbolism at the same time that it also opens toward African American associations: for example, trees on African-American graves connote connection between roots, earth, and heaven (Thompson 1983:38–39); thus the tree metaphor of the crucifixion builds in the idea of rebirth. Trees are also ancestral altars, spirit abodes, and surrogates for the person in Africa (for wide geographic distribution, see Partridge 1905:271–273, MacGaffey 1977:149, and Little 1967:219–220) and the United States (Gundaker 1993). Trees were and are often special sites for prayer (see Sims 1981; Rawick 1972 19:8–9; Brewer 1958:7, 15–17; and Day 1955:39, 43). Trees are also replete with crossmark imagery of traffic between worlds because of the many intersections created by their roots and branches.

2. Roman Catholic yard shrines convey the general idea that God is watching. Statues of St. Joseph stand guard in front of some houses. St. Joseph is a popular protector among black as well as white Catholics in Louisiana. See, especially, Newbell Niles Puckett and Murray Heller's account of giving small statues of the saint to conjurers in mainly Protestant Mississippi (1926:563–565). Some Catholics also favor various eye talismans. But so far I have not

encountered a European American parallel to the four-eyes sign in actual use in the United States. An English crossmark garden charm was observed in England:

> In Herefordshire on May morning seedbeds were spiked with small protective crosses of rowan and birch. . . . Ruth Tongue remembers helping an old Somerset cottager in his garden and at his request making the charm sign, a heart between crosses, with a hazel stick on the newly turned earth of the spring seedbed. She had seen this sign once or twice thereafter tucked away discreetly in a secret corner of a cottage garden, against the depredations of "vairies." (Baker 1978:123)

3. Eagle weather vanes on homes, especially over the front door, overlook all four directions and can connote special powers of sight.

4. On grave decoration, see Nichols 1989, Lawton 1939:185–222, Thompson 1983:132–142, Thompson and Cornet 1981:181–203, Vlach 1978:139–147, Bolton 1891, Michael 1943, Little 1989, Fenn 1985, Ingersoll 1892, and Brannon 1925.

5. Harriet Powers's Bible quilt from the Boston Museum of Fine Arts is reproduced often; see Livingston and Beardsley 1982:35 (black and white); Grudin 1990:6 (color); and Fry 1990:88 (excellent color). Adams (1977), Perry (1976), and Fry (1976, 1990:84–91) review biographical information on Harriet Powers and the quilter's own reading of her work.

6. The hand is a common gravestone motif. Usually hands on markers take one of the following forms: a single *hand pointing heavenward* (very common in the nineteenth century); *clasped hands* (frequent in the last quarter of the nineteenth century); occasionally, a *hand reaching out of the clouds*, suggesting heaven and the hand of God; and more rarely, a *hand holding an object* like a Bible or flower. I assume that the hand pointing at the sun is fairly unusual, since I have visited dozens of European and African American cemeteries, yet only seen it on one group of markers, apparently made by one craftsperson.

7. Probably there is a connection between the injunctions against drawing crossmarks, stepping on crossmarks, and crossing the legs during the ring shout when the performance is a sacred one (Gordon 1973:448; Puckett 1926:60). Another crossmark variation: if a woman burns the four corners off a love letter and returns it to the writer, this shows that she "didn't want to be bothered" and gives the writer bad luck (Hyatt 1970–78, vol. 3:3592).

Among contemporary young men (mainly urban, often gang members), a protective sign resembling the four-eyes sign appears in a scarification or tattoo. Often the sign marks the point on the hand where an imaginary perpendicular line from the forefinger crosses a horizontal line parallel to the extended thumb:

```
o ¦ o
---¦---
o ¦ o
```

In a 1987 photograph, a rapper has a crossmark scarification at the base of his right forefinger (Beckman and Adler 1991:108). I have observed this sign on hands in New Haven. According to Karen Davalos some Mexican American young men wear the sign above in a similar position, and have done so since zoot suit days (personal communication, July 1992).

8. Compare the crossmarks that all participants in the Vodou ceremony of degradation make on a *canari* (a clay vessel filled with food offerings) after the death of an important or specially talented person. "It is this act which will

217

NOTES TO
PAGES
67–78

constitute proof against the dead in the future in case a new demand is made" by the deceased on his or her relatives (Simpson 1946, quoted in Courlander 1976:40).

9. On a dire confrontation with a plat-eye brought on by the theft of a bottle from a grave mound, see Hayward (1929).

10. On protective blue, see Crum (1940:40, 85), Cooley (1926:53), McTeer (1970:19), and Thompson (1989:118, 140). Blue is the spirit eye/vision color in Muslim charms (see the color photos appended to Koenig 1975). Blue eye color is a sign of special sight in African American rootwork and healing traditions. Among the Bamileke of Cameroon, blue is the color of death and of water; therefore widows wear deep blue (de Rosny 1985:184). From this perspective, blue predicts the near future of trespassers and thieves: dead.

11. Another variation on this theme was the clover-filled yard of visionary artist and preacher Sister Gertrude Morgan. Her yard cross-referenced the Christian cross, the Afro-Atlantic crossmark, and the blockage of negative influences through the sign "4 × 4," the four-eyes sign, and lucky four-leaf clover.

> From house to street the narrow front yard is completely carpeted with four-leaf clovers. Although her neighbors' garden patches in this drab ghetto area of New Orleans bristle with predictable assortments of substandard shrubs, disiccated grasses, and coarse weeds, Sister Gertrude regards the remarkable horticultural event that has taken place outside her own door without astonishment. . . . [S]he views the unlikely greenery as further testimony to her very special and intimate relationship with the deity. (Horwitz 1975:25)

12. On pipes as conduits in African American grave decoration, see Thompson and Cornet (1981:193–194) and chapter 6. The following account of a pipe conduit is especially vivid. (It may reinterpret a hospital drip tube.)

> One night I remember I was sick and the doctors said I couldn't live. During this time I lay on the bed with my arms folded. To my mind, in the spirit, a little silver pipe was let down from the top of the ceiling and three angels came down. On this little silver pipe I could hear their little wings flapping, click, click.
>
> The doctors wouldn't allow me to eat. I'd be so hungry and thirsty and these little angels would come down loaded with food. They gave me water out of a little silver pipe. I could feel each drop on my tongue. They told me this was the water of life. Some nights I'd be so cold and they would huddle close to me and warm me in my dreams.
>
> One day I told them I wanted to die. They told me to be ready the next time they came after me and they came . . . [they] told me that the good Lord wasn't ready for me. Then they flew up the pipe. As they reached the ceiling all six of them pulled the gates apart and Oh! how beautiful. I saw the souls of my friends lying under the altar. (Rawick 1972 vol. 19:69)

Recently, white PVC plastic pipe has become popular. Ideally, the pipe should be long enough to touch the coffin underground (Johnson Smith, personal communication, March 6, 1991).

13. According to Mary Ethel Smith of Lumberton, Mississippi, the outside of the house reflects the inside: if the yard is a mess, passersby will assume that it also is a mess inside (personal communication, December 3, 1990).

14. Not accidentally, this woven diamond resembles Mexican "God's Eyes" of woven yarn, which are descended from the African Muslim all-seeing-eye horse trappings that crossed the Atlantic with the Spanish.

15. For example, shortly after his birth, the nurse of John Sale, the son of a Mississippi slaveholder, planted a tree bearing his name and timed the planting for daybreak in order to catch the strength of the rising sun (Sale 1929:15–17).

16. See also the illustration of a red-and-white crib quilt "showing strong African influence" with crossmarks, circles, and coffin-diamonds in the personal collection of Gladys-Marie Fry (1990:44). Fry says that Robert Farris Thompson interpreted this quilt as a memorial for a dead child or an amulet to assist a sick child. Whereas a popular type of crib quilt today is gendered pink or blue satin that suggests infants' softness, vulnerability, and need for protection, the African American quilt actively asserts forces at the boundary of worlds through its strong color and clearcut design.

17. A few sources on cross-rhythms and the break principle are Benitez-Rojo (1992, especially his introduction), Snead (1990), and Thompson (1987).

18. *Mojo* is a term for charm, *trick, gris-gris, root, hand*: all manner of tied, wrapped, packaged, activated, fed, personalized objects of power, aggression, and protection. Possible contents include bits or small amounts of mirror, foil, grave dirt, red and white clay, bones, tree stumps, lightning-struck wood, hair, feathers, writing, seeds, blood, and so forth.

19. In this section I have focused on only a portion of the network of signs that allude to clairvoyance and double worlds. We might as easily look at material objects like clocks; silvery objects and twisted wood that connote water; or fans, wheels, graveyard allusions, and several species of plants that have similar connotations. (See Thompson 1983, 1988, 1993; Thompson and Cornet 1981; Gundaker 1993.) In keeping with the insight that ethnographic writing involves fictions, and fiction is (or can be) ethnographic, many of the most accurate accounts of the phenomena I discuss occur in stories and reminiscences. Especially thick descriptive fictions in this vein are Henry Dumas's story "The Ark of Bones" (1988) involving a clairvoyant character named Headeye, and A. R. Flowers's novel *De Mojo Blues* (1985). The Mississippi River is a Kalunga line and threshold for crossover knowledge in both works.

♪ NARRATIVES OF LITERACY ACQUISITION AND USE

1. The first narrator I discuss, John Jea, was born in Africa and considered himself African, not American.

An excellent and thought provoking discussion of some of the same material as in this chapter appeared after this book was completed. See Mullin (1996).

2. Among other sources, see Anderson (1988), Webber (1978), and Cornelius (1991).

3. To compare literacy among regions, whites and blacks, and changes over time, see the U.S. census reports (Department of Commerce 1919:403–435), bearing in mind an important problem that Harvey Graff discusses (1988): differences among definitions of literacy and their use as measures in research. Kenneth Lockridge estimates that about two-thirds of white men and a higher percentage of women were illiterate in New England during the colonial period (1974:73–87). The proportion in the South has remained greater than the North.

Whatever the statistics, reading and writing were such potent symbols of white dominance that, for blacks, learning that some whites could not read or write could be quite a revelation. Interviewed in the 1930s, Joanna Thompson Isom of Lafayette, Mississippi, commented (poor dialect transcription):

> Since I been doin' dis beggin'—dat's what I calls dis here "relief", I goes up to de office an ses so many ole white folks what caint read and write—dey don't know one single letter; I ses to myself; "White folks iz all born free how cum dey caint read an' write; hit looks lak sum body woul' hev learned dem sumthin'. I ses: "Niggers aint de onliest fools in de world. Dere aint no diffrunce twixt niggers an' white folks, 'cept dey color . . . ef you cuts dey finger, dey both bleeds alike." (Rawick 1977 vol. 8:1101)

4. Robert Starobin discusses the practicality of slaves knowing how to read (1974). The following passages are reminders that some masters required the assistance of slaves because for one reason or another they could not read and write themselves.

> Marse Jones had us slaves taught how to read an' write. He didn't want us not to know nothin'. He couldn't read [at] all on account of his bad eyes so he use to hab me set by him an' read to him. I could read purty good den an' I would set fer hours on a stretch an' read to him. Some times from de Bible an' again from farm papers, mostly 'bout hogs. (Rawick 1977 vol. 8:1292)

> I heard, when at Mobile, of an intelligent young negro lad who had run away from his master. . . . His master was so uneducated, that he employed this slave in writing his business letters, and had become sensible of the danger of losing him, after teaching him what he had never been taught himself. (Lewis 1845:176)

5. See Thompson 1969:133–134.
6. Dave (the) Potter's word choice is suggestive. "Nation" is a common term for African ethnic groups in the New World (see Thornton 1992:196–204). Clubs and regional settlements based on such nation/ethnic identity were widespread in Cuba, Brazil, and Haiti. In Carriacou, the Nation Dance celebrates ethnicity. In New Orleans's Congo Square, space was divided among different dances and nations. In the United States, nations were not widely recognized groupings, especially outside the cities. However, the term has been prevalent enough that Dave Potter may well have been making a double-entendre—or a single entendre that whites may not have grasped. Groups like the Mardi Gras Indians of New Orleans result from a composite of the idea of the nation (parallel to Indian tribes) and the mutual aid society, which continues to be nation-based and nation-named in other parts of the diaspora, such as Cuba. On nation and nation language in the Caribbean, see Brathwaite (1984). The following passage, which Brathwaite uses as a lead quote, illustrates a traditional African American usage of nation:

> "And what does that mean: Congo. What does it mean when you say Congo?
> *Congo is the nation*
> Which nation, the Congo nation?
> *The Congo nation*
> And everybody here know what nation they belong to?

Yes. Everybody know what is a nation . . .
What is your nation?
Kromantee and Tembe
Are you a Congo?
Kromantee.

(Alan Lomax in Carriacou in the 1950s,
quoted in Brathwaite 1984:4)

7. See Rawick (1972 vol. 4 pt. 1:110, 141–142) and Blassingame (1977:130, 347–348, 465, 478).

8. See Cornelius for a survey of accounts of multilation and threats of mutilation for slaves' reading, writing, or teaching others (1983:173–174). Writing was worse than reading from the master's point of view. FWP interviewer Ethel Fleming reported the following about the former slave James Lucas:

His first master was Bill Stamps, who would get drunk and finally lost all of his property. . . . [James Lucas] never went to school a day in his life but can scribble his name. The slaves were not allowed to have a book or a piece of paper with print on it. His master bought eight slaves from Baltimore and some from Virginia. Those that came from Baltimore were sent back as they could read and write and were too smart. His master hung the best slave he had for trying to teach the others how to spell. (Rawick 1977 vol. 8:1328–1329)

Sarah Benjamin, enslaved in Louisiana, reported, "Dey in't larn us nothin' and iffen you did larn to write you better keep it to yourse'f, cause some slaves got e thumb or finger cut off for larnin' to write" (Rawick 1972 vol. 4 pt. 1:71).

9. This kind of writing seems to be a white parallel to tying and wrapping; see chapter 2.

10. Restrictions on slave literacy and serious reprisals for possession of any written matter followed Nat Turner's rebellion. A freedman narrator believed to be Rev. Fields Cook, who was an unsuccessful congressional candidate for a Virginia district in 1869, recalled the tensions of the period:

I went to work . . . to try what I could do for myself in the way of learning but I had many things to contend with at this undertaking for I was a boy about the time of Nat Turner's insurrection who had better never been born than to have left such a curse upon his nation I say that had better never been born: for at that time I was living in the country and we poor colored people could not sleep at nights for the guns and swords being stuck in at our windows and doors to know who was there and what their business was and if they had a passport and so forth and at that time a colored person was not to be seen with a book in his hand: but all the Books I had had been given to me by my owners and therefore I kept them though many a poor fellow burned his books for fear. (Bratton 1980:93)

11. I used, and quote here, the copy in the rare book room of Butler Library, Columbia University, printed circa 1815.

12. Jea seems to interpret the destruction of the master's crops from an African perspective.

In a word, the spirits of God, gods, and ancestors working together are considered the most powerful forces in the universe. In this respect, Africans are power worshipers. They seek power in all things and respect power potential wherever it is made manifest. While there is a difference in kind and degree of power in the spirits of ancestors, animals, nature and God, all power gains its dynamic nature from God, the supreme power. Power is perceived as active, diffused, exoteric, and universal. Since power is differentiated and therefore not perceived as uniform in all things, its individualistic potential in a given spirit is indeterminable. Nevertheless, all powers of spirits are mutually penetrable, interactive, and infectious. Most of all, religions in Africa are pragmatic or basically utilitarian in that they are not concerned with the future but with the effect of the spirits which live after death upon present human conditions and circumstances. (Washington 1972:27)

13. Compare with the account of slave religion that Andrew Jackson Tyner of Murphreesboro, North Carolina, gave to E Roy Turner:

"The Bible was the great fetish; as a book it was holy. A Christian did not necessarily have to read it to obtain its power. Some blacks only had to hold it in their hands and look heavenward to receive the messages as set forth in it by inspiration of the Holy Spirit. Thus one could read the Bible while being unable to recognize a word in a secular book." (Johnson 1970:40)

14. Moderate as opposed to the strong-consequence alphabetic literacy of Walter J. Ong (1982), at the extreme of which Robert K. Logan (1987) asserts that the finer-grained segmentation of the alphabet, compared to logographic and syllabic systems, promotes both finer-grained cognitive processing and left hemisphere dominance in the brain, which accounts for the emergence of scientific rationalism and democratic institutions in the West, beginning in ancient Greece. This view accords to some extent with the position that digital, serial processing in artificial intelligence research is sufficient to in due course account for higher cognitive processes in humans. In this approach, questionable connections between communicative or cognitive complexity and the alphabet abound and are often inverted to account for presumed failures, lacks, and deficits. For example, S. I. A. Kotei closes an article, "The West African Autochthonous Alphabets," with the following explanation of the fact that many African societies did not use alphabetic scripts: "[A]lphabets failed to develop because the function of communication was not complex enough to necessitate their development into more expansive forms" (1977:70).

15. This difference of opinion over spirit possession and ecstatic worship is, for example, the subject of a gospel song performed by Shirley Caesar. "Hold My Mule!" says an elderly man named John, who descends from this stubborn and rural animal to attend an uppity church. There he persists in feeling the Spirit and falling into trance, much to the dismay of the higher-class worshippers.

A former slave, Cordelia Jackson, of Spartanburg, South Carolina, associates the religion of whites with *narrative about* and the religion of blacks with *participation in* religious experience.

White folks tell stories about 'ligion. Dey tells stories 'bout kaise dey's 'fraid of it. I stays independent of what white folks tells me when I shouts. De Spirit moves me every day, dats how I stays in. White folks don't feel sech as I do; so dey stays out. (Rawick 1972 vol. 3:5)

Callie Gray of Marshall County, Mississippi, recalled:

> I wuz put in the field when I wuz big 'nough to hoe. . . . Hit wuz work but us got some enjiment outen hit too. De slaves would tell tales an' ghos' stories an' all 'bout cunjerin' an' hoo-doo-in'. Den dey would git to singin', prayin', an' shoutin'. . . . Dat was de onliest time de slaves could worship lak dey wanted to, 'cause us didn' hab no church. Us went to de white folks' church, an' sit on back seats, but didn't jine in de worship. You see, de white folks don't git in de spirit, dey don't shout, pray, hu[m], and sing all through de services lak us do. Dey don't believe in a heap o' things us niggers knows about. (Rawick 1977 vol. 8:892)

16. It is interesting that the name Shaker has been given to Black sects in Trinidad, St. Vincent, Dominica, Barbados, and Guyana, as well as the United States. In Grenada, says Smith, "[o]ccupying the folk pole of extreme Protestant sectarianism are the Shouters, Shakers or Spiritual Baptists who combine spirit-possession, divination, the use of cabalistic signs and other differentiae (1963:7)."

17. See, for example, Henry Mitchell (1978) on relative "blackness" and "blackenizing" (1978:20) in African American worship and Black preaching.

18. A quotation from Hyatt expresses self-possession as holding the space one occupies. The grandson of Bill Jones, a nineteenth-century spiritual doctor in Georgia, quoted his grandfather: "I can keep every bit of the ground I stand on. . . . I've traveled the four corners of the world (1970–78, vol. 2:1744)."

19. I have photographed small white figures—some are plaster figures, others are homemade dolls—that suggest that the maker selected the white skin tone of the doll. These figures were placed on the graves of African American adults in Baxterville, Mississippi; Ooltewah, Tennessee; and near Snow Hill, Maryland. One of the most striking, a little figure of a white man on a grave, was placed in the bowl of a white porcelain toilet near Sunbury, Georgia (see Bragg 1962:21). Ely Green recalled the testimony of black church converts to visions in which a "little white man . . . placed a small stone on their tongue" (1990:79). Victor Turner carried out extensive comparisons between European and African, specifically Ndembu, white symbolism and ambivalence toward whiteness in both culture areas (1975:178–203).

6 ALTERNATIVE MODES OF PARTICIPATION WITH TEXT AND ARTIFACTS OF LITERACY

1. A nagging problem for students of popular religion and healing involves distinguishing whether such stigmatization is a perception of medical and economic exploitation or is a reaction to practices that appear marginal because of their cultural orientation—their "difference."

2. For various perspectives on the relationship between African traditions and African American folk religion, see Herskovits (1958), Raboteau (1978), Stuckey (1987), Levine (1977), Sobel (1979, 1987), Ahlo (1976), and Creel (1988, 1990).

3. For example, Black (1962), Lakoff and Johnson (1980), Ricoeur (1975), and Fernandez (1974, 1991).

4. I take language from Bateson, but one could equally well look to Bakhtin, cross-referencing his ideas of double voicing and heteroglossia in the novel with creolization, and enlarging on his point that traditional stylistics

223

NOTES TO
PAGES
115–126

and its categories and methods—"poetic language," "image," "symbol," and so on—

> as well as the entire set of concrete stylistic devices subsumed by these categories (no matter how differently understood by individual critics), are all equally oriented toward the single-language and single-styled genres, toward the poetic genres in the narrow sense of the word. . . . All these categories, and the very philosophical conception of poetic discourse in which they are grounded, are too narrow and cramped, and cannot accommodate the artistic prose of novelistic discourse. (Bakhtin 1981:266)

In other words, the concept of poetic discourse and categories like "symbol" orient toward monologic utterances and genres: discourse that is underwritten by, indeed enforced by, concepts of standard language and conventional literacy. Similarly—following Garfinkel's critique—these traditional stylistic concepts and categories are grounded in a notion of "shared understandings" devolving upon "sets" (domains of symbols, relations expressed in terms of "origin" and "derivation") rather than emergent "rules" (domains/strips of activity, relations expressed in terms of coproduction and mobility among multiple realities).

5. Ironically, now some literary critics and even some anthropologists are calling themselves priests, shamans, and diviners. Is this, then, an invocation of "primitivism" as route to true meanings? And is this another way of "fetishizing" writing?

6. The concept, metaphor, is a useful tool for talking about creolization because it falls on an intermediate level of organization between "systems" like "culture" or "tradition" and lexical creolization via loan-translations and calques.

7. The shoe is an enduring African American metaphor for knowledge. Among certain Trinidadian Spiritual Baptists, a shoe beside the door indicates that a spiritual counselor occupies the premises (Ann Thomas, personal communication, November 1988). Dilmus Hall, of Athens, Georgia, known for his good counsel, placed a shoe that "rode a tornado" into his yard in a box in front of his house, along with an identifying sign (Judith McWillie, personal communication, April 1988). In Chattanooga, Tennessee, a Holiness preacher and his wife, both counselors and community leaders, placed a table with one heavy leather work boot on it next to their front steps; it remained there for about six months, along with other object-signs in the yard. In his autobiography the television personality Mr. T explained that he always wore his father's work boots (Mr. T 1984:6). Charley Williams of Oklahoma, an ex-slave, told an interviewer in the 1930s: "If you want Negro history you will have to get someone who wore the shoe and by and by from one to the other you will get a book" (Rawick 1972 vol. 7, part 1:334).

8. See Thompson for a related complex of symbolic whips, writing, and violence as these relate to the Ejagham Ngbe, the Cuban Abaqua, nsibidi, and anaforuana writing and whips as badges of society membership (1983:227–267, 298).

9. Beyond their obvious abusiveness, I wonder if these welts revolted some recent arrivals all the more because the randomness and imprecision of the whip marks contrasted so thoroughly with African traditions of scarification. In many places scarification, with its orderly composition and semasiographic coding, signaled a body that had been "civilized" through personal

endurance. Raised scarifications were designed to appeal to the tactile sense as well as the eye.

10. The work crew is a venerable African American tradition of communal labor found in variations across the diaspora, for example, the *combite* of Haiti. Alan Lomax has made an excellent case for transatlantic continuities in the work crew, and for the work crew as source of African influences on African American performance style (1968). For an Ibo comparison, see Uchendu (1965:76–77).

11. Handkerchief, flag, umbrella—these three items, quite different in function and distinct in a European visual/material vocabulary, appear interchangeably or in clusters in certain African American settings. For example, Puckett remarked that, although he assumed the belief derived from the European notion that a sharp object severs lovers' affections, he could find no European parallel to the black folk notion that bad luck follows "a man giving a woman an umbrella." He continues, "it is hard to see why some Georgia Negroes think the giving of handkerchiefs also causes loss of affection" (1926:431). On the surface, the association may be between handkerchiefs and tears. But another connotation when the umbrella and handkerchief appear in the same circumstances is of spirit presence outside the body and death. John Bennett retells a black folktale from South Carolina in which a woman receives an umbrella from a ghost at a "remember service" for the forgotten dead (1946:193–196). For Old World precedents in southeastern Nigeria, see the photo in Talbot 1912 following page 260, of an umbrella over a torso silhouette with extended arms, captioned "mourning emblems at house of dead chief," and "material *nsibidi*, funereal motifs" in Thompson (1983:258–259).

12. Puckett recognized that Fancy Talk was/is important in certain settings, but he misunderstood the talk as imitative.

> Both in Africa and in America the Negro seems to find a decided pleasure in altiloquent speech. Perhaps this bombast is partly due to the fact that the long and unusual word has a sort of awe-inspiring, almost fetishistic significance to the uneducated person, and with the Negro, at least, it indicated a desire to approximate the white man in outward signs of learning. . . . A loquacious old slave in my locality always comes forth with, "Underneath de ole foundations whar imputations rivals no gittin' long," when he especially desires to impress his audience. (Puckett 1926:28)

13. The account of the ABCs performed at a child's funeral (chapter 3) comes from the same era and place. It was recorded by one of the teacher-missionaries to the freedpeople.

14. The following passage describes sight-recognition in the Bible in a couple's devotions. The passage, part of the life history of Josh Horn as told by himself to Ruby Pickens Tartt during the 1930s, does not mention the Horns incorporating devotional sight-recognition into the shout, but it does mention that shouting was part of their prayer practice. The passage is especially valuable because it touches on the history of both conventional and vernacular approaches to reading, writing, and text in one family across the generations.

> Me and [Alice Horn] didn't neither one have no book learnin' 'cause us come along in slavery time and warn't 'lowed to have no schoolin then. . . .
> Me and Alice had children fast—sixteen of 'em . . . and us . . . give

them fourteen what us raised a little schoolin, much as us could. You see, schoolin helps a heap of folks, and I is glad the children is got some. But I been thinkin—it ain't always book learnin that counts the most; sometimes it's learnin what you gets just studyin what other folks *does*, that lets in the light. It's mighty nice though when us gets letters from the children and Alice can tell by how it looks which one it's from. Us knows Birmingham, and Detroit and Chattanooga every time us sees it.

Now the children done showed us how to find most any little verse us knows in the Bible, by what it look like on the page. Tain't exactly like readin, I know, but me and Alice pleasures us-selves mightily with it. (Brown and Owens 1981:103)

15. The following passage has been cited as a description of the communal creation process from which spirituals emerged (see Levine 1977:26). It also, however, illustrates the incorporation of text from the Bible into the Shout tradition and contributes to a pattern, when placed alongside the search for J-E-S-U-S and the account of "Aunt Deborah." Jeanette Robinson Murphy credits the passage to "a rare old singer, a Kentucky mammy, whom everybody loved."

Us ole heads use ter make 'em up on de spurn of de moment, arter we wrassle wid de Sperit and come thoo. But the tunes was brung from Africa by our granddaddies. . . . [I]n de ole days dey call 'em spirituals, case de Holy Spirit done revealed 'em to 'em. Some say Moss Jesus taught 'em, and I's seed 'em start in meetin'. We'd all be at the "prayer house" de Lord's Day, and de white preacher he'd splain de word and read whar Ezekial done say—

Dry bones gwine ter lib ergin.

And, honey, *de Lord would come a-shinin' thoo dem pages* and revive dis ole nigger's heart, and I'd jump up dar and en and holler and shout and sing and pat, and dey would cotch all de words and I'd sing it to some ole shout song I'd heard 'em sing from Africa, and dey'd all take it up and keep at it, and keep a-addin' to it, and den it would be a spiritual. Dese spirituals am de best moanin' music in de world, case dey is de whole Bible sung out and out. Notes is good enough for you people, but us likes a mixtery. (Murphy 1899:662, reprinted in Jackson 1967:328–329, my emphasis)

16. Another variation of this shout occurs in the third and fourth verses of "Lonesome Valley," recorded on the Sea Island of St. Helena, South Carolina, in the nineteenth century.

When Johnny brought a letter
When Johnny brought a letter, my Lord
When Johnny brought a letter
    He meet my Jesus dere.

An' Mary and Marta read 'em
An' Mary and Marta read 'em, Lord
An' Mary and Marta read 'em
    Dey meet my Jesus dere.
           (Spaulding 1863:199;
             Jackson 1967:72)

Harold Courlander assembled several spirituals combining the theme of writing with John the Baptist ("John saw that number way in the middle of the air") and John the Revelator ("Don't seal up your book, John, till you can sign my name"). His comments on the relation of the spirituals to particular Bible verses are well worth reading (1976:327–333).

17. See Mahiri (1991) for a good description of how vernacular practices and conventional literate skills intertwine among preadolescent black males in a basketball league. Along with displaying complex language skills on and off the court, Mahiri noted that participants closely read newspapers, analyzed statistics on players and teams, discussed basketball cards, and "eagerly devoured 20- to 30-page video game manuals" (1991:310).

18. Jackson surveys filter and counting-charm beliefs (1967:293); also see Hyatt (1970–78, vol. 1:160) and Puckett (1926:163–165).

19. Surely this protection is one reason why finely woven red-and-white checked shirts are favored for school uniforms in Haiti. Thompson traces this pattern back to checked fabric associated with the Fon thunder deity of Dahomey (lecture, November 1, 1988).

20. On offbeat and break-patterns, see chapter 4, note 18.

21. Since hoodoo sometimes employs powders on the ground, and since spirit influences for good or bad can arise from the ground (often in contrast to airy European spirits), insulating the shoe sole beneath the foot is a sensible precaution. See also note 7.

22. Bessie Jones recalled her father using a sifter and her mother spreading newspapers around the bed to keep away a spirit (1983:73–74).

From John Barlow Martin's description of The Mecca, a palatial apartment building in Chicago with between fourteen and twenty-four hundred black residents, comes this paragraph:

> In the flat, wallpaper hangs from the walls in great sheets. Clean newspapers are spread on the floor. Over the dresser are some artificial flowers, and a transparent plastic wrapper covers the bed. The sideboard, radio, and table are cluttered with family photographs. Mottos and pictures are hung on the walls, a picture of Jesus Christ and a crucifix put out by a large liquor store, a plaque, "My Help cometh from the Lord," and also secular shrines: a large frame holding the pictures of Abraham Lincoln and Frederick Douglass flanked by Booker T. Washington, Paul Lawrence Dunbar, W. E. B. Du Bois, and other race leaders. . . . She calls Lincoln "Abraham." She was born in Alabama. She is bent and stooped, aged. She says, "I live here all by myself, me and my Lord." (Martin 1954:355–356)

23. The fact that tenements were also drafty, however, does not fully explain how newspapers on walls became an icon of African American occupancy for artists who painted African American life in urban centers like Harlem.

24. I drew this sketch and figure 6.6 from memory.

25. I do not want to bog down in anthropological debates about what is properly defined as religion or magic. The African American activities that concern me presuppose supernatural agency with a visible outcome. Participants rarely use the word "magic"; rather, they say *fix, work, cross/uncross, hurt,* or *tie,* depending on the geographic region and what the specific case involves. In religion, such activity is associated with a community of worship and prayer. In hoodoo, it is directed toward personal gain. Although speakers distinguish between them, in practice religion and hoodoo can overlap.

26. For a discussion of contemporary Voodoo and hoodoo in one state—

Louisiana—see Bodin (1990); for an updating of African American traditional formuli for benign purposes, see Teish (1985).

27. Hyatt (1970–78, vol. 1:58) gives a U.S. variation from St. Petersburg, Florida.

28. Although the preselected invisible ink messages that Hyatt observed seem patently fraudulent, they can also be interpreted as props that make the doctor's reading of the client's problem graphically and physically present. This interpretation accords with the drift of the interview as a whole because the informant states quite clearly that he also uses a crystal ball and reads cards and palms. These, he says, are props in magic shows for entertainment: "dat's all trickery." Fortunetelling with cards is also fraudulent, because "somebody will tell yo' one card represent one thing, and another say it represent another" (Hyatt 1970–78, vol. 2:1323). While criticisms of this sort obviously downgrade the informant's competitors, they also could imply that he operates primarily on intuition and suits the material trappings of his trade to the consumer. Since most of his clients have trouble with money, love, or jealous neighbors, the demands on his intuition would not be very great.

Spiritual doctors often distinguish different degrees of efficacy and authenticity among divinatory and healing rites that skeptics view as equally fraudulent. For example, a Mississippi freedman, retired farmer, and former schoolteacher told an interviewer in the 1930s: "I am now a healer. That is I have power to cure any kind of sickness and stop any pain by looking at the person afflicted. I don't use any voodoo or charm. Don't believe in nothing like that. I have power to change water into medicine, the only medicine I ever use. I could do so much more for humanity if people didn't have such false ideas" (Rawick 1979 vol. 8:1209).

Beryl Bellman helps to resolve the dilemma implicit in these remarks in his work on Kpelle secrecy in Liberia. He points out that there is a "Western interpretive bias that magic is always accomplished through deception. Instead, the so-called trick is better considered to be a member's knowledge that is obtained in the course of ritual activity and instruction" (1984:147). Since the example he gives in support of this conclusion involves divination with a book, it is worth quoting at length.

> I learned medicines from a Zo named Kutupu. . . . Kutupu ran a medicine practice analogous to Western mission hospitals. He sat on a raised pedestal with his patients seated before him. Each, in turn, would . . . state his troubles. Kutupu would ask for a sum of money . . . and place it under the cover of the Koran. He then placed a medicine horn, or *mina*, on top of the book and discussed the patient's troubles with him or her. After a while, he picked up the book and used it as an oracle. He would say, "If the person's troubles are the result of his/her having broken a food taboo, then the money should disappear." He then passed the book three times around his back for a woman and four for a man. If the money was still there, he would choose another cause [for example, someone making bad medicine or a malefic spirit]. . . .
>
> Kutupu then turned the book behind his back so the other side was face up. When he opened the book the money seemed to have disappeared. Then he would discuss how to cure the patient; to show the effectiveness of the diagnosis, he made the money reappear by again turning the book behind his back. Because I was "apprenticing" under Kutupu, I sat to his side and was able to see how he performed his oracle.

A short time [later] . . . I visited some Kpelle college students . . . [and] showed the oracle. All present were astonished that I made the money disappear, and no one appeared to notice when I turned the book behind my back. Finally, I announced how I made the money disappear. Instead of destroying the illusion that I created, my friend stated, "Yes, of course, but Kuputu knows *when* to turn the book." The fact that I showed them the trick did not disturb their belief in the oracle. (1984:147)

29. The following story involves some of the same ingredients:

The Farmer and the G.P.C.

One time dere was a man what was a farmer. One year he had a real good crop. But dis man was kinda lazy, and when it come time to gather de crop he tole de ole lady he could not he'p gather de crop cause he felt de Lord was callin' him to go preach. He tole her to look up in de sky, and he pointed out de letters GPC, which he say meant, "Go Preach Christ" and he had to go.

But de ole lady she was too much fer him. "Dose letters don't mean "Go Preach Christ," she said. "Dey mean, "Go Pick Cotton." (Browne 1954:133)

30. See Pelton's summary of the literature and commentary on Legba and Eshu; he terms them "writers of destiny" (1980:71–163). Another summary is Gates's, incorporated into his theory of literary criticism (1988:3–43).

31. On sacrifices, see also Haskell (1891).

32. Consider this speculative question: Did Prays Services—gatherings centered on the ring shout—ever *begin* with a shout focused on John the Revelator? That is, did the Revelator "open the gate" (break the seal) as Eshu/Ellegua/Legba does in Afro-Caribbean religions? Or was no particular sequence followed in these performances?

33. Notice the possibility, however remote, of wordplay here, punning watch (ye therefore) and watch (wrist, pocket).

34. Another artist who associated writing with revelation in her work was the late Sister Gertrude Morgan (Horwitz 1975:25–30; Rosenak and Rosenak 1990:219–220; Livingston and Beardsley 1982:97–103, 183–184.)

35. For a humorous treatment of this theme, with double-voiced seriousness built into the narrative, see the story "John's Watch" (Courlander 1976:436–437).

36. Perpetual motion was a problem that attracted the alchemically inclined around the turn of the century. However, I strongly suspect that John Martin was more than a mere hobbyist. Compare Martin's interests with the quotation from Boyd, p. 101.

7 CONTRASTING AND COMPLEMENTARY SCRIPTS AND GRAPHIC SIGNS

1. This openness is one reason that Egyptian hieroglyphics were superior to Roman script in the opinion of some Renaissance thinkers. Since hieroglyphics were not decoded until the eighteenth century, Renaissance neoplatonists did not know that the script was phonological. For Renaissance interpretations of hieroglyphics see Wittkower (1972).

2. On *simbi*, see MacGaffey (1986), Thompson (1983:191; 1988).

3. On vèvè and their role in Haitian Vodou, see, among others, Brown (1975), Deren (1953), Rigaud (1969, 1975), and Cosentino (1995).

4. Illustrations of these signs appear in Simpson (1966:547), and Thompson (1983:112).

5. At least a hint of the variety of uses for scripts and graphic systems along the borders of magic and religion may be gathered from Keith Basso and Ned Anderson's description of the Western Apache script of Silas John (1973); Carlo Severi's account of the oral and pictographic "chemin des metamorphoses" of Cuna healers (1982); C. Hooykaas's collection of drawings in Balinese sorcery (1980); William Shaw's discussion of talismans for invulnerability in the Malay Peninsula (1971); and M. Meggitt's discussion of the uses of literacy in New Guinea and Melanesia (1968). Aesthetic aspects of such scripts are of course especially developed in cultures with rich calligraphic and manuscript traditions (Safadi 1978; Mercier 1979). Rappaport analyzes Paez Indian understandings of their history and functions of the written word in relation to the larger Colombian society (1987).

6. Perhaps some of the problems in appreciating Fancy Talk in its cultural context result from its being confused with similar language in European and American "avant-garde" traditions, which arises from different aims.

7. Mary Helms investigates the relation of power, knowledge, and geographical distance in *Ulysses Sail* (1988). Claude Levi-Strauss's account in *Tristes Tropiques* of the chief who imitated his writing is classic. Also in this vein is the white anthropologist character in Ibo masquerade who writes in a notebook (Clifford 1988: cover). An interesting article by Moshe Barasch explores an aspect of this problem from the perspective of Renaissance art: pseudoinscriptions—nondecodable script—of Hebrew and Kufic appearance in paintings and sculptures (1989).

8. On Minnie Evans, see Starr (1969), Kahan (1986), and McWillie (1991).

9. On "writing in the spirit," also called "writing in an unknown tongue," see McWillie (1987, 1991) and Thompson (1983:108–116, 284–285, 288–289). A Osman El-Tom mentions writing by "non-human beings" among the Berti (1987:225).

Recent work on African American writing in unknown tongues and personal scripts should shed some light on the graphic system developed by Leroy Person, a resident of eastern North Carolina (see Manley 1989:102). According to at least one account, Person taught this script to his family and used it for practical purposes. If that is the case, his graphic system seems to parallel the pattern of emergence of the Hmong script (Smalley, Vang, and Yang 1990). Shong Lue, the Hmong script's inventor, crafted a decodable script in a region that already had a tradition of mediumistic and diagnostic writing in unknown tongues. Like Shong Lue, Leroy Person seems to have fit the general profile of writers in unknown tongues, and both men then took the practice one step further. Obviously, Person would have had continual exposure to Roman script throughout his life. However, he also used traditional African American iconography in pieces like his Blue Throne, which is bordered in a wheel motif and has his personal script underneath the seat.

This book discusses a situation similar in some ways to conditions prior to the development of the Hmong alphabet. This alphabet appears to occupy a special place in the history of writing systems because it may be the only alphabet developed by a person who could not read or write. There is a possibility that Leroy Person shares a similar distinction.

10. Compare with southern Italian vernacular Catholicism. A man named

"Domenico Masselli of Stornarella . . . (born about 1922) first saw Mary in 1959, when she appeared to him and told him of the need to urge repentance upon the world" (Carroll 1992:55). From that day forward, he spoke directly with Mary on the first three Fridays of every month. With offerings collected from his followers, Masselli was able to construct an oratory (consisting of one large room) dedicated to San Gerardo Maiella, who is one of the most popular saints in the region; in this oratory these dialogues with Mary took place:

> Supplicants would write letters to Mary outlining their concerns; they would then place these letters, properly sealed in envelopes carrying the normal postage, at the base of the Madonna's altar. The service would start with a recitation of the rosary and the singing of hymns. Masselli would then. . . . "see" the Madonna and begin to speak to her. He would then open each of the letters and begin writing on a blank sheet (which each supplicant had enclosed in their letter) the response dictated by the Madonna. Subsequently, he would read the message aloud. (Carroll 1992:56).

11. Artists also deserve credit for challenging rationalist conventions about naturalness, and they mirror theories of reference in speech and writing. Raymond Williams points out:

> [O]f course the use of material sound and of rhythm, in both general communication and the many forms of drama, narrative, lyric, ritual and so on, is in no way a modernist discovery and is, moreover, never reducible, in another direction, to simplified accounts of meaning in language. . . . What is different, in some modernist and *avant-garde* theory and practice, is the attempt to rationalize it for specific ideological purposes of which the most common—though it has never been more than an element of these movements—is the deliberate exclusion or devaluing of all or any referential meaning. (1987:36)

The modernist challenge included assaults on conventional literacy that drew on the work of anthropologists like Lucien Levi-Bruhl and influenced others like Levi-Strauss. In the long run, the concepts the artists (for example, André, Breton, François Picabia, and Marcel Duchamp) depended on—primary process, primitivism, and the like—remained mired in Eurocentrism. But their efforts deserve mention as challenges to the authority of "purism," as responses to the felt presence of people of African descent in the Europe of the time, and, ironically, as proponents of one of conventional literacy's bedrock assumptions: the great cognitive divide.

Artists like the surrealists sought alternative grounding for concepts of nature through a fascination with psychoanalytic interpretation and non-European peoples, Africans and African Americans among them. For example, André Breton wrote: "Surrealism is allied with peoples of colour, first because it has sided with them against all forms of imperialism . . . and secondly because of the profound affinities between surrealism and 'primitive' thought" (1978:256). The same interests also led dada and surrealist artists to delve into automatic writing as a tool that not only disrupted conventional rationalist literacy but promised a direct channel to the psyche.

Here an interesting twist occurred, all too typical of naturalizing processes: a recursive reentrenchment of the very assumptions the surrealists tried to subvert. Along with predecessors as remote in most respects as the British essayists, who sought a perfect fit between words and referents, Breton and others sought—and believed that they had found in automatic writing—a new purity of fit between language and thought. Breton quotes Maurice Blanchot: "Thanks to automatic writing [in surrealism] . . . language has benefited by the highest promotion. Language is now merged with 'thought'; it is bound to the only true spontaneity, human freedom in action." Before surrealism, Breton continues, "the secret of this identification . . . was lost" (1978:257). This identification, externalized through automatic writing, bridged the gap between the world of primary process and the everyday world, confronting that world with texts that were "rationally" unintelligible yet "natural." Thus, whereas the British essayists strove for perfect referentiality in an objective world, the surrealists thought they had pushed beyond referentiality and objectivity using rationalism's greatest tool, the pen. Unfortunately the scale of this achievement was precisely the ascribed distance between "rational" and "primitive" thought, a divide that anthropologists, most notably the surrealists' sometime companion, Levi-Strauss, attributed largely to writing and print (1992).

12. The criterion of individual/private versus group/public orientation is what usually distinguishes hoodoo from Voodoo. In Louisiana and the Gulf Coast region during the nineteenth and early twentieth centuries, Voodoo ceremonies related to Haitian Vodou, as well as Fon, Kongo, and—probably to a lesser extent—several other African belief systems, involved at first large and then gradually dwindling numbers of participants and onlookers. The Voodoo queens and kings who officiated at these ceremonies, like the famous Marie Laveaus and Dr. Johns, also carried on private consultations, and consultants who consider themselves part of this tradition continue their work today. Although both public and private aspects of Voodoo were related, the private side of the religion proved more durable than the public side—at least on the surface. In practice, although the Fon-derived serpent seems to have disappeared from rituals, spirit possession, spirit guides and guards, and a performance-oriented worship style remain important in numerous African American religious congregations, the Spiritual churches among them.

13. See Coleman for a discussion of Mary Gladdy's narrative in relation to other slave (and other) narratives of encounters with spirits and the Spirit (1991).

14. It is tempting to try to dispense with the notion of compensation altogether, but doing so would not only erase the social and economic benefits of literacy, but mask the two-sidedness—the both/and—that promotes the transformation of a significant negative into an even more farreaching positive.

15. According to Murray, his writing was decodable not into spoken sounds but rather into messages for the spiritually prepared. Scholars have long recognized that the conventions that govern spoken and written language differ from yet interpenetrate each other; for example, see Tannen (1987).

16. Dual scripts parallel the political and social differentiations among speakers of one language. For the Renaissance and early modern England, respectively, see Goldberg (1990) and Thomas (1986). In England during these periods, "scripts" meant calligraphers' hands, not writing systems. While such scripts comprise different registers and mark different statuses, scribes do not seem to have style-shifted between them in one document, as some African Americans have done.

17. Similarly, people in possession do not remember what their bodies do during the time that the spirit is manifest; other participants tell them later.

18. Sally and Richard Price have discussed another contact situation involving ideas about conventional literacy that interact with local, vernacular signs. They resided in Surinam among the inland Maroons, about thirty years after the Herskovitses conducted their research nearer the coast. Price and Price explain Maroon attitudes toward graphic inscription as follows:

> Maroons . . . have always had a very real respect for the power of writing and believe on an abstract level that any marking at all may carry a message, if only one knew how to read it. This almost mystical belief in the power of writing was undoubtedly involved in the invention of Afaka's "Djuka script." . . . It also explains why maroons use totally blank calabash bowls in ritual contexts; they reason that a bowl with the usual decorative markings might convey an inappropriate message that would offend one of the spirits in attendance, and that since they do not know how to "read" the markings, it is safer to use a blank calabash. (1980:190)

This description comes from a longer passage in which Price and Price discuss Maroon responses to "literate outsiders," whom, the Prices say, "see Maroon symbolism where it simply does not exist" (1980:191). Price and Price argue that while these outsiders expect designs on fabric, furniture, and calabashes to yield one-to-one translations, the Maroons have no such expectation. Instead, objects' meanings involve complex associations among their makers, owners, histories, and contexts of use. Many designs are decorative "filler." Discrete marks that identify an object's owner contrast with fluid lines. These emblematic marks stand for names, not words or concepts. According to the Prices, misinterpretations of Maroon arts result in part because of "Maroon notions about their position as illiterate people in a literate world," a situation that opens the way for imposed interpretations when Maroons obligingly "read" meanings into marks for interested outsiders whose expectations are shaped by conventional literacy (1980:190).

The situation that Price and Price describe seems quite similar to the distribution of writing and marking—among narrative, tying, and emblematic functions—that I have outlined. Since the category "literacy" comes preloaded with exclusionary assumptions, and conventionally fits only the narrative, segmentable, and sequential aspects of marks that encode sounds, it is not surprising that the Maroons would seem to subscribe to a have/have-not outlook when they compare themselves with outsiders. However, a distinction that David Dalby has drawn places some of the Prices' observations and the Maroons' markings in another light.

> A . . . distinction needs to be made between the *secular* use of graphic symbols as a means of communication and their various *magical* uses (as means of propitiation, prophylaxis, sorcery, divination, etc.). The clear dichotomy between textual and contextual graphic systems and between coherent systems and isolated symbols, tends to break down when they are used for magical or ritual purposes, and the distinction between secular and magical use is itself blurred when symbols acquire a quasi-cryptographic, quasi-mystical function. (1968:159n.9)

Dalby stresses the tendency of scripts and graphic functions to blur as contexts change from sacred to secular. However, the Prices mention both sacred and secular functions without telling us where different sorts of marking fall in the Maroon graphic economy. It would be interesting and useful for comparative purposes to hear more: if inscription among the Maroons is structured by insider-outsider relations on one hand and insiders' intracultural relations and "almost mystical belief in the power of writing" on the other, we need to know more about how the Maroons deploy these dual frames of reference.

19. Not all historians take this view, and not all revolts conform to this pattern. For example, Hilary Beckles has specifically excluded esoteric practices from roles in certain slave uprisngs in Barbados. Nevertheless, in accounts of revolts, the interaction of literacy with vernacular practice and ideology is a pertinent issue. When historians characterize participants in revolts, literacy, lack of literacy, and mobilization of vernacular resources are intimately bound up with the vastly complicated issues of nationhood and independence—from slavery, from colonial powers, and from alien languages and values.

20. It is not clear that literacy was a significant factor in the Southampton revolt.

21. Stephen B. Oates, in his history of the Southampton Rebellion, states that whites had heard about Nat Turner's visions and tried to discredit him: "Blood on the corn indeed. Angels in the sky indeed. What humbuggery. One white later charged that Nat secretly arranged the leaves in the woods, painted these and the corn with pokeberry juice, then showed the Negroes such skulduggery as proof of his divine importance" (1975:44).

22. Philip Curtin calculates that approximately one-fourth of all slaves brought to the North American mainland came from Congo-Angola (1969:157). In a 1977 lecture at Yale University he estimated one-third (cited in Thompson 1988:57).

23. Maturity is an especially important criterion for deep knowlege of any kind in African American thought. Recall the emphasis on white hair like lamb's wool in interpretations of Revelation in chapter 6. In European American Judeo-Christian tradition, childlike innocence is sometimes a channel for special insight. In African American tradition this theme seems to appear far less frequently; rather, the innocent child is more like Mark Twain's *Mysterious Stranger*, an angel that caused damage because it had not tasted knowledge— had not grown up.

24. Many points of view on Turner and the Rebellion are represented in John Hendrik Clarke *William Styron's Nat Turner: Ten Black Writers Respond* (1968) and in Duff and Mitchell (1971), another collection of papers gathered in response to Styron's book.

25. Unfortunately, several important sections of the Throne are in storage and inaccessible to scholars. Neither the part-to-whole relations of the entire ensemble nor the corpus of Hampton's written signs have been fully assessed. Nevertheless, curator Lynda Hartigan has made an impressive amount of information about the Throne available. A color photo appears in Gould (1987:48).

26. John Szwed has pointed out that African American calls for a new alphabet or new code of representation often coincide with references to space travel, as his biography of the musician Sun Ra demonstrates (1997).

27. Johnson Smith explained criteria for a good grave mound during visits to several graveyards that we made in the summer of 1991. He also pointed out a bad grave mound for comparison. Because the dirt had not been tamped down thoroughly after interment, this mound had sunk into a concave pit filled with rank grass. In Smith's opinion, this bad grave showed that either the person buried there had no surviving relatives or he or she had behaved so badly in life that now no one cared to tend the grave.

28. Sources on African American naming traditions include Hudson (1938), Puckett (1937, 1938), Dillard (1968), and Joyner (1984:217–222).

29. African American church names have been documented by Noreen (1965), Fairclough (1960), and Dillard (1968), among others. Dillard noticed that the length of certain church names is organized around a core, expanding outward. The names of two churches in New Haven illustrate this expansiveness: Third Star of Jacob Christian Church Assembly of God, and Greater Mount Zion Apostolic Church of the First Born. I would add the suggestion that this expansiveness hints at a general predisposition toward omnidirectionality and enclosure—draw it out and tie it up—that comes to the fore when Roman alphabetic literacy and African American vernacular concerns interact.

30. Sources on graffiti include Reisner (1971), Smith (1985), Hess (1987), Kohl (1972), deAk (1983), l'Argenton (1988), Hager (1984), and, with color photographs, Cooper and Chalfont (1984) and Schwartzman (1985).

31. Unhampered by any knowledge of Peru, I infer that the trend at work here seems to be a shift in popularity away from the kinds of vehicle names that predominate among African Americans and Africans to those that predominate in the forms of popular Catholicism that are more like European forms. This phenomenon leads me to wonder if vehicle naming in Peru started among African descendents, then spread to the population at large. For essential reading, see Thompson (1996).

32. Punctuation marks the intersection of vision and voice in the organization of text. Not decodable in themselves—and thus indelibly contextual [?(.)?]—punctuation marks indicate modes of relating: possession, transition. They divide scriptural differences-that-make-a-difference into packages that promise coherence and comprehension of meaning, even if the written text itself belies these qualities: Hub tha twiat, mae sun mork vacet!

References

Abimbola, 'Wande
  1977   *Ifa Divination Poetry*. New York: Nok.

Abrahams, Roger D.
  1970–71   "Talking my Talk": Black English and social segmentation in Black American communities. *African Language Review* 9:227–254.

  1983   *The Man of Words in the West Indies: Performance and the Emergence of Creole Culture*. Baltimore: Johns Hopkins University Press.

  1992   *Singing the Master: The Emergence of African American Culture in the Plantation South*. New York: Pantheon.

Abrahams, Roger D., and John F. Szwed, eds.
  1983   *After Africa: Extracts from British Travel Accounts and Journals of the Seventeenth, Eighteenth, and Nineteenth Centuries concerning the Slaves, their Manners, and Customs in the British West Indies*. New Haven: Yale University Press.

Adams, Marie Jeanne
  1977   The Harriet Powers pictorial quilts. *Black Arts Magazine* 3(4): 12–28.

Ahlo, Olli

1976   *The Religion of the Slaves: A Study of the Religious Tradition and Behavior of Plantation Slaves in the United States, 1830–1865.* Folklore Fellows Communications no. 17. Helsinki: Folklore Fellows.

Akinnaso, F. Niyi

1992   Schooling, language, and knowledge in literate and nonliterate societies. *Comparative Studies in Society and History* 34:68–109.

Alford, Terry

1977   *Prince among Slaves.* New York: Oxford University Press.

Andersen, Oivind

1989   The significance of writing in early Greece—a critical appraisal. In *Literacy and Society,* edited by Karen Schousboe and Mogens Trolle Larsen, pp. 73–88. Center for Research in the Humanities, Copenhagen University. Copenhagen: Akademisk Forlag.

Anderson, James D.

1988   *The Education of Blacks in the South, 1860–1935.* Durham, N.C.: Duke University Press.

Andersson, E.

1958   *Messianic Popular Movements in the Lower Congo.* Studia Ethnographica Upsaliensia 6. Uppsala, Sweden.

Andrews, William L.

1986   *To Tell a Free Story: The First Century of Afro-American Autobiography, 1760–1865.* Urbana: University of Illinois Press.

Aptheker, Herbert

1943   *American Negro Slave Revolts.* New York: Columbia University Press.

Austin, Allan D.

1984   *African Muslims in Antebellum America: A Sourcebook.* New York: Garland.

Baker, Houston A., Jr.

1987   *Modernism and the Harlem Renaissance.* Chicago: University of Chicago Press.

Baker, Margaret

1978   *Gardener's Magic and Folklore.* New York: Universe Books.

Bakhtin, M. M.

1981   Discourse in the novel. In *The Dialogic Imagination,* translated by Caryl Emerson and Michael Holquist. Austin: University of Texas Press.

Bales, Mary Virginia

1928   Some Negro folk songs of Texas. In *Follow the Drinkin' Gou'd,* edited by J. Frank Dobie, pp. 85–112. Publications of the Texas Folk-Lore Society 7. Austin: Texas Folk-Lore Society.

Banks, Frank D., and Portia Smiley

1973   Old-time courtship conversation. In *Mother Wit from the Laughing Barrel: Readings in the Interpretation of Afro-American Folklore*, edited by Alan Dundes, pp. 251–257. Englewood Cliffs, N.J.: Prentice Hall. Original article, *Southern Workman* 24 (1895):14–15, 78.

Barasch, Moshe

1989   Some Oriental pseudo-inscriptions in Renaissance art. *Visible Language* 23(2/3):170–187.

Barrett, Leonard

1976   *The Sun and the Drum.* Kingston: Sangster's Bookshop.

Barthes, Roland

1983   *The Fashion System.* Translated by Matthew Ward and Richard Howard. Berkeley: University of California Press.

Barton, Paul Alfred

1991   *Afrikuandika: The African Hieroglyphic Writing System.* New York: Vantage Press.

Bascom, William

1969   *Ifa Divination: Communication between Gods and Men in West Africa.* Bloomington: Indiana University Press.

1980   *Sixteen Cowries: Yoruba Divination from Africa to the New World.* Bloomington: Indiana University Press.

Bass, Ruth

1973   The little man. In *Mother Wit from the Laughing Barrel: Readings in the Interpretation of Afro-American Folklore*, edited by Alan Dundes, pp. 388–396. Englewood Cliffs, N.J.: Prentice Hall.

Basso, Keith H.

1974   The ethnography of writing. In *Explorations in the Ethnography of Speaking*, edited by R. Bauman and J. Sherzer, 425–432. Cambridge: Cambridge University Press.

1976   "Wise words" of the Western Apache: metaphor and semantic theory. In *Meaning in Anthropology*, edited by Keith H. Basso and Henry A. Selby, pp. 93–121. Albuquerque: University of New Mexico Press.

Basso, Keith H., and Ned Anderson

1973   A Western Apache writing system: the symbols of Silas John. *Science* 180 (June 8):1013–1021.

Bastide, Roger

1978   *The African Religions of Brazil.* Translated by Helen Sebba. Baltimore: Johns Hopkins University Press.

Bateson, Gregory

    1971   Communication. Chap. 1 in *The Natural History of an Interview*, pp. 1–33. Chicago: University of Chicago Library Microfilm Collection of Manuscripts in Cultural Anthropology, series 15, nos. 95–98.

    1972   *Steps to an Ecology of Mind.* New York: Ballantine.

Bauman, Richard

    1977   *Verbal Art as Performance.* Prospect Heights, Ill.: Waveland Press.

Béart, Ch.

    1955   *Jeux et Joets de l'Oest Africain.* 2 vols. Memoirs de l'Institut Français d'Afrique Noire 42. Dakar: IFAN.

Beckman, Janette, and B. Adler

    1991   *Rap! Portraits and Lyrics of a Generation of Black Rockers.* New York: St. Martin's Press.

Beckwith, Martha Warren

    1929   *Black Roadways: A Study of Jamaican Folk Life.* Chapel Hill: University of North Carolina Press.

Bellman, Beryl L.

    1984   *The Language of Secrecy: Symbols and Metaphors in Poro Ritual.* New Brunswick, N.J.: Rutgers University Press.

Benedict, Ruth

    1945   *Race: Science and Politics.* Revised edition with *The Races of Mankind* by Ruth Benedict and Gene Weltfish. New York: Viking Press.

Benitez-Rojo, Antonio

    1992   *The Repeating Island: The Caribbean and the Postmodern Perspective.* Durham, N.C.: Duke University Press.

Bennett, John

    1946   *The Doctor to the Dead: Grotesque Legends and Folk Tales of Old Charleston.* New York: Rinehart.

Bennett, Lerone

    1966   *Before the Mayflower.* New York: Penguin.

Bernal, Martin

    1987   *Black Athena: The Afroasiatic Roots of Western Civilization.* Vol. 1. New Brunswick, N.J.: Rutgers University Press.

Berry, Brewton

    1963   *Almost White.* New York: Macmillan.

Bickerton, Derek

    1975   *Dynamics of a Creole System.* New York: Cambridge University Press.

REFERENCES

Black, Max
    1962   *Models and Metaphors.* Ithaca, N.Y.: Cornell University Press.

Blassingame, John W., ed.
    1975   Using the testimony of ex-slaves: approaches and problems. *Journal of Southern History* 41:473–492.
    1977   *Slave Testimony.* Baton Rouge: Louisiana State University.

Bledsoe, Caroline H., and Kenneth M. Robey
    1986   Arabic literacy and secrecy among the Mende of Sierra Leone. *Man* (n.s.) 21:202–226.

Blier, Rudolph
    1991   Diviners as alienists and annunciators among the Batammaliba of Togo. In *African Divination Systems*, edited by Philip M. Peek, pp. 73–90. Bloomington: University of Indiana Press.

Bloxam, G. W.
    1887   Exhibition of West African symbolic messages. *Journal of the Anthropolical Institute* 16:294–299.

Bodin, Ron
    1990   *Voodoo Past and Present.* Louisiana Life Series no. 5, Center for Louisiana Studies. Lafayette: University of Southwestern Louisiana.

Bolton, H. Carrington
    1891   Decoration of graves of Negroes in South Carolina. *Journal of American Folklore* 4:214.

Boone, Sylvia Ardyn
    1986   *Radiance from the Waters: Ideals of Feminine Beauty in Mende Art.* New Haven: Yale University Press.

Borgatti, Jean
    1983   *Cloth as Metaphor: Nigerian Textiles from the Museum of Cultural History.* Monograph Series no. 20. Los Angeles: Museum of Cultural History, University of California at Los Angeles.

Botume, Elizabeth Hyde
    1893   *First Days among the Contrabands.* Boston: Lee and Shepherd.

Boyd, Boston Napoleon Bonoparte
    1924   *Revised Search Light on the Seventh Day Bible and X-Ray.* Greenville, N.C.: Boston N. B. Boyd.

Bragg, Lillian Chaplin
    1962   Two Savannah cemeteries. *Georgia Magazine* 5:20–21.

Brannon, P. A.
    1925   Central Alabama superstitions. *Birmingham News*, January 18, p. 15.

Brantley, Daniel
  1987   Blacks and Louisiana constitutional development, 1890-present: A study in southern political thought and race relations. *Phylon* 48:51–61.

Brathwaite, Edward Kamau
  1971   *The Development of Creole Society in Jamaica.* New York: Oxford University Press.

  1974   *Contradictory Omens: Cultural Diversity and Integration in the Caribbean.* Mona: Savacou Publications.

  1977   Caliban, Ariel, and Unprospero in the conflict of creolization: A study of the slave revolt in Jamaica in 1831–32. In *Comparative Perspectives on Slavery in New World Plantation Societies,* edited by V. Rubin and A. Tuden. Annals, New York Academy of Science.

  1981   Caribbean history and culture. Paper delivered June 24, 1980, Ubermuseum and University of Bremen.

  1984   *The History of the Voice: The Development of Nation Language in Anglophone Caribbean Poetry.* London: New Beacon Books.

Bratton, Mary J., ed.
  1980   Field's observations: The slave narrative of a nineteenth-century Virginian. *Virginia Magazine of History and Biography* 88(1):75–93.

Bravmann, René A.
  1983   *African Islam.* Washington, D.C.: Smithsonian Institution Press.

Braxton, Joanne M.
  1993   Introduction to *The Collected Poetry of Paul Laurence Dunbar,* ed. Joanne M. Braxton. Charlottesville: University Press of Virginia.

Bredo, Eric, Mary Henry, and R. P. McDermott
  1990   The cultural organization of learning and teaching. *Harvard Educational Review* 60 (2).

Brenner, Louis, and Murray Last
  1985   The role of language in West African Islam. *Africa* 55:432–446.

Breton, André
  1978   *What Is Surrealism? Selected Writings.* Edited by Franklin Rosemond. New York: Monad.

Brewer, John Mason
  1958   *Dog Ghosts and Other Texas Negro Folk Tales.* Austin: University of Texas Press.

Brown, Joseph Augustine
  1984   Harmonic circles: Afro-American religious heritage and American aesthetics. Ph.D. diss., Yale University.

Brown, Karen McCarthy
  1975   The vèvè of Haitian Vodou: a structural analysis of visual imagery. Ph.D. diss., Philadelphia, Temple University.

1991   *Mama Lola: A Vodou Priestess in Brooklyn.* Berkeley: University of California Press.

Brown, Virginia Pounds, and Laurella Owens
1981   *Toting the Lead Row: Ruby Pickens Tartt, Alabama Folklorist.* University: University of Alabama Press.

Browne, Ray B.
1954   Negro folklore from Alabama. *Southern Folklore Quarterly* 28(2):133.

Bruce, Dickson D.
1989   *Black American Writing from the Nadir: The Evolution of a Literary Tradition 1877–1915.* Baton Rouge: Louisiana State University Press.

Brunvand, Jan Harold
1960   A note on names for cars. *Names* 10:279–284.

Bryant, William Cullen
1850   *Letters of a Traveller.* New York: G. P. Putnam.

Bullock, Henry Allen
1970   *A History of Negro Education in the South.* New York: Praeger.

Burley, Dan
1944   *Dan Burley's Original Handbook of Harlem Jive.* New York: Author.

1973   The technique of jive. In *Mother Wit from the Laughing Barrel: Readings in the Interpretation of Afro-American Folklore*, edited by Alan Dundes, pp. 206–221. Englewood Cliffs, N.J.: Prentice Hall.

Burton, Orville Vernon
1985   *In My Father's House Are Many Mansions: Family and Community in Edgefield, South Carolina.* Chapel Hill: University of North Carolina Press.

Byers, Paul
1992   The spiritual in the classroom. *Holistic Education* (Spring).

Cabrera, Lydia
1954   *El Monte.* Havana: Editiones C.R.

1970   *La Sociedad Secreta Abakua: Narrada por Viejos Adeptos.* Miami: Colection del Chicherebu.

1975   *Anaforuana: Ritual y Simbolos de la Initiation en la Sociedad Secreta Abakua.* Madrid: Ediciones R.

Calame-Griaule, G., and P.-F. Lacroix
1986   *Words and the Dogon World.* Philadelphia, Pa.: Institute for the Study of Human Issues (ISHI). Original edition, Paris: Editions Gallimard, 1965.

1969   Graphies et signes africains. *Semiotica* 1:256–272.

Camitta, Miriam

1993   Vernacular writing: Varieties of literacy among Philadelphia high school students. In *Cross-Cultural Approaches to Literacy*, edited by Brian V. Street, pp. 228–246. Cambridge: Cambridge University Press.

Campbell, John

n.d.   *Obeah Yes or No? A Study of Obeah and Spiritualism in Guyana.* Georgetown: Labour Advocate Job Printing.

Carpentier, Alejo

1966   *La Cuidad de las Columnas. Tientos y Diferencias.* Havana: Ediciones Union.

Carroll, Michael P.

1992   *Madonnas that Maim: Popular Catholicism in Italy since the Fifteenth Century.* Baltimore: Johns Hopkins University Press.

Cissé, Youssouf

1973   Signs graphiques, représentations, concepts et tests relatifs a la personne chez lees Malinke et les Bambara du Mali. In *La Notion de Personne en Afrique Noire.* Colloques Internationaux du Centre National de la Recherche Scientifique no. 544, pp. 131–179. Paris: Éditiones du Center National de la Recherche Scientifique.

Clanchy, M. T.

1979   *From Memory to Written Record.* Cambridge: Harvard University Press.

1988   Hearing and seeing *and* trusting writing. In *Perspectives on Literacy,* edited by Eugene R. Kintgen, Barry M. Kroll, and Mike Rose, pp. 135–158. Carbondale: Southern Illinois University Press.

Clarke, John Hendrik, ed.

1968   *William Styron's "Nat Turner": Ten Black Writers Respond.* Boston: Beacon Press.

Clark, Vé Vé A.

1984   Fieldhands to stagehands in Haiti: The measure of tradition in Haitian popular theatre. Ph.D. diss., University of California, Berkeley.

1991   Diaspora literacy and Marasa consciousness. In *Comparative American Identities: Race, Sex, and Nationality in the Modern Text,* edited by Hortense J. Spillers, pp. 40–61. New York: Routledge.

Clifford, James

1988   *The Predicament of Culture.* Cambridge: Harvard University Press.

Clifford, James, and George E. Marcus

1986   *Writing Culture: The Poetics and Politics of Ethnography.* Berkeley: University of California Press.

Coe, Michael D.

1992   *Breaking the Maya Code.* New York: Thames and Hudson.

Coleman, Will
    1991   "Coming through 'ligion'": Metaphor in non-Christian and Christian experiences with the spirit(s) in African American slave narratives. In *Cut Loose Your Stammering Tongue: Black Theology in the Slave Narratives*, edited by Dwight N. Hopkins and George Cummings, pp. 67–102. Maryknoll, N.Y.: Orbis Books.

Conklin, Harold
    1949   Bamboo literacy in Mindoro. *Pacific Discovery* 3:4–11.

Connor, Kimberly Rae
    1994   *Conversions and Visions in the Writings of African-American Women*. Knoxville: University of Tennessee Press.

Cooley, Rossa Belle
    1926   *Homes of the Freed*. New York: New Republic.

Cooper, Carolyn
    1993   *Noises in the Blood: Orality, Gender and the "Vulgar" Body of Jamaican Popular Culture*. London: Macmillan Caribbean.

Cooper, Martha, and Henry Chalfont
    1984   *Subway Art*. New York: Henry Holt.

Cornelius, Janet Duitsman
    1983   "We slipped and learned to read": Slave accounts of the literacy process, 1830–1865. *Phylon* 44:171–186.

    1991   *When I Can Read My Title Clear: Literacy, Slavery, and Religion in the Antebellum South*. Columbia: University of South Carolina Press.

Cornet, Joseph
    1975   *Art from Zaire*. New York: African-American Institute.

    1980   *Pictographies Woyo*. Quaderni Poro 2. Milan: PORO, Associazione degli Amici dell'Arte Extraeuropea.

Cosentino, Donald J.
    1988   Divine horsepower. *African Arts* 21(3):39–42.

Cosentino, Donald J., ed.
    1995   *The Sacred Arts of Haitian Vodou*. Los Angeles: Fowler Museum of Cultural History, University of California at Los Angeles.

Coulmas, Florian
    1989   *The Writing Systems of the World*. Oxford: Basil Blackwell.

Courlander, Harold
    1976   *A Treasury of Afro-American Folklore*. New York: Crown.

Craton, Michael
    1982   *Testing the Chains: Resistance to Slavery in the British West Indies*. Ithaca, N.Y.: Cornell University Press.

Creel, Margaret Washington

    1988   *"A Peculiar People": Slave Religion and Community Culture among the Gullahs.* New York: New York University Press.

    1990   Gullah attitudes toward life and death. In *Africanisms in American Culture*, edited by Joseph E. Holloway, pp. 69–97. Bloomington: Indiana University Press.

Crum, Mason

    1940   *Gullah: Negro Life in the Carolina Sea Islands.* Durham, N.C.: Duke University Press.

Crystal, David

    1987   *The Cambridge Encyclopedia of Language.* Cambridge: Cambridge University Press.

Curtin, Philip D.

    1969   *The African Slave Trade: A Census.* Madison: University of Wisconsin Press.

Curtin, Philip D., ed.

    1967   *Africa Remembered: Narratives by West Africans from the Era of the Slave Trade.* Madison: University of Wisconsin Press.

Dalby, David

    1967   A survey of the indigenous scripts of Liberia and Sierra Leone: Vai, Mende, Loma, Kpelle and Bassa. *African Language Studies* 8:1–51.

    1968   The indigenous scripts of West Africa and Surinam: Their inspiration and design. *African Language Studies* 9:156–197.

    1969   Further indigenous scripts of West Africa: Manding, Wolof and Fula alphabets and Yoruba "holy" writing. *African Language Studies* 10:161–185.

    1970   The historical problem of the indigenous scripts of West Africa and Surinam. In *Language and History in Africa*, pp. 109–119. New York: Africana.

    1970–71   The place of Africa and Afro-America in the history of the English language. *African Language Review* 9:280–298.

    1986   L'Afrique et la Lettre/Africa and the Written Word. Lagos: Centre Culturel Francais and Paris: Fete de la Lettre.

Dalton, Karen C. Chambers

    1991–92   "The alphabet is an abolitionist": Literacy and African Americans in the emancipation era. *Massachusetts Review* 32:545–580.

Davis, Gerald L.

    1985   *I Got the Word in Me and I Can Sing It, You Know: A Study of the Performed African-American Sermon.* Philadelphia: University of Pennsylvania Press.

Day, Beth

    1955   *The Little Professor of Piney Woods: The Story of Professor Laurence Jones.* New York: Julian Messner.

Dayrell, Elphinstone
    1910   Some "Nsibidi" signs. *Man* 67–68:113–114.

    1911   Further notes on Nsibidi signs with their meanings from the Ikom district, S. Nigeria. *Journal of the Royal Anthropological Institute* 41:521–540.

deAk, Edit
    1983   Train as book. *Artforum* 21(9):88–94

DeCamp, David
    1960   Cart names in Jamaica. *Names* 8:15–23.

de Certeau, Michel
    1984   The practice of everyday life. Translated by Steven Rendell. Berkeley: University of California Press.

DeFrancis, John
    1989   *Visible Speech: The Diverse Oneness of Writing Systems.* Honolulu: University of Hawaii Press.

de Ganay, S.
    1950   Graphies Bambara des nombres. *Journal de le Societe des Africanistes 20(2).*

Delafosse, Maurice
    1899   Les Vai: leur langue et leur systeme d'ecriture. *L'Anthropologie* 10:129–151, 294–314.

    1922   Naissance et evolution d'un systeme d'ecriture de creation contemporaine. *Revue d'Ethnographie et des Traditions Populaires* 3(9–12):11-36.

Denyer, Susan
    1978   *African Traditional Architecture: An Historical and Geographic Perspective.* New York: Africana Publishing

Deleuze, Gilles and Felix Guattari
    1987   *A Thousand Plateaus: Capitalism and Schizophrenia.* Translated by Brian Massumi. Minneapolis: University of Minnesota Press.

Deren, Maya
    1953   *The Divine Horseman: The Living Gods of Haiti.* New Paltz, N.Y.: McPherson.

de Rosny, Eric
    1985   *Healers in the Night.* Translated by Robert R. Barr. Maryknoll, N.Y.: Orbis Books.

Derrida, Jacques
    1976   *Of Grammatology.* Translated by Gayatri Chakravorty Spivak, Baltimore: Johns Hopkins University Press.

Desmangles, Leslie Gerald

1977   African interpretations of the Christian cross in Vodun. *Sociological Analysis* 38:13–24.

Dillard, J. L.

1965   Afro-American vehicle names and other names. Special Studies 1. Rio Piedras: Institute of Caribbean Studies, University of Puerto Rico.

1968 On the grammar of Afro-American naming practices. *Names* 16:230–237.

1970   Names or slogans: Some problems from the Cameroun, the Caribbean, Burundi, and the United States. *Caribbean Studies* 9:104–110.

1972   *Black English*. New York: Vintage.

Diop, Cheikh Anta

1974   *The African Origin of Civilization: Myth or Reality?* Translated by M. Cook. Westport, Conn.: L. Hill.

1978   *Black Africa: The Economic and Cultural Basis for a Federated State.* Translated by Harold Salemson, Westport, Conn.: L. Hill.

Diringer, David

1948   *The Alphabet*. New York: Philosophical Library.

Dobbin, Jay D.

1986   *The Jombee Dance of Monserrat: A Study of Trance Ritual in the West Indies.* Columbus: Ohio State University Press.

Dornseiff, Franz

1925   *Das Alphabet in Mystik und Magie.* Berlin: Verlag und Druck von B. G. Teubner.

Drummond, Lee

1980   The cultural continuum: a theory of intersystems. *Man* (n.s.) 15:352–374.

Dubelaar, C. N., and Ándré Pakosie

1993   Kago Buku: Notes by Captain Kogo from Tabiki, Tapahoni River, Suriname, written in Afaka script. *New West Indian Guide/Nieuwe West-Indische Gids* 67(3 and 4):239–279.

Du Bois, W. E. B.

1938   *The Souls of Black Folk*. Chicago: McClurg.

Duff, John B., and Peter M. Mitchell, eds.

1971   *The Nat Turner Rebellion: The Historical Event and the Modern Controversy.* New York: Harper & Row.

Dugast, I., and M. D. W. Jeffreys

1950   L'Ecriture des Bamum. Bulletin de l'Insitut Français d'Afrique Noire (IFAN). Centre du Cameroun Duala. Memoires Series: Populations 4.

Dumas, Henry
  1988 *Goodbye, Sweetwater.* Edited by Eugene B. Redmond. ed. New York: Thunder Mouth Press.

Dundes, Alan
  1969 The devolutionary premise in folklore theory. *Journal of the Folklore Institute* 6:5–19.

Dundes, Alan, ed.
  1973 *Mother Wit from the Laughing Barrel: Readings in the Interpretation of Afro-American Folklore.* Englewood Cliffs, N.J.: Prentice Hall.

Early, Gerald
  1989 *Tuxedo Junction: Essays on American Culture.* New York: Ecco Press.

Egerton, Douglas R.
  1991 "Fly across the river": The Easter slave conspiracy of 1802. *North Carolina Historical Review* 68:87–110.

Elkins, W. F.
  1986 William Lauron DeLaurence and Jamaican folk religion. *Folklore* 97(2):215–218.

Ellison, Ralph
  1964 *Shadow and Act.* New York: Random House.

El-Tom, A. Osman
  1985 Drinking the Koran: The meaning of Koranic verses in Berti Erasure. *Africa* 55(4):414–431.
  1987 Berti Qur'anic amulets. *Journal of Religion in Africa* 17(3):224–244.

Emmons, Martha
  1969 *Deep Like the Rivers: Stories of my Negro Friends.* Austin: Encino.

Faïk-Nzuji, Clémentine
  1992 *Symboles Graphique en Afrique Noire.* Paris: Éditions Kathala pour CILTADE, Louvain.

Fairclough, G. Thomas
  1960 "New Light" on "Old Zion." *Names* 8:75–85.

Fauset, Arthur Huff
  1925 American Negro folk literature. In *The New Negro*, edited by Alain Locke, pp. 238–249. New York: Boni.
  1944 *Black Gods of the Metropolis: Negro Religious Cults in the Urban Northeast.* Philadelphia: American Anthropological Society.

Fenn, Elizabeth
  1985 Honoring the ancestors: Kongo-American graves in the American south. *Southern Exposure* 13 (5): 42–47.

Ferguson, Leland

1989   The cross is a magic sign: Marks on eighteenth century bowls from South Carolina. Paper presented at symposium, Digging the American Past, May 17–21, University of Mississippi.

1992   *Uncommon Ground: Archeology and Early African America, 1650–1800.* Washington, D.C.: Smithsonian Institution Press.

Fernandez, James

1974   The mission of metaphor in expressive culture. *Current Anthropology* 15(2):119–146.

Fernandez, James, ed.

1991   *Beyond Metaphor: The Theory of Tropes in Anthropology.* Stanford: Stanford University Press.

Ferris, William R.

1972   The Rose Hill service. *Mississippi Folklore Register* 6:37–56.

Fisher, Miles Mark

1953   *Slave Songs in the United States.* Ithaca, N.Y.: Cornell University Press.

Flowers, A. R.

1985   *De Mojo Blues: De Quest of HighJohn de Conqueror.* New York: E. P. Dutton.

Ford, Theodore P.

1939   *God Wills the Negro.* Chicago: Geographical Institute Press.

Foucault, Michel

1973   *The Order of Things.* New York: Viking.

1973   *The Birth of the Clinic: An Archaeology of Medical Perception.* Translated by A. M. Sheridan Smith. New York: Pantheon.

Frake, Charles

1983   Did literacy cause the Great Cognitive Divide? *American Ethnologist* 11:368–371.

Franklin, C. L.

1989   *Give Me This Mountain: Life History and Selected Sermons.* Edited by Jeff Todd Titon. Urbana: University of Illinois Press.

Frazier, E. Franklin

1963   *Black Bourgeoisie: The Rise of a New Middle Class in the United States.* New York: Crowell-Collier.

Freire, Paulo

1970   *Pedagogy of the Oppressed.* New York: Seabury.

Fry, Gladys-Marie

1976   Harriet Powers: portrait of a Black quilter. In *Missing Pieces: Geor-*

gia Folk Art 1770–1976, edited by Anna Wadsworth. Atlanta: New York Historical Society.

1990   *Stitched from the Soul: Slave Quilts from the Ante-Bellum South.* New York: Dutton Studio Books in association with the Museum of American Folk Art.

Garfinkel, Harold
1986   Remarks on ethnomethodology. In *Directions in Sociolinguistics: The Ethnography of Communication*, edited by John J. Gumperz and Dell Hymes, pp. 301–324. Original edition, New York: Holt, Rinehart and Winston, 1972.

Gates, Henry Louis, Jr.
1985–86   Writing "race" and the difference it makes. In *"Race," Writing, and Difference*, pp. 1–20. Chicago: University of Chicago Press.

1987   *Figures in Black: Words, Signs, and the "Racial" Self.* New York: Oxford University Press.

1988   *The Signifying Monkey: A Theory of African-American Literary Criticism.* New York: Oxford University Press.

Gates, Henry Louis, Jr., ed.
1987   *The Classic Slave Narratives: The Life of Olaudah Equiano, The History of Mary Prince, Narrative of the Life of Frederick Douglass, Incidents in the Life of a Slave Girl.* New York: Mentor.

Gelb, I. J.
1963   *A Study of Writing.* 2d ed. Chicago: University of Chicago Press.

Georgia Writers Project
1940   *Drums and Shadows: Survival Studies among the Georgia Coastal Negroes.* Athens: University of Georgia Press. (Reprint, 1986.)

Gibson, Gordon D., and McGurk, Cecilia
1977   High status caps of the Kongo and Mbundu peoples. *Textile Journal* 4(4):71–96.

Gilroy, Paul
1991   *"There Ain't No Black in the Union Jack": The Cultural Politics of Race and Nation.* Chicago: University of Chicago Press.

Glazier, Stephen D.
1985   Mourning in the Afro-Baptist tradition: A comparative study of religion in the American south and Trinidad. *Southern Quarterly* 23(3):141–156.

Goffman, Erving
1973   *The Presentation of Self in Everyday Life.* New York: Overlook.

Goldberg, Jonathan
1990   *Writing Matters: From the Hands of the English Renaissance.* Stanford: Stanford University Press.

Gonggrijp, J. W.

1960   The evolution of a Djuka-script in Surinam. *West-Indische Gids.* 40:63–72.

Goody, Jack

1968   Restricted literacy in northern Ghana. In *Literacy in Traditional Societies*, edited by Jack Goody and Ian Watt. Cambridge: Cambridge University Press.

1977   *The Domestication of the Savage Mind.* Cambridge: Cambridge University Press.

1986   Writing, religion, and revolt in Bahia. *Visible Language* 20:318–343.

1987   *The Interface between the Oral and the Written.* Cambridge: Cambridge University Press.

Goody, Jack, and Ian Watt

1963   The consequences of literacy. *Comparative Studies in Society and History* 5:304–345.

Goody, Jack, Michael Cole, and Sylvia Scribner

1977   Writing and formal operations: a case study among the Vai. *Africa* 47(3):289–304.

Gordon, Robert Winslow

1973   Negro "shouts" from Georgia. In *Mother Wit from the Laughing Barrel: Readings in the Interpretation of Afro-American Folklore*, edited by Alan Dundes, pp. 445–451. Englewood Cliffs, N.J.: Prentice Hall.

Gould, Stephen Jay

1987   James Hampton's Throne and the dual nature of time. *Smithsonian Studies in American Art* 1:47–57.

Graff, Harvey J.

1988   The legacies of literacy. In *Perspectives on Literacy*, edited by Eugene R. Kintgen, Barry M. Kroll, and Mike Rose, pp. 82–91. Carbondale: Southern Illinois Press.

Graham, Effie

1914   *Aunt Liza's Praisin' Gate.* Chicago: McClurg.

Gray, Thomas R.

1968   The confessions of Nat Turner, the leader of the late insurrection in Southampton, Va. In *William Styron's "Nat Turner": Ten Black Writers Respond*, edited by J. H. Clarke, pp. 94–117. Boston: Beacon Press.

Green, Ely

1990   *Ely: An Autobiography.* Athens: University of Georgia Press. Original edition, New York: Seabury, 1966.

Greenberg, Joseph H.

1940   The decipherment of the "Ben-Ali Diary." *Journal of Negro History* 25:372–375.

Griaule, Marcel, and Germaine Dieterlen
    1951   *Signes Graphiques Soudanais*. L'Homme, Cahiers d' Ethnologie, de
    Geographie, et de Linguistique. No. 3. Paris: Ecole Practique des Hautes
    Etudes.

Grudin, Eva Unger
    1990   *Stitching Memories: African-American Story Quilts*. Williams-
    town, Ma.: Williams College Museum of Art.

Gundaker, Grey
    1993   Tradition and innovation in African American yards and gardens in
    the southeastern United States. *African Arts* 26(2):58–71, 94–96.

    1994   Halloween in two southern settings. In *Celebrations of Life and
    Death*, edited by Jack Santino. Knoxville: University of Tennessee Press.

Haas, William
    1982   Introduction: on the normative character of language. In *Standard
    Languages: Spoken and Written*, edited by W. Haas, pp. 1–36. Manchester,
    England: University of Manchester Press.

Hagège, Claude
    1990   *The Dialogic Species*. Translated by Sharon L. Shelly. New York:
    Columbia University Press.

Hager, Steven
    1984   *Hip Hop: The Illustrated History of Breakdancing, Rap Music, and
    Graffiti*. New York: St. Martin's Press.

Hair, P. E. H.
    1963   Notes on the discovery of the Vai script, with a bibliography. *Sierra
    Leone Language Review* 2:36–51.

    1965   Sierra Leone items in the Gullah dialect of American English. *Sierra
    Leone Language Review* 4:79–84.

Hall, Michael D.
    1988   *Stereoscopic Perspective: Reflections on American Fine and Folk
    Art*. Ann Arbor: UMI Research Press.

Halverson, John
    1992   Havelock on Greek orality and literacy. *Journal of the History of
    Ideas* 53(1):143–163.

Handloff, Robert E.
    1982   Prayers, amulets, and charms: health and social control. *African
    Studies Review* 25(2/3):185–194.

Hannerz, Ulf
    1969   *Soulside*. New York: Columbia University Press.

    1987   The World in creolisation. *Africa* 57(4):546–559.

Haraway, Donna

1989   *Primate Visions: Gender, Race, and Nature in the Modern World and Modern Science.* New York: Routledge.

Hartigan, Lynda Roscoe

1977   *The Throne of the Third Heaven of the Nations Millenium General Assembly.* Boston: Museum of Fine Arts.

Haskell, Joseph A.

1891   Sacrificial offerings among North Carolina Negroes. *Journal of American Folklore* 4(14):267–269.

Hauenstein, Alfred

1966–67   Considerations sur le motif decoratif croix ainsi differentes coutumes a accompagnees de gestes cruciformes chez quelques tribus d'Angola. *Bulletin der Schweizerischen Gesellschaft fur Anthropologie und Ethnologie* 43.

1984   L'eau et les cours d'eau an differents rites et coutumes en afrique occidentale. *Anthropos* 79:569–585.

Havelock, Eric A.

1963   *Preface to Plato.* Cambridge: Harvard University Press.

1976   *The Origin of Western Literacy.* Toronto: Ontario Institute for the Study of Education.

1986   *The Muse Learns to Write.* New Haven: Yale University Press.

Hayward, Du Bose

1929   *The Half Pint Flask.* New York: Farrar and Rinehart.

Heath, Shirley Brice

1984   *Ways with Words: Language, Life, and Work in Communities and Classrooms.* Cambridge: Cambridge University Press.

1990   The children of Trackton's children. *Cultural Psychology: Essays on Comparative Human Development*, edited by James W. Stigler, Richard A. Shweder and Gilbert H. Herdt. New York: Cambridge University Press, pp. 296–319.

Hebdige, Dick

1978   *Subculture: The Meaning of Style.* London: Routledge.

Helms, Mary W.

1988   *Ulysses' Sail: An Ethnographic Odyssey of Power, Knowledge, and Geographical Distance.* Princeton: Princeton University Press.

Hemenway, Robert

1984   Introduction to *Dust Tracks on a Road*, 2d ed., by Zora Neale Hurston, pp. ix–xxxix. Urbana: University of Illinois Press.

Heninger, S. K., Jr.

1974   *Touches of Sweet Harmony: Pythagorean Cosmology and Renaissance Poetics.* San Marino, Calif.: Huntington Library.

Henney, Jeannette Hillman
1968   Spirit possession belief and trance behavior in a religious group in St. Vincent, British West Indies. Ph.D. diss., Ohio State University.

Herskovits, Melville J.
1941   *The Interdisciplinary Aspects of Negro Studies.* Washington, D.C.: American Council of Learned Societies Bulletin no. 32.

1958   *The Myth of the Negro Past.* Boston: Beacon Press.

1966   *The New World Negro.* Bloomington: University of Indiana Press.

Herskovits, Melville J., and Frances S. Herskovits
1936   *Suriname Folk-Lore.* Columbia Contributions in Anthropology 27. New York: Columbia University.

Hess, Elizabeth
1987   Graffiti R.I.P.: how the art world loved 'em and left 'em. *Village Voice*, December 22, 1987, pp. 37–40.

Hodgson, William Brown
1844   *Notes on Northern Africa, the Sahara, and the Sudan.* New York: Ethnological Society of New York.

Hogg, Donald William
1960   The Convince Cult in Jamaica. In *Papers in Caribbean Anthropology,* compiled by Sidney W. Mintz. New Haven: Department of Anthropology, Yale University.

1961   Magic and "science" in Jamaica. *Caribbean Studies* 1(2):1–5.

Holloway, Joseph E.
1990   The origins of African-American culture. In *Africanisms in American Culture,* edited by Joseph E. Holloway, pp. 1–18. Bloomington: University of Indiana Press.

Holm, John
1988   *Pidgins and Creoles.* Vol. 1, *Theory and Structure.* New York: Cambridge University Press.

1989   *Pidgins and Creoles.* Vol. 2, *Reference Survey.* New York: Cambridge University Press.

Holsoe, Svend E.
1977   Slavery and economic response among the Vai (Liberia and Sierra Leone). In *Slavery in Africa: Historical and Anthropological Perspectives,* edited by Suzanne Miers and Igor Kopytoff, pp. 287–303. Madison: University of Wisconsin Press.

Hooykaas, C.
1980   *Drawings of Balinese Sorcery.* Leiden: E. J. Brill.

Hopkins, Dwight N., and George Cummings
1991   *Cut Loose Your Stammering Tongue: Black Theology in the Slave Narratives.* Maryknoll, N.Y.: Orbis Books.

Hornell, J.

    1928   The string games and tricks of Sierra Leone. *Sierra Leone Studies* 13, n.p.

Horwitz, Elinor Lander

    1975   *Contemporary American Folk Artists.* Philadelphia: Lippincott.

Houlberg, Marilyn

    1979   Social hair: Tradition and change in Yoruba hairstyles. In *The Fabrics of Culture*, edited by Justine M. Cordwell and Ronald A. Schwarz, pp. 349–397. The Hague: Mouton.

Hudson, Arthur Palmer

    1938   Some curious Negro names. *Southern Folklore Quarterly* 2:179–193.

Hunter, Carmen, and David Harmon

    1979   *Adult Illiteracy in the United States.* New York: McGraw-Hill.

Hurston, Zora Neale

    1935   *Mules and Men.* Philadelphia: Lippincott. Reprint, Bloomington: University of Indiana Press, 1978.

    1942   *Dust Tracks on a Road.* Philadelphia: Lippincott.

Hyatt, Harry Middleton

    1970–1978   *Hoodoo—Conjuration—Witchcraft—Root Work.* 5 vols. Hannibal, Mo.: Western.

Hymes, Dell, ed.

    1971   *Pidginization and Creolization of Languages.* New York: Cambridge University Press.

    1981   *"In Vain I Tried to Tell You": Essays in Native American Ethnopoetics.* Philadelphia: University of Pennsylvania Press.

Ibn Wahshiya

    1977   La connaissance des alphabets occultes devolee. In *La Magie Arabe Traditionelle*, edited by S. Matton. Paris: Retz.

Ingersoll, Ernest

    1892   Decoration of Negro graves. *Journal of American Folklore* 5:68–69.

Imes, G. Lake

    1917   The last recruits of slavery. *Southern Workman* 46:355–359.

Jackson, Bruce

    1967   *The Negro and His Folklore in Nineteenth Century Periodicals.* Austin: University of Texas Press.

Jackson, Rebecca Cox

    1981   *Gifts of Power: The Writings of Rebecca Jackson, Black Visionary, Shaker Eldress.* Edited by Jean McMahon Humez. Amherst: University of Massachusetts Press.

Jacobs, Claude F., and Andrew J. Kaslow
    1991   *The Spiritual Churches of New Orleans: Origins, Beliefs, and Rituals of an African-American Religion.* Knoxville: University of Tennessee Press.

James, G. G. M.
    1954   *Stolen Legacy.* New York: Philosophical Library.

James, C. L. R.
    1963   *Black Jacobins.* New York: Vintage.

Janzen, John M.
    1985   The consequences of literacy in African religion. In *Theoretical Explorations in African Religion,* edited by Wim van Binsbergen and Matthew Schoffeleers, pp. 225–252. London: Kegan Paul.

Janzen, John M., and Wyatt MacGaffey
    1974   *An Anthology of Kongo Religion: Primary Texts from Lower Zaire.* University of Kansas Publications in Anthropology no. 5. Lawrence: University of Kansas.

Jarmusch, Ann
    1986   Mysterious stranger. *ArtNews,* October, p. 166.

Jea, John
    1815?   *The Life, History, and Unparalleled Sufferings of John Jea, The African Preacher; Compiled and Written by Himself.* Portsea, England: Williams.

Jeffreys, M. D. W.
    1939   Some notes on the Ekoi. *Journal of the Royal Anthropological Institute* 69:95–108.

Johnson, F. Roy
    1970   *The Nat Turner Story: History of the South's Most Important Slave Revolt, with New Material Provided by Black Tradition and White Tradition.* Murfreesboro, N.C.: Johnson Publishing.

Johnson, Guy B.
    1927–28   Double meaning in the popular Negro blues. *Journal of Abnormal Psychology* 22:12–20.

Johnson, James Weldon, and J. Rosamond Johnson
    1925, 1926   *The Books of Negro Spirituals.* New York: Viking Press. Reprint, New York: De Capo, 1989.

Johnston, Harry
    1906   *Liberia.* 2 vols. London: Hutchinson.

Jones, Bessie
    1983   *For the Ancestors: Autobiographical Memories.* Collected and edited by John Stewart. Urbana: University of Illinois Press.

Jopling, Carol
1988   *Puerto Rican Houses in Sociohistorical Perspective.* Knoxville: University of Tennessee Press.

Joyner, Charles
1984   *Down by the Riverside: A South Carolina Slave Community.* Urbana: University of Illinois Press.

Judy, Ronald A. T.
1993   *(Dis)Forming the American Canon: African-Arabic Slave Narratives and the Vernacular.* Minneapolis: University of Minnesota Press.

Kahan, Mitchell
1986   *Heavenly Visions: The Art of Minnie Evans.* Raleigh: North Carolina Museum of Art.

Kahn, M. C.
1931   *The Djuka, The Bush Negroes of Dutch Guiana.* New York: Viking Press.

Kalu, Ogbu U. [Kenneth Ogbu]
1978   Nsibidi: pictographic communication in pre-colonial Cross-River societies (Nigeria). *Cahiers des Religions Africaines* 12:97–106.

Kittay, Jeffrey
1990   Thinking through literacies. In *Literacy and Orality*, edited by David R. Olson and Nancy Torrance, pp. 165–173. Cambridge: Cambridge University Press.

Kohl, Herbert, and James Hinton
1972   Names, graffiti, and culture. In *Rappin' and Stylin' Out: Communication in Urban Black America*, edited by Thomas Kochman, pp. 109–133.

Kotei, S. I. A.
1977   The West African autochthonous alphabets: An exercise in comparative paleography. *Advances in the Creation and Revision of Writing Systems*, edited by Joshua Fishman. The Hague: Mouton. (Originally published in *Ghana Social Science Journal* 2:98–110, 1972.)

Kubik, Gerhard
1984   African graphic systems: A reassessment. *Mitteilungen der Anthropologischen Gelleschaft in Wein* 114:71–107.

1986   African graphic systems with particular reference to the Benue-Congo or "Bantu" languages zone. *Muntu: Revue Scientifique et Culturelle du CICIBA* 4–5:71–135.

Kulick, Don, and Christopher Stroud
1990   Christianity, cargo, and ideas of self: Patterns of literacy in a Papua New Guinea village. *Man* (n.s.) 25:70–88.

Kus, James S.
1979   Peruvian religious truck names. *Names* 27:179–187.

Kuyk, Betty M.
1983   The African derivation of Black fraternal orders in the United States. *Comparative Studies in Society and History* 25:559–592.

Labouret, H.
1935   L'Ecriture Bamum. *Togo-Cameroun* (April–July): 127–133.

Lachman, Richard
1988   Graffiti as career and ideology. *American Journal of Sociology* 94(2):229–50.

Lakoff, George, and Mark Johnson
1980   *Metaphors We Live By.* Chicago: University of Chicago Press.

Lakoff, George, and Mark Turner
1989   *More than Cool Reason: A Field Guide to Poetic Metaphor.* Chicago: University of Chicago Press.

Laman, Karl
1957, 1962   The Kongo. Vols. 2 and 3. Uppsala, Sweden: Studia Ethnographia Upsaliensia.

Lancy, David F.
1975   The social organization of learning: initiation rituals and the public schools. *Human Organization* 34:457–68.
1980   Becoming a blacksmith in Gbarngasuakwelle. *Anthropology and Education Quarterly* 11:266–74.

l'Argenton, Francoise Robert
1988   Graffiti: tags et grafs. *Communication et Langages* 85(3):58–71.

Lave, Jean
1988   *Cognition in Practice.* Cambridge: Cambridge University Press.

Lawton, Samuel Miller
1939   The religious Life of South Carolina coastal and Sea Island Negroes. Ph.D. diss., George Peabody College for Teachers.

Lehiste, Ilse
1988   *Lectures on Language Contact.* Cambridge, Mass.: M.I.T. Press.

Leiris, Michel
1960   On the use of Catholic religious prints by practitioners of Voodoo in Haiti. *Evergreen Review* 4(13):84–94.

Leon, Eli
1987   *"Who'd A Thought It": Improvisation in African American Quiltmaking.* San Francisco: San Francisco Craft and Folk Art Museum.

Levine, Lawrence W.

 1977 *Black Culture and Black Consciousness: Afro-American Folk Thought from Slavery to Freedom.* Oxford: Oxford University Press.

Lévi-Strauss, Claude

 1992 *Tristes Tropiques.* Translated by John and Doreen Weightman. New York: Penguin.

Levy-Bruhl, Lucien

 1923 *The Primitive Mentality.* New York: Macmillan.

Lewis, George

 1845 *Impressions of America and the American Churches.* Edinburgh: W. P. Kennedy.

Little, Kenneth

 1967 *The Mende of Sierra Leone.* London: Routledge and Kegan Paul.

Little, M. Ruth

 1989 Afro-American grave markers in North Carolina. In *Markers VI: The Journal of the Association for Gravestone Studies,* pp. 103–134. Boston: University Press of America.

Littlefield, Daniel

 1981 *Rice and Slaves: Ethnicity and the Slave Trade in Colonial South Carolina.* Baton Rouge: Louisiana State University Press.

Livingston, Jane, and John Beardsley

 1982 *Black Folk Art in America, 1930–1980.* Jackson: University Press of Mississippi.

Lockridge, Kenneth

 1974 *Literacy in Colonial New England: An Enquiry into the Social Context of Literacy in the Early Modern West.* New York: Norton.

Logan, Robert K.

 1987 *The Alphabet Effect: The Impact of the Phonetic Alphabet on the Development of Western Civilization.* New York: St. Martin's Press.

Lomax, Alan

 1968 *Folksong Style and Culture.* Washington, D.C.: American Association for the Advancement of Science.

Lowery, Irving E.

 1911 *Life on the Old Plantation in Ante-Bellum Days, or, A Story Based on Facts.* Columbia, S.C.: State Company.

MacGaffey, Wyatt

 1977 The black loincloth and the son of Nzambi Mpungu. In *Forms of Folklore in Africa: Narrative, Poetic, Gnomic, Dramatic,* edited by Bernth Lindfors, pp. 144–151. Austin: University of Texas Press.

1986   *Religion and Society in Central Africa: The BaKongo of Lower Zaire.* Chicago: University of Chicago.

1988a   Bakongo cosmology. *The World and I* (September): 512–521.

1988b   Complexity, astonishment and power: The visual vocabulary of Kongo minkisi. *Journal of Southern African Studies* 14(2):188–203.

1991   *Art and Healing of the Bakongo Commented by Themselves: Minkisi from the Laman Collection.* Stockholm: Folkens Museum— Etnografiska.

MacGregor, J. K.
1909   Some notes on Nsibidi. *Journal of the Royal Anthropological Institute* 1 (39):209–219.

MacRae, David
1870   *The Americans at Home: Pen and Ink Sketches of American Men, Manners, and Morals.* Volume 2. Edinburgh: Edmonston and Douglas.

Mahiri, Jabari
1991   Discourse in sports: Language and literacy features of preadolescent African American males in a youth basketball program. *Journal of Negro Education* 60: 305–313.

Malcolm, L. W. G.
1920–21   Short notes on the syllabic writing of the Eghap—Central Cameroons. *Journal of African Society* 20:127–129.

Manley, Roger
1989   *Signs and Wonders: Outsider Art in North Carolina.* Raleigh: North Carolina Museum of Art.

Marks, Morton.
1971   Performance rules and ritual structure in Afro-American music. Ph.D. diss., University of California at Berkeley.

Marques-Riviere, Jean
1950   *Amulettes, Talismans et Pentacles dans les Traditions Orientales et Occidentales.* Paris: Payot.

Martin, John Bartlow
1954   The Mecca. In *Sidewalks of America*, edited by B. A. Botkin, pp. 352–360. Indianapolis: Bobbs-Merrill.

Martins, P. Joachim
1968   *Sabedoria Cabinda: Simbolos E Proverbios.* Lisbon: Junta de Investigacoes do Ultramar.

Massaquoi, M.
1911   The Vai people and their syllabic writing. *Journal of the African Society* 9:459–466.

Maultsby, Portia K.
1986–87   The use and performance of hymnody, spirituals and Gospels in the Black Church. *Journal of the Interdenominational Theological Center* 14:141–159.

McCall, George J.
1963   Symbiosis: The case of hoodoo and the numbers racket. *Social Problems* 10:361–371.

McDermott, R. P.
1987   The explanation of minority school failure, again. *Anthropology and Education Quarterly* 18:361–364.

n.d.   *Culture, Literacy, and Learning.* Unpublished ms., Teachers College, Columbia University.

McDermott, R. P., and Shelley Goldman
1983   Teaching in multicultural settings. In *Multicultural Education,* edited by L. van de Berg-Eldering, F. de Rijcke, and L. Zuck. Dordrecht, Netherlands: Foris Publications.

McHugh, Peter
1968   *Defining the Situation: The Organization of Meaning in Social Interaction.* New York: Bobbs-Merrill.

McTeer, J. E.
1970   *High Sheriff of the Low Country.* Beaufort, S.C.: Beaufort Book Company.

McWillie, Judith
1987   Another face of the diamond. *The Clarion* 12(4):42–53.

1990   *Even the Deep Things of God: A Quality of Mind in Afro-Atlantic Traditional Art.* Exhibition catalog. Pittsburgh, Pa.: Pittsburgh Center for the Arts.

1991   Writing in an unknown tongue. In *Cultural Perspectives on the American South,* edited by Charles Reagan Wilson, pp. 103–117. New York: Gordon and Breach.

1992   The migrations of meaning. In *The Migrations of Meaning,* edited by Judith McWillie and Inverna Lockpez, pp. 7–17. New York: INTAR Latin American Gallery.

Meggitt, M.
1968   Uses of literacy in New Guinea and Melanesia. In *Literacy in Traditional Societies,* edited by J. Goody. Cambridge: Cambridge University Press.

Melmed, P. J.
1973   *Black English Phonology: The Question of Reading Interference.* Berkeley: Language-Behavior Research Laboratory, University of California.

Mercier, Jacques
    1979   *Ethiopian Magic Scrolls.* Translated by Richard Purvear. New York: George Braziller.

Metraux, Alfred
    1959   *Voodoo in Haiti.* New York: Oxford University Press.

Mezzrow, Mezz, and Bernard Wolfe
    1946   *Really the Blues.* New York: Random House. Reprint, New York: Citadel Press, 1990.

Michael, Dorothy Jean
    1943   Grave decoration. *Publications of the Texas Folklore Society* 18: 129–136.

Milburn, S.
    1964   Kisimi Kamara and the Mende script. *Sierra Leone Language Review* 3:20–23.

Miller, Christopher L.
    1990   *Theories of Africans: Francophone Literature and Anthropology in Africa.* Chicago: University of Chicago Press.

Miller, Randall M., ed.
    1978   *Dear Master: Letters of a Slave Family.* Ithaca, N.Y.: Cornell University Press.

Mintz, Sidney W.
    1970   Creating culture in the Americas. *Columbia Forum* 13:4–11.

    1990   Introduction to *The Myth of the Negro Past*, by Melville Herskovits. Washington, D.C.: American Council of Learned Societies Bulletin no. 32.

Mintz, Sidney W., and Richard Price
    1976   *An Anthropological Approach to the Afro-American Past.* ISHI Occasional Papers in Social Change 2. Philadelphia: Institute for the Study of Human Issues.

    1992   Preface to *The Birth of African-American Culture*, edited by Sidney W. Mintz and Richard Price, pp. vii–viv. Boston: Beacon Press.

Mitchell, Henry
    1975   *Black Belief: Folk Beliefs of Blacks in America and West Africa.* New York: Harper & Row.

    1978   *Black Preaching.* San Francisco: Harper & Row.

Mitchell-Kernan, Claudia
    1972   Signifying and marking: Two Afro-American speech acts. In *Directions in Sociolinguistics*, edited by John J. Gumperz and Dell Hymes, pp. 161–179. New York: Holt, Rinehart and Winston.

Mommersteen, Geert

    1988   "He has smitten her heart with love": The fabrication of an Islamic love-amulet in West Africa. *Anthropos* 83:501–510.

Moneyhon, Carl H.

    1985   Black politics in Arkansas during the Gilded Age, 1876–1900. *Arkansas Historical Quarterly*.

Monteil, Victor

    1965   Les manuscrits historiques arabo-africains. *Bulletin de l'Institut Français d'Afrique Noire* (IFAN) (ser. B) 27:531–542.

    1966   Les manuscrits historiques arabo-africains (2). *Bulletin de l'IFAN* (ser. B) 28:668–675.

    1967a   Les manuscrits historiques arabo-africains (3). *Bulletin de l'IFAN* (ser. B) 29:599–603.

    1967b   Analyse de 25 documents arabes des Males de Bahia (1835). *Bulletin de l'IFAN* (ser. B) 29:88–98.

Morris, Robert C.

    1982   *Reading, Writing, and Reconstruction: The Education of Freedmen in the South, 1861–1870.* Chicago: University of Chicago Press.

Morrish, Ivor

    1982   *Obeah, Christ and Rastaman: Jamaica and Its Religion.* Cambridge: James Clark.

Mr. T

    1984   *Mr. T: The Man with the Gold, an Autobiography.* New York: St. Martin's Press.

Mufwene, Salikoko S., ed.

    1993   *Africanisms in Afro-American Language Varieties.* Athens: University of Georgia Press.

Mullin, Gerald W.

    1972   *Flight and Rebellion: Slave Resistance in Eighteenth Century Virginia.* New York: Oxford University Press.

Mullin, Harryette

    1996   African signs and spirit writing. *Callaloo* 19:670–689.

Murphy, Jeannette Robinson

    1899   The survival of African music in America. *Popular Science Monthly* 55:660–672.

Myrdal, Gunnar

    1944   *An American Dilemma.* New York: Harper & Row.

Neeley, Bobby Joe

    1988   Contemporary Afro-American Voodooism (black religion): The retention and adaptation of the ancient African-Egyptian mystery system. Ph.D. diss., University of California at Berkeley.

Newton, Mary Mann-Page
    1891   Aunt Deborah goes visiting: a sketch from Virginia life. *Journal of American Folklore* 4(15):354–356.

Nichols, Elaine, ed.
    1989   *The Last Miles of the Way: African-American Homegoing Traditions 1890–Present*. Columbia: South Carolina State Museum.

Nketia, J. H. Kwabena
    1972   Surrogate languages of Africa. *The Conch* 4(2):11–48.

Noll, Joyce Elaine
    1991   *Company of Prophets: African American Psychics, Healers and Visionaries*. St. Paul, Minn.: Llewellyn.

Nooter, Mary
    1993   *Secrecy: African Art that Conceals and Reveals*. New York: Museum for African Art and Munich: Prestel.

Noreen, Robert G.
    1965   Ghetto worship: A study of the names of Chicago storefront churches. *Names* 13:19–38.

North American Review
    1865   The freedmen at Port Royal. 101:1–28.

Oates, Stephen B.
    1975   *The Fires of Jubilee: Nat Turner's Fierce Rebellion*. New York: Mentor.

Obenga, Theophile
    1973   *L'Afrique dans L'Antiquite: Egypte Pharonique—Afrique Noire*. Paris: Presence Africaine.

Ogbu, John
    1978   *Minority Education and Caste: The American System in Cross-cultural Perspective*. New York: Academic Press.

    1991   Minority status and literacy in comparative perspective. In *Literacy: an Overview by Fourteen Experts*, edited by Stephen R. Graubard, pp. 141–165. New York: Hill and Wang.

Olmsted, Frederick Law
    1861   *The Cotton Kingdom: A Traveller's Observations on Cotton and Slavery in the American Slave States*. Vol. 1. New York: Mason.

Olson, David R.
    1977   From utterance to text: The bias of language in speech and writing. *Harvard Educational Review* 47:257–281.

    1989   Literate thought. In *Understanding Literacy and Cognition*, edited by C. K. Leong and B. S. Randhawa, pp. 3–15. New York: Plenum Press.

Omarr, Sydney
    1990   Your horoscope. *Chattanooga Times*, March 21, 1990, p. B6.

Ong, Walter J.
　　1982　*Orality and Literacy*. New York: Methuen.

Ottenberg, Simon, and Linda Knudsen
　　1985　Leopard society masquerades: Symbolism and diffusion. *African Arts* 28(2):37–44, 93.

Owen, Charles L.
　　1986　Technology, literacy, and graphic systems. In *Towards a New Understanding of Literacy*, edited by Merald E. Wrolstad and Dennis F. Fisher. New York: Praeger.

Owen, Mary Alicia
　　1893　*Voodoo Tales as Told among the Negroes of the Southwest*. New York: G. P. Putnam.

Parrish, Lydia
　　1942　*Slave Songs of the Georgia Sea Islands*. Athens: University of Georgia Press

Partridge, Charles
　　1905　*Cross River Natives: Being Some Notes on the Primitive Pagans of Obdura Hill District, Southern Nigeria*. London: Hutchinson.

Pearson, Elizabeth Ware, ed
　　1906　*Letters from Port Royal*. Boston: W. B. Clarke.

Peek, Philip M.
　　1991　African divination systems: Non-normal modes of cognition. In *African Divination Systems*, pp. 193–212. Bloomington: University of Indiana Press.

Pelton, Robert D.
　　1980　*The Trickster in West Africa: A Study in Mythic Irony and Sacred Delight*. Berkeley: University of California Press.

Pelton, Robert W.
　　1972　*The Complete Book of Voodoo*. New York: Berkley.

Pennington, Patience
　　1913　*A Woman Rice Planter*. New York: Macmillan.

Perani, Judith, and Norma Wolff
　　1992　Embroidered gown and equestrian ensembles of the Kano aristocracy. *African Arts* 25(3):70–81, 102–104.

Perdue, Charles L., Jr.
　　1976　Introduction to *Weevils in the Wheat: Interviews with Virginia Ex-Slaves*, edited by Charles L. Perdue, Jr., Thomas E. Barden, and Robert K. Phillips, pp. xi–xiv. Charlottesville: University Press of Virginia.

Perdue, Charles L., Jr., Thomas E. Barden, and Robert K. Phillips, eds.
1976 *Weevils in the Wheat: Interviews with Virginia Ex-Slaves*. Charlottesville: University Press of Virginia. Reprint, Bloomington: University of Indiana Press, 1980.

Perrin, Michel
1986 "Savage" points of view on writing. In *Myth and the Imaginary in the New World*, edited by Edmundo Magana and Peter Mason, pp. 211–231. Latin American Studies 34. Amsterdam: CEDLA Centre for Latin American Research and Documentation.

Perry, Reginia
1976 Harriet Powers, 1837–1910. *Selections of Nineteenth-Century Afro-American Art*. New York: Metropolitan Museum of Art.

Petesch, Donald A.
1989 *A Spy in the Enemy's Country: The Emergence of Modern Black Literature*. Iowa City: University of Iowa Press.

Pierre, Roland
1977 Caribbean religion: The Voodoo case. *Sociological Analysis* 38(1): 25–36.

Piestrup, A.
1973 *Black Dialect Interference and Accommodation of Reading in the First Grade*. Monograph no. 4. Berkeley: Language-Behavior Research Laboratory, University of California.

Pipes, William H.
1951 *Say Amen, Brothers: Old-Time Negro Preaching*. New York: William-Frederick. Reprint, Detroit: Wayne State University Press, 1992.

Pitts, Walter
1986 Linguistic variation as a function of ritual frames in the Afro-Baptist church in central Texas. Ph.D. diss., University of Texas at Austin.

1989 "If you caint get a boat, take a log": Cultural reinterpretation in the Afro-Baptist Ritual. *American Ethnologist* 16(2):279–293.

1991 Like a tree planted by the water: The musical cycle in the African-American Baptist ritual. *Journal of American Folklore* 104(413):318–340.

1993 *Old Ship of Zion: The Afro-Baptist Ritual in the African Diaspora*. New York: Oxford University Press.

Price, Richard
1976 *The Guiana Maroons: A Historical and Bibliographical Introduction*. Baltimore: Johns Hopkins University Press.

Price, Sally, and Richard Price
1980 *Afro-American Arts of the Suriname Rain Forest*. Berkeley: University of California Press.

Prussin, Labelle
1986   *Hatumere: Islamic Design in West Africa.* Berkeley: University of California Press.

Puckett, Newbell Niles
1926   *Folk Beliefs of the Southern Negro.* Chapel Hill: University of North Carolina Press.

1937   Names of American Negro slaves. In *Studies in the Science of Society,* edited by George Peter Murdock, pp. 471–494. New Haven: Yale University Press.

1938   American Negro names. *Journal of Negro History* 33:35–48.

Puckett, Newbell Niles, and Murray Heller
1975   *Black Names in America: Origins and Usage.* Boston: G. K. Hall.

Quinn, Naomi
1991   The cultural basis of metaphor. In *Beyond Metaphor: The Theory of Tropes in Anthropology,* edited by James W. Fernandez, pp. 56–93. Stanford: Stanford University Press.

Raboteau, Albert
1978   *Slave Religion: The "Invisible Institution" in the Antebellum South.* New York: Oxford University Press.

1995   *A Fire in the Bones: Reflections on African American Religious History.* Boston: Beacon Press.

Rachal, John
1986   Gideonites and freedmen: Adult literacy education at Port Royal, 1862–1865. *Journal of Negro Education* 55:453–469.

Rampini, Charles
1873   *Letters from Jamaica.* Edinburgh: Edmoston and Douglas.

Rappaport, Joanne
1987   Mythic images, historical thought, and printed texts: The Paez and the written word. *Journal of Anthropological Research* 43:43–61.

Raum, O. F.
1943   The African chapter in the history of writing. *African Studies* 2:178–192.

Rawick, George P., ed.
1972   *The American Slave: A Composite Autobiography.* 19 vols. Contributions in Afro-American and African Studies 11. Westport, Conn.: Greenwood Press.

1977   *The American Slave: A Composite Autobiography.* Supplement, series 1. 12 vols. Contributions in Afro-American and African Studies 35. Westport, Conn.: Greenwood Press.

1979   *The American Slave: A Composite Autobiography.* Supplement, series 2. 10 vols. Contributions in Afro-American and African Studies 49. Westport, Conn.: Greenwood Press.

Rawley, James A.
1981   *The Trans-Atlantic Slave Trade.* New York: Norton.

Reed, Ishmael
1972   *Mumbo Jumbo.* New York: Atheneum.

Reichert, Rolf
1967   L'Insurrection d'esclaves de 1835 a la lumiere des documents arabes des Archives Publique e l'Estat de Bahia. *Bulletin de l'Institut Français d' Afrique Noire (IFAN)* (ser. B) 24:99–140.

Reis, João José
1982   Slave rebellion in Brazil: The African Muslim uprising in Bahia, 1835. Ph.D. diss., University of Minnesota.

1993   *Slave Rebellion in Brazil: The Muslim Uprising of 1835 in Bahia.* Translated by Arthur Brakel. Baltimore: Johns Hopkins University Press.

Reisman, Karl
1965   "The island is full of voices": A study of Creole in the speech patterns of Antigua, West Indies. Ph.D. diss., Harvard University.

1970   Cultural and linguistic ambiguity in a West Indian village. In *Afro-American Anthropology*, edited by N. Whitten and J. Szwed, pp. 129–144. New York: Free Press.

Reisner, Robert
1971   *Graffiti: Two Thousand Years of Wall Writing.* New York: Cowles.

Ricoeur, Paul
1975   *The Rule of Metaphor: Multidisciplinary Studies of the Creation of Meaning in Language.* Toronto: University of Toronto Press.

Rigaud, Milo
1969   *Secrets of Voodoo.* New York: Arco.

1975   *Vè-Vè: Diagrammes Rituels du Vodou.* New York: French and European Publications.

Riva, Anna
1974   *The Modern Herbal Spellbook.* Tohica Lake, Calif.: International Imports.

Roberts, Allen F.
1995   The irony of System D. Paper presented at the annual meeting of the American Folklore Society, Lafayette, La. October 1995.

Roberts, Mary Nooter, and Allen F. Roberts
1996   Memory: Luba art and the making of history. *African Arts* 24(3):22–35, 101–103.

Roberts, Peter A.
1988   *West Indians and Their Language.* Cambridge: Cambridge University Press.

Rose, Willie Lee

    1964   *Rehearsal for Reconstruction: The Port Royal Experiment.* New York: Oxford University Press.

Rosen, Norma

    1989   Chalk iconography in Olokun worship. *African Arts* 22(3):44–53, 88.

Rosenak, Chuck, and Jan Rosenak

    1990   *Museum of American Folk Art Enclyclopedia of Twentieth-Century American Folk Art and Artists.* New York: Abbeville Press.

Rosenberg, Bruce

    1988   *Can These Bones Live? The Art of the American Folk Preacher.* Rev. ed. Urbana: University of Illinois Press. Original edition, New York: Oxford University Press, 1970.

Rossi-Landi, Ferruchio

    1973   *Ideologies of Linguistic Relativity.* The Hague: Mouton.

Safadi, Yasin Hamid

    1978   *Isamic Calligraphy.* London: Thames and Hudson.

Sale, John

    1929   *The Tree Named John.* Chapel Hill: University of North Carolina Press.

Saussure, Ferdinand de

    1983   Course in General Linguistics. Edited by Charles Bally and Albert Sechehaye. Translated by Roy Harris. London: Duckworth.

Schieffelin, Bambi B., and Rachelle Charlier Doucet

    1994   The "real" Haitian Creole: ideology, metalinguistics and orthographic choice. *American Ethologist* 21:176–200.

Schmidtt, Alfred

    1963   *Die Bamum-Schrift.* 3 vols. Weisbaden: Harrassowitz.

    1967   Die Bamum-Schrift. *Studium Generale* 20(9):594–604.

Schultz, Emily A.

    1990   *Dialogue in the Margins: Whorf, Bakhtin, and Linguistic Relativity.* Madison: University of Wisconsin Press.

Schutz, Alfred

    1962   *Collected Papers.* Vol. 1, *The Problem of Social Reality.* The Hague: Martinus Nijhoff.

Schwartz, Jack

    1963   Mens' clothing and the Negro. *Phylon* 24:224–231.

Schwartzman, Allan

    1985   *Street Art.* Garden City, N.Y.: Dial Press.

Scribner, Sylvia, and Michael Cole
    1981   *The Psychology of Literacy*. Cambrige: Harvard University Press.

Sea Island Singers
    1994   Read 'em John *Sea Island Songs*, m:80278-2. New York: New World Records.

Severi, Carlo
    1982   Le chemin des metamorphoses; un modele de connaissance de la folie dans un chant shamanique Cuna. *Res* 3:31–67.

Shaw, Rosalind
    1991   Splitting truths from darkness: Epistemological aspects of Temne divination. In *African Divination Systems*, edited by Philip M. Peek, pp. 137–152. Bloomington: University of Indiana Press.

Shaw, William
    1971   Invulnerability. *Federation Museums Journal* 16:3–28.

Shuman, Amy
    1986   *Storytelling Rights: The Uses of Oral and Written Texts by Urban Adolescents*. Cambridge: Cambridge University Press.

Simpson, George Eaton
    1946   Four Vodun ceremonies. *Journal of American Folklore* 59:154–167.

    1966   "Baptism," "Mourning," and "Building" ceremonies of the Shouters of Trinidad. *Journal of American Folklore* 79:537–550.

    1970   *Religious Cults of the Caribbean*. Rio Piedras: University of Puerto Rico.

Simpson, Robert
    1985   The Shout and Shouting in the Slave Religion of the United States. *Southern Quarterly* 23(3):34–48.

Sims, Barbara
    1981   Facts in the life of a Mississippi-Lousiana healer. *Mississippi Folklore Register* 15(2):63–69.

Sixth and Seventh Books of Moses, The
    n.d.   Chicago: Regan. (The editions usually referred to were published by DeLaurence Company, Chicago.)

Smalley, William A., Chia Koua Vang, and Gnia Yee Yang
    1990   *Mother of Writing: The Origin and Development of a Hmong Messianic Script*. Chicago: University of Chicago Press.

Smith, Duncan
    1985   The truth of graffiti. *Art and Text* 17:84–90.

Smith, M. G.
    1960   The African heritage of the Caribbean. In *Caribbean Studies: A Symposium*. Seattle: University of Washington Press.

1963   *Dark Puritan*. Kingston: Department of Extra-Mural Studies, University of the West Indies.

1965   *The Plural Society in the British West Indies*. Berkeley: University of California Press.

Smith, Michael
1978   *The Ethnography of a Vai Town*. Vai Literacy Project Working Paper no. 1, Laboratory of Comparative Human Cognition, Rockefeller University.

Smith, Michael P.
1984   *Spirit World: Pattern in the Expressive Folk Culture of Afro-American New Orleans*. New Orleans: New Orleans Folklife Society.

Smith, Theophus H.
1994   *Conjuring Culture: Biblical Formations of Black America*. New York: Oxford University Press.

Snead, James A.
1990   Repetition as a figure of Black culture. In *Out There: Marginalization and Contemporary Cultures*, edited by Russell Ferguson, Martha Gever, Trin T. Minh-Ha, and Cornel West, pp. 213–230. New York: New Museum of Contemporary Art and M.I.T. Press.

Snowden, Frank M. S.
1970   *Blacks in Antiquity: Ethiopians in the Greco-Roman Experience*. Cambridge: Harvard University Press.

1983   *Before Color Prejudice: The Ancient View of Blacks*. Cambridge: Harvard University Press.

Sobel, Mechal
1979   *Trablin' On: The Slave Journey to an Afro-Baptist Faith*. Westport, Conn.: Greenwood.

1987   *The World They Made Together: Black and White Values in Eighteenth Century Virginia*. Princeton: Princeton University Press.

Spalding, Henry D., ed.
1990   *The Encyclopedia of Black Folklore and Humor*. Middle Village, N.Y.: Jonathan David. Original edition, 1972.

Spaulding, H. G.
1863   Under the palmetto. *Continental Monthly* 4:188–203.

Spence, Muneera Umedaly
1979   Nsibidi and Vai: A survey of two indigenous West African scripts. Master's thesis, Yale University.

Spencer, Jon Michael
1995   *The Rhythms of Black Folk*. Trenton, N.J.: Africa World.

Spillers, Hortense J., ed.
1991 *Comparative American Identities: Race, Sex, and Nationality in the Modern Text.* New York: Routledge.

Starobin, Robert, ed.
1971 *Denmark Vesey: The Slave Conspiracy of 1822.* Englewood Cliffs, N.J.: Prentice Hall.

1974 *Blacks in Bondage: Letters of American Slaves.* New York: Viewpoints.

Starr, Nina Howell
1969 The lost world of Minnie Evans. *Bennington Review* (Summer): 40–58.

Steiner, Roland
1899 Superstitions and beliefs from central Georgia. *Journal of American Folklore* 12(47):261–271.

1901 "Seeking Jesus": A religious rite of Negroes in Georgia. *Journal of American Folklore* 14(54):172.

1901 Observations on the practice of conjuring in Georgia. *Journal of American Folklore* 14(54):173–180.

Stepto, Robert B.
1979a *From Behind the Veil: A Study of Afro-American Narrative.* Urbana: University of Illnois Press.

1979b I thought I knew these people: Richard Wright and the Afro-American literary tradition. In *Chant of Saints: A Gathering of Afro-American Literature, Art, and Scholarship.* Urbana: University of Illinois Press.

Stewart, Gail
1967 Notes on the present-day usage of the Vai script in Liberia. *African Language Review* 6:71–74.

Stewart, Gail, and P. E. H. Hair
1969 A bibliography of the Vai language and script. *Journal of West African Languages* 6(2):109–124.

Stewart, Robert J.
1992 *Religion and Society in Post-Emancipation Jamaica.* Knoxville: University of Tennessee Press.

Stewart, William
1975 Teaching Black children to read against their will. In *Linguistic Perspectives on Black English,* edited by Philip A. Luelsdorff. Münster Verlag Hans Carl Regensberg.

Street, Brian V.
1984 *Literacy in Theory and Practice.* Cambridge: Cambridge University.

Street, Brian V., ed.

1993   *Cross-Cultural Approaches to Literacy.* Cambridge: Cambridge University Press.

Stuckey, Sterling

1987   *Slave Culture: Nationalist Theory and the Foundations of Black America.* New York: Oxford University Press.

Studsill, John D.

1979   Education in a Luba secret society. *Anthropology and Education Quarterly* 10:67–79.

Suggs, Redding S., Jr.

1963   "Heaven Bound." *Southern Folklore Quarterly* 27:249–266.

Suttles, William C., Jr.

1971   African religious survivals as factors in American slave revolts. *Journal of Negro History* 56:97–104.

Szwed, John F.

1981   The ethnography of literacy. In *Writing.* Vol. 1, *Variation in Writing: Functional, Linguistic, and Cultural Differences,* edited by M. Farr-Whiteman. Hillside, N.J.: Lawrence Erlbaum.

1992   Vibrational affinities. In *The Migrations of Meaning,* pp. 59–67. New York: INTAR.

1996   Metaphors of incommensurability. Unpublished paper.

1997   *Space is the Place: The Lives and Times of Sun Ra.* New York: Pantheon.

Szwed, John F., and Roger D. Abrahams

1978   *Afro-American Folk Culture: An Annotated Bibliography of Materials from North, Central and South America and the West Indies.* Philadelphia: Institute for the Study of Human Issues (ISHI).

Szwed, John F., and Morton Marks

1988   The Afro-American transformation of European set dances and dance suites. *Dance Research Journal* 20(1):29–36.

Talbot, P. Amaury

1912   *In the Shadow of the Bush.* New York: George H. Doran.

Tallmadge, William H.

1968   The responsorial and antiphonal practice in Gospel song. *Ethnomusicology* 12:219–238.

Tannen, Deborah

1987   The orality of literature and the literacy of conversation. In *Language, Literacy, and Culture: Issues of Society and Schooling,* edited by J. Langer, pp. 67–88. Norwood, N.J.: Ablex.

Taulbert, Clifton L.

    1989   *Once Upon A Time When We Were Colored.* Tulsa, Okla.: Council Oak Books.

Teish, Luisah

    1985   *Jambalaya: The Natural Woman's Book of Personal Charms and Practical Rituals.* San Francisco: Harper & Row.

Thomas, Keith

    1986   The meaning of literacy in early modern England. In *The Written Word in Transition,* edited by Gerd Baumann. Oxford: Clarendon Press.

Thompson, Robert Farris

    1969   African influence on the art of the United States. In *Black Studies in the University: A Symposium,* by Armstead L. Robinson et al. New Haven: Yale University Press.

    1974   *African Art in Motion.* Los Angeles: University of California Press.

    1978   Black ideographic writing: Calabar to Cuba. *Yale Alumnae Magazine* 42(2)29–33.

    1983   *Flash of the Spirit: African and Afro-American Art and Philosophy.* New York: Random House.

    1987   From the first to the final thunder: African-American quilts, monuments of cultural assertion. Preface to *Who'd A Thought It: Improvisation in African-American Quiltmaking,* by Eli Leon, pp. 12–21. San Francisco: San Franscisco Craft and Folk Art Museum.

    1988   The circle and the branch: Renascent Kongo-American art. In *Another Face of the Diamond: Pathways through the Black Atlantic South.* New York: INTAR Latin American Gallery.

    1989   The song that named the land: The visionary presence of African-American art. In *Black Art: Ancestral Legacy.* Dallas: Dallas Museum of Art.

    1991   *Dancing between Two Worlds: Kongo-Angola Culture and the Americas.* New York: Caribbean Cultural Center.

    1993   Face of the Gods: Art and Altars of Africa and the African Americas. New York: Museum for African Art; Munich: Prestel.

    1996   TAP-TAP, FULA-FULA, KIA-KIA: The Haitian bus in Atlantic perspective. *African Arts* 24(2):36–45.

Thompson, Robert Farris, and Joseph Cornet

    1981   *The Four Moments of the Sun: Kongo Art in Two Worlds.* Washington, D.C.: National Gallery of Art.

Thornton, John

    1992   *Africa and Africans in the Making of the Atlantic World, 1400–1680.* Cambridge: Cambridge University Press.

Todd, Loreto

    1974   *Pidgins and Creoles.* London: Routledge and Kegan Paul.

Torday, Emil
    1928   Dualism in Western Bantu religion and social organization. *Journal of the Royal Anthropological Institute* 58:225–245.

Tragle, Henry I.
    1971   *The Southampton Slave Revolt of 1831: A Compilation of Source Material.* Amherst: University of Massachusetts Press.

Turner, Lorenzo Dow
    1949   *Africanisms in the Gullah Dialect.* Chicago: University of Chicago Press.

Turner, Victor
    1975   *Revelation and Divination in Ndembu Ritual.* Ithaca, N.Y.: Cornell University Press.

Twining, Mary Arnold
    1977   An examination of African retentions in the folk culture of the South Carolina and Georgia Sea Islands. Ph.D. diss., Indiana University.

Uchendu, Victor C.
    1965   *The Igbo of Southeast Nigeria.* New York: Holt, Rinehart and Winston.

Udal, J. S.
    1915   Obeah in the West Indies. *Folk-Lore* 26(3):255–295.

U.S. Department of Commerce. Bureau of the Census.
    1918   *Negro Population 1790–1915.* Washington, D.C.

Varenne, Hervé, and R. P. McDermott
    1986   "Why" Sheila can read: Structure and indeterminacy in the reproduction of familial literacy. In *Acquisition of Literacy*, edited by B. Schiefflen and P. Gilmore. Norwood, N.J.: Ablex.

Vass, Winifred Kellersberger
    1979   *The Bantu-Speaking Heritage of the United States.* Los Angeles: Center for Afro-American Studies, University of California at Los Angeles.

Vaz, Jose Martins
    1970   *Filosofia Tradicional dos Cabindas.* Lisbon: Agencia-geral do Ultramar.

Vlach, John Michael
    1978   *The Afro-American Tradition in Decorative Arts.* Cleveland: Cleveland Museum of Art.

Volosinov, V. N.
    1986   *Marxism and the Philosophy of Language.* Translated by Ladislav Matejka and I. R. Titunik. Cambridge: Harvard University Press.

Vygotsky, L. S.
    1978   *Mind in Society.* Edited by M. Cole, V. John-Steiner, S. Scribner, and E. Souberman. Cambridge: Harvard University Press.

1986   *Thought and Language.* Translated by Alex Kozulin. Cambridge, Mass.: M.I.T. Press.

Wahlman, Maude Southwell
1986   African symbolism in Afro-American quilts. *African Arts* 20: 68–76, 99.

Wahlman, Maude Southwell, and John Scully
1983   Aesthetic principles in Afro-American Quilts. In *Afro-American Folk Art and Crafts*, edited by William Ferris. Boston: G. K. Hall.

Walker, Wyatt Tee
1979   *Somebody's Calling My Name.* Valley Forge, Pa.: Judson.

Washington, Joseph R.
1972   *Black Sects and Cults.* Garden City, N.Y.: Doubleday.

Waterman, Richard Alan
1952   African influence on the music of the Americas. In *Acculturation in the Americas*, edited by Sol Tax, pp. 207–18. Chicago: University of Chicago Press.

Webber, Thomas L.
1978   *Deep Like the Rivers: Education in the Slave Quarter Community, 1831–1835.* New York: Norton.

Wertsch, James V.
1991   *Voices of the Mind: A Sociocultural Approach to Mediated Action.* Cambridge: Harvard University Press.

Wesling, Donald
1987   Writing as power in the slave narrative of the Early Republic. *Michigan Quarterly Review* 26:459–472.

Williams, Brackette F.
1987   Humor, linguistic ambiguity, and disputing in a Guyanese community. *International Journal of the Sociology of Language* 65:79–94.

1991   *Stains on My Name, War in My Veins: Guyana and the Politics of Cultural Struggle.* Durham, N.C.: Duke University Press.

Williams, Charles
1982   The conversion ritual in a rural Black Baptist church. In *Holding on to the Land and the Lord: Kinship, Ritual, Land Tenure, and Social Policy in the Rural South*, edited by R. L. Hall and C. B. Stack. Athens: University of Georgia Press.

Williams, Joseph J.
1934   *Psychic Phenomena of Jamaica.* New York: Dial Press.

Williams, Raymond
1987   Language and the avant-garde. In *The Linguistics of Writing: Arguments between Language and Literature*, edited by Nigel Fabb, Derek At-

tridge, Alan Durant, and Colin MacCabe, pp. 33–47. Manchester: Manchester University Press.

Willis, Paul
1977   *Learning to Labor.* Westmead, UK: Saxon House.

Wilson, Peter J.
1969   Reputation versus respectability: a suggestion of Caribbean ethnography. *Man* (n.s.) 4:70–84.

Wilson, Peter Lanborn
1993   Lost/found Morrish timelines in the wilderness of North America. In *Sacred Drift: Essays on the Margins of Islam,* pp. 15–50. San Francisco: City Light Books.

Wittkower, Rudolf
1972   Hieroglyphics in the Early Renaissance. In *Developments in the Early Renaissance,* edited by Bernard Levy. Albany: State University of New York Press.

Wood, Peter H.
1974   *Black Majority: Negroes in Colonial South Carolina from 1670 through the Stono Rebellion.* New York: Norton.

Woods-Elliot, Claire, and Dell H. Hymes
n.d.   Issues in literacy: Different lenses. University of Pennsylvania Graduate School of Education. Photocopy.

Woodson, Carter G.
1915   *Education of the Negro Prior to 1861.* Washington, D.C. Reprint, New York: Arno Press, 1968.

1933   *The Mis-Education of the Negro.* Washington, D.C.: Associated Publishers. Reprint, Trenton, N.J.: Africa World, 1990.

Yetman, Norman R.
1967   The background of the Slave Narrative Collection. *American Quarterly* 19:540–41.

Zahan, Dominique
1950   Pictographic Writing in the Western Sudan. *Man* 219:136–138.

Zaslavsky, Claudia
1979   *Africa Counts: Number and Pattern in African Culture.* Westport, Conn.: Lawrence Hill. Original edition, Boston: Prindle, Weber and Schmidt, 1973.

Index

ABCs. *See* Alphabet
Abolition(ists), 96
Abrahams, Roger, 136–138, 207n9
Abstraction, 7
Acculturation, 4, 18
Aesthetic(s), 84, 95, 97, 201n1
Afaka, 37, 56
African diaspora, 3–4, 20, 27, 29,
   33, 35, 37, 64, 92, 101, 117,
   120, 153, 172, 174, 187
   theories of, 7, 19. *See also*
   Creolization; Culture;
   Intercultural relations;
   Transatlantic connection
Africa(ns), 44–45, 64, 153, 160,
   167
   Central, 8, 28, 33, 36, 42, 44–46,
   52, 58, 116, 124, 152–154
   West, 8, 28, 29, 33, 36–37, 39, 42,
   46, 52, 54, 57–58, 116, 124,
   150, 152–154, 171, 183
   orientation, 19, 38, 64, 66, 75,
   110–119, 135, 143, 155,
   177–183

Afrikuandika, 55–56
Afro-Cuban, 66
   prenda, 46
   religion, 35
Akinnaso, F. Niyi, 58–59
Alabama, 41, 55, 85–86, 89, 146,
   188
Allah, 29, 34, 51
Alphabet(s), 8, 36–39, 42, 49, 51,
   60–61, 64, 96, 98–101, 108,
   120, 121, 124, 173, 225n13
   efficiency or explicitness of, 7, 22,
   37–38, 55, 108
   mystical, 51
   Roman, 12, 28, 37, 49, 51, 54, 58,
   76, 79, 102, 147, 163–199
Ambiguity, 6, 20, 22, 24, 37–40,
   52–53, 55, 63, 99, 114, 128,
   131, 137, 144, 155–156, 164
Ambivalence. *See* Ambiguity
*American Freedman's Inquiry
   Commission*, 97
American Negro Spirituals, 76
Anaforuana, 35, 165–168

Ancestor(s), 7, 18, 35, 71, 116
  relations with, 24, 95, 114, 119
Andrews, William L., 97
Angola, 44, 178
Anthropology, 5, 27–28, 58, 111,
  210n25, 227n25
Arabic, 34, 42, 51–52, 150–151,
  171, 183, 213n4
  literacy, 33, 36–37, 46–52, 54, 57,
  202n5 *See also* Alphabet;
  Writing systems
Arawak, 66
Arbitrariness, 7
Armstrong, Z. B., 159–160, 198
Art, 48, 65, 96, 184
  African, 10
  folk, 28, 41, 183
  market, 28–29, 41, 174, 183,
  185
  venues, 29
Artis, Maggie, 100
Assimilation, 4
Astronomy, 91
Atahualpa, 102
Atcherson, Ma Sue, 100–101
Austin, Allan D., 47
Autobiography. *See* Narrative

Bahamas, 79–80, 160, 169
Bakhtin, M. M., 20, 102, 105
Balmyard(s), 44, 116
Bambara, 42
Bamum, 36
Bantu, 44
Barbados, 177
Barrett, Leonard, 127
Barton, Paul Alfred, 55–56
Bassa, 36
Bateson, Gregory, 126, 201n1,
  204n9
Beaufort, 58
Bellman, Beryl, 55
Benedict, Ruth, 210n25
Benitez-Rojo, Antonio, 66, 121,
  214n6
Bernal, Martin, 203n8
Biafra, Bight of, 58
Bible, 9, 12, 24, 48, 52–53, 57, 96,
  100–109, 118, 120, 134, 139,
  141–144, 150, 152–162, 173,
  220n4, 222n13, 225n14,
  226n15

Bilali (of Sapelo), 47–49, 57, 216n23
Bird(s), 67, 69
Black, 90
Black Gods of the Metropolis, 149
Black Hawk, 155
Black(ness), 19, 189
Blood, 121
Blue, 79–82, 86, 156, 194, 208n15,
  218n10
Blue-back speller, 57, 109
Blues, 47, 156
Body, 64, 150, 224–225n9
  inscription on, 34, 36, 65,
  129–130
  parts, 21, 46
  substitutes for, 144, 151–153
Book(s), 15, 37, 58, 84, 100–109,
  113–114, 116–118, 126, 132,
  134, 170
  eat(ing), 157
  Talking, 102–109, 113
Boone, Sylvia Ardyn, 54
Boyd, Boston B. Napoleon, 45
Brathwaite, Edward Kamau, 18–19,
  22, 26, 177, 220n6
Braxton, Joanne, 20
Brazil, 44, 49, 119
Break(s), 91, 111, 116, 120, 182
  patterning, 95–96, 104, 131, 144,
  146–147, 219n17
Brewer, J. Mason, 130, 131
Britain, 177
  government of, 18
Brown, Joseph A., 115
Bryant, William Cullen, 132,
  135–136
Building(s), 34, 36, 44, 65, 68, 77,
  83–89, 107, 116, 126, 141, 144,
  147, 185–186, 193, 195–199,
  213n4, 214n6, 227n22
Bullock, James, 164
Bunseki, Fu-Kiau Kia, 95
Butler, Ellen, 98

Cabrera, Lydia, 167
Calabar, 42, 104, 109, 167
California, 92
*Cambridge Encylclopedia of
  Language*, 124
Cameroon, 36, 42, 64
Canada, 97
Candomblé, 126

Carnival, 19, 111

Caul, 22

Cemetery. *See* Grave

Certeau, Michel de, 5, 111, 126

Chalfont, Henry, 186

Charleston, 49, 58, 177

Charm(s), 4, 13, 30, 36, 49–50, 76,
82, 116, 123, 143–153, 173,
215n19

Chattanooga, 25–26, 68, 147, 157,
160, 193

Chinese, 171–172

Christian(ity), 15, 45, 47, 49, 60,
65, 73, 99, 101, 104–121, 141,
185

Chromolithograph(s), 127, 133, 135

Church, 19, 52, 71–72, 86, 88, 91–
92, 107, 116, 131, 133–134,
138, 173, 192

   African Methodist Episcopal
(A.M.E.), 114–115

   Baptist(s), 18, 71, 110, 140, 142,
209n23

   Presbyterian, 140

   Roman Catholic, 126–127, 135,
171, 173, 216n2, 231n10

   Spiritual, 155

   United House of Prayer for All
People, 149–150

Civil War, 132

Clairvoyance, 22, 219n19. *See also*
Double vision; Four eyes

Clark, Henry Ray, 183

Clark, Susan, H., 139

Clark, Vè Vè, 203n6, 207n9

Class, 11, 17, 20, 131

Classification systems, 3, 5–6, 42,
111

Claud, Persie, 100

Clock(s), 159–162

Clothing, 19, 25, 34, 36, 43, 111,
137, 160, 206n6

Code(s), 16, 44, 54, 59, 115, 126,
154, 164, 189, 206n4

Coding, 7–9, 13, 37–38, 53, 96,
104, 124–125, 150. *See also*
Decoding, Script, Style switch,
Writing systems

Cole, Michael, 56, 171

Colonialism, 3, 16–17, 27, 31, 58

Colono ware, 46

Color(s), 17, 26, 43

Communication, 3, 6, 9–10, 16, 19,
25, 34, 36, 42, 44, 52, 54, 56 60,
82, 98, 106, 110, 112, 128–129,
152–154, 171, 173, 202n5

   sender-receiver model of, 9–10,
108, 111, 164

Composite words, 137, 155,
188–189

Conduit, 82, 129, 144, 147–152,
184, 218n12

Configuration(s), 26–27, 30, 33, 111

Conflict, 11

Congo-Angola, 58, 64, 92, 140

Congregation, 15, 24

Conjure, 22, 75–79, 120, 130, 143,
150, 207n14

Context(s), 8, 11, 22, 33, 35–36, 38,
40, 54, 199

   dependence, 9, 59, 128

   independence, 7

   intercultural, 11, 90, 126

Contextual(ization), 12, 93, 130,
164

Continuities. *See* Transatlantic
connections

Continuum. *See* Evolution(ism);
Progression

Control-signs, 129–131

Conversion, 103–110, 116–117,
119, 139

Cool, 25

Coolen, Michael, 47

Cooper, Carolyn, 3

Cooper, Martha, 186

Cornelius, Janet, 57, 96, 99, 134,
215n16

Cornet, Joseph, 71, 208n15

Cornshucking, 132–133, 135–136,
141, 143

Cosmogram, 9, 12, 44–45, 63, 66,
71–75, 93–94, 96, 116,
161–162, 164

Counterclockwise, 46, 116

Covering. *See* Mask and Masking

Craton, Michael, 177

Creel, Margaret Washington, 46,
140

Creole(s), 56–57. *See also* Gullah;
Kweyol

   language(s), 17–19, 38, 204n9,
205n2

Creolization, 10–12, 17, 31, 33, 35,
    43, 54, 56, 124–132, 137, 151,
    172–173, 181
  negative or regressive, 18
  primastic view of, 18
  as research paradigm, 17, 28,
    205n2, 206n3
Cross(ed), 25–26, 65–66, 73–83,
    97, 153, 161
Crossmark, 12, 46, 66, 75–83, 85,
    93–94, 96–97, 114, 130, 144,
    147, 161, 167–170, 217n7,
    218n11
Cross River, 42, 64–66, 104, 167
Crossroad(s), 46, 55, 66, 76, 92, 156,
    169
Cuba, 64, 126, 154, 165
Cugoano, Ottobah, 102
Culture(s), 16, 27, 103, 105, 128,
    132, 144, 161, 164
  American, 6
  contact. See Intercultural
  deterritorialization of, 16
  popular, 65
  systems of, 11, 38, 119, 143
  theories of, 6, 11, 27, 125,
    205–206n3
Cycle(s), 45–46, 71–75, 86, 158,
    160–162, 196

Dahomean, 45, 51, 65, 73, 77, 157,
    207n9
Dalby, David, 36–37, 116
Damballah, 51, 133, 157
Dance, 111, 115, 146. See also Ring
    Shout; Shout
  country, 19
  quadrille, 19
Daniel, 53
Dasent, Theophilus, 169–170
Dave (the potter or Potter), 97,
    220n6
Davenport, Elijah, 71
Davis, Claude, 29, 53, 192–195
Decoding, 9, 26, 48, 124
Delaware, 95
Deloatch, Willie, 67–68, 71
Derrida, Jacques, 129
Devil, 15, 65
Dialogue, 20
Diamond. See Star
Directions. See Spatial, orientation

Divides, 4–6, 110, 138
Divination, 8–9, 12–13, 49, 58, 123,
    125, 152–154, 165, 208n15,
    208n18
  definition of, 151, 172
  Ifa, 59, 154
Divine Spiritual Church of Christ,
    51
Djuka, 37, 183
Dog(s), 67–70, 94, 196–197
Dogon, 35
Dominica, 79–80
Double consciousness, 8, 10, 20, 22,
    164
Double sight. See Double vision
Double vision, 10–13, 23–24, 31,
    35, 44, 66, 93, 101, 106, 114,
    116, 126–128, 135, 162–199
  definition of, 11, 22
Double voicing, 10–12, 20–22, 25,
    31, 35, 64, 75–76, 91, 99, 105,
    127, 131, 135, 145, 155–156,
    163–199
  definitions of, 11, 102
Doubling, 8, 10–11, 18–19, 21–22,
    25–26, 156–158, 164–199,
    206n4
Douglass, Frederick, 104
Drawing, 53
Dress. See Clothing
Drummond, Lee, 124, 205n2
Du Bois, W. E. B., 8, 20, 145, 207n10
Dumas, Henry, 15, 219n19
Dunbar, Paul Laurence, 20
Dundas, Alan, 139
Dust Tracks on a Road, 22, 207n12
Dutch, 102–103

Early, Gerald, 21
Edo, 44
Education, 4, 6, 43, 48, 56, 61,
    109–112, 118, 120–121, 202n5,
    204n9
Egypt(ian), 158, 229n1
  hermetic traditions, 51–52
Ejagham, 42–43, 167
Elaborate speech, 136–138,
    171–172, 225n12
Ellison, Ralph, 206n9
Emblem(s), 8–9, 19, 29–30, 34, 36,
    134–135, 163–164, 167, 175,
    177, 185, 187, 191, 198

Enclosure, 9, 28–29, 41, 44, 49–50, 159, 185. *See also* Tying and wrapping
  as safety zone, 29
Encode. *See* Coding
English, 37, 102–103, 160, 177, 189
  Renaissance, 129
  Standard. *See* Language, standard
Environment. *See* Context; Spatial
Equiano, Olaudah, 102
Essay
  British tradition of, 38, 55
  genre, 20–21
Ethnography, 10, 28, 101
Eurocentrism, 4, 13
European (American) orientation, 19, 38, 55, 65–66, 75, 92, 96, 110–121, 127, 135, 143, 155, 177–183
Evans, Minnie, 154, 171–172
Evolution(ism), 7, 35, 37–38, 105, 139, 163, 203n6, 203n7
Expressive, 52, 137, 160
  culture, 4, 16, 61, 154, 172, 185, 201n1
  modes and/or forms, 17–18, 26, 41, 43, 45, 63, 68–69, 114, 141, 184
  repertoire, 7, 9–10, 12–13, 26, 31, 38, 49, 94, 119, 147, 175
Eye(s), 88, 92, 108, 174, 208n15, 208n22, 219n14
  All-seeing, 66, 82, 86, 128

Fall(ing) out, 25
Fancy talk. *See* Elaborate speech
Faucet, Arthur Huff, 149
Ferguson, Leland, 46
Filter, 144–147
Fisk University, 109, 117
Flight to Canada, 97
Floating signifiers, 4, 17
Florida, 48
Folk, 124
  speech styles, 24
Folklore, 22, 65–66, 76, 120, 139
Fon, 17, 156
Food, 26
Ford, Theodore, 216n1
Four cardinal points. *See* Spatial, orientation
Four corners, 130

Four-eyes, 135, 164, 167, 197, 207n15
  sign, 12, 63–71, 75, 92–94, 96, 114, 126, 175
  term, 22
Four moments of the sun. *See* cosmogram
Franklin, C. L., Rev., 24, 67, 159–160
Fraternal organization(s), 40, 60, 66, 165, 216n26
Freedom, 18, 22, 26
French, 17, 31, 177
Functional groupings of modes of inscription, 8–9, 28
Function(s), 9, 11, 33, 36, 38, 51, 54, 65, 123, 126, 130, 188
Funeral, 132–136

Garden, 100
Gates, Henry Louis, Jr., 97, 102–109, 113
Gender, 3, 11, 39, 96, 112
Genesis, 101, 113
Georgia, 47–49, 57, 68–71, 77, 79, 81–83, 92, 99, 100, 141–142, 146–147, 149, 151, 159, 163, 173–175, 184
Gesture, 6, 8, 29, 44, 52, 132–143, 164
Ghosts, 22
Gifts of Power, 111–116
Gilmore, Ruby, 68, 70, 195–199
Gilroy, Paul, 11
Gladdy, Mary, 173–174
Glossolalia, 49
Glyph, 55–56
God, 25, 37, 51, 67, 77, 84, 86, 92, 102–104, 106–112, 117, 120, 128, 139, 147, 149–150, 154–160, 163, 165, 174, 185, 194
God Struck Me Dead, 117
Goldberg, Jonathan, 129
Gold Coast, 58
Golson, Letha, 144
Goody, Jack, 15, 202n5
Grace, Daddy, 149
Grace Magazine, 149
Graffiti, 175, 185–187, 189, 193, 235n30
  tags, 9, 29

Grammatology, Of, 129
Graphemes, 16, 42, 71–72, 167
Graphic practices, 6, 12, 17, 36–37,
    39–41, 43–44, 52, 63–94, 131,
    201n1
    ideologies of. *See* Literacies, ide-
        ology of
    repertoire of. *See* Expressive
        repertoire
    vernacular, 28, 31
Graphic signs. *See* Signs
Graphic system(s), 12, 16, 33,
    35–46, 52, 142, 163–199. *See
    also* Graphic practices;
    Logographs; Scripts; Sign sys-
    tems
Grave(s), 30, 63, 71, 73–75, 77–78,
    82–84, 90, 95, 119, 130, 185,
    197, 217n4, 218n12, 234n27
Gray, Thomas, R., 99–100
Great Chain of Being, 96
Greece, 5
Greek, 60, 64, 177, 204n8
Green, Elder, 109–112, 117, 133,
    135, 145, 163
Greenburg, Joseph, 48
Green Thursday, 75
Grenada, 101, 117
Gronniosaw, James Albert
    Ukawsaw, 102
Gullah, 57, 140
    Jack, 178

Hair, 82, 170
    style of, 30, 34
Haiti(an), 44, 51–52, 65, 77, 79,
    119, 126, 145, 165, 167, 177,
    207n15
    Creole, 16
Hall, C. L., 97
Halloween, 66
Hampton, James, 4, 49, 154, 160,
    181–182, 198
Handerchief, 132, 134–135, 225n11
Harris, Washington, Bishop, 44
Hausa, 34, 49, 177
Havana, 64
Havelock, Eric, 164
Head, 63, 68, 90, 170
    coverings for, 34, 209n24, 213n5
Healing, 13, 28, 44, 52, 76, 79, 82,
    100, 127–130, 149–150, 153,
    167, 172–175, 180–181,
    223n1, 228n28
Hearts Cologne, 82
Hemenway, Robert, 207n12
Herbs. *See* Healing
Herskovits, Frances S., 45, 175–176
Herskovits, Melville J., 45, 58,
    175–176, 209n25
Hiding. *See* Masks and masking
Hip Hop, 160
History, 26, 46, 64, 86, 92, 95, 111,
    119, 159–162, 164, 177–183
    conflict in, 16, 27
    durability in, 8, 33, 66, 71, 83
    as God's clock, 159–160
    relation of old and new in, 7–8,
        22, 31
Hmong script, 230n9
Hoodoo, 22, 51, 76, 130, 167, 171,
    173, 232n12 *See also* Conjure;
    Magic; Obeah
Hopeton Plantation, 57
House. *See* Building; Yard
Houston, Edward, 41, 54, 86
Howells, William Dean, 20
Humez, Jean McMahon, 115
Humphrey, Olivia, 147–148
Hurston, Zora Neale, 21–23, 31,
    207n12, 207n13
Hyatt, Harry Middleton, 76,
    150–153, 156
Hybridity, 11

Ibrahima, Abd Rahman, 47
Identity, 5, 8, 16, 19, 21, 84, 93, 96,
    126, 164, 186
Ideologies of inscription. *See*
    Literacies, ideologies of
Imitation of Christ, The, 152
Improvisation, 137
Indigenous terms and concepts,
    5–6, 8, 28, 54, 91, 93
Indirection, 30, 38–40, 53, 55,
    63–64, 83, 114, 164
Initiation, 9, 25, 28, 31, 39–42, 44,
    54, 116, 118, 124, 140, 165,
    167, 209n23
Insider(s), 19, 26, 126, 131, 135,
    172, 175
    and/or outsider(s), 3, 12, 16,
        18, 22, 110, 116, 146, 186–
        187

Intercultural processes, 3, 11, 18, 37, 124–162. *See also* Culture; Double consciousness; Double vision; Double voicing; Doubling
  interaction in, 8, 10–11, 16
  theories of, 6, 18, 31
Interference, 6, 8, 31, 199, 204n9. *See also* Creolization; Culture; Sound; Stuttering
  cultural, 17
Intersystems, 17
Invocation, 8–9
Ireland, 133
Isaiah, 159–160
Islam, 15, 29, 34, 37, 51, 57, 150, 215n17
Isom, Joanna Thompson, 76
Ityopia, 18

Jack o' Lantern, 66, 196
Jackson, Rebecca Cox, 111–119, 128, 135, 139–140, 145, 150, 174, 192
Jamaica(n), 3, 18, 26, 44, 116, 177, 187–188
James, C. L. R., 177
James, William, 172
Japanese, 189
Jasper, John, 45, 75
Jazz, 10
Jea, John, 102–111, 135, 140, 145, 208n22, 221n12
Jebu, 39
Jesus Christ, 25–26, 28, 73, 139, 141–142, 155, 158, 179–180
Jes-Us, 25–26, 131
Jewish, 215n19
  mysticism, 51–52
Jihad, 47
John
  the Apostle, 155–156, 160
  the Baptist, 155
  Canoe, 155
  Doctor, 155
  Gospel of, 102–104, 108
  plantation story character, 155
  the Revelator, 142, 154–158, 160
Johnson, Ernest J., Archbishop, 51
Johnson, F. Roy, 100

Jones, Bessie, 185, 206–207n9
Jones, Mandy, 60
Jopling, Carol, 86
Jordan River, 66
Judy, Ronald A. T., 48
July 4th, 97
Junkanoo. *See* John Canoe
Justice, 25, 160–161
Just-Ice, 25

Kabbalah, 51
Kalunga, 44, 65–66, 71, 158, 178
Khan, Hazrat Inayat, 21
KiKongo, 17, 90
Kittay, Jeffrey, 16
Knowledge, 7, 9, 12, 25–26, 43, 96, 120, 128, 135, 151, 194
  deep or stratified, 28, 43, 44, 54, 59, 61, 93, 113–114, 119, 146, 157, 165, 182–183, 186–187, 202n5
  represented by shoe, 224n7
  scientific, 121
  spiritual, 59, 113, 120, 140, 170–171, 209n22
Kongo, 30, 35, 44–46, 64–66, 68, 71, 73, 77, 86, 91–92, 130, 134, 142, 165
Kpelle, 36, 54, 59, 228–229n28
Kubik, Gerhard, 44
Kweyol, 56

Labeled groups, 6
Laman, Karl, 77, 90
Language(s), 20, 27, 38, 44, 51, 57, 111, 156, 202n5
  dependent or independent, 40
  dialects and varieties, 10, 25, 38, 55–56, 79
  emergence of, 11
  interaction of, 16
  metropolitan, 17, 31
  misuse of, 137–139
  standard, 17, 20, 38, 105, 136–137
Latin, 60, 171, 177
Laveau, Marie, 77–78, 155
Lawton, Samuel Miller, 117–118, 209n22
Leadership, 133–134, 177–181
Learning. *See* Literacies, acquisition of

Legba, 79, 155, 165, 173, 229n30

Leiris, Michel, 126–127

Letter(s), 54, 104, 130, 137–138, 142–143, 145, 154, 170, 175–176, 226n15. *See also* Alphabet; Messages; Writing systems

Liberia, 55–56, 58, 60, 116, 140

Light, Joe, 44

Linguistic(s), 16–17
  creole, 17, 204n9
  relativity, 38
  structural, 17, 27

Literacies, 3, 21, 36, 46–48, 54, 56–61, 95, 124, 132, 134
  acquisition of, 4, 6, 12, 24, 33, 36, 57–61, 95–121, 134
  artifacts of, 4, 12–13, 16, 57, 105, 127, 132–143
  "conventional," 3, 5–6, 9–10, 12–13, 16, 25–26, 33, 35, 38 60–61, 63, 95, 97, 103–121, 123–162
  and freedom, 12, 96–121, 145, 177–181
  ideologies of, 4–5, 8–10, 12, 18, 33–36, 38, 52, 55, 133, 222n14
  miraculous acquistion of, 99–109, 111–119
  plural, 3, 7, 56, 144
  research on, 4, 6
  "vernacular," 3, 5–6, 9–10, 16, 26, 33, 35, 60, 63–95, 103–121, 123–162

Literacy. *See* Literacies
  Literature, 21, 95–97, 102, 112–114

Littlefield, Daniel, 58

Loan words, 26

Logograph, 181

Logos (of products), 9, 34, 79, 82, 163–164, 191

Logos, the, 104

Loma, 36–37

Louisiana, 66, 79, 81, 87–88

Low, Harvey, 147–148

Lowery, I. E., 207n11

Luba, 35, 59

Lucky Heart, 79, 82

Lusane, Bennie, 79, 82

MacGaffey, Wyatt, 44, 90

Magic, 33, 49, 51–52, 82, 91–92, 124, 150–152, 167, 233n18
  squares, 37, 191–192

Mali, 42, 54

Mande, 54, 116

Mandinga, 47

Mark(ing), 31, 52, 105, 126, 129–131, 147, 153, 159, 170
  and mock, 130–131, 171

Markedness, 20

Maroon(s), 18, 37

Marrant, John, 102

Martin, John, 161–162

Masks and masking, 19, 21, 49, 96, 98, 111, 114, 116, 126, 133, 157, 162, 197

Mason(ic), 52, 66, 73, 91

Massina, 57

Material culture, 4, 6, 8, 13, 23, 29–30, 39–41, 44–45, 52, 60, 64–93, 124, 126, 144, 153–162, 185–199

Matthews, John, 155

Mayflower, the, 8

Mbute, 201n1

McRae, David, 140

McTeer, J. E., 76

McWillie, Judith, 71, 84, 146, 172, 174

Mediation, 64, 93–94, 108, 123, 128, 147, 153–155, 158, 164–165

Melancon, Victor, 53–54

Memphis, 44, 86, 89, 92–93

Mende, 30, 54, 150–151

Message(s), 8, 28, 31, 34, 39–40, 55, 59, 79, 84, 112, 145, 147, 150, 156, 165, 177, 184–185, 198
  leaf, 38
  propositional, 9

Metacommentary, 3, 11, 193

Metaphor(s), 6, 11, 13, 20, 109, 124–132, 224n6
  definitions of, 125–126

Metraux, Oscar, 156

Miami, 35

Miller, Christopher L., 35, 54, 215n22

Missionaries, 18

Mississippi, 23–24, 30, 60, 70–71, 73–76, 79–80, 83, 92, 137, 147–148, 152, 154–155, 161–162, 167, 184, 195–199
Missouri, 65
Mitchell-Kernan, Claudia, 131
Modernism, 231n11
Mojo, 66, 92–93, 219n18
Monroe, Fortress, 139, 150, 174
Monserrat, 19
Montgomery, Robert, 160–161
Moore, Ruby A., 44
Moorish Science, 49
Moses, 51–52
Mullin, Gerald W., 204n9
Murray, J. B., 70, 174–175
Music, 4, 6, 47, 65, 111, 115, 141, 144
Muslim. *See* Islam
Mutilation, 221n8

Nam, 19
Name(s), 9, 21, 46, 130, 151, 153–154, 163, 185–191
   book, 37, 47–49
   church, 235n29
   daynames, 26, 215n17
   vehicle, 186–191
Naming, 102, 105, 219n15, 235n28, 235n31
Narrative(s), 4, 8–9, 12, 13, 37, 44, 86, 96–119, 128, 133, 147, 163, 181, 193–194
Nation, 97, 167, 220–221n6
Nationalism, 17–19
Nation of Islam, 49
Ndembu, 152
Ndjuka, 37, 56
Nevis, 169
New England, 57, 219n3
New Haven, 189–190
New Orleans, 51, 77–78, 85, 91–92, 120, 134, 144, 155–156, 167, 208n15
Newspaper(s), 18, 22
New Testament. *See* Bible
New York, 35
   state of, 102, 107–108
Ngbe society, 43, 64
Nigeria, 39–40, 42, 44, 51, 64–65, 104, 146

Noll, Joyce Elaine, 172–173
North Carolina, 76, 100
Not-reading, 4, 12, 95–96, 103–121, 123, 135–136, 175. *See also* Not-writing
Not-writing, 4, 12, 95–96, 135–136. *See also* Not-reading
Novel, 20
Nsibidi, 42–44, 53, 59, 64, 92, 167, 214n11
   translation of term, 43
Number(s), 147, 149, 152–153
Numerology, 52
Nyombo, 90

Obeah, 51, 167–171
Object(s), 12, 22, 24, 26, 28–31, 39–41, 44, 54, 64–93, 114, 116, 123–124, 134, 144, 195–199
Offering(s), 77–78
Oklahoma, 92
Oliver, Paul, 47
Olmsted, Frederick Law, 131–136
Olson, David, 164
Olukum, 44
Oral, 5, 102, 111, 133, 136, 207n13. *See also* Sound versus literate, 6, 35, 59, 61, 104–105, 110, 136–139, 191, 199
Orators, 24
Orthography, 16–17, 48, 150
Oshun, 66, 117
Other(ing), 5, 7, 18
Outsider(s). *See* Insider
Owen, Mary Alicia, 65

Palm reading, 125–126
Pan-African(ism), 56
Paris, 36
Parrish, Lydia, 47, 145–146
Pass(es), 97
Patmos, 155
Paul, Norman, 101, 117, 167–168
Peek, Philip, 59
Performance, 3–4, 6, 13, 19, 24, 43, 46, 52, 91, 96, 106, 111, 113–117, 119, 123, 131–143, 164, 172, 189, 199, 208n19
   reading in, 4, 9, 106
   writing in, 4, 9

Person, Leroy, 48
Peterkin, Julia, 75
Philadelphia, 115
Photograph(s), 147, 151
Pictogram. *See* Graphic systems;
    Signs
Pitts, Walter, 209n23
Plantation, 7, 17, 98, 105, 107, 109,
    129–30, 172, 204–205n9
    literature, 20
Planters, 15
Poetry, epic, 20
Point, 78, 104, 164–167
    definition of, 46
Polarities, 11, 61
Policy playing. *See* Numbers
Poro society, 37, 58–59, 140
Port Royal, 140, 143
Powers, Harriet, 71, 73, 92, 184,
    217n5
Prayer cloth, 134
Preacher(s), 15, 24–25, 107–110,
    122–134
Preliterate, 7, 15, 61, 123, 139,
    203n6
Presbyterian, 107
Price, Richard, 233n18
Price, Sally, 233n18
Primer, 57
Print, 20, 34, 38, 51, 53, 105–106,
    144, 146–147, 153, 174,
    197–199
    appearance of dialect in, 20, 105
Progress, 7
Progression, 7, 13
Protection, 64, 68–71, 82–83, 93,
    97–98, 144–149, 170, 193–199
Proverb(s), 8, 34, 39, 44, 129, 191
Puckett, Newbell Niles, 22, 75, 120,
    129
Puerto Rico, 86
Pun(s), 8, 26, 39–41, 54, 127, 189,
    192
Punctuation, 235n32
Pwe. See Point

Quilt(s), 29, 71, 73
Qu'ran, 29, 49, 57

Raboteau, Albert, 139–140, 207n9
Race, 11
Racism, 7

Rap, 25
Rastafari, 18
Reading, 16, 25, 54, 77, 96, 98, 109,
    113, 124, 126, 131–132, 154
    aloud, 12
    as verbal art form, 22
Reason, 7
Rebus(es), 39–40
Reconfiguration, 17, 104, 119, 124,
    165, 192
Recurrence, 7
Recursive(ness), 7, 31, 154
Red, 41, 43, 85–86, 90, 179, 189, 94
Reed, Ishmael, 97
Reinterpretation, 19, 31, 54
Reisman, Karl, 18
Religion(s), 12, 45–46, 48, 51, 53,
    57–58, 65, 101, 118, 123–124,
    134–135, 140–144, 155,
    222n12, 222n14
Remodelled, 142
Representation(s), 40, 53–54
    and identity, 16, 58
    modes of, 28
    orthodoxies of, 10
Reptile, 90
Resistance, 6, 204n9
Resource(s), 17, 26, 33, 35, 54, 59,
    172, 199
    definition of, 12
Retention(s), 30
Revelation(s), 13, 37, 40, 118, 123,
    128, 152, 154–162
    book of, 65, 113
    definition of, 154
Revolt, 19. *See also* Slave revolt
Rhythm, 24, 33, 48, 115, 141–143
Ring shout, 46, 91, 116, 141–143,
    154–155, 185, 229–232
Rita, Mother, 127–128, 140
Ritual, 43, 46, 49, 116, 118, 130,
    132–143, 209n23
Roberts, Allen, 29
Root(s). *See* Conjure
Rossi-Landi, Ferruccio, 38

Said, Oman Ibn, 49
Saints, 156
Salih Bilali, 47, 57, 216n22
Sande society, 36, 58–59, 140
Santeria, 126, 156
Saussure, Ferdinand de, 27

School(ing), 56–61, 95, 101, 109–110, 131, 133, 140, 164, 173, 184, 204n9

Scribner, Sylvia, 56, 171

Script(s), 4, 8, 11–12, 24, 37–38, 48, 51–52, 56, 105–106, 116, 126, 133, 163–199. *See also* Writing systems

definition of, 36

nondecodable, 13, 48–49

placement of. *See* Spatial

Sea Island(s), 46–49, 57–58, 117, 146

Sea Island Singers, 142, 145

Seal(s), 51, 82, 107, 157–158, 160, 198

Seeing, 22, 24, 54, 67–68, 84, 90, 106, 158

Seeking, 140–141

Senegambia(n), 47, 57, 65

Sermon(s), 45, 67, 75, 131–137, 157, 208n19

genre of, 21

sung style of, 24, 115

Seventh Day Adventist, 101

Shaker(s), 111–116

Shango, 126, 157, 173

Sharpe, Sam, 18, 177

Shout, 132, 142. *See also* Ring shout

Sierra Leone, 56, 58, 140

Signifying, 20, 24, 102–109, 135, 156

Signifying Monkey, The, 113

Sign(s), 31, 33, 34, 42–46, 100, 105, 114, 131

deep, 36, 42, 55

on the ground, 44, 77, 129, 167–168, 214n12

ideographic, 54, 213n2

mnemonic, 36

protective, 46

semasiographic, 36, 40–46, 55, 61, 63–94, 198–199, 212n2

systems of, 11–13, 35, 38, 40, 59, 219n19

vernacular, 24

Sixth and Seventh Books of Moses, 51, 120, 143, 168

Slave revolt, 96, 177–183, 221n10, 234n19–23

in Jamaica, 18

Slave Songs of the Georgia Sea Islands, 47

Slave trade, 28, 35–36, 46–47, 58, 214n13, 234n22

Smith, Johnson, 23–24, 31, 75, 137

Smith, M. G., 101

Smith, Mary Tillman, 28–29, 44

Snoopy. *See* Dog

Sobel, Mechal, 117, 160

Soul(s), 41, 44–45, 54, 76, 90–92, 103, 107–108, 118–119

Souls of Black Folk, The, 20

Sound

encoding and/or decoding of, 7, 42, 55, 163

units of, 7, 37

South Carolina, 46, 57–58, 74, 92, 95, 97, 139–140, 142, 178

Southern United States, 8, 15, 61, 96, 132, 134, 219n3

people from, 21–22

speech of, 131

Spatial

arrangements, 52, 54

distance, 30, 170–171, 230n7

limits, 60

orientation, 6, 9, 12, 41, 44–45, 65, 76–77, 82, 96, 110, 115–116, 141–143, 158–162, 167, 175, 179–180

position, 36, 84, 91, 118, 146, 159, 223n18

Speakerly text, 6

Specifying, 22

Speechmaking, 132–143

Spiral, 44–45

Spirit(s), 8, 19, 37, 52, 64, 73, 100, 116–120, 129, 134, 142–145, 150, 152–153, 169, 172–183, 204n9

Holy, 24–25, 107–110, 115, 135, 155, 179–180

possession, 24, 99, 115–116, 140, 155, 173, 175–176, 232n17

vodu, 45

Spiritual Baptist, 51, 117, 168, 223n16

Spiritualism, 119, 172–173

Spirituals. *See* Music

Stained glass, 53, 72, 86

Standardization of orthography, 17

Star(s), 41, 44, 73, 82–92, 164–165, 169

Steiner, Roland, 76
Stepto, Robert, 145
Stereoscope, 23
Stereotypes, 7, 20, 132–134
Street, Brian V., 9
St. Lucia(n), 56
Stono Rebellion, 97
St. Simon's Island, 47
Stuckey, Sterling, 46
Studsill, John D., 58
Sturghill, Annie, 67–69, 147
Stuttering, 204n9
St. Vincent, 117, 152
Style switching, 6, 8, 12, 19–20, 24,
    26, 44, 96, 110–121, 126, 131,
    150, 171, 175, 177–183
Sudan(ese), 42
Sun, 23, 71–75, 174, 180
    four moments of the. See
    Cosmogram
Sunbury, 77–78
Sundi, 90
Surinam, 37, 175–176, 183,
    233n18
Surrealism, 231–232n11
Syllabaries, 7–8, 36–39, 54, 61,
    204n8
Syllogism, 7
Symbol(s). See Graphic systems;
    Objects; Representations;
    Writing systems
Syncretism, 18, 21, 124
Szwed, John, 204n9, 234n26

Tacit, 193
    practices, 8, 18, 27
    premises, 7, 27
Talbot, P. Amaury, 43
Talismans. See Charms
Tartt, Ruby Pickens, 130
Tennessee, 25, 30, 44, 86, 89, 92,
    147, 157, 160
Texas, 95
Textiles, 8
That Talk, 29, 93, 131
Therapy. See Healing
Thing(s). See Object(s)
Thomas à Kempis, 152
Thompson, Robert Farris, 44–46, 68,
    71, 134, 145, 201n1
Threshold, 86
Time, 158–162

Titon, Jeff Todd, 24
Toasts, 20–21
Toma, 37
Townsend, Johnny, 189–190
Transatlantic connections, 7–8,
    11–12, 30, 34–36, 40, 44,
    60–61, 63–94, 114–121, 126,
    137, 151, 210–211n25, 223n2.
    See also Creolization; Culture;
    Intercultural
    debates about, 26–28
    diversity of, 8
    theories of, 11
Trinidad(ian), 78, 126, 173
Turner, Nat, 4, 99–101, 178–181
Turner, Victor, 152, 154
Tusona, 44
Tying and wrapping, 8–9, 26,
    28–31, 36, 49, 82, 93, 116, 130,
    144–147, 159–162, 170–171,
    185–199, 211n25
Typologies. See Classifications

Udall, S., 169–170
Umbanda, 119, 126
Umbrella, 134–135
Unconscious. See Tacit
Unkas, 156

Vai, 35–37, 42, 54, 56–57, 60,
    213n3
Values, 8, 10, 12, 24, 30, 35, 38, 56,
    97, 104, 110, 127, 163, 171, 198
Verbal art(s), 6, 21–22, 35, 57, 102,
    105, 130–131, 136–138, 185
Vernacular repertoire, 6, 8, 13, 105
Vesey, Denmark, 177–178
Vèvè, 9, 52, 165–167, 230n3
Virgen de la Caridad del Cobre,
    66
Virginia, 66–69, 71–72, 86, 88,
    99–100, 132, 142, 160, 204n9
Virgous, Felix, 86
Vodou, 44, 51–52, 65, 77, 79, 116,
    126–127, 133, 135, 156, 165,
    207n15, 217n8
Volosinov, V. N., 202n3
Voodoo, 77–78
    death, 64

Ware, Harriet, 58
Warner, Pecolia, 71

Washington, Booker T., 133
Watch(ing). *See* Seeing, Time
Watchdog. *See* Dog
Watch Men, 160
Water, 44, 46, 72, 82, 153, 155, 163
Western Apache, 230n5
West Georgia College, 101
Wheatley, Phillis, 96
White(ness), 25, 37, 41, 43, 71, 79,
    84, 90, 114, 116–118, 128, 153,
    165, 170, 189, 223n19
Williams, Charles, 191–192
Williams, Emporer, Rev., 97
Window, stained glass, 53–54
Winti, 175–176
Wordplay, 13, 21–22, 38–40,
    190–192
Writing, 9, 16, 25, 31, 37, 51,
    96–98, 109, 112, 124, 128–132,
    137–138, 153–154, 157,
    163–199
  automatic, 172–173

danger and duplicity of, 22, 55, 98,
    108
instrumentality of, 9, 13, 22,
    165–172
modes and varieties of, 9, 11
revealed, 13, 36–37, 154,
    181–183
surface and deep, 53–55, 59
in the unknown tongue, 71,
    172–176. *See also* Glossalalia;
    Script, nondecodable,
Writing systems, 5–6, 33, 35–44,
    46–61, 63, 116. *See also*
    Alphabets; Scripts; Signs;
    Syllabaries

Yard(s), 23–24, 26, 28–29, 41, 84,
    86–87, 126, 130, 174, 195–199,
    218n13
Yellow, 84
Yoruba, 30, 49, 66, 104, 117, 156,
    177, 203n5, 208n21

DATE DUE